ENCYCLOPEDIA OF RACISM IN THE UNITED STATES

ENCYCLOPEDIA OF RACISM IN THE UNITED STATES

VOLUME THREE, S–Z, WITH PRIMARY DOCUMENTS AND ORIGINAL WRITINGS

Edited by Pyong Gap Min

GREENWOOD PRESS
Westport, Connecticut • London

Library of Congress Cataloging-in-Publication Data

Encyclopedia of racism in the United States / edited by Pyong Gap Min.
    p. cm.
  Includes bibliographical references and index.
  ISBN 0-313-32688-6 (set : alk. paper) — ISBN 0-313-33249-5 (vol. 1 : alk. paper)
— ISBN 0-313-33250-9 (vol. 2 : alk. paper) — ISBN 0-313-33555-9 (vol. 3 : alk.
paper) 1. Racism—United States—Encyclopedias. 2. United States—Race
relations—Encyclopedias. 3. United States—Ethnic relations—Encyclopedias.
4. Minorities—United States—Social conditions—Encyclopedias. I. Min, Pyong Gap,
1942–
  E184.A1E773 2005
  305.8'00973'03—dc22   2005008523

British Library Cataloguing in Publication Data is available.

Library of Congress Catalog Card Number: 2005008523
ISBN: 0–313–32688–6 (set)
      0–313–33249–5 (vol. I)
      0–313–33250–9 (vol. II)
      0–313–33555–9 (vol. III)

First published in 2005

Greenwood Press, 88 Post Road West, Westport, CT 06881
An imprint of Greenwood Publishing Group, Inc.
www.greenwood.com

Printed in the United States of America

The paper used in this book complies with the
Permanent Paper Standard issued by the National
Information Standards Organization (Z39.48–1984).

10 9 8 7 6 5 4 3 2 1

CONTENTS

Preface   vii

Acknowledgments   xi

Introduction   xiii

List of Editors, Advisory Board Members, and Contributors   xxvii

Chronology of Race and Racism in the United States   xxxiii

List of Entries   xlvii

Guide to Related Entries   lv

Encyclopedia of Racism in the United States   1

Appendix   659

Primary Documents

1. Slave Codes of the State of Georgia, 1848
2. Excerpts from Treaty of Guadalupe Hidalgo (1848)
3. The Emancipation Proclamation (1863)
4. Fourteenth Amendment (June 1866)
5. The Chinese Exclusion Act of 1882
6. Excerpt from the Indian Allotment Act (1887)
7. *Plessy v. Ferguson* (1896)
8. The National Origins Act of 1924 (Johnson-Reed Act)
9. Executive Order 9066 (February 1942)
10. *Brown v. Board of Education* (May 1954)

11. The Civil Rights Act of 1964

12. Excerpt from the Immigration and Naturalization Act of 1965

13. Voting Rights Act of 1965

14. Executive Order 11246 (1965), as Amended

15. Excerpt from the Kerner Commission Report (1968)

Original Writings

16. Excerpt from President Abraham Lincoln's "Letter to James C. Conkling" (August 26, 1863)

17. Excerpt from W.E.B. Du Bois's *The Souls of Black Folk* (1903)

18. Excerpts from Madison Grant's *The Passing of the Great Race* (1916)

19. Excerpt from Gunnar Myrdal's *An American Dilemma: The Negro Problem and Modern Democracy* (1944)

20. Excerpt from Martin Luther King Jr.'s "Letter from a Birmingham Jail" (1963)

21. Excerpt from Martin Luther King Jr.'s "I Have a Dream" Speech (1963)

22. Excerpt from Malcolm X's *The Autobiography of Malcolm X* (1965)

23. Excerpt from James Mooney's *The Ghost-Dance Religion and the Sioux Outbreak of 1890* (1965)

24. Excerpt from the Aryan Nations Platform

25. Excerpt from the American Sociological Association's "The Importance of Collecting Data and Doing Social Scientific Research on Race" (2003)

26. Poem by Haunani-Kay Trask, "Settlers, Not Immigrants" (2000)

Selected Bibliography   755

Index   769

PREFACE

The racial and ethnic diversity caused by the influx of new immigrants, the expansion of ethnic-studies programs in colleges and universities, and the gradual shift since the 1970s in the government's policy from Anglo-conformity to multiculturalism have contributed to the phenomenal increase in the number of high school and college courses relating to immigration, ethnicity, and racial- and ethnic-minority relations. These courses are offered in the disciplines of sociology, urban studies, anthropology, and history, as well as in various ethnic-studies programs. To meet the increasing demand, a number of encyclopedias covering new immigrant and minority groups and multicultural education have recently been published. Many high school and college students who study American history, immigration, ethnicity, and racial and ethnic relations need to understand concepts, theories, issues, and historical events related to racism. However, despite this need, no encyclopedia of racism in the United States existed.

Several recently published books focus on racism.[1] Some of them offer conceptual and theoretical clarifications relating to racism, and others concentrate attention on white racism against blacks, drawing on ethnographic research or public documents. But none of them is a reference work offering a comprehensive list of concepts, theories, and historical events relating to racism in the United States. Information about historical events that reflect prejudice, discrimination, and physical violence against minority racial groups can be found in books that cover the histories of particular minority groups. But none provides a comprehensive list of historical events pertaining to various racial and ethnic minority groups in the United States. Several handbooks and encyclopedias, such as the *Encyclopedia of the Civil Rights Movement* and the *Encyclopedia of Indian Holocaust*, specialize in racial issues relating to particular minority groups, but no comprehensive encyclopedia covering racial victimization for all racial and ethnic minority groups in the United

States had been published before this book, the *Encyclopedia of Racism in the United States.*

SCOPE OF COVERAGE AND CLASSIFICATION OF ENTRIES

To prepare the *Encyclopedia*, I reviewed most of the major books that specialize in race and ethnic relations or that focus on particular minority groups in the United States. In consultation with a five-member advisory board, a list of entries was devised for inclusion in the *Encyclopedia.* The selected entries, whether directly or indirectly related to racism in the United States, can be broadly classified into the following six categories:

1. Social-science terms, concepts, and theories related to racism
2. Historical and contemporary events, figures, and organizations reflecting or supporting racial discrimination and racial violence against minority groups
3. Racial prejudice and discrimination in employment, housing, and other areas
4. Reactions of minority groups to racial discrimination and of minority leaders who have fought against racism
5. Governmental measures, programs, and agencies, and court cases related to either discrimination or prevention of racial discrimination against minority groups
6. Major books either supporting or exposing racism

Most entries also refer to particular racial and ethnic minority groups. The groups are broadly divided into the following eight categories:

1. Native Americans/American Indians (terms used interchangeably)
2. African Americans
3. Hispanics/Latinos (terms used interchangeably)
4. Asian Americans and Pacific Islanders
5. Muslims, Arabs, and Middle Easterners
6. White ethnic groups (e.g., Jews, Italians, Irish)
7. Immigrants and their children
8. All ethnic groups

Many entries, such as Derogatory Terms and Hate Crimes, fall into category 8; that is, they relate to all racial and ethnic minority groups. These two ways of classifying entries, which are clearly reflected in the "Guide to Related Entries," will help users of the *Encyclopedia* trace broad themes and topics across the entries and will also assist readers who are searching for related groups of topics that interest them or that meet their study or research needs.

The *Encyclopedia of Racism in the United States* is heavily cross-referenced. For instance, readers searching for an organization by acronym, such as AIM, will encounter a cross-reference that sends them to the main entry under the full name of the organization—in this case, they will be instructed to *See* the American Indian Movement. A reader searching for the term *all-weather bigots* will be instructed to *See* Bigots, Types of, the entry in which "all-weather bigots" are described and discussed. The ends of most of the entries also feature *See also* cross-references that list other, related entries. Most entries also conclude with a "Further Reading" section that lists references the reader can turn to for more detailed information on the entry subject. A detailed person and subject index offers greater access to terms and concepts within entries. The *Encyclopedia* also includes an introduction that traces the history of American racism, a general bibliography of important and useful works on racism and minority and ethnic groups, a brief chronology of racism in the United States, and a selection of the full text or excerpts of important primary documents relating to U.S. racism.

Of the *Encyclopedia*'s 447 entries, 25 (e.g., Affirmative Action) are longer entries of 2,000–3,000 words covering complex topics or concepts, while about 180 are midsized entries of 500–1,000 words. The remainder are entries on issues, people, events, or organizations for which basic information and importance can be conveyed in fewer than 500 words. Each contributor to the *Encyclopedia* committed to write one long essay and several medium and short entries on topics within his or her particular field of expertise, and a continuity of thought and style across many related entries is the result.

PRACTICAL VALUE OF THE *ENCYCLOPEDIA* FOR MODERATION OF RACISM

Despite all the democratic ideals emphasized in the Declaration of Independence, the U.S. Constitution, and many other government documents, the United States has probably been the most racist country in the world, with the exception of South Africa under apartheid between 1948 and 1994, and Nazi Germany. Although federal and local governments have made significant changes since 1970 in support of multiculturalism, they have done little to achieve racial equality and to moderate institutional racism during the same period. White Americans are receptive to ethnic and racial diversity to a much grater extent than they were in 1970, but they do not always accept African Americans as friends, as members of their social clubs, or even as neighbors.

Given the seriousness of the problem of racism and racial inequality in contemporary American society, it is important for everyone to join the effort to moderate it. To moderate racism and racial inequality, education of the general public, especially high school and college students, about historical cases of racial injustices and contemporary forms of racism is needed. Students can learn as much about racism from researching a chosen topic as from listening to lectures.

I undertook the extremely difficult task of editing the *Encyclopedia* mainly because of its practical value for contributing to the moderation of racism. I hope the *Encyclopedia* will be helpful to high school and college students who are conducting research on race-related and minority issues and that it will serve as a valuable resource for graduate students and faculty members who teach and conduct research on race relations, racial inequality, and particular minority groups in social science, history, and ethnic studies programs.

NOTE

1. See Eduardo Bonilla-Silva, *Racism without Racists: Color-Blind Racism and the Persistence of Racial Inequality in the United States* (New York: Rowman & Littlefield, 2003); Benjamin P. Bowser and Raymond G. Hunt, *Impacts of Racism on White Americans*, 2nd ed. (Thousand Oaks, CA: Sage Publications, 1996); Martin Bulmer and John Solomon, *Racism* (New York: Oxford University Press, 1999); Christopher Bates Doob, *Racism: An American Caludron*, 3rd ed. (New York: Longman, 1999); Joe Feagin and Melvin P. Sikes, *Living with Racism: The Black Middle-Class Experience* (Boston: Beacon Press, 1994); Andrew Hacker, *Two Nations: Black and White, Separate, Hostile, Unequal*, 2nd ed. (New York: Random House, 1995); Paula S. Rotenberg, *White Privilege: Essential Readings on the Other Side of Racism* (New York: Worth Publishers, 2002); Neil J. Smelser, William J. Wilson, and Faith Mitchell, eds., *America Becoming: Racial Trends and Their Consequences*, vol. 2 (Washington, DC: National Research Council, 2001).

ACKNOWLEDGMENTS

I would like to acknowledge my gratitude to a number of people who helped me complete this encyclopedia project. First of all, I am grateful to the contributors, especially the main contributors, who wrote one or two sets of sixteen to eighteen entries, for their commitment to and personal sacrifice in completing their essays. In particular, I feel obligated to express my deep gratitude to Mikaila Arthur and Dong Ho-Cho, who each wrote essays for thirty-six entries, or approximately seventy manuscript pages. Their contribution to the encyclopedia has been enormous. I also appreciate the gracious cooperation of the encyclopedia's contributors during the revision process.

I would like to thank the five members of the advisory board for reviewing the original list of entries. Their suggestions and additions have made the list of entries more comprehensive and balanced. In particular, I am grateful to Charles Jaret for his invaluable assistance in shaping the final list of entries, finding two contributors for me, writing essays on a set of entries, and supporting my career activities, both as my dissertation advisor at Georgia State University and as one of my closest friends.

I received the Queens College Presidential In-Residence Release-Time Award in the 2003 fall semester for my book project comparing Indian Hindus and Korean Protestants. But I spent much of the released time in completing this encyclopedia project. I express my sincere gratitude to the president of Queens College and the award committee for granting me release-time that was indispensable to completing the project.

Four students at Queens College—Keiko Hirota, Tiffany Vélez, Kelly Corcorom, and Soyoung Lee—aided me in creating the original list of entries, editing entries by contributors, collecting original documents, reviewing copy-edited manuscripts, and/or communicating with contributors through e-mail. Their aid was essential because the project was completed with no institutional monetary support.

I started this encyclopedia project three years ago when Wendi Schnaufer, acquisitions editor at Greenwood Press, encouraged me to initiate it. I wish to acknowledge that she helped me create the list of entries and collect primary documents, and she edited the final version of the entire manuscript. I also owe my gratitude to John Wagner, development editor at Greenwood Press, who edited every essay, took care of format and references, and arranged all entries in alphabetical order.

Finally, I need to acknowledge my heartfelt thanks to my wife, Young Oak, for spending a great deal of time and energy editing many essays, classifying entries, and reading page proofs. Moreover, her loving support and encouragement were essential to completing probably the most difficult project in my career in sociology.

INTRODUCTION

THE PREVALENCE OF RACISM IN EARLY U.S. HISTORY

African Americans

In its classic form, racism refers to the belief that on the basis of their genetic difference some racial groups are innately superior to other racial groups in intelligence, temperament, and attitudes. Racist ideology began to develop during the fifteenth century, the Age of Discovery, when white Europeans began encountering large numbers of non-white peoples in the New World, Asia, and Africa. In North America, South America, the Caribbean Islands, and South Africa, European colonial rulers established slavery as an effective way to control and exploit African workers on plantations. White racial supremacy was institutionalized with the establishment of the racial slavery system. To justify this system, European Christian settlers emphasized their cultural and moral superiority to African blacks. To perpetuate the system, Europeans tightly supervised and controlled the behaviors and movements of African slaves.

By far, the most rigid form of racial slavery developed in the American South. It has been noted that the absence of a substantial intermediate group of free people of color set the stage for a sharp dichotomy between whites and blacks in the antebellum South.[1] Meanwhile, less restrictive manumission requirements enabled more sizable and socially significant free colored groups to develop in the slave societies of South America, the Caribbean, and South Africa. The racial caste system characterized the form of slavery in the American South, but it did not fit the other three slave societies, where many free blacks married white settlers and thereby gained higher status.

Black slaves in the American South were liberated from slavery after the Civil War, in 1865. But the white violence and physical intimidation—especially with the rise of the Ku Klux Klan during Reconstruction (1865–1877)—effectively prevented black men from competing with white workers in the labor market. Thus, African Americans endured worse economic conditions during Reconstruction than they had under slavery. Moreover, the failure of Reconstruction in 1877 led to the establishment by Southern states of Jim Crow segregation laws to control the black threat to the economic and social advantages of white Americans. Jim Crow segregation laws and other statutes that disenfranchised blacks helped maintain the de facto racial caste system in the South until the early 1960s. In 1903, when black nationalist W.E.B. Du Bois wrote that "the problem of the twentieth century is the problem of the color line," he was mainly concerned about racial separation and inequality as it existed at the time in the United States. The United States preserved a very rigid racial caste system for more than three centuries, from the time of the agrarian economy of the eighteenth and nineteenth centuries into the industrial economy of the twentieth. Only the apartheid system established in South Africa in 1948 was more rigid than the racial caste system in the United States.

As Michael Roberts points out in his entry Race Riots in this encyclopedia, African Americans are mistakenly understood to be mainly responsible for race riots in the United States because race is usually ascribed to minority groups rather than to whites. However, race riots of the Jim Crow era were almost always white-on-black riots, that is, the attempts of "white mobs . . . to maintain the status quo of Jim Crow." Most of these riots occurred when white workers attacked black workers, who were often used by white business owners or managers as strikebreakers. Approximately 250 race riots occurred between 1898 (Wilmington, Delaware) and 1943 (Detroit), claiming the lives of approximately 4,300 blacks. Also, numerous minorities, mostly blacks, were victimized by lynching, another common form of white-on-minority violence. More than 3,500 instances of lynching occurred in the United States between 1885 and 1914.[2]

Native Americans

Other racial minority groups in the United States, while spared slavery, were subjected to other forms of racial prejudice and discrimination. Ethnocentrism, conquest, and racial domination-subordination strongly characterized the relationship between European whites and Native Americans. From the beginning of their encounters, European white Protestant settlers perceived Native Americans as uncivilized and intellectually and morally inferior. Plantation owners in the South used some Indians as slaves but preferred blacks to Indians because in the case of Indian servitude white physical security and control could not be guaranteed: Indian slaves could obtain help and support from their own, nearby peoples and territories.[3] White settlers initially tried to solve the "Indian problem" by killing them all.[4] When this failed, the U.S. government tried by force to remove Indian tribes from their native lands in the East and relocate them to unfamiliar and barren lands west of the Mississippi. In the process, many Indians died and most Indian tribes lost all or a portion of their lands. In the late nineteenth century, a change in government

Indian policy from separation to assimilation only ended up taking more lands from Indians, who were also left culturally uprooted.

Mexican Americans

Mexican Americans, who account for approximately 60 percent of the Latino population in the United States, also were initially absorbed into American society as a conquered group, a fact that set the stage for the colonial pattern of their race relations with American Anglos. Texas, which won its independence from Mexico in 1836, was annexed, over Mexican objections, by the United States in 1845. About half of the remaining Mexican territory, including California and New Mexico, came to the United States at the end of the Mexican-American War (1846–1848). Under the terms of the Treaty of Guadalupe Hidalgo, which ended the war, the U.S. government guaranteed the Mexican residents of these territories political and property rights and promised to safeguard their culture, especially by guaranteeing the right to use the Spanish language and to practice the Catholic religion. However, English gradually replaced Spanish as the standard language, and Anglos in the Mexican states began to develop and exhibit prejudice against Mexican Catholics. Moreover, Anglos gradually took the property of Mexicans through official and unofficial means and through fraud, thus transforming the Mexicans into a colonial work force.

By virtue of their in-between racial status, Mexican Americans and other Latinos have been treated better than African Americans in terms of selection of residential areas, public accommodation, and access to social-club membership. Yet, their physical and cultural differences and generally low economic status have also subjected them to prejudice, discrimination, police harassment, and racial violence. According to a study of a South Texas community, Anglos believed Mexicans to be unclean, prone to drunkenness and criminality, hostile, and unpredictable.[5] The lynching of Mexicans was common in the mining camps of Los Angeles in the nineteenth century.[6]

Asian Americans

The migration of Asians to the United States started after the California Gold Rush of 1848–1849, when Chinese farmers were recruited to California to work in mining and railroad construction. Initially, Californians praised Chinese immigrants as "hard-working" and "compliant." Yet, white workers came to believe that industrious Chinese immigrants were a threat to their employment; thus, prejudice against and stereotypes of Chinese immigrants quickly developed among whites. Lobbying by white workers, and the overall anti-Chinese sentiment on the West Coast, led to passage of the Chinese Exclusion Act in 1882, which prohibited the immigration of Chinese for more than sixty years.[7] The Chinese Exclusion Act is the only U.S. government measure to ban the immigration of a particular national-origin group.

Enforcement of the Chinese Exclusion Act led to the recruitment of Japanese and other Asian workers in Hawaii and California. But these groups also encountered a series of immigration restrictions by the U.S. government, which culminated in the National Origins Act of 1924.[8] Moreover, Asian immigrants were not allowed to be American citizens until 1952. In 1913, California passed the Alien Land Law to prohibit Japanese immigrants from owning farmland, and other West Coast states passed similar laws targeting Japanese and other immigrants. California and other states later used the law to prevent Asian immigrants from purchasing real estate. As noncitizen residents, Asian immigrants before World War II did not receive legal protection even if they were victimized by racial violence. Finally, all Japanese Americans living on the West Coast (excluding Hawaii), including native-born citizens, were incarcerated in internment camps during World War II for "security" reasons. Because of their incarceration, innocent Japanese Americans in relocation camps incurred not only monetary and property losses but also psychological damage.

White Immigrant Groups

Catholic, Jewish, and Eastern Orthodox Americans of heavily eastern and southern European ancestry have today been incorporated into mainstream white American society. But, when large numbers of these non-Protestant European immigrants arrived in the United States at the end of the nineteenth and beginning of the twentieth century, they were considered physically different from native-born Anglos and thus were subjected to prejudice, discrimination, and racial violence.[9] Southern Italians suffered not only antagonism directed against Catholics in general but also severe anti-Italian sentiments because of their peasant background. Italians suffered physical violence as well as negative images and stereotypes. Killings and lynchings of Italian immigrants occurred in the United States, especially in the South, between 1890 and 1910.[10] Nicola Sacco and Bartolomeo Vanzetti, two Italian immigrants, were charged with and found guilty of murder and armed robbery and executed in 1927, even though numerous witnesses testified that they were not involed in the crime.

For many centuries, Jews suffered negative stereotypes, prejudice, and discrimination, including legal discrimination, in European Christian countries. Although American Jews fared better than European Jews in terms of legal discrimination, they also encountered anti-Semitism in different forms.[11] Anti-Semitism in the United States increased in the 1880s with the influx of eastern European Jewish immigrants and reached its high point in the 1920s and the 1930s. The Ku Klux Klan and some white industrialists, such as Henry Ford, filled the media with anti-Semitic propaganda, spreading the idea of a "world Jewish conspiracy."[12] Jews were often denied accommodation at hotels and admission to social clubs. As the number of Jewish students in prestigious universities and professional schools increased, the latter took measures to restrict Jewish admissions. Jewish Americans were also subjected to discrimination in professional occupations, especially in law, medicine, and academia.

Nativist reactions to and prejudice against Jewish, Catholic, and Asian immigrants in the United States in the first decade of the twentieth century contributed to the development of "biological racism," a racist ideology that sees so-called Nordic races as genetically—and therefore also intellectually and morally—superior to other races, including eastern and southern Europeans, African Americans, Mexicans, and Asians.[13] Such well-known psychologists as Lewis Terman and C. W. Gould argued that based on scores of IQ tests, eastern and southern European immigrants and African Americans had lower levels of intellectual ability but tended to "outbreed" people of "Nordic" races. Their arguments supported the eugenics movement, which emerged after World War I. These ideas also contributed to the passage of discriminatory immigration laws in the early 1920s, which severely reduced immigration from eastern and southern European countries and entirely banned Asian immigration.

THE PERSISTENCE OF RACISM IN THE POST–CIVIL RIGHTS ERA

The passage of civil rights laws, including affirmative action programs, in the 1960s may lead many people to believe that racism is no longer an important factor for the adjustment of minorities in the twenty-first century. The ethnic and racial diversities created by the influx of Third World immigrants, the increasing emphasis on multiculturalism by government and schools, and the increase in intermarriages since the early 1970s may further enhance the belief about the insignificance of racism in contemporary American life. Jews, Italians, and other turn-of-the-century white immigrant groups have been incorporated into mainstream America.[14] However, the social-science literature accumulated since the 1980s reveals that African Americans still suffer high levels of racial prejudice and discrimination in all aspects of their lives, and other nonwhite minority groups also experience different forms of unequal treatment because of their nonwhite status.[15] Based on their findings, the authors of these studies have suggested that the color line continues to divide American society in the twenty-first century, just as it did in the twentieth.

Although legal discrimination against African Americans ended with the civil rights legislation of the early 1960s, enough evidence exists to support the view that African Americans still have to deal with racism—both individual and institutional—on a daily basis. Many people tend to believe that racial prejudice and discrimination are problems confronted only by poor blacks concentrated in inner-city neighborhoods and that well-educated, middle-class blacks do not have to deal with it. However, based on personal interviews with middle-class blacks, two social scientists, Joe Feagin and Melvin Sikes, have challenged this view. They conclude that "racism is the everyday experience" for middle-class blacks as well and that experiences with serious racial discrimination "have a cumulative impact on particular individuals, their families, and their communities."[16] Summing up his view of white-black separation in contemporary America, political scientist Andrew Hacker similarly commented that "America's version of apartheid, while lacking overt legal sanction, comes closest to the system even now being overturned in the land of its invention" (South Africa).[17]

Sociological studies show that the high level of segregation for African Americans has not been moderated since the 1970s.[18] Housing discrimination by real estate agents, commercial banks, and local white community leaders, and the racial gap in socioeconomic status are partly responsible for what has been called "American apartheid."[19] But racial prejudice against blacks on the part of white Americans is mainly responsible for racial segregation. Residential isolation, in turn, further enhances antiblack racial prejudice and creates further socioeconomic disadvantages for African Americans.[20] Segregated black neighborhoods are characterized by all kinds of social ills, such as high poverty and unemployment rates, high mortality and crime rates, and poor educational and health-care facilities.

Since the 1978 publication of his controversial book, *Declining Significance of Race*, William Wilson has paid keen attention to the class division within the African American community and focused on poverty among residents in inner-city black neighborhoods.[21] He has argued that the disappearance of blue-collar jobs from black neighborhoods, which is a result of deindustrialization rather than racism, is the main cause of poverty among inner-city black residents. However, various studies reveal that regardless of their class background, blacks experience racial discrimination in the labor market.

No doubt, deindustrialization, along with the poor school performance overall of black children, is an important contributing factor to the exceptionally high unemployment and poverty rates among young blacks. But the preference of employers for Latino legal and illegal workers over black workers is also responsible for the difficulty young blacks have finding employment. Studies by Roger Waldinger and Michael Richter have found that regardless of industry, employers and managers prefer Latino immigrants to blacks because they perceive the former to be more "subservient" and "docile."[22] Moreover, Feagin and Sikes have shown that black professionals also encounter discrimination in finding employment and in salaries, evaluations, and promotions.[23] According to an analysis of census data by Hacker, black men with a bachelor's degree earned $764 for every $1,000 earned by their white counterparts.[24] It can be argued that the racial gap in earnings is caused mainly by racial discrimination.

The influx of immigrants from the Caribbean Islands since the 1970s has contributed to a phenomenal increase in the black immigrant population.[25] Unlike African Americans whose ancestors were brought to the United States by force for economic exploitation, Caribbean immigrants are voluntary migrants who came here for better economic and educational opportunities. An interesting question is: will the adaptation of Caribbean black immigrants and their descendants follow the pattern taken by voluntary minority groups or by colonial minority groups?[26] Mary Waters' 1999 study of Caribbean immigrants in New York City reveals that the children of lower-class immigrants assimilate quickly, becoming African American children.[27] This finding indicates the importance of race as well as class for the racialization of Caribbean immigrants.

Although Latinos in the United States are currently better accepted than African Americans, they are also subjected to prejudice, stereotypes, and discrimination. Their in-between physical characteristics and their generally lower economic class and immigrant backgrounds enhance the negative image of Latinos. The influx of legal and illegal Mexicans immigrants during recent years has led to stereotypes of native-born Mexican Americans as undocumented residents and manual laborers.[28] Because of a long history of Anglo-Mexican racial stratification, Mexicans in Texas, in particular, still experience semi-involuntary segregation in using public facilities and racial harassment by the police similar to that experienced by African Americans.[29] Probably because of their darker skin, Puerto Ricans experience residential segregation from white Americans that is more similar to that of African Americans than to other Latino groups. Moreover, Puerto Ricans, regardless of generational status, exhibit low educational and occupational levels and a high poverty rate comparable to African Americans.

Most Asian-American groups currently have a higher socioeconomic status than whites.[30] Moreover, approximately 40 percent of U.S.-born Asian Americans engage in intermarriages, in most cases with white partners.[31] These facts have led some social scientists to predict that Asian Americans are likely to be incorporated into white society in the near future.[32] However, contemporary Asian immigrants are socio-economically polarized, with one group representing professional and business classes and the other group consisting of poor refugees from Indochina and working-class migrants.[33] Moreover, the social-science literature on Asian Americans indicates that not only Asian immigrants but also U.S.-born Asian Americans encounter racial violence, racial discrimination, and rejection because of their nonwhite racial characteristics. In the past two decades, dozens of incidents of racial violence against Asian Americans have occurred in many U.S. cities, killing a dozen people. Studies based on personal interviews with or personal narratives by second-generation Asian Americans reveal that most informants experienced rejection, with such taunts as "Go back to your country" or "What country are you from?"[34] Third- and fourth-generation white Americans have an option to choose their ethnic identity or not, because they are accepted as full American citizens.[35] However, one ethnographic study showed that society forces most third- or fourth-generation Japanese and Chinese Americans to accept their ethnic and racial identities, even though they, like multigeneration white Americans, are thoroughly acculturated to American society.[36]

The influx of large numbers of Latino, Caribbean, and Asian immigrants into a predominantly white society since the 1970s has increased anti-immigrant prejudice and actions, including a resurgence of white supremacist groups.[37] In particular, Mexican immigrants, accounting for about one-fifth of total immigrants, have been subjected to nativist attacks for serving the interest of their homeland, not being assimilable, and taking welfare monies.[38] In the late 1980s and early 1990s, California, Florida, and other states passed referenda making English the standard language, which partly reflects anti-immigrant attitudes toward Latino immigrants. In 1994, Californians also passed Proposition 187, which was intended to make the children of illegal residents ineligible for free medical treatment and education. Although the proposition was invalidated, it targeted mainly Mexican illegal residents.

Although the separation of church and state and the emphasis on religious pluralism have helped many ethnic groups preserve their ethnic traditions through the practice of religious faith and rituals, white racism and Protestantism, as the foundational elements of American culture, have served each other since the colonial era (see the entry Religion and Racism, by Khyati Josh). At the end of the nineteenth and beginning of the twentieth century, Jewish and Catholic immigrants from eastern and southern Europe suffered prejudice and racial discrimination by native Protestants. At the beginning of the twenty-first century, Muslim, Sikh, and Hindu immigrants from South Asia and the Middle East are experiencing prejudice and discrimination by white Christians, especially by white evangelical Protestants. As documented in detail by Bozorgmehr and Bakalian in this encyclopedia, many Middle Eastern and South Asian Muslims and Sikhs have been subjected to two types of discrimination and physical violence in the post–September 11 era. First, they have become targets of hate crimes and bias incidents, such as arson, assaults, and shootings perpetrated by ordinary American citizens. Second, they have been subjected to supervision, detentions, and other forms of civil rights violations carried out by the U.S. government at the federal and local levels. Although Jewish Americans have successfully assimilated into white society, they are not safe from hate crimes either. Several white supremacist organizations, such as the Ku Klux Klan, the Christian Identity Movement, and skinheads, target Jews as well as other racial minority groups.[39]

CONTEMPORARY FORMS OF RACISM

To better understand the contemporary forms of racism in the United States, we need to make a series of distinctions among different types of racism. Until the 1960s, social scientists focused on individual racism, the belief that some racial groups are morally, intellectually, or culturally superior to other races. However, following the path-breaking book *Black Power* (1967) by Stokely Carmichael and Charles Hamilton, two black-nationalist leaders, social scientists now usually distinguish between individual racism and institutional racism. Institutional racism means that social institutions are arranged in such a way that they are disadvantageous to minority racial groups.[40] According to one source, "Institutional racism, unlike individual racism, is not an immediate action but the legacy of a past racist behavioral pattern."[41] Specifically, institutional racism refers to "the discriminatory racial practices built into such prominent structures as the political, economic, and educational system."

Racial minority groups in the United States, especially African Americans in the post–civil rights era, suffer more from institutional racism than from individual racism. As shown by Francois Pierre-Louis in his essay on this topic (Institutional Racism) in this encyclopedia, there are many examples of institutional racism, such as cultural biases in intelligence tests and the low quality of schools in inner-city black neighborhoods that keep children of lower-income black families at a disadvantage. The 1973 Rockefeller Drug Laws in New York state are another salient example of institutional racism. The laws have imposed severe penalties on those who have sold or possessed narcotic drugs and crack cocaine, and as a result of these laws, the state's prison population has increased rapidly. Most of the prisoners are African American men because users of crack cocaine are heavily concentrated in this population.[42]

Social scientists also tend to divide individual racism into two types: biological racism and symbolic racism.[43] As previously noted, biological racism, which emphasizes the intellectual superiority of northwestern Europeans, was popular in the first decade of the twentieth century. By contrast, symbolic racism focuses on a racial minority group's purported behavioral deficiencies, such as being welfare dependent, lazy, and criminally oriented, which conflict with traditional American values such as hard work and self-reliance.[44] Individual racism against minority groups in the post–civil rights period usually takes the form of symbolic racism. That is, white Americans generally attribute the lower socioeconomic status and poverty of African Americans and other minority groups to the latter's lack of motivation and work ethic, and to their unstable families. Most white Americans seem to accept the culture-of-poverty thesis endorsed by conservative scholars and policymakers.

Given the contemporary knowledge of human development, few people could persuasively argue for the genetic basis of the intellectual superiority of particular racial groups. Nevertheless, biological racism has reemerged among academics in contemporary America. In his controversial 1969 article, Arthur Jensen, an educational psychologist, argued that Asians have the highest level of cognitive abilities, blacks have the lowest, and whites are in the middle, and that these differences were largely determined by biology. Based on his findings, Jensen suggested that the Head Start program that was created at that time to boost the IQ of minority children would have a limited impact. About twenty-five years later, Richard Herrnstein and Charles Murray made a similar argument for biologically determined differences in cognitive abilities among Asians, whites, and blacks.[45] They further claimed that the differences in the cognitive abilities account for some of the social stratification among the three groups.

Joel Kovel made a distinction between dominative racism and aversive racism.[46] This distinction is also of great use for understanding the nature of racial separation in contemporary America. While dominative racism involves unfair treatment of minority members, "aversive racism" refers to the tendency to try to avoid contact with blacks and other minority members. This form of racism is the main cause of the high level of residential segregation of African Americans from white Americans and the lack of white-black social interactions at the personal level. Since the unwillingness of white Americans to contact minority members at the personal and neighborhood levels does not involve civil rights violations, the government cannot use any short-term measures to facilitate interracial friendship and dating.

Finally, most contemporary Americans can be said to commit color-blind racism, which is a form of racism that serves to maintain the racial dominance of whites by ignoring the continuing effects of historical prejudice on the life chances of minority members.[47] Many whites believe that because minority members have enjoyed equal opportunity since the enforcement of the civil rights laws the racial category should no longer be considered as a factor in college admission or employment. They claim that the United States should be a color-blind society that gives reward only based on individual merits. Those who embrace color-blind racism argue that race-based affirmative action programs are not only unfair to white Americans, they are also demeaning to minority members of society because they imply that minorities are not equal to white Americans. The main problem with their argument is that they ignore how minorities' opportunities for socioeconomic attainment have been affected by past and current racial discrimination.

Color-blind racism can be said to be "unintentional racism" in that some white Americans do not pay attention to the current status of racial inequality and the special needs of American society's minority members mainly because they are ignorant of the lingering effects of past racial discrimination and of different forms of current racial discrimination. But many other white conservatives intentionally avoid discussion of racial issues and vaguely emphasize meritocracy to protect their racial privileges.

The "California Ballot Initiative to Ban Racial Data," or California Ballot Proposition 54, was the most exemplary public expression of color-blind racism. This proposition, made by University of California regent Ward Connerly in 2002, would have prohibited state and local governments in California from classifying students, contractors, or employees by race, ethnicity, or national origin. This initiative was an effort to block researchers' and policymakers' access to racial data in employment, public education, and governmental contracts. California voters defeated the proposition in October 2003. If it had been approved, researchers and policymakers would not have information about how underrepresented blacks or Latinos are, for example, in the Los Angeles Police Department or in the student body of the University of California system.

Opponents of racial data collection argue that any kind of racial classification is arbitrary because the human species is biologically and anatomically diverse, and that it "foments separatist racial identities and promotes practices of ingroup/outgroup inclusion and exclusion."[48] But the ulterior motivation of many of the opponents is to control information about the levels of direct and indirect racial discrimination taking place in employment, education, heath care, law enforcement, and other public settings. Racial classification in public documents, however arbitrary it may be, is necessary to understanding the level and nature of racial discrimination and racial inequality, because "race serves as a basis for the distribution of social privileges and resources."[49]

NOTES

1. George Frederickson, *White Supremacy: A Comparative Study of American and South African History* (New York: Oxford University Press, 1981).

2. Terry Ann Knopf, *Rumors, Race and Riots* (New Brunswick, NJ: Transaction Books, 1975).

3. Pierre van den Berghe, *The Ethnic Phenomenon* (New York: Elsevier, 1981).

4. Russell Thornton, *American Indian Holocaust Survival: A Population History since 1492* (Norman: University of Oklahoma Press, 1987).

5. Ozie G. Simmons, "The Mutual Image and Expectations of Anglo-Americans and Mexican-Americans," in *Chicanos: Social and Psychological Perspectives,* ed. Nathaniel N. Wagner and Marsha J. Haug (St. Louis, MO: Mosby, 1971).

6. Carey McWilliams, *North from Mexico: The Spanish-Speaking People of the United States* (New York: Greenwood Press, 1968).

7. Alexander Saxton, *The Indispensable Enemy: The Labor and the Anti-Chinese Movement in California* (Berkeley, CA: University of California Press, 1971); Ronald

Takaki, *Strangers from a Different Shore: A History of Asian Americans* (Boston: Little, Brown, 1989).

8. Bill Ong Hing, *Making and Remaking of Asian America through Immigration Policy* (Stanford, CA: Stanford University Press, 1993).

9. Noel Ignatiev, *How the Irish Became White* (New York: Routledge, 1995).

10. Richard Gambino, *Vendetta* (Garden City, NY: Doubleday, 1977).

11. Frederic Cople Jaher, *A Scapegoat in the New Wilderness: The Origins and Rise of Anti-Semitism in America* (Cambridge, MA: Harvard University Press, 1994); Louise A. Mayo, *The Ambivalent Image: Nineteenth-Century America's Perception of the Jew* (Rutherford, NJ: Fairleigh Dickenson University Press, 1988); Stephen L. Slavin and Mary A. Pratt, *The Einstein Syndrome: Corporate Anti-Semitism in America Today* (New York: World Publishers, 1982).

12. Martin Marger, *Race and Ethnic Relations: American and Global Perspectives*, 5th ed. (Belmont, CA: Wadsworth, 2000).

13. Madison Grant, *The Passing of the Great Race* (New York: Charles Scribner's Sons, 1916); John Higham, *Strangers in the Land* (New York: Atheneum, 1955).

14. Nancy Foner, *From Ellis Island to J.F.K. Airport: Immigrants to New York City* (New Haven, CT: Yale University Press, 2001); Ignatiev, *How the Irish Became White*.

15. Benjamin P. Bowser and Raymond G. Hunt, *Impacts of Racism on White Americans*, 2nd ed. (Thousand Oaks, CA: Sage Publications, 1996); Joe Feagin, "The Continuing Significance of Race: Anti-Black Discrimination in Public Places," *American Sociological Review* 56 (1991): 101–116; Joe R. Feagin and Karyn D. McKinney, *The Many Costs of Racism* (Lanham, MD: Rowman & Littlefield, 2003); Joe Feagin and Melvin P. Sikes, *Living with Racism: The Black Middle-Class Experience* (Boston: Beacon Press, 1994); Andrew Hacker, *Two Nations: Black and White, Separate, Hostile, Unequal,* 2nd ed. (New York: Random House, 1995); Douglas S. Massey and Nancy Denton, *American Apartheid: Segregation and the Making of the Underclass* (Cambridge, MA: Harvard University Press, 1993); Paula S. Rotenberg, *White Privilege: Essential Readings on the Other Side of Racism* (New York: Worth Publishers, 2002); Howard Schuman, Charlotte Steeh, Lawrence Bobo, and Maria Krysan, *Racial Attitudes in America: Trends and Interpretations*, rev. ed. (Cambridge, MA: Harvard University Press, 1997); Stephen Steinberg, *The Ethnic Myth: Race, Ethnicity, and Class in America*, 2nd ed. (Boston: Beacon Press, 1988); Roger Waldinger, *Still the Promised City? African Americans and New Immigrants in Postindustrial New York* (Cambridge, MA: Harvard University Press, 1996); Cornel West, *Race Matters* (New York: Vintage Books, 1994).

16. Feagin and Sikes, *Living with Racism*, 15–16.

17. Hacker, *Two Nations*, 4.

18. Reynolds Farley, Charlotte Steeh, Maria Krysan, Tara Jackson, and Keith Reeves, "Stereotypes and Segregation: Neighborhoods in the Detroit Area," *American Journal of Sociology* 100 (1994): 750–780; Massey and Denton, *American Apartheid*.

19. Massey and Denton, *American Apartheid*.

20. Ibid.

21. William Wilson, *The Declining Significance of Race* (Chicago: University of Chicago Press, 1978); Ibid., *The Truly Disadvantaged: The Inner City, the Underclass, and Public Policy* (Chicago: University of Chicago Press, 1987); Ibid., *When Work Disappears: The World of the New Urban Poor* (New York: Knopf, 1996).

22. Waldinger, *Still the Promised City*; Roger Waldinger and Michael I. Richter, *How the Other Half Works: Immigration and the Social Organization of Race* (Berkeley: University of California Press, 2003).

23. Feagin and Sikes, *Living with Racism*.

24. Hacker, *Two Nations*, 101.

25. Philip Kasinitz, *Caribbean New York: Black Immigrants and the Politics of Race* (Ithaca, NY: Cornell University Press, 1992); Mary Waters, *Black Identities: West Indian Immigrant Dreams and American Realities* (New York: Russell Sage Foundation, 1999).

26. Robert Blauner, *Racial Oppression in America* (New York: Harper and Row, 1972); John Ogbu, "Immigrant and Involuntary Minorities in Comparative Perspective," in *Minority Status and Schooling: A Comparative Study of Immigrant and Involuntary Minorities*, ed. Margaret Gibson and John Ogbu (New York: Garland Publishing, 1991).

27. Waters, *Black Identities*.

28. Min Zhou, "The Changing Face of America: Immigration, Race/Ethnicity, and Social Mobility," in *Mass Migration to the United States: Classical and Contemporary Periods*, ed. Pyong Gap Min (Walnut Creek, CA: AltaMira Press, 2002), 82.

29. Leo Grebler, Joan W. Moor, and Ralph C. Guzman, *The Mexican-American People: The Nation's Second Largest Minority* (New York: Free Press, 1970).

30. Arthur Sakamoto and Chomghwan Kim, "The Increasing Significance of Class, the Declining Significance of Race, and Wilson's Hypothesis," *Asian American Policy Issue* 12 (2003): 19–41; Arthur Sakamoto, Jeng Liu, and Jessie Tzeng, "The Declining Significance of Race among Chinese and Japanese American Men," *Research in Social Stratification and Mobility* 16 (1998):225–246.

31. Sharon Lee and Marilyn Fernandez, "Trends in Asian American Racial/Ethnic Inter-Marriage: A Comparison of 1980 and 1990 Census Data," *Sociological Perspectives* 41 (1998): 323–342.

32. Herbert Gans, "The Possibility of a New Racial Hierarchy in the Twentieth-First Century United States," in *The Cultural Territories of Race: Black and White Boundaries*, ed. Mechele Lamont (Chicago: University of Chicago Press, 1999).

33. Pyong Gap Min, "An Overview of Asian Americans" in *Asian American: Contemporary Trends and Issues* (Thousand Oaks, CA: Sage Publications, 1995).

34. Pyong Gap Min and Rose Kim, eds., *Struggle for Ethnic Identity: Narratives by Asian American Professionals* (Walnut Creek, CA: AltaMira Press, 1999); Pyong Gap Min, *The Second Generation: Ethnic Identity among Asian Americans* (Walnut Creek, CA: AltaMira Press, 2002).

35. Mary Waters, *Ethnic Options: Choosing Identities in America* (Berkeley: University of California Press, 1990).

36. Mia Tuan, *Forever Foreigners or Honorary Whites? The Asian Ethnic Experience Today* (New Brunswick, NJ: Rutgers University Press, 1999).

37. Charles Jaret, "Troubled by Newcomers: Anti-immigrant Attitudes and Action During Two Eras of Mass Immigration to the United States," *Journal of American Ethnic History* 18 (1999): 9–39.

38. Richard D. Lamm and Gary Imhoff, *The Immigration Time Bomb: The Fragmenting of America* (New York: Truman Talley, Dutton, 1985).

39. Amy Ferber, *White Man Falling: Race, Gender, and White Supremacy* (New York: Rowman & Littlefield, 1998); Slavin and Pratt, *The Einstein Syndrome*.

40. Christopher Bates Doob, *Racism: An American Cauldron*, 3rd ed. (New York: Longman), 8; Joe Feagin, *Discrimination, American Style* (Englewood, NJ: Prentice Hall, 1978); Feagin and Sikes, *Living with Racism*, 3; Thomas Pettigrew, ed., *Racial Discrimination in the United States* (New York: Harper and Row, 1975), x.

41. Doob, *Racism*, 8.

42. Aaron Wilson, "Rockefeller Drug Laws Information Sheet," Partnership for Responsible Drug Information, 2000.

43. Doob, *Racism*, 15; Hacker, *Two Nations*, 23–27; David Sears, "Symbolic Racism,"

in *Eliminating Racism: Profiles in Controversy*, ed. Phyllis Katz and Dalmas Taylor (New York: Plenum, 1988).

44. Sears, "Symbolic Racism."

45. Richard J. Herrnstein and Charles Murray, *The Bell Curve: Intelligence and Class Structure in American Life* (New York: Free Press, 1994).

46. Joel Kovel, *White Racism: A Psychohistory* (New York: Pantheon, 1970).

47. Eduardo Bonilla-Silva, *Racism without Racists: Color-Blind Racism and the Persistence of Racial Inequality in the United States* (New York: Rowman & Little-field, 2003).

48. Yehudi Webster, "Racial Classification: A Wrong Turn," *Footnotes* 31 (January 2003): 8–9.

49. American Sociological Association, "The ASA Statement on the Importance of Collecting Data and Doing Social Science Research on Race," American Sociological Association, February 2002.

LIST OF EDITORS, ADVISORY BOARD MEMBERS, AND CONTRIBUTORS

EDITOR

Pyong Gap Min

Professor
Queens College and CUNY Graduate Center

ADVISORY BOARD MEMBERS

Steven Gold

Professor and the Acting Chair
Department of Sociology
Michigan State University

Ramon Gutierrez

Professor and Endowed Chair
Ethnic Studies Department
University of California at San Diego

Charles Jaret

Professor
Department of Sociology
Georgia State University

Ronald Taylor

Professor
Department of Sociology
Vice Provost, Multicultural and International Affairs
University of Connecticut

Min Zhou

Professor
Department of Sociology
Chair, Asian American Studies Interdepartmental Degree Program
University of California at Los Angeles

MAIN CONTRIBUTORS

Each main contributor wrote a series of at least 14 entries of varying lengths, including one long essay on a broad topic of special significance. Each contributor's long essay topic is listed below.

Daisuke Akiba

Assistant Professor
Elementary and Early Childhood Education
Queens College
Japanese American Internment

Mikaila Mariel Lemonik Arthur

Doctoral Student
Department of Sociology
New York University
Anti-Semitism in the United States

Anny Bakalian

Associate Director
The Middle East and Middle Eastern American Studies Center
September 11th (2001) Terrorism, Discriminatory Reactions to

Sandra L. Barnes

Assistant Professor
Department of Sociology
Purdue University
Culture of Poverty Thesis

Mehdi Bozorgmehr

Associate Professor
Co-Director, The Middle East and Middle Eastern American Studies Center
Hunter College and the Graduate Center of City University of New York (CUNY)
September 11th (2001) Terrorism, Discriminatory Reactions to

Fairleigh Dickenson University
Multiculturalism

Kwang Chung Kim

Emeritus Professor
Department of Sociology and Anthropology
Western Illinois University
Immigration Act of 1965

Shin Kim

Professor Emeritus
Department of Economics
Chicago State University
Immigration Act of 1965

Heon Cheol Lee

Associate Professor
Department of Sociology
University of North Carolina at Ashvillle
Nativism and the Anti-Immigrant Movements

Rebekah Lee

Assistant Professor
Department of Sociology
University of London
Derogatory Terms

Romney S. Norwood

Assistant Professor
Department of Sociology
Georgia State University
Residential Segregation

Sookhee Oh

Doctoral Student
Milano Graduate School of Management and Urban Policy
New School University
Jim Crow Laws

Francois Pierre-Louis

Assistant Professor
Department of Political Science
Queens College
Institutional Racism

Michael Roberts

Assistant Professor
Department of Sociology
San Diego State University
Race Riots

Robin Roger-Dillon

Assistant Professor
Department of Sociology
Queens College of CUNY
Biological Racism

Benjamin F. Shearer

Independent Scholar
Tallahassee, Florida
Financial Institutions and Racial Discrimination

Philip Yang

Associate Professor
Department of Sociology and Social Work
Texas Woman's University
Affirmative Action

OTHER CONTRIBUTORS

Nicholas Alexiou

Adjunct Professor
Department of Sociology
Queens College of CUNY

Jane Davis

Associate Professor
Department of English Literature
Iowa State University at Ames

On Kyung Joo

Library Media Specialist
Davison Avenue School
Long Island, New York

Rose Kim

Doctoral Student
Sociology Program
The Graduate Center of CUNY

Etsuko Maruoka-Ng

Doctoral Student
Department of Sociology
State University of New York (SUNY)—Stony Brook

Victoria Pitts

Associate Professor
Department of Sociology
Queens College of CUNY

Tiffany Vélez

Graduate Student
Department of Speech Pathology
Queens College

Barbara J. Webb

Associate Professor
Department of English Literature
Hunter College and the Graduate Center of CUNY

CHRONOLOGY OF RACE AND RACISM IN THE UNITED STATES

1790	Congress passes the Naturalization Act establishing the first rules and procedures to be used in granting citizens to immigrants
1800	Gabriel Prosser leads slave uprising in Virginia
1820	Congress enacts the Missouri Compromise by admitting Missouri as a slave state but prohibiting slavery in Louisiana Purchase territories north of Missouri's southern boundary
1822	Denmark Vesey leads a slave insurrection in Charleston, South Carolina
1824	Bureau of Indian Affairs (BIA) is created as part of the U.S. War Department to manage encounters and interactions with Native Americans
1831	In *Cherokee Nation v. Georgia*, the U.S. Supreme Court declares Georgia laws confiscating Cherokee lands unconstitutional
1831	Nat Turner leads a slavery uprising in Virginia
1833	American Anti-Slavery Society is formed in Philadelphia
1835	Publication of Alexis de Tocqueville's *Democracy in America*, an analysis of the nature of American democracy in the early nineteenth century
1836	New Philadelphia, the earliest known black town, is established in Pike County, Illinois
1838–1839	Trail of Tears: U.S. government forcibly removes the Cherokee from their lands in Georgia to Oklahoma
1845	Publication of the *Narrative of the Life of Frederick Douglass*, the autobiography of ex-slave abolitionist Frederick Douglass

1845	Term *Manifest Destiny* is coined by journalist John L. O'Sullivan in the July–August edition of the *United States Magazine and Democratic Review*
1845	United States annexes Texas
1848	Signing of the Treaty of Guadalupe Hidalgo, ending the Mexican-American War
1849	Bureau of Indian Affairs (BIA) is transferred to the U.S. Department of the Interior
1850	Congress passes a new Fugitive Slave Act as part of the Compromise of 1850
1850	Know-Nothing Party, a nativist, anti-immigrant political party, is founded
1852	Publication of Harriet Beecher Stowe's novel *Uncle Tom's Cabin*
1852	California enacts the Foreign Miners License Tax to protect white miners from foreign competition, especially from Chinese immigrants
1854	Kansas-Nebraska Act repeals the Missouri Compromise and opens all territories to the possibility of slavery
1857	In the Dred Scott Decision, the U.S. Supreme Court strikes down the Missouri Compromise (1820), declaring that Congress has no power to prohibit slavery
1859	Abolitionist John Brown raids the federal arsenal at Harper's Ferry, Virginia, in an effort to initiate a slave uprising
1862	President Abraham Lincoln issues the Emancipation Proclamation
1863	Believing they are being forced to fight and die for African Americans, with whom they are in competition for jobs, Irish immigrants riot against the Civil War draft in New York City
1865	Thirteenth Amendment is ratified, abolishing slavery in the United States
1865	Freedmen's Bureau is established by Congress to oversee all matters relating to war refugees and freed slaves
1865	Ku Klux Klan is founded in Tennessee
1866	Race riots erupt in Memphis, Tennessee, when white mobs attack African American soldiers and residents
1868	Fourteenth Amendment is ratified, requiring equal protection under the law for all citizens
1871	Anti-Chinese race riot erupts in Los Angeles after a white man is accidentally killed while trying to stop a dispute between two Chinese men
1877	To settle the disputed presidential election of 1876, the Democrats concede victory to Republican Rutherford B. Hayes, who

in turn withdraws federal troops from the South, thereby allowing white governments to overturn the political and social advances made by blacks during Reconstruction

1877–1950s Southern states and municipalities pass and enforce a series of enactments known as Jim Crow Laws, which are designed to create and maintain racial segregation and to discriminate against blacks

1882 Congress passes the Chinese Exclusion Act, which prohibits Chinese laborers from entering the United States and denies naturalized citizenship to Chinese already in the country

1884 Publican of Mark Twain's novel *Adventures of Huckleberry Finn*

1887 Congress passes the Indian Allotment Act, known as the Dawes Act, to distribute parcels of tribal land to each tribal member or family on the reservation

1890 U.S. troops massacre Lakota Sioux Indians at Wounded Knee, South Dakota

1894 Immigration Restriction League is founded in Boston to protect the American way of life from and influx of "undesirable immigrants," mainly Jews and Catholics from southern and eastern Europe

1896 In *Plessy v. Fergusson*, the U.S. Supreme Court declares the separate but equal doctrine constitutional

1898 United States annexes Hawaii

1903 Publication of W.E.B. Du Bois's classic work, *The Souls of Black Folk*

1905 Asiatic Exclusion League, originally called the Japanese and Korean Exclusion League, is formed by white nativist labor unions

1905 Niagara Movement is founded by W.E.B. Du Bois to advocate full civil rights and full manhood suffrage for African Americans

1906 San Francisco School Board orders the segregation of Japanese and Korean children in the city's schools

1907 Bellingham Riots begin when a mob of white men, who fear the loss of their jobs to immigrants, attacks a Hindu community in Bellingham, Washington

1908 Japan accepts the so-called Gentlemen's Agreement, agreeing to issue no passports for immigration to the United States except to relatives of Japanese workers already in the country

1909 National Association for the Advancement of Colored People (NAACP) is founded by an interracial group of citizens in Springfield, Illinois

1911 Dillingham Report on immigration to the United States is issued by the U.S. Commission on Immigration, a congressional commission chaired by Senator William P. Dillingham

1913	Alien Land Law is passed in California to prevent immigrants from owning or leasing land for more than three years
1913	Anti-Defamation League of B'nai Brith is founded to combat prejudice, discrimination, and violence against Jews
1915	Release of D. W. Griffith's film, *Birth of a Nation*, a racist view of U.S. history that is instrumental in the revival of the Ku Klux Klan
1915	Leo Frank, a Jew convicted of murdering a girl in Georgia in 1913, is abducted from prison and lynched, despite the existence of evidence that casts doubt on his guilt
1915	Ku Klux Klan is refounded in Georgia by William J. Simmons
1916	New York chapter of the Universal Negro Improvement Association (UNIA) is established by organization founder Marcus Garvey
1916	Publication of Madison Grant's widely read *The Passing of the Great Race*, which argues that race is a primary factor in differences in intelligence, work ethic, and social and psychological characteristics
1917	Congress prohibits all immigration from the "Asiatic Barred Zone," which includes various parts of Asia and the Middle East
1917	Competition for jobs leads to a deadly white-on-black race riot in St. Louis, Missouri
1920	American Civil Liberties Union (ACLU) is established
1922	In *Ozawa v. United States*, the U.S. Supreme Court declares that a Japanese person is not eligible for citizenship in the United States
1923	In *United States v. Thind*, the U.S. Supreme Court denies citizenship to Asian Indian immigrants
1924	Congress passes the National Origins Act, severely restricting the flow of immigrants to the United States
1924	Congress passes the Indian Citizenship Act, granting U.S. citizenship to all Native Americans who are not already citizens under some other law or treaty
1927	Execution of Nicola Sacco and Bartolomeo Vanzetti, two Italian American anarchists convicted, on largely circumstantial evidence, of two murders committed during a robbery in 1920
1928	Meriam Report on Indian reservations is issued to the Secretary of the Interior
1929	League of United Latin American Citizens (LULAC) is founded to advocate for Hispanic civil rights
1930	Japanese American Citizens League (JACL) is founded to protect the civil rights of Japanese and other Asian Americans
1930	Nation of Islam (Black Muslims) is founded in Detroit by Wallace D. Fard

1932–1972   U.S. Public Health Service conducts and funds the Tuskegee Study of Untreated Syphilis in the Negro Male, which exploits and misleads hundreds of African American men in the name of science

1934   Federal Housing Administration (FHA) is created

1934   Congress passes the Indian Reorganization Act, also known as the Wheeler-Howard Act, to increase Native American self-governance and to foster tribal economic independence

1934   Congress passes the federal Anti-Lynching Law in response to the racially motivated murders of African Americans

1935   Congress passes the Wagner Act, also known as the National Labor Relations Act, giving workers the right to independent, union representation for purposes of collective bargaining with their employers

1942   Emergency Labor Program, popularly called the Bracero Program, is established to allow Mexican workers into the United States to meet the labor needs of southwestern agriculture growers during World War II

1942   Congress of Racial Equality (CORE) is founded as a pacifist group seeking to fight racism, integrate public facilities, and work for civil rights for African Americans

1942   President Franklin D. Roosevelt signs Executive Order 9066, clearing the way for internment of Japanese Americans

1942   War Relocation Authority (WRA) is established by executive order of President Roosevelt as the government agency responsible for removing persons believed to be threats to national security

1943   Detroit Race Riot comprises a series of violent encounters, sparked by competition for jobs and housing, between whites and African Americans in Detroit, Michigan

1943   Zoot Suit Riots, consisting of white attacks on Mexican American youths, erupt in Los Angeles

1944   In *Korematsu v. United States*, the U.S. Supreme Court case upholds the internment of Japanese Americans during World War II

1944   National Congress of American Indians (NCAI) is founded to lobby for Native American rights and causes

1946   Congress creates the Indian Claims Commission (ICC) to hear and determine claims against the U.S. government made by any Native American tribe or group

1947   Jackie Robinson joins the Brooklyn Dodgers, becoming the first African American player in major-league baseball

1948   President Harry S. Truman issues Executive Order 9981 racially integrating the U.S. military

1948	In *Shelley v. Kraemer*, the U.S. Supreme Court rules that the equal protection clause of the Fourteenth Amendment prevents racially restrictive housing covenants from being enforceable
1948	American GI Forum, an organization devoted to securing equal rights for Hispanic American veterans, is founded by Hector P. Garcia
1948	In *Oyama v. California*, the U.S. Supreme Court strikes down California's Alien Land Laws as unconstitutional
1952	Congress passes the McCarran-Walter Act, which eases certain restrictions on immigrants of particular national origins
1954	In *Brown v. Board of Education of Topeka*, the U.S. Supreme Court declares racial segregation in schools unconstitutional
1954	Publication of Gordon Allport's *The Nature of Prejudice*, an influential work examining and defining the nature of racial prejudice
1954	U.S. Immigration and Naturalization Service launches the controversial paramilitary repatriation program, "Operation Wetback," which targets Mexicans working "illegally" in the agricultural industry of the Southwest
1955	African American Rosa Parks refuses to give up her seat on a Montgomery, Alabama, bus to a white passenger, thereby initiating the Montgomery Bus Boycott
1955	Publication of John Higham's *Strangers in the Land*, a classic analysis of nativism in the United States
1956	Publication of Kenneth Stampp's *The Peculiar Institution*, which views slavery as a coercive and profit-seeking regime, a significant revision in the way historians have previously seen the institution
1957	Southern Christian Leadership Conference (SCLC) is created in New Orleans by a group of ministers, labor leaders, lawyers, and political activists concerned about the impact of segregation on their communities
1957	U.S. Commission on Civil Rights (USCCR) is created by the Civil Rights Act of 1957 as an independent, fact-finding arm of the federal government
1957	President Dwight D. Eisenhower sends federal troops to protect from angry whites nine black students attempting to integrate Central High School in Little Rock, Arkansas
1958	John Birch Society is founded by Robert Welch to advocate limited government, anticommunism, and American isolationism
1959	American Nazi Party is founded by George Lincoln Rockwell
1960	Student Nonviolent Coordinating Committee (SNCC) is founded at Shaw University in Raleigh, North Carolina, to coordinate nonviolent protest actions against racial segregation

1960	Publication of John Howard Griffin's *Black Like Me*, the story of the extensive loss of rights and privileges suffered by a white man who darkened his skin to pass for black
1961	President John F. Kennedy issues Executive Order 10925, which makes first use of the term *affirmative action* in calling on government contractors to treat employees "without regard to their race, creed, color, or national origin"
1961	Freedom Riders, blacks and whites who travel together across the South in buses, protest racial segregation
1961	Release of *West Side Story*, a groundbreaking film about white–Puerto Rican race relations
1962	National Farm Workers Association (NFWA), later the United Farm Workers (UFW), is founded by Cesar Chavez and Dolores Huerta
1963	March on Washington is organized to bring attention to the lack of job opportunities and civil rights for African Americans
1963	Martin Luther King Jr. delivers his "I Have a Dream" speech before the Lincoln Memorial in Washington, DC
1963	Martin Luther King Jr. writes his "Letter from a Birmingham Jail" while incarcerated for his role in antisegregation demonstrations in Birmingham, Alabama
1963	Reies Lopez Tijerina founds the Alianza Federal de Pueblos Libres (Federal Alliance of Land Grant) to reclaim Spanish and Mexican land grants held by Mexican and Native Americans before the Mexican-American War (1846–1848)
1964	Congress passes the Civil Rights Act to end the deeply entrenched practices of racial segregation and other forms of racial discrimination
1964	Bracero Program, which has allowed Mexican workers into the United States since 1942, is ended
1964	Organization of Afro-American Unity (OAAU) is founded by Malcolm X to coordinate political action and self-organization among blacks toward the goal of racial equality
1964	Harlem riot begins when a white police officer shoots and kills an African American youth in Yorkville, New York
1965	Congress creates the federal Department of Housing and Urban Development (HUD)
1965	Publication of Paul M. Siegel's groundbreaking article, "On the Cost of Being a Negro," which examines the true extent of the income gap between blacks and whites
1965	El Teatro Campensino, the Farmworkers Theater, is founded by Luis Valdez as part of the organizing effort of Cesar Chavez's United Farm Workers union

1965	Congress passes the Voting Rights Act, which requires certain state and local jurisdictions to get federal approval before altering their voting procedures
1965	Congress passes the Immigration Act, phasing out national-origin quotas and emphasizing the reunification of families
1965	Race riots erupt in the Watts neighborhood of Los Angeles
1965	Publication of Daniel Patrick Moynihan's *The Negro Family in America: The Case for National Action*, which blames the poverty and social problems afflicting African Americans on the breakdown of the family
1966	Black Panther Party for Self-Defense is formed by Huey Newton, Bobby Seale, and other radical black activists
1966	In *Miranda v. Arizona* (1966), the U.S. Supreme Court establishes suspects' right to an attorney and to be informed of their rights before questioning by police
1966	Maulana Karenga, professor of black studies at California State University, develops Kwanzaa as a cultural holiday to promote the African American experience
1967	Race riot erupts in Newark, New Jersey
1967	Publication of *Black Power: The Politics of Liberation in America* by Stokely Carmichael and Charles V. Hamilton
1967	Discrimination and poor housing for blacks spark violent race riots in Detroit, Michigan
1967	National Advisory Commission on Civil Disorders (the Kerner Commission) is formed by President Lyndon B. Johnson to investigate the causes and implications of the urban riots occurring in black sections of many major cities
1968	American Indian Movement (AIM) is founded
1968	Congress passes another Civil Rights Act to ensure fair housing practices (Title VIII, known as the Fair Housing Act) and confer various civil rights on Native Americans
1968	Bilingual Education Act is passed by Congress
1968	Kerner Commission (the National Advisory Commission on Civil Disorders) issues its report on the series of urban race riots that occurred in 1967
1968	Mexican American Legal Defense and Education Fund (MALDEF) is founded in San Antonio, Texas, to protect the civil rights of Latinos and promote their empowerment and full participation in society
1969	Arthur Jensen publishes a widely cited article in the *Harvard Education Review* attacking Head Start programs and claiming that African American children have a low average IQ that cannot be improved by social engineering

1969	MEChA (Spanish acronym for "The Chicano Student Movement of Aztlán"), a national college student organization for Chicano/as, is founded
1969	Native American activists begin a nineteen-month occupation of Alcatraz Island in San Francisco Bay
1970	National Chicano Moratorium demonstration against the Vietnam War and discrimination against Hispanics at home occurs in Los Angeles
1971	Alaska Native Claims Settlement Act is passed by Congress to resolve Native Alaskan claims to lands appropriated by the federal government
1971	United Farm Workers (UFW) is created from a merger of the Agricultural Workers Organizing Committee, founded in 1959, and the National Farm Workers Association, founded in 1962
1971	Arab Community Center for Economic and Social Services (ACCESS), an Arab American support and advocacy organization, is established
1971	*All in the Family*, Norman Lear's groundbreaking sit-com about bigot Archie Bunker, premiers on CBS
1972	Congress passes the Equal Employment Opportunity Act to amend the 1964 Civil Rights Act, making it more effective in ensuring equal job opportunities
1972	In *Furman v. Georgia*, the U.S. Supreme Court declares the death penalty "capricious and arbitrary" and thus unconstitutional
1972	Publication of Robert Blauner's *Racial Oppression in America*, which challenges the traditional theoretical paradigm of racial relations in the United States, that is, the classical assimilation theory, and proposes instead the internal-colonialism paradigm
1973	Organization of Chinese Americans, Inc. (OCA), a national nonprofit, nonpartisan advocacy organization of concerned Chinese and Asian Americans, is founded
1973	American Indian Movement members occupy Wounded Knee, South Dakota
1973	In *Lau v. Nichols*, the U.S. Supreme court rules that the San Francisco public school system violated the Civil Rights Act of 1964 by denying non-English-speaking students of Chinese ancestry a meaningful opportunity to participate in public education
1974	Publication of Nathan Glazer's *Affirmative Discrimination: Ethnic Inequality and Public Policy*, which argues that affirmative action is actually "affirmative discrimination" against individuals

1974	Asian American Legal Defense and Education Fund (AALDEF) is founded to protect the legal rights of Asian Americans
1975	Aryan Nations, a white-supremacist, anti-Semitic group, is founded by Richard G. Butler
1975	Congress amends the Voting Rights Act of 1965 to protect the voting rights of citizens of certain ethnic groups whose first language is not English
1975	Congress passes the Indian Self-Determination and Education Assistance Act to implement tribal self-determination in matters relating to delivery of educational, health, and other services to Native Americans
1976	In *Gregg v. Georgia*, the U.S. Supreme Court reinstates the death penalty
1976	Publication of Alex Haley's *Roots: The Saga of an American Family*, a semiautobiographical history of Haley's family and their experiences as slaves
1978	In *Regents of the University of California v. Bakke*, the U.S. Supreme Court upholds the concept of affirmative action
1978	Publication of William J. Wilson's influential *The Declining Significance of Race*, a polemic on the relative importance of race and class for life chances of African Americans
1978	Publication of Joe Feagin's *Discrimination, American Style*, which argues that racial discrimination is embedded in institutions and policies designed to address the concerns of white European males
1980	American-Arab Anti-Discrimination Committee is established
1981	U.S. Department of Education formulates a clear policy that Ebonics is a form of English, not a separate language, and thus not eligible for public funding
1982	Vincent Chin is murdered in Detroit, Michigan, by two white autoworkers who mistake him for Japanese and blame him for the loss of American jobs
1983	Publication of Thomas Sowell's *Economics and Politics of Race*, in which a conservative social scientist argues that culture makes a difference in the success of an ethnic group and that racial strife has affected human society throughout history
1984	Publication of Charles Murray's *Losing Ground: American Social Policy, 1950–1980*, a controversial examination of U.S. government social programs
1985	Arab American Institute is established to represent the interests of Americans of Arab descent in politics and to foster their civic and political empowerment
1985	Rainbow Coalition is founded by Reverend Jesse Jackson to unite people of diverse ethnic, religious, economic, and political backgrounds in a push for social, racial, and economic justice

1986	Howard Beach incident occurs, in which Michael Griffith, a black Trinidadian immigrant, is killed after he and two other men are attacked by a gang of white teenagers in the white Howard Beach neighborhood in Queens, New York
1986	Publication of Michael Omi and Howard Winant's *Racial Formation in the United States: From the 1960s to the 1980s*, a groundbreaking work on racial theory
1987	Dot-buster attacks occur, in which Latino gangs in Jersey City, New Jersey, threaten violence and vandalism against Asian Indian residents who do not leave the city
1988	Osama Bin Laden, the son of a Saudi billionaire, forms Al Qaeda, an organization that develops in the 1990s into a global terrorist network that promotes an extremist and militant form of Islam and attacks U.S. global interests
1988	Bensonhurst incident occurs, in which black teenager Yusef Hawkins is beaten to death by white youths in Bensonhurst neighborhood of Brooklyn, New York
1988	Congress passes the Fair Housing Amendments Act to strengthen provisions of the Fair Housing Act of 1968 by giving the Department of Housing and Urban Development (HUD) greater power to enforce the earlier legislation
1988	Congress approves the Civil Liberties Act, authorizing redress payments to Japanese Americans interned during World War II
1989	Publication of Stephen Steinberg's *Ethnic Myth: Race, Ethnicity and Class in America*, which challenges various prevailing ideas about race and ethnicity in the United States
1989	In *City of Richmond v. J.A. Croson Company*, the U.S. Supreme Court rules that a city affirmative action program violates the equal protection clause of the Fourteenth Amendment
1990	Congress passes the Hate Crimes Statistics Act, which requires the Department of Justice to compile annual national data on hate crimes and publish an annual summary of findings
1991	Yankel Rosenbaum, a Jewish yeshiva student, is murdered by a black mob in Crown Heights, New York
1991	Los Angeles police officers are taped beating Rodney King, an African American motorist, after King refuses to be pulled over
1991	Congress passes another Civil Rights Act to reverse recent court rulings that seem to weaken enforcement of earlier civil rights legislation
1992	Riots erupt in Los Angeles after the acquittal of the police officers accused in the Rodney King beating incident
1994	California voters pass Proposition 187, the Save Our State Initiative, which denies publicly funded nonemergency medical care, education, and social services to illegal immigrants and their foreign-born children

1994	Council on American Islamic Relations (CAIR) is to advocate for the civil rights of Muslim Americans
1994	Publication of scholar Cornel West's *Race Matters*, which examines the role of race in shaping the African American experience
1995	Minister Louis Farrakhan of the Nation of Islam sponsors the Million Man March on Washington to support African American families
1995	Publication of *Black Wealth/White Wealth: A New Perspective on Racial Inequality*, a book by Melvin L. Oliver and Thomas M. Shapiro detailing disparities in wealth between whites and blacks
1995	Right-wing extremists bomb the Alfred P. Murrah Federal Building in Oklahoma City
1995	O. J. Simpson, an African American football legend, is acquitted of murdering his wife, Nicole Brown Simpson, and Ron Goldman, who were both white
1995	Publication of John Yinger's *Closed Doors, Opportunities Lost: The Continuing Costs of Housing Discrimination*, examining various housing studies to determine how closely the housing industry is adhering to the Fair Housing Act of 1968
1996	Richard J. Herrnstein and Charles Murray publish *The Bell Curve: Intelligence and Class Structure in American Life*, in which they present statistical evidence that supposedly supports the notion of racial superiority based on IQ
1996	California voters pass Proposition 209, the California Civil Rights Initiative, which repeals affirmative action in public employment, education, or contracting
1996	In *Shaw v. Hunt*, the U.S. Supreme Court declares that race cannot be the sole factor in redrawing congressional districts
1997	California voters pass Proposition 227, the English Language Education for Children in Public Schools Initiative, which eliminates bilingual education in California public schools
1998	James Byrd Jr., a black man, is murdered in Jasper, Texas, by three white racists who slit his throat and drag his body behind a truck
1999	Publication of Mary Waters's *Black Identities: West Indian Immigrant Dreams and American Realities*, an award-winning book that explores the experiences of West Indian immigrants in New York
1999	Amadou Diallo, an immigrant working as a street vendor in New York, is shot by four undercover police officers, who mistake him for a rape suspect
1999	Wen Ho Lee, a Chinese American engineer working at the Los Alamos Research Laboratory, is accused of spying by the government and fired from his job in violation of his civil rights. He is later cleared of all charges

2001   Members of the militant Islamist organization Al Qaeda, acting on orders of the group's leader, Osama Bin Laden, launch terrorist attacks on New York City and Washington, DC, that kill almost 3,000 people

2001   Patriot Act is passed in the wake of the September 11, 2001, terrorist attacks to increase the effectiveness of U.S. law enforcement in detecting and preventing further acts of terrorism

2003   U.S. Supreme Court renders decisions in two University of Michigan affirmation action cases—*Grutter v. Bollinger* and *Gratz v. Bollinger*—declaring that race can be considered in university admissions decisions but cannot be a "deciding factor"

2003   California voters reject Proposition 54, the Racial Privacy Initiative (RPI), which would have banned the use and production of racially coded data by various state and municipal agencies

LIST OF ENTRIES

Abolitionist Movement

Academic Racism

"Acting White" Stage of Life

Adaptive Discrimination

Affirmative Action

Affirmative Action, University of Michigan Ruling on

Affirmative Discrimination: Ethnic Inequality and Public Policy

Afrocentrism

Alaska Native Claims Settlement Act of 1971

Alien Land Laws on the West Coast

All-Black Resorts

Al Qaeda

American-Arab Anti-Discrimination Committee (ADC)

American Civil Liberties Union (ACLU)

American Dream Ideology

American GI Forum (AGIF)

American Indian Movement (AIM)

American Literature and Racism

American Nazi Party (ANP)

American "Obsession with Race"

Americanization Movement

Anglo Conformity

Anti-Catholicism in the United States

Anti-Defamation League of B'nai Brith (ADL)

Anti-Semitism in the United States

Arab American Institute (AAI)

Arab Community Center for Economic and Social Services (AC-CESS)

Arab/Muslim American Advocacy Organizations, Responding to the Backlash

Archie Bunker Bigotry

Aryan Nations

Asian American Legal Defense and Education Fund (AALDEF)

Asian Americans, Discrimination against

Asian Americans for Equality (AAFE)

Asian Americans, Perceptions of as Foreigners

Asian Americans, Violence against

Asiatic Barred Zone

Asiatic Exclusion League (AEL)

Assimilation Theory

Back-to-Africa Movement

Barrios

Bellingham Riots

Bensonhurst Incident

Bigots, Types of

Bilingual Education

Biological Racism

Black Anti-Semitism

Black Conservatives

"Black English" (Ebonics)

Black Family Instability Thesis

Black Identities: West Indian Immigrant Dreams and American Realities

Black-Korean Conflicts

Black Nationalist Movement

Black Panther Party

Black Political Disenfranchisement

Black Power: The Politics of Liberation in America

Black Wealth/White Wealth: A New Perspective on Racial Inequality

Blacks, Wage Discrimination against

Blaming-the-Victim Argument

Block-busting

Boycotts

Bracero Program

Brown v. Board of Education of Topeka

Buffalo Soldiers

Bureau of Indian Affairs (BIA)

Busing

Byrd, James Jr.

California Ballot Proposition 54

California Ballot Proposition 187

California Ballot Proposition 209

California Ballot Proposition 227

Caló

Campus Ethnoviolence

Capitalism and Racial Inequality

Capital Punishment and Racial Inequality

Caribbean Immigrants, Attitudes toward African Americans

Caribbean Immigrants, Class Differences in the Second Generation

Caribbean Immigrants, Experience of Racial Discrimination

Carmichael, Stokely

Chavez, Cesar

Cherokee Nation v. Georgia

Chicano Movement

Chin, Vincent

Chinese Exclusion Act of 1882

Chinese Immigrants, Adaptation of to Female Jobs

Chinese Immigrants and Anti-Chinese Sentiments

Civil Rights Act of 1964

Civil Rights Act of 1968

Civil Rights Act of 1991

Civil Rights Movement

Civil War and the Abolition of Slavery

Closed Doors, Opportunities Lost: The Continuing Costs of Housing Discrimination

College Admission, Discrimination in

Colonization Complex

Colonized versus Immigrant Minorities

Color-Blind Racism

Color Hierarchy

Color Line

Columbus Day Controversy

Congress of Racial Equality (CORE)

Coolie

"Cost of Being a Negro"

Council on American Islamic Relations (CAIR)

Covert versus Overt Discrimination

Creation Generation

Crime and Race

Criminal Justice System and Racial Discrimination

Cultural Genocide

Culture of Poverty Thesis

Declining Significance of Race, The

Deindustrialization and Racial Inequality

De Jure and De Facto Segregation

Democracy in America

Derogatory Terms

Detroit Race Riot of 1943

Detroit Race Riot of 1967

Diallo, Amadou

Dillingham Report

Discrimination, American Style

Diversities, Ethnic and Racial

Dot Buster Attacks

Douglass, Frederick

Draft Riot of 1863

Dred Scott Decision

Driving while Black, Stopping People for

Dual Housing Markets

Du Bois, W.E.B

Duke, David

Economics and Politics of Race

Economics of Discrimination

Education and Racial Discrimination

El Teatro Campensino

Emancipation Proclamation

English-Only Movement

Environmental Racism

Equal Employment Opportunity Act of 1972

Ethnic Myth: Race, Ethnicity, and Class in America

Ethnic Options

Ethnic Retention and School Performance

Ethnic Studies

Ethnocentrism

Ethnogenesis

Eugenics Movement

Executive Order 9066

Executive Order 9981

Expatriation

Exposure Index

Fair Housing Act of 1968

Fair Housing Amendments Act of 1988

Fair-Housing Audit

Fair-Weather Liberals

Farrakhan, Louis

Federal Housing Administration (FHA)

Films and Racial Stereotypes

Financial Institutions and Racial Discrimination

Ford, Henry

Foreign Miners License Tax

Fourteenth Amendment

Frank, Leo

Freedmen's Bureau

Freedom Riders

Free Persons of Color in the Antebellum North

Fu Manchu

Furman v. Georgia

Garvey, Marcus

Genotype versus Phenotype

Gentlemen's Agreement of 1908

Gerrymandering, Racial

Ghost Dance Religion

Goddard, Henry H.

Godfather, The

Gonzales, Rodolfo "Corky"

Government Initiatives after the September 11, 2001, Attack on the United States

"Green Menace"

Guadalupe Hidalgo, Treaty of

Gulf War

Gutierrez, Jose Angel

Haitians, Discrimination against in Refugee Policy

Harlem Renaissance

Harlem Riot of 1964

Hate Crimes

Hate Crimes Statistics Act of 1990

Hawaii, Annexation of

Hayes-Tilden Compromise of 1877

Hereditarians versus Environmentalists

Hidden Curriculum

Hispanics, Prejudice and Discrimination against

Hollywood and Minority Actors

Homelessness and Minority Groups

Housing Discrimination

Howard Beach Incident

Identity Politics

"I Have a Dream" Speech

Illegitimacy and Race

Immigrant Preference in Employment

Immigration Act of 1965

Immigration Restriction League of 1894

Indentured Servants

Index of Dissimilarity

Indian Allotment Act of 1887

Indian Citizenship Act of 1924

Indian Claims Commission (ICC)

Indian Occupation of Alcatraz Island

Indian Reorganization Act of 1934 (IRA)

Indian Reservations

Indian Self-Determination and Education Assistance Act of 1975 (ISDEAA)

Institutional Racism

Intelligence and Standardized Tests, Cultural Biases in

Intelligence Tests and Racism

Intermarriage

Internal Colonialism

Internalized Racism

Iran Hostage Crisis and Anti-Iranian Stereotypes

Irish Immigrants, Prejudice and Discrimination against

Islamic Jihad

Italian Americans, Prejudice and Discrimination against

Italian Americans, Violence against

Jackson, Jesse

Japan Bashing

Japanese American Citizens League (JACL)

Japanese American Internment

Japanese Americans, Redress Movement for

Jeffries, Leonard

Jensen, Arthur

Jewish-Black Conflicts

Jewish Defense League (JDL)

Jihad

Jim Crow Laws

John Birch Society

Journalism and Racial Stereotypes

Kerner Commission Report

King, Martin Luther Jr.

Know-Nothing Party

Korematsu v. United States

Ku Klux Klan (KKK)

Kwanzaa

Labor Movement, Racism in

Laissez-Faire Racism

La Raza Unida

Lau v. Nichols

League of United Latin American Citizens (LULAC)

Lee, Wen Ho

Legacy of Past Discrimination Argument for Affirmative Action

"Letter from a Birmingham Jail"

Liberal and Conservative Views of Racial Inequality

Lincoln, Abraham, and the Emancipation of Slaves

Literacy Test

Little Rock (Arkansas) Central High School, Integration of

Los Angeles Riot of 1871

Los Angeles Riots of 1992

Losing Ground: American Social Policy, 1950–1980

Lynching

Malcolm X

Manifest Destiny

March on Washington

March on Washington Movement

McCarran-Walter Act of 1952

Melting Pot

Memphis Race Riot of 1866

Meriam Report

Mestizo

Mexican American Legal Defense and Education Fund (MALDEF)

Mexican-American War

Mexican Americans, Prejudice and Discrimination against

Mexican Americans, Violence against

Mexican Illegals, Labor Exploitation of

Mexican Repatriations

Middle Easterners, Historical Precedents of Backlash against

Middle Easterners, Stereotypes of

Middleman Minorities

"Migrant Superordination and Indigenous Subordination"

Million Man March on Washington

Minstrelsy

Mismatch Hypothesis

Missouri Compromise

Model Minority Thesis

Modern Racism

Montgomery Bus Boycott

Morrison, Toni

Muhammad, Elijah

Mulatto

Multiculturalism

Music Industry, Racism in

Muslim Philanthropic Organizations, Closure of after September 11, 2001

Muslims, Prejudice and Discrimination against

Muslims, Terrorist Image of

Nation of Islam

National Advisory Commission on Civil Disorders

National Association for the Advancement of Colored People (NAACP)

National Chicano Moratorium

National Congress of American Indians (NCAI)

National Crime Victimization Survey (NCVS)

National Origins Act of 1924

Native Americans, Conquest of

Native Americans, Forced Relocation of

Native Americans, Prejudice and Discrimination against

Nativism and the Anti-Immigrant Movements

Naturalization Act of 1790

Nature of Prejudice, The

Negative Self-Image among Minorities

Negro Family: The Case for National Action, The

Neocolonialism

Neo-Nazism

Newark Riot of 1967

Niagara Movement

Nigger

Noble Savage

Non-Judeo-Christian Immigrant Groups, Violence against

Nonwhite Racism

Nordic Superiority

Oklahoma City Federal Building Bombing

One-Drop Rule

Operation Wetback

Oppositional Identity

Organization of Afro-American Unity (OAAU)

Organization of Chinese Americans (OCA)

Orientalism

"Origin of Ethnic Stratification"

Ozawa v. United States

Paine, Thomas

Pan-Asian Solidarity

Pan-ethnic Movements

Parks, Rosa

Passing of the Great Race, The

Passing, Psychosocial

Peculiar Institution: Slavery in the Ante-bellum South, The

Philippine-American War

Plantation System

Political Correctness (P.C.)

Poll Tax

Powell, Colin

Prejudice, Cognitive and Emotional Dimensions of

Proximal Host

Race Card in Political Campaigns

Race Matters

Race Relations, Paternalistic versus Competitive

Race-Relations Cycle

Race Riots

Racial Classification of Population

Racial Difference in Poverty Rate

Racial Differences in Property Holding

Racial Earnings Gap

Racial Formation in the United States: From the 1960s to the 1980s

Racial Ghettoes

Racialism

Racialization

Racial Oppression in America

Racial Purity

Racial Segregation, White and Black Preferences as a Cause of

Racial Socialization

Racial Stigmatization

Racism, Aversive versus Dominative

Rainbow Coalition

Randolph, A. Philip

Rape and Racism

Reconstruction Era

Redistricting

Redlining

Red Power Movement

Regents of the University of California v. Bakke

Religion and Racism

Religious Right

Reparations for African Americans

Residential Segregation

Restrictive Covenants

Reverse Discrimination

Richmond v. Croson

Robinson, Jackie

Rodney King Beating

Role-Model Argument for Affirmative Action

Roots

Sacco and Vanzetti Case

San Francisco School Board Crisis of 1906

Scapegoat Theory of Racial Prejudice

School Segregation

"Second-Generation Decline"

Segmented-Assimilation Theory

Segregation, Voluntary versus Involuntary

Self-Fulfilling Prophecy

Separate but Equal Doctrine

September 11, 2001, Terrorism, Discriminatory Reactions to

Sharecropping

Shaw v. Hunt

Shelley v. Kraemer

Simpson, O.J.

Sioux Outbreak of 1890

Sit-ins

Skinheads

Slave Auctions

Slave Codes

Slave Families

Slave Revolts and White Attacks on Black Slaves

Slave Trade

Slavery and American Indians

Slavery in the Antebellum South

Social Construction of Whiteness

Social Darwinism

Social Distance

South Asians, Ambiguity in Racial Identity among

Southern Christian Leadership Conference (SCLC)

Spanish-American War

Spencer, Herbert

Sports and Racism

Sports Mascots

St. Louis Riot of 1917

Statistical Discrimination

Strangers in the Land: Patterns of American Nativism, 1860–1925

Student Nonviolent Coordinating Committee (SNCC)

Symbolic Racism

Television and Racial Stereotypes

Television Drama and Racism

Terman, Lewis

Texas, Annexation of

Texas Rangers

Texas Rebellion

Third World Movement of the 1960s

Thomas, Clarence

Thurmond, Strom

Tijerina, Reies Lopez

Tokenism

Toxic Neighborhoods

Tracking

Tuskegee Syphilis Experiment

Underground Railroad

Undocumented Immigrants

United Farm Workers (UFW)

United States v. Thind

U.S. Border Patrol

U.S. Commission on Civil Rights (USCCR)

U.S. Department of Housing and Urban Development (HUD)

Voting Rights Act of 1965

Voting Rights Amendments of 1975

Wagner Act

Wallace, George

War and Racial Inequality

War on Poverty and the Great Society

War Relocation Authority (WRA)

Washington, Booker T.

WASPs

Welfare Dependency

West Side Story

White Flight

White-Supremacist Movement in the United States

White-Supremacist Underground

Yellow Peril

Yellows

Zionist Occupied Government (ZOG)

Zoot Suit Riots

GUIDE TO RELATED ENTRIES

African Americans

"Acting White" Stage of Life

Affirmative Action

Afrocentrism

All-Black Resorts

Back-to-Africa Movement

Bensonhurst Incident

Black Anti-Semitism

Black Conservatives

"Black English" (Ebonics)

Black Family Instability Thesis

Black-Korean Conflicts

Black Nationalist Movement

Black Panther Party

Black Political Disenfranchisement

Black Power: The Politics of Liberation in America

Black Wealth/White Wealth: A New Perspective on Racial Inequality

Blacks, Wage Discrimination against

Block-busting

Brown v. Board of Education of Topeka

Buffalo Soldiers

Busing

Byrd, James Jr.

Caribbean Immigrants, Attitudes toward African Americans

Carmichael, Stokely

Civil Rights Movement

Color Line

"Cost of Being a Negro"

Culture of Poverty Thesis

Diallo, Amadou

Douglass, Frederick

Driving while Black, Stopping People for

Du Bois, W.E.B.

Expatriation

Farrakhan, Louis

Freedmen's Bureau

Freedom Riders

Free Persons of Color in the Antebellum North

Garvey, Marcus

Harlem Renaissance

"I Have a Dream" Speech

Jackson, Jesse

Jewish-Black Conflicts

Jim Crow Laws

King, Martin Luther Jr.

Kwanzaa

"Letter from a Birmingham Jail"

Literacy Test

Little Rock (Arkansas) Central High
School, Integration of

Lynching

Malcolm X

March on Washington

March on Washington Movement

Million Man March on Washington

Minstrelsy

Montgomery Bus Boycott

Morrison, Toni

Mulatto

National Association for the Advancement of Colored People
(NAACP)

*Negro Family: The Case for Na-
tional Action, The*

Niagara Movement

Nigger

Oppositional Identity

Organization of Afro-American
Unity (OAAU)

Parks, Rosa

Passing, Psychosocial

Poll Tax

Powell, Colin

Randolph, A. Philip

Reparations for African Americans

Robinson, Jackie

Roots

Separate but Equal Doctrine

Sharecropping

Simpson, O. J.

Southern Christian Leadership Conference (SCLS)

Thomas, Clarence

Tuskegee Syphilis Experiment

Washington, Booker T.

**Asian Americans and Pacific
Islanders**

Asian American Legal Defense and
Education Fund (AALDEF)

Asian Americans, Discrimination
against

Asian Americans for Equality
(AAFE)

Asian Americans, Perceptions of as
Foreigners

Asian Americans, Violence against

Asiatic Barred Zone

Bellingham Riots

Black-Korean Conflicts

Chin, Vincent

Chinese Exclusion Act of 1882

Chinese Immigrants, Adaptation of
to Female Jobs

Chinese Immigrants and Anti-
Chinese Sentiments

Coolie

Dot Buster Attacks

Executive Order 9066

Foreign Miners License Tax

Fu Manchu

Gentlemen's Agreement of 1908

Hawaii, Annexation of

Japan Bashing

Japanese American Citizens League
(JACL)

Japanese American Internment

Japanese Americans, Redress Movement for

Korematsu v. United States

Lau v. Nichols

Lee, Wen Ho

Organization of Chinese Americans (OCA)

Orientalism

Ozawa v. United States

Pan-Asian Solidarity

San Francisco School Board Crisis of 1906

South Asians, Ambiguity in Racial Identity among

United States v. Thind

War Relocation Authority (WRA)

Yellow Peril

Books, Articles, Reports, and Other Documents

Affirmative Discrimination: Ethnic Inequality and Public Policy

Black Identities: West Indian Immigrant Dreams and American Realities

Black Power: The Politics of Liberation in America

Black Wealth/White Wealth: A New Perspective on Racial Inequality

Closed Doors, Opportunities Lost: The Continuing Costs of Housing Discrimination

"Cost of Being a Negro"

Declining Significance of Race, The

Democracy in America

Dillingham Report

Discrimination, American Style

Economics and Politics of Race

Ethnic Myth: Race, Ethnicity and Class in America

Kerner Commission Report

"Letter from a Birmingham Jail"

Losing Ground: American Social Policy, 1950–1980

Meriam Report

"Migrant Superordination and Indigenous Subordination"

Nature of Prejudice, The

Negro Family: The Case for National Action, The

"Origin of Ethnic Stratification"

Passing of the Great Race, The

Peculiar Institution: Slavery in the Ante-bellum South, The

Race Matters

Racial Formation in the United States: From the 1960s to the 1980s

Racial Oppression in America

Roots

Strangers in the Land: Patterns of American Nativism, 1860–1925

Civil Rights

American Civil Liberties Union (ACLU)

Boycotts

Brown v. Board of Education of Topeka

Busing

Carmichael, Stokely

Civil Rights Act of 1964

Civil Rights Act of 1968

Civil Rights Act of 1991

Civil Rights Movement

De Jure and De Facto Segregation

Driving while Black, Stopping People for

Du Bois, W.E.B.

Fourteenth Amendment

Freedom Riders

Garvey, Marcus

"I Have a Dream" Speech

Jackson, Jesse

Jim Crow Laws

King, Martin Luther Jr.

"Letter from a Birmingham Jail"

Literacy Test

Little Rock (Arkansas) Central High
School, Integration of

Lynching

Malcolm X

March on Washington

March on Washington Movement

Montgomery Bus Boycott

National Association for the Advancement of Colored People (NAACP)

Parks, Rosa

Poll Tax

Racial Segregation, White and Black
Preferences as a Cause of

Randolph, A. Philip

Residential Segregation

Rodney King Beating

School Segregation

Segregation, Voluntary versus Involuntary

Separate but Equal Doctrine

Sit-ins

Southern Christian Leadership Conference (SCLS)

U.S. Commission on Civil Rights
(USCCR)

Voting Rights Act of 1965

Voting Rights Amendments of 1975

Concepts, Beliefs, and Theories

"Acting White" Stage of Life

Afrocentrism

American Dream Ideology

American "Obsession with Race"

Anglo Conformity

Assimilation Theory

Black Family Instability Thesis

Blaming-the-Victim Argument

Colonization Complex

Color Hierarchy

Color Line

Culture of Poverty Thesis

Ethnic Options

Ethnocentrism

Ethnogenesis

Exposure Index

Genotype versus Phenotype

Hereditarians versus Environmentalists

Identity Politics

Index of Dissimilarity

Internal Colonialism

Kwanzaa

Laissez-Faire Racism

Legacy of Past Discrimination Argument for Affirmative Action

Manifest Destiny

Melting Pot

Mismatch Hypothesis

Model Minority Thesis

Multiculturalism

Neocolonialism

Neo-Nazism

Nordic Superiority

One-Drop Rule

Oppositional Identity

Passing, Psychosocial

Political Correctness (P.C.)

Proximal Host

Race-Relations Cycle

Racialism

Racialization

Racial Purity

Racial Socialization

Racial Stigmatization

Reparations for African Americans

Role-Model Argument for Affirmative Action

Scapegoat Theory of Racial Prejudice

"Second-Generation Decline"

Segmented-Assimilation Theory

Self-Fulfilling Prophecy

Separate but Equal Doctrine

Social Construction of Whiteness

Social Darwinism

Social Distance

Tokenism

WASPs

Welfare Dependency

White Flight

Court Cases

Affirmative Action, University of Michigan Ruling on

Brown v. Board of Education of Topeka

Cherokee Nation v. Georgia

Dred Scott Decision

Furman v. Georgia

Korematsu v. United States

Lau v. Nichols

Ozawa v. United States

Regents of the University of California v. Bakke

Richmond v. Croson

Sacco and Vanzetti Case

Separate but Equal Doctrine

Shaw v. Hunt

Shelley v. Kraemer

United States v. Thind

Derogatory or Stereotypical Words and Terms

Coolie

Derogatory Terms

Fu Manchu

Journalism and Racial Stereotypes

Nigger

Yellow Peril

Yellows

Discrimination and Prejudice

Adaptive Discrimination

Affirmative Discrimination: Ethnic Inequality and Public Policy

Anti-Catholicism in the United States

Anti-Semitism in the United States

Archie Bunker Bigotry

Asian Americans, Discrimination against

Asiatic Exclusion League (AEL)

Bigots, Types of

Black Anti-Semitism

Blacks, Wage Discrimination against

Caribbean Immigrants, Experience of Racial Discrimination

Closed Doors, Opportunities Lost: The Continuing Costs of Housing Discrimination

College Admission, Discrimination in

Covert versus Overt Discrimination

Criminal Justice System and Racial Discrimination

De Jure and De Facto Segregation

Discrimination, American Style

Driving while Black, Stopping People for

Economics of Discrimination

Education and Racial Discrimination

Fair-Weather Liberals

Haitians, Discrimination against in Refugee Policy

Hispanics, Prejudice and Discrimination against

Housing Discrimination

Intermarriage

Irish Immigrants, Prejudice and Discrimination against

Italian Americans, Prejudice and
Discrimination against

Jim Crow Laws

Legacy of Past Discrimination Argument for Affirmative Action

Literacy Test

Mexican Americans, Prejudice and
Discrimination against

Muslims, Prejudice and Discrimination against

Native Americans, Prejudice and
Discrimination against

Nature of Prejudice, The

Prejudice, Cognitive and Emotional
Dimensions of

Redlining

Reverse Discrimination

Rodney King Beating

Scapegoat Theory of Racial Prejudice

September 11, 2001, Terrorism, Discriminatory Reactions to

Statistical Discrimination

Economics and Labor

*Black Wealth/White Wealth: A New
Perspective on Racial Inequality*

Blacks, Wage Discrimination against

Boycotts

Capitalism and Racial Inequality

*Closed Doors, Opportunities Lost:
The Continuing Costs of Housing Discrimination*

"Cost of Being a Negro"

Culture of Poverty Thesis

Deindustrialization and Racial Inequality

Dual Housing Markets

Economics and Politics of Race

Economics of Discrimination

Financial Institutions and Racial
Discrimination

Foreign Miners License Tax

Immigrant Preference in Employment

Labor Movement, Racism in

Laissez-Faire Racism

Mexican Illegals, Labor Exploitation
of

Racial Difference in Poverty Rate

Racial Earnings Gap

Sharecropping

United Farm Workers (UFW)

Wagner Act

War on Poverty and the Great Society

Welfare Dependency

Education

Bilingual Education

"Black English" (Ebonics)

*Brown v. Board of Education of
Topeka*

Busing

Campus Ethnoviolence

College Admission, Discrimination
in

Education and Racial Discrimination

English-Only Movement

Ethnic Retention and School Performance

Ethnic Studies

Hidden Curriculum

Intelligence and Standardized Tests,
Cultural Biases in

Intelligence Tests and Racism

Lau v. Nichols

Multiculturalism

Oppositional Identity

Political Correctness (P.C.)

San Francisco School Board Crisis of 1906

School Segregation

Tracking

Hispanic Americans

American GI Forum (AGIF)

Barrios

Bilingual Education

Bracero Program

California Ballot Proposition 187

California Ballot Proposition 227

Caló

Chavez, Cesar

Chicano Movement

Creation Generation

El Teatro Campensino

English-Only Movement

Gonzales, Rodolfo "Corky"

Guadalupe Hidalgo, Treaty of

Gutierrez, Jose Angel

Hispanics, Prejudice and Discrimination against

La Raza Unida

League of United Latin American Citizens (LULAC)

Manifest Destiny

Mestizo

Mexican American Legal Defense and Education Fund (MALDEF)

Mexican-American War

Mexican Americans, Prejudice and Discrimination against

Mexican Americans, Violence against

Mexican Illegals, Labor Exploitation of

Mexican Repatriations

National Chicano Moratorium

Operation Wetback

Texas, Annexation of

Texas Rangers

Texas Rebellion

Tijerina, Reies Lopez

United Farm Workers (UFW)

Zoot Suit Riots

Housing and Real Estate

Block-busting

Closed Doors, Opportunities Lost: The Continuing Costs of Housing Discrimination

Dual Housing Markets

Fair Housing Act of 1968

Fair Housing Amendments Act of 1988

Fair-Housing Audit

Federal Housing Administration (FHA)

Homelessness and Minority Groups

Housing Discrimination

Racial Differences in Property Holding

Racial Ghettoes

Racial Segregation, White and Black Preferences as a Cause of

Redlining

Residential Segregation

Restrictive Covenants

Shelley v. Kraemer

Toxic Neighborhoods

U.S. Department of Housing and Urban Development (HUD)

White Flight

Immigration and Immigrants

Asiatic Barred Zone

Asiatic Exclusion League (AEL)

Black Identities: West Indian Immigrant Dreams and American Realities

California Ballot Proposition 187

California Ballot Proposition 227

Caribbean Immigrants, Attitudes toward African Americans

Caribbean Immigrants, Class Differences in the Second Generation

Caribbean Immigrants, Experience of Racial Discrimination

Chinese Exclusion Act of 1882

Chinese Immigrants, Adaptation of to Female Jobs

Chinese Immigrants and Anti-Chinese Sentiments

Colonized versus Immigrant Minorities

Dillingham Report

Diversities, Ethnic and Racial

Expatriation

Foreign Miners License Tax

Gentlemen's Agreement of 1908

Haitians, Discrimination against in Refugee Policy

Immigrant Preference in Employment

Immigration Act of 1965

Immigration Restriction League of 1894

Irish Immigrants, Prejudice and Discrimination against

McCarran-Walter Act of 1952

Melting Pot

National Origins Act of 1924

Nativism and the Anti-Immigrant Movements

Naturalization Act of 1790

Non-Judeo-Christian Immigrant Groups, Violence against

Operation Wetback

Proximal Host

"Second-Generation Decline"

Strangers in the Land: Patterns of American Nativism, 1860–1925

United States v. Thind

Undocumented Immigrants

U.S. Border Patrol

Individuals

Byrd, James Jr.

Carmichael, Stokely

Chavez, Cesar

Chin, Vincent

Diallo, Amadou

Douglass, Frederick

Du Bois, W.E.B.

Duke, David

Farrakhan, Louis

Ford, Henry

Frank, Leo

Garvey, Marcus

Goddard, Henry H.

Gonzales, Rodolfo "Corky"

Gutierrez, Jose Angel

Jackson, Jesse

Jeffries, Leonard

Jensen, Arthur

King, Martin Luther Jr.

Lee, Wen Ho

Lincoln, Abraham, and the Emancipation of Slaves

Malcolm X

Morrison, Toni

Muhammad, Elijah

Paine, Thomas

Parks, Rosa

Powell, Colin

Randolph, A. Philip

Robinson, Jackie

Simpson, O.J.

Spencer, Herbert

Terman, Lewis

Thomas, Clarence

Thurmond, Strom

Tijerina, Reies Lopez

Wallace, George

Washington, Booker T.

Jews

Anti-Defamation League of B'nai
  Brith (ADL)

Anti-Semitism in the United States

Aryan Nations

Black Anti-Semitism

Frank, Leo

Jewish-Black Conflicts

Jewish Defense League (JDL)

Zionist Occupied Government
  (ZOG)

Laws, Treaties, Propositions, Constitutional Amendments, and Executive Orders

Alaska Native Claims Settlement
  Act of 1971

Alien Land Laws on the West Coast

Asiatic Barred Zone

California Ballot Proposition 54

California Ballot Proposition 187

California Ballot Proposition 209

California Ballot Proposition 227

Chinese Exclusion Act of 1882

Civil Rights Act of 1964

Civil Rights Act of 1968

Civil Rights Act of 1991

Equal Employment Opportunity
  Act of 1972

Executive Order 9066

Executive Order 9981

Fair Housing Act of 1968

Fair Housing Amendments Act of
  1988

Fourteenth Amendment

Guadalupe Hidalgo, Treaty of

Hate Crimes Statistics Act of 1990

Immigrant Act of 1965

Indian Allotment Act of 1887

Indian Citizenship Act of 1924

Indian Reorganization Act of 1934
  (IRA)

Indian Self-Determination and Educational Assistance Act of 1975
  (ISDEAA)

Jim Crow Laws

McCarran-Walter Act of 1952

Missouri Compromise

National Origins Act of 1924

Naturalization Act of 1790

Voting Rights Act of 1965

Voting Rights Amendments of 1975

Wagner Act

Movements

Abolitionist Movement

Afrocentrism

Americanization Movement

Back-to-Africa Movement

Black Nationalist Movement

Chicano Movement

Civil Rights Movement

English-Only Movement

Eugenics Movement

Expatriation

Freedom Riders

Harlem Renaissance

Japanese Americans, Redress Movement for

Labor Movement, Racism in

March on Washington Movement

Nativism and the Anti-Immigrant Movements

Niagara Movement

Pan-ethnic Movements

Red Power Movement

Third World Movement of the 1960s

White-Supremacist Movement in the United States

Muslims, Arabs, and Middle Easterners

Al Qaeda

American-Arab Anti-Discrimination Committee (ADC)

Arab American Institute (AAI)

Arab Community Center for Economic and Social Services (AC-CESS)

Arab/Muslim American Advocacy Organizations, Responding to the Backlash

Asiatic Barred Zone

Council on American Islamic Relations (CAIR)

Farrakhan, Louis

Government Initiatives after the September 11, 2001, Attack on the United States

"Green Menace"

Gulf War

Iran Hostage Crisis and Anti-Iranian Stereotypes

Islamic Jihad

Jihad

Middle Easterners, Historical Precedents of Backlash against

Middle Easterners, Stereotypes of

Muhammad, Elijah

Muslim Philanthropic Organizations, Closure of after September 11, 2001

Muslims, Prejudice and Discrimination against

Muslims, Terrorist Image of

Nation of Islam

September 11, 2001, Terrorism, Discriminatory Reactions to

Native Americans

Alaska Native Claims Settlement Act of 1971

American Indian Movement (AIM)

Buffalo Soldiers

Bureau of Indian Affairs (BIA)

Cherokee Nation v. Georgia

Columbus Day Controversy

Ghost Dance Religion

Indian Allotment Act of 1887

Indian Citizenship Act of 1924

Indian Claims Commission (ICC)

Indian Occupation of Alcatraz Island

Indian Reorganization Act of 1934 (IRA)

Indian Reservations

Indian Self-Determination and Educational Assistance Act of 1975 (ISDEAA)

Meriam Report

National Congress of American Indians (NCAI)

Native Americans, Conquest of

Native Americans, Forced Relocation of

Native Americans, Prejudice and Discrimination against

Noble Savage

Red Power Movement

Sioux Outbreak of 1890

Slavery and American Indians

Organizations, Groups, and Government Agencies

Al Qaeda

American-Arab Anti-Discrimination Committee (ADC)

American Civil Liberties Union (ACLU)

American GI Forum (AGIF)

American Indian Movement (AIM)

American Nazi Party (ANP)

Anti-Defamation League of B'nai Brith (ADL)

Arab American Institute (AAI)

Arab Community Center for Economic and Social Services (AC-CESS)

Arab/Muslim American Advocacy Organizations, Responding to the Backlash

Aryan Nations

Asian American Legal Defense and Education Fund (AALDEF)

Asian Americans for Equality (AAFE)

Asiatic Exclusion League (AEL)

Black Panther Party

Bureau of Indian Affairs (BIA)

Congress of Racial Equality (CORE)

Council on American Islamic Relations (CAIR)

Federal Housing Administration (FHA)

Freedmen's Bureau

Freedom Riders

Immigration Restriction League of 1894

Indian Claims Commission (ICC)

Islamic Jihad

Japanese American Citizens League (JACL)

Jewish Defense League (JDL)

John Birch Society

Know-Nothing Party

Ku Klux Klan (KKK)

La Raza Unida

League of United Latin American Citizens (LULAC)

Mexican American Legal Defense and Education Fund (MALDEF)

Muslim Philanthropic Organizations, Closure of after September 11, 2001

Nation of Islam

National Advisory Commission on Civil Disorders

National Association for the Advancement of Colored People (NAACP)

National Congress of American Indians (NCAI)

Organization of Afro-American Unity (OAAU)

Organization of Chinese Americans (OCA)

Rainbow Coalition

Southern Christian Leadership Conference (SCLC)

Student Nonviolent Coordinating Committee (SNCC)

Texas Rangers

United Farm Workers (UFW)

U.S. Border Patrol

U.S. Commission on Civil Rights (USCCR)

U.S. Department of Housing and Urban Development (HUD)

War Relocation Authority (WRA)

Policies, Programs, and Government Acts

Affirmative Action

Affirmative Action, University of Michigan Ruling on

Anglo Conformity

Asiatic Barred Zone

Boycotts

Bracero Program

Busing

Government Initiatives after the September 11, 2001, Attack on the United States

Haitians, Discrimination against in Refugee Policy

Hawaii, Annexation of

Hayes-Tilden Compromise of 1877

Indian Reservations

Legacy of Past Discrimination Argument for Affirmative Action

Literacy Test

Little Rock (Arkansas) Central High School, Integration of

National Crime Victimization Survey (NCVS)

Poll Tax

Racial Classification of Population

Rodney King Beating

Role-Model Argument for Affirmative Action

Texas, Annexation of

Tuskegee Syphilis Experiment

War on Poverty and the Great Society

Politics

Black Conservatives

Black Panther Party

Black Political Disenfranchisement

Black Power: The Politics of Liberation in America

Busing

Columbus Day Controversy

Crime and Race

Economics and Politics of Race

Fair-Weather Liberals

Gerrymandering, Racial

Hawaii, Annexation of

Hayes-Tilden Compromise of 1877

Identity Politics

"I Have a Dream" Speech

Iran Hostage Crisis and Anti-Iranian Stereotypes

Know-Nothing Party

Liberal and Conservative Views of Racial Inequality

Manifest Destiny

Missouri Compromise

Political Correctness (P.C.)

Powell, Colin

Race Card in Political Campaigns

Redistricting

Religious Right

Thurmond, Strom

Racism and Race

Academic Racism

American Literature and Racism

Archie Bunker Bigotry

Bigots, Types of

Biological Racism

Capitalism and Racial Inequality

Capital Punishment and Racial Inequality

Color-Blind Racism

Crime and Race

Criminal Justice System and Racial Discrimination

Declining Significance of Race, The

Deindustrialization and Racial Inequality

Diversities, Ethnic and Racial

Economics and Politics of Race

Environmental Racism

Ethnic Myth: Race, Ethnicity and Class in America

Eugenics Movement

Exposure Index

Films and Racial Stereotypes

Financial Institutions and Racial Discrimination

Gerrymandering, Racial

Hate Crimes

"I Have a Dream" Speech

Illegitimacy and Race

Institutional Racism

Intelligence Tests and Racism

Internalized Racism

Journalism and Racial Stereotypes

Ku Klux Klan (KKK)

Labor Movement, Racism in

Laissez-Faire Racism

Liberal and Conservative Views of Racial Inequality

Literacy Test

Little Rock (Arkansas) Central High School, Integration of

Modern Racism

Music Industry, Racism in

Neo-Nazism

Nonwhite Racism

Nordic Superiority

Race Card in Political Campaigns

Race Matters

Race-Relations Cycle

Race Relations, Paternalistic versus Competitive

Race Riots

Racial Classification of Population

Racial Difference in Poverty Rate

Racial Differences in Property Holding

Racial Earnings Gap

Racial Ghettoes

Racialism

Racialization

Racial Purity

Racial Segregation, White and Black Preferences as a Cause of

Racial Socialization

Racial Stigmatization

Racism, Aversive versus Dominative

Rape and Racism

Religion and Racism

Skinheads

Social Darwinism

Sports and Racism

Symbolic Racism

War and Racial Inequality

Religion

Anti-Catholicism in the United States

Anti-Semitism in the United States

Black Anti-Semitism

Ghost Dance Religion

Know-Nothing Party

Nation of Islam

Nativism and the Anti-Immigrant Movements

Non-Judeo-Christian Immigrant Groups, Violence against

Religion and Racism

Religious Right

United States v. Thind

WASPs

Riots

Bellingham Riots

Detroit Race Riot of 1943

Detroit Race Riot of 1967

Draft Riot of 1863

Harlem Riot of 1964

Los Angeles Riot of 1871

Los Angeles Riot of 1992

Memphis Race Riot of 1866

Newark Riot of 1967

Race Riots

St. Louis Riot of 1917

Zoot Suit Riots

Slavery, Abolition, and Reconstruction

Abolitionist Movement

Civil War and the Abolition of Slavery

Douglass, Frederick

Dred Scott Decision

Emancipation Proclamation

Fourteenth Amendment

Freedmen's Bureau

Free Persons of Color in the Antebellum North

Guadalupe Hidalgo, Treaty of

Hayes-Tilden Compromise of 1877

Indentured Servants

Ku Klux Klan (KKK)

Lincoln, Abraham, and the Emancipation of Slaves

Literacy Test

Manifest Destiny

Missouri Compromise

Peculiar Institution: Slavery in the Ante-bellum South, The

Plantation System

Reconstruction Era

Roots

Sharecropping

Slave Auctions

Slave Codes

Slave Families

Slave Revolts and White Attacks on Black Slaves

Slavery and American Indians

Slavery in the Antebellum South

Slave Trade

Underground Railroad

Sports, Entertainment, Culture, and Leisure

All-Black Resorts

El Teatro Campensino

Films and Racial Stereotypes

Fu Manchu

Godfather, The

Harlem Renaissance

Hollywood and Minority Actors

Minstrelsy

Morrison, Toni

Multiculturalism

Music Industry, Racism in

Robinson, Jackie

Simpson, O. J.

Sports and Racism

Sports Mascots

Television and Racial Stereotypes

Television Drama and Racism

West Side Story

Terrorism and 9/11

Al Qaeda

Arab/Muslim American Advocacy Organizations, Responding to the Backlash

Cultural Genocide

Government Initiatives after the September 11, 2001, Attack on the United States

"Green Menace"

Islamic Jihad

Middle Easterners, Historical Precedents of Backlash against

Muslim Philanthropic Organizations, Closure of after September 11, 2001

Muslims, Terrorist Image of

Oklahoma City Federal Building Bombing

September 11, 2001, Terrorism, Discriminatory Reactions to

Violent, Acts and Victims of

Asian Americans, Violence against

Bellingham Riots

Bensonhurst Incident

Byrd, James Jr.

Campus Ethnoviolence

Chin, Vincent

Cultural Genocide

Diallo, Amadou

Dot Buster Attacks

Frank, Leo

Hate Crimes

Howard Beach Incident

Italian Americans, Violence against

Ku Klux Klan (KKK)

Little Rock (Arkansas) Central High School, Integration of

Lynching

Mexican Americans, Violence against

Native Americans, Forced Relocation of

Non-Judeo-Christian Immigrant Groups, Violence against

Oklahoma City Federal Building Bombing

Rape and Racism

Rodney King Beating

Slave Revolts and White Attacks on Black Slaves

Wars and Military

American GI Forum (AGIF)

Buffalo Soldiers

Civil War and the Abolition of Slavery

Draft Riot of 1863

Executive Order 9066

Executive Order 9981

Guadalupe Hidalgo, Treaty of

Gulf War

Japanese American Internment

Mexican-American War

Native Americans, Conquest of

Philippine-American War

Sioux Outbreak of 1890

Spanish-American War

Texas Rebellion

War and Racial Inequality

War Relocation Authority (WRA)

White Supremacy

Aryan Nations

Duke, David

Ku Klux Klan (KKK)

Neo-Nazism

Nordic Superiority

Oklahoma City Federal Building Bombing

Skinheads

White-Supremacist Movement in the United States

White-Supremacist Underground

Zionist Occupied Government (ZOG)

S

Sacco and Vanzetti Case

Nicola Sacco and Bartolomeo Vanzetti were two Italian immigrant anarchists who were convicted of murder, sentenced to death on circumstantial evidence, and executed in 1927. On April 15, 1920, a paymaster and his guard were shot to death during the robbery of a shoe factory in South Braintree, Massachusetts. Three weeks later, despite there being little evidence against them, Sacco, a shoe worker, and Vanzetti, a fish peddler, were accused and arrested for the crime. After a seven-week trial rife with circumstantial evidence, Sacco and Vanzetti were convicted of the murder and sentenced to death. Seven years later, on August 23, 1927, both men were executed, in spite of numerous appeals and worldwide protests. The Sacco and Vanzetti Case is considered as "the case that will never die" because of the many controversies that surround it.

The fundamental controversy is that their conviction was based less on evidence than on racial prejudice and bias against their radical political views and their Italian background. The overall indications support the view that the two men did not receive a fair trial in light of the anti-immigrant sentiment of the 1920s. This period is characterized as a turbulent decade of social unrest, during which numerous southern and eastern European immigrants, mostly Catholic, Jewish, and Eastern Orthodox, were discriminated against for their political or religious beliefs and ethnicity. It was a decade of intense nationalism, in which the rights of immigrants were violated in such events as the Red Scare and Palmer Raids. In August 1977, Massachusetts governor Michael Dukakis signed a proclamation that recognized the faults of the trial and cleared the names of both men. August 23 has been established as "Sacco-Vanzetti Memorial Day" in Massachusetts. The execution of Sacco and Vanzetti is an extreme example of prejudice, discrimination, and racial violence against Italian immigrants.

Italian immigrants Nicola Sacco and Bartolomeo Vanzetti stand in handcuffs with unidentified escorts, Massachussetts, circa 1927.

AP/Wide World Photos.

See also Italian Americans, Prejudice and Discrimination against; Italian Americans, Violence against.

Nicholas Alexiou

San Francisco School Board Crisis of 1906

In 1906, the San Francisco School Board ordered the segregation of Japanese and Korean children in the San Francisco city school system (Chinese children already attended separate schools). At the time of this decision, there were only ninety-three Japanese American students attending public school in San Francisco, and they were scattered across the city's twenty-three schools. The decision was related to the anti-Asian movement then gaining strength in California (and across the United States), particularly among labor groups. This movement came about from the belief that Asian immigration was a threat to the entire nation and its way of life.

This resulted in a diplomatic crisis between the United States and Japan, which was outraged about how its citizens and their children were being treated. President Theodore Roosevelt convinced the school board to back down and allow Japanese children to attend school with white children, but only by promising Californians an end to Japanese immigration, the result of which was the Gentlemen's Agreement, which barred Japanese laborers from migrating to the United States. This agreement also stopped the immigration of Japanese by way of Canada, Mexico, and Hawaii.

See also Asian Americans, Discrimination against; Education and Racial Discrimination.

Further Reading

Wollenberg, Charles. *All Deliberate Speed: Segregation and Exclusion in California Schools, 1855-1975.* Berkeley: University of California Press, 1976.

Mikaila Mariel Lemonik Arthur

Save Our State Initiative

See California Ballot Proposition 187.

Scapegoat Theory of Racial Prejudice

The scapegoat theory of racial prejudice is a psychological theory that attempts to explain individual prejudice within personality dynamics. This personality-centered explanation of prejudice links prejudice to the individual's needs to deal with frustration and express aggression against a substitute target or a "scapegoat." The theory asserts that when individuals find themselves in circumstances in which the cause of frustration is unavailable or inappropriate, a process called displacement might occur. In this case, the frustrated individuals find a substitute target or a "scapegoat" against whom they transfer their hostility and aggression. This theory also suggests that the level of prejudice that exists in a society will reflect the level of individual frustration. In this respect, periods of difficult socioeconomic and political conditions, such as high inflation or unemployment, are usually characterized by an increase in displaced aggression and expressions of prejudice against a subordinate group.

Most frequently, groups that have been targeted are economically or politically weak. Moreover, preexisting stereotypes against certain ethnic/racial groups supply oversimplifications about those groups and make the scapegoating process easier. For example, in many different times and countries, Jews have been held responsible for economic crises and unemployment of a society, as a whole, while in the U.S., blacks have been blamed for high crime rates. Typically, by scapegoating others, the group that does the blaming fails to realize and analyze the existing social and economic realities that contribute to their misfortunes.

The scapegoat theory has been criticized for being overly simplistic. Some critics argue that aggression is not an automatic or unvarying reaction to frustration and also that the likelihood of displacement varies widely for different types of individuals. Although the scapegoat hypothesis provides some insights into one cause of prejudice, it does not adequately explain the complexity of many other possible variables and factors involved in any general explanation of prejudice.

See also Prejudice, Cognitive and Emotional Dimensions of.

Nicholas Alexiou

School Performance

See Ethnic Retention and School Performance.

School Segregation

School segregation refers to the separation of students in schools by race either by government actions and law (de jure) or by individual actions (de facto). The U.S. Supreme Court's decision in the 1954 *Brown v. Board of Education* case defined school segregation as state actions that explicitly created dual systems of education based on race.

One of the earliest court decisions that dealt with de jure school segregation was the *Robert v. City of Boston* case in 1848. Five-year-old Sarah Robert was barred from the local primary school because she was black. Her father sued the city. The lawsuit was part of an organized effort by the African American community to end racially segregated schools. In 1855, Boston's black community finally reaped the rewards of their years of struggle for equal school rights when racially segregated schools were abolished by the Massachusetts State Legislature. In 1896, during the Jim Crow era, the Supreme Court, however, decided in *Plessy v. Ferguson* that separate facilities for blacks and whites were justified. Separate schools for white and colored children soon became a legitimate part of everyday life in the South for the next half century.

The 1938 Supreme Court began to change course, starting with *Missouri ex rel. Gaines v. Canada*. In this decision, the Court ruled that graduate and professional schools for blacks could not possibly be both separate and equal and that, therefore, blacks had the right to be admitted to white programs and schools. In 1954, *Brown v. Board of Education* finally ended this long history of legal school segregation by declaring school segregation unconstitutional.

In 1968, after the *Brown* ruling, the court turned its attention to the remedy for this violation of the Constitution in *Charles C. Green v. County School Board of New Kent County* and defined what it meant by desegregation. School segregation, the Court said, was reflected not only in enrollments by race, but also in the district's success in desegregating and eliminating discrimination in terms of faculty, staff, transportation, extracurricular activities, and facilities. The Court's guidelines mandated massive integration from 1968 to 1973 because the Court placed an affirmative duty on school boards to integrate.

Laws can be changed, but people's attitudes linger. De facto school segregation results not from laws but primarily from individuals' actions or residential choices. This kind of school segregation occurs when a neighborhood is racially homogeneous. De facto segregation generally stems from a variety of residential patterns, population migration, and economic and political factors.

The Supreme Court first used the term *de facto* in the 1971 *Swann* decision, when it said that de facto school segregation did not require court action. In 1973, however, after hearing the *Keyes* case in Denver, the court found that many governmental actions (in this case, the actions of urban-development agencies) had led to de facto school segregation. So even though de facto school segregation may not be the result of explicit state or local government actions, government policies can reinforce it. For example, white flight into suburban areas combined with the Supreme Court's *Milliken v. Bradley* ruling in 1974, which prevented a multidistrict desegregation plan, increased disparities in racial composition between the city and suburban districts.

Racial integration of schools, or school desegregation, is important for three major reasons. First, the racial integration of schools is considered the most effective method to equalize educational resources across racial groups. Second and more importantly, the racial integration of schools can contribute to overall racial integration in society. White students who have attended an in-

White and African American fourth graders at St. Martin School dash for the playground at recess, September 1954.

AP/Wide World Photos.

tegrated school are more likely to accept minority members as their coworkers or neighbors than are those who have attended an all-white school. Third, there is considerable evidence that students who attend integrated schools have more access to social networks that may have both economic and social influence in the lives of young people than those who attend segregated schools.

But black students still attend highly segregated schools. A 2003 Harvard study (Frankenberg et al. 2003) found that American schools have become segregated although the nation's minority student enrollment has approached 40 percent of all public school students. For example, 70 percent of black students now attend school where minority enrollment is over 50 percent. About 37 percent of Latino students go to schools where less than 10 percent of the school population is white. White students on average attend schools in which 80 percent of the students are white.

See also Education and Racial Discrimination; Ethnic Retention and School Performance; Race Riots; San Francisco School Board Crisis of 1906; Segregation, Voluntary versus Involuntary.

Further Reading

Clotfelter, Charles. *Public School Segregation in Metropolitan Areas.* Working paper 6779, National Bureau of Economic Research, 1998.

Frankenberg, Erika, Chungmei Lee, and Gary Orfield. *A Multiracial Society with Segregated Schools: Are We Losing the Dream?* The Civil Rights Project, Harvard University, 2003.

Raffel, Jeffrey. *Historical Dictionary of School Segregation and Desegregation: The American Experience.* Westport, CT: Greenwood Press, 1998.

Sookhee Oh

SCLC

See Southern Christian Leadership Conference (SCLC).

"Second-Generation Decline"

As the children of post–1965 immigrants reach adulthood and enter the workforce, the economic experiences of these second-generation Americans, particularly those of racialized minorities, have become important research and policy topics. Are second-generation Americans following the historic assimilation and mobility trajectories of earlier European immigrant groups? How will the assimilation process be affected by changes in the economic "context of reception," especially by the declining need for physical labor?

One scholar, Herbert Gans, fears that some members of the second generation, including the Vietnamese, Salvadorans, Haitians, and others from Asia, Latin America, the Caribbean and Africa, especially those whose parents are among the working poor, may end up in persistent poverty, following the patterns of native-born blacks, Puerto Ricans, Mexicans, and other Hispanics. There are several reasons for his prediction of the economic decline of the second generation. The first is limited job opportunities due to the restructuring of the American economy that has resulted in massive deindustrialization and the loss of entry-level manufacturing jobs that may not require English language proficiency or skills. Second, the children of these lower-class immigrants of color may not receive a good education and thus may lack the skills and connections necessary to do better economically than their parents. Moreover, they may be unwilling to work at immigrant wages and hours. Subsequently, these second-generation members will join the jobless and/or occupy marginal economic positions, maybe even losing out to newer immigrant workers who are ready to work at low wages and long hours in the next period of economic growth.

Traditional theories of immigrant acculturation and assimilation were based on the experiences of southern and eastern European immigrants of the last great wave during a period of economic expansion and growth at the end of the nineteenth and the beginning of the twentieth century. The most popular theory of immigrant incorporation is the "straight-line" theory of assimilation that proposes each native-born generation acculturates more and improves its status relative to the previous one. The straight-line theory is problematic because how the economic context shapes opportunities for incorporation is not considered. In addition, the straight-line trajectory or progression toward complete assimilation is a myth and minimizes the role of human choices or agency in the formation of one's identity, including ethnic identity. Gans has noted that many still identify with an ethnic group even though it may be mostly symbolic, indulging for example, in "familial and leisure-time ethnicity." He suggests that the process of assimilation is more like a "bumpy-line" than a "straight line."

See also Deindustrialization and Racial Inequality; Segmented-Assimilation Theory.

Further Reading

Gans, Herbert J. "Second Generation Decline: Scenarios for the Economic and Ethnic Futures of the Post–1965 American Immigrants." *Ethnic and Racial Studies* 15, no. 2 (April 1992): 173–192.

Portes, Alejandro, and Min Zhou. "The New Second Generation: Segmented Assimilation and Its Variants." *Annals of the American Academy of Political Science* 530 (1993): 74–96.

Waldinger, Roger, and Joel Perlmann. "Second Generations: Past, Present, Future." *Journal of Ethnic and Migration Studies* 24, no. 1 (1998): 5–24.

Tarry Hum

Segmented-Assimilation Theory

The theory of segmented assimilation was first formulated by Alejandro Portes and Min Zhou (1993) and further elaborated later (e.g., Zhou 1997). It was an attempt to challenge the classic assimilation theory and to address the processes and outcomes of second-generation adaptation to the United States.

According to the classic assimilation theory, second-generation Americans, or children of immigrants, will inevitably become assimilated into the mainstream middle-class American culture and social structure and move up the socioeconomic ladder. Assimilation is a straight-line process, and its outcome is uniform upward mobility for all new groups (Gordon 1964).

However, since the 1960s this orthodox approach has met growing challenges. For example, recent studies have found that longer U.S. residence is associated with maladjustment such as poor school performance, low aspirations, and deviant behaviors—substance abuse, violence, delinquency, premarital sex. Studies have also revealed diverse generational differences in socioeconomic performance. Herbert Gans (1992), for example, speculated that children of poor, especially dark-skinned, immigrants would be trapped in high rates of unemployment, crime, drug use, alcoholism, and other pathologies associated with poverty and that there was little hope of their upward mobility over their immigrant parents. Gans dubbed this phenomenon "second-generation decline." On the other hand, some immigrants of middle-class or upper-class backgrounds, as well as their children, bypass the traditional bottom-up path and jump several steps ahead.

Built on the new empirical evidence, the segmented assimilation theory rejects both the straight-line process and uniform upward mobility as the only outcome of assimilation prescribed by the classic assimilation theory. The basic idea of this new theory is that the processes and outcomes of second-generation adaptation are diverse and segmented, and not all groups or individuals will experience upward mobility. American society consists of segregated and unequal segments, so the outcomes of second-generation adaptation depend on which segment of society one assimilates to. According to Portes and Zhou (1993), there are three possible multidirectional outcomes of mobility: (1) upward mobility into normative, middle-class America; (2) downward mobility into the underclass; and (3) economic upward mobility into middle-class America, with lagged acculturation and deliberate preservation of the immigrant community's cultures and institutions.

The segmented assimilation theory also seeks to explain what factors determine which segment of American society a particular immigrant group assimilates to. Zhou (1997) highlights two categories of factors: (1) factors intrinsic to the group, such as financial and human capital upon arrival, family structure, community organization, and networks of social support and control; (2) structural/contextual factors, including economic opportunities, racial stratification, residential segregation, and family socioeconomic backgrounds. It is the interaction of these two categories of factors that accounts for the diverse outcomes of second-generation adaptation.

The segmented assimilation theory appears to offer a viable framework for explaining the diverse patterns of intergenerational mobility in contemporary America and has gained growing recognition in the fields of immigration and ethnic/racial studies. What is needed in future research is to expand the current theory to explain vertical outcomes (especially nonlinear outcomes) of *intergenerational* mobility rather than just a horizontal array of outcomes for second generation, and to take into account how gender intersects with generation, class, and race to generate differential outcomes. In addition, such bidirectional terms as *adaptation*, *integration*, or *incorporation* more accurately reflect changes from two-way interactions between immigrants and their children and the host society than *assimilation*, which implies unidirectional change.

See also Assimilation Theory; Oppositional Identity; Race-Relations Cycle.

Further Reading

Gans, Herbert. "Second Generation Decline: Scenarios for the Economic and Ethnic Futures of the Post–1965 American Immigrants." *Ethnic and Racial Studies* 15 (1992): 173–192.

Gordon, Milton. *Assimilation in American Life*. New York: Oxford University Press, 1964.

Portes, Alejandro, and Min Zhou. "The New Second Generation: Segmented Assimilation and Its Variants among Post–1965 Immigrant Youth." *Annals of the American Academy of Political and Social Science* 530 (1993): 74–98.

Zhou, Min. "Growing Up American: The Challenge Confronting Immigrant Children and Children of Immigrants." *Annual Review of Sociology* 23 (1997): 63–95.

Philip Yang

Segregation, Voluntary versus Involuntary

Segregation refers to members of two or more ethnic/racial groups and/or classes maintaining separation in residential patterns, schools, and social interactions. Voluntary segregation occurs when people with a common culture or common interests group together in areas of residence, leisure, schools, and so forth. Involuntary segregation occurs when the state actively enforces policies of rigorous separation of members of a group and other people or when economic disparity and/or social stigma causes a group to be isolated.

Voluntary and involuntary segregation are often related to each other because what appears to be voluntary segregation may be caused by underlying social and economic forces imposing involuntary segregation on people. For example, though there is a notable trend of the African American middle class choosing to live in segregated suburban enclaves, it is more often the case that residential segregation among African Americans is not voluntary. Rather, it is usually caused by a lack of financial resources, as well as a history of social stigmatization that results in African Americans not being accepted by white neighbors (e.g., "white flight"). Likewise, many immigrant groups segregate in residence and business enterprise to form immigrant enclaves initially because they may not have the language or cultural skills to maneuver through the mainstream society. However, often these immigrants voluntarily remain in these enclaves even when they have the financial resources to move into other neighborhoods. In these cases, the commonality of culture and language in these enclaves outweighs the allure of living in a traditional, largely white, middle-class environment.

In U.S. history, various types of involuntary segregation have occurred, such as the forced segregation of Native Americans and the internment of Japanese

American citizens during World War II. But involuntary segregation most often refers to a systematic and historical pattern of isolation that has affected African Americans long after slavery. In the United States, post–Civil War policies of forced segregation permeated all facets of existence for freed African American slaves and their children. Even after the Jim Crow era, when official policies of involuntary segregation in schools, residences, and other venues were made illegal, African Americans in all parts of the country were forced by intimidation, violence, prejudice, and ongoing poverty to remain segregated in squalid neighborhoods with inferior public resources and schools. This legacy of isolation continues in contemporary America, where lower-income African Americans are often trapped in a form of involuntary segregation, which, while not enforced by law or legislation, is born out of a history of oppression, poverty, and social stigmatization.

Voluntary segregation, on the other hand, can be seen as a means to empowerment. For example, many immigrant communities find strength, as well as social capital, in their shared values and culture. Likewise, African Americans often voluntarily segregate themselves—in schools, college campuses, and leisure associations—for political and cultural reasons, citing the preservation of group identity as justification. Historically, the feeling of black solidarity has been the basis of black cultural expression. The history of racial oppression that perpetuated involuntary segregation between blacks and whites served to create a black culture founded on difference from, as well as defiance against, white institutions.

Class is a key factor in looking at voluntary segregation among African Americans. The middle-class African Americans who choose to segregate from whites are not representative of the kind of segregation associated with most African Americans. More often, "voluntary" segregation, especially in housing and schools, is a result of low-income African Americans' lack of economical resources, rather than their act of racial solidarity. While African Americans may justifiably prefer to live in separate racial enclaves with access to black institutions, churches, and businesses, according to scholar Charles Abrams, "The test is not whether a group is segregated but whether there are elements of compulsion which keep its members in place when they are ready, willing and able to live elsewhere."

See also De Jure and De facto Segregation; Housing Discrimination; Jim Crow Laws; Residential Segregation; White Flight.

Further Reading

Abrams, Charles. *The City is the Frontier*. New York: Harper Colophon, 1965.

Finkenstaedt, Rose L. H. *Face-to-Face: Blacks in America: White Perceptions and Black Realities*. New York: William Morrow, 1994.

Meyer, Stephen Grant. *As Long as They Don't Move Next Door: Segregation and Racial Conflict in American Neighborhoods*. Lanham, MD: Rowman & Littlefield, 2000.

Rabinowitz, Howard N. *Race Relations in the Urban South, 1865–1890*. New York: Oxford University Press, 1978.

Tracy Chu

Self-Fulfilling Prophecy

The self-fulfilling prophecy refers to a process by which a person or group internalizes and then exhibits those qualities that others maintain that person or group has. It can have an especially destructive impact on minority groups, particularly when dominant groups create stereotypes (inaccurate generalizations regarding an entire group) about the minority group. This can happen in at least two ways. First, a dominant group may generalize that all members of a certain group lack the ability to perform a certain task. Eventually, from repeated exposure to the idea, and, subsequently, internalization of the idea that they cannot perform the task (even though the group actually has the ability to perform the task), the group develops an inability to perform the task.

Another way in which the self-fulfilling prophecy can hurt minorities is through the reaction by those in power to the stereotype. Dominant groups will emphasize the false stereotypical image. They will attempt to foster that image in the minority group by denying them opportunities that do not fit the stereotype. For example, the stereotypical image of black athletic superiority can hurt blacks in at least two ways. First, repeated exposure to this stereotype may prevent blacks themselves from developing intellectual skills in favor of athletics. Second, blacks will be denied opportunities by dominant groups, such as entrance into advanced learning programs.

However, the impact of the self-fulfilling prophecy is more complicated than this short essay may suggest. Sociologist Edwin Schur, for example, suggests that those who are stigmatized can overcome it. Indeed, there have been attempts by minority groups to overcome stereotypes. An example in the 1960s and 1970s is the popular euphemism that "black is beautiful."

John Eterno

Separate but Equal Doctrine

The separate but equal doctrine is typically mentioned in discussions involving the rights of people of color in educational settings; however, it originated in a U.S. Supreme Court case involving public transportation in a Southern state. While traveling in Louisiana in 1892, Homer Plessy was seated in a railroad cabin designated for whites, despite the fact that one of his great grandparents was "colored," which made him African American according to Louisiana law at that time. He was tried and convicted of having violated a local law intended to maintain complete segregation between white Americans and African Americans; similar ordinances were emerging throughout Southern states following the end of slavery. In the 1896 case *Plessy v. Ferguson*, the Supreme Court ruled that Louisiana's law to require that railroad service providers establish separate cabins for white American and African Americans was constitutional. The doctrine of separate but equal stems directly from the decision in this case.

Associate Justice Henry Billings Brown indicated that if the public services provided to white Americans and African Americans were comparable, it was lawful for a state to require race-based segregation in public facilities. He further added that the decision might seem only unjust to individuals who choose to perceive racial injustice by placing "that construction on it," since segregation did not designate one race superior to another if comparable services were to be rendered. In other words, any perceived injustice associated with segregation was attributed to African Americans' allegedly "paranoid" thinking, rather than to the reality of racial discrimination.

The sole dissenter, Justice John M. Harlan, expressed his discontent by stating that the U.S. Constitution was meant to be color-blind and it would not support any legal decisions to create classes among the citizens based on race. He also speculated that this decision would have devastating ramifications for segregation not only in transportation-related spheres but also in a wide variety of other social settings. His vision proved to be prophetic.

This doctrine was frequently cited in the subsequent decades to justify racial segregation in various settings, primarily involving schools, even in the face of the fact that the facilities for African Americans were decidedly inferior in every way to those designed for white Americans. For example, although all students had access to "comparable" public education, African American children attended public schools with outdated facilities and educational materials, and perhaps under-trained teachers, in economically depressed neighborhoods. By contrast, their white American counterparts, in general, attended better-equipped public schools in less distressed neighborhoods, or had the option of attending private schools. This discrepancy within the supposed "equality" contributed to maintaining and widening the social positions of these two groups for decades.

In fact, it was not until 1954 that this doctrine was rejected in another Supreme Court case, *Brown v. Board of Education of Topeka*. However, by that time, the long divide had perpetuated the shadows of slavery, marked by the insurmountable differences in social positions between white Americans and African Americans. For example, White Americans and African Americans continued to be far divided in housing, schooling, and economics, with African Americans collectively and consistently at a disadvantage. This served to impede African Americans' efforts to contribute to the American society to a greater degree.

Aside from these devastating consequences of the separate but equal doctrine, one may criticize this policy on a more fundamental level. For example, if the provision of separate facilities based on race were not racially motivated, why would it be necessary for policymakers to require that African Americans and white Americans be given separate accommodations in the first place? The separate but equal doctrine, therefore, represents a less blatant form of racism, often called "aversive racism," whose consequences are sometimes as harmful as—if not more harmful than—blatant forms of racism.

See also Brown v. Board of Education of Topeka; School Segregation.

Further Reading

Anderson, Wayne. *Plessy v. Ferguson: Legalizing Segregation*. New York: Rosen Publishing Group, 2003.

Gillette, William. *Retreat from Reconstruction, 1869–1879.* Baton Rouge: University of Louisiana Press, 1979.

Lofgren, Charles A. *The Plessy Case.* New York: Oxford University Press, 1987.

Daisuke Akiba

September 11, 2001, Attack on the United States

See Al Qaeda; Arab/Muslim American Advocacy Organizations, Responding to the Backlash; Government Initiatives after the September 11, 2001, Attack on the United States; Middle Easterners, Historical Precedents of Backlash against; Muslim Philanthropic Organizations, Closure of after September 11, 2001; Muslims, Terrorist Image of; September 11, 2001 Terrorism, Discriminatory Reactions to.

September 11, 2001, Terrorism, Discriminatory Reactions to

On Tuesday September 11, 2001, at 8:45 a.m., a plane crashed into the North Tower of the World Trade Center in New York City. Then at 9:03 a.m., a second plane hit the South Tower. At 9:43 a.m. a third plane flew into the Pentagon in Washington, DC. A fourth plane went down near Somerset County, Pennsylvania, near Pittsburgh, as passengers struggled with the highjackers who had commandeered United Airlines 93 toward a more strategic target. The "Attack on America" is the most heinous terrorist act ever to have occurred on U.S. soil, killing 2,819 innocent men and women. As the world watched in horror the collapse of the Twin Towers on television screens repeatedly following this tragedy, retaliatory acts of bias and discrimination escalated against Middle Eastern and South Asian Americans. This backlash was based on the news that Al Qaeda had masterminded the highjacking of these commercial U.S. planes. Individuals who looked Middle Eastern, or had Arabic- or Islamic-sounding names, became the scapegoats of citizens' anger and vengeance. Hate crimes and bias incidents skyrocketed in the weeks after 9/11. Balbir Singh Sodhi was the first murder victim of the backlash, evidently because his traditional Sikh looks—turban and unshorn hair—were confused with Al Qaeda leader Osama Bin Laden's *kafieh* and beard. Ironically, Sikhs are neither Arab nor Muslim—the identity of most of the Al Qaeda terrorists.

Men and women of Middle Eastern ancestry have not been immune to stereotyping and discrimination in U.S. history. However, after September 11, the exponential increase in hate crimes and bias incidents is correlated with the gravity of the terrorist attacks, the targeting of Arabs and Muslims by government initiatives, and the continued climate of insecurity in the country. Hate-motivated incidents peaked immediately after 9/11 and then declined but remained at higher rates than the pre-9/11 period. This was probably due to the cautionary appeals of public officials, including the president of the United States, who condemned all vigilante-style acts of retaliation and hate crimes as soon as the backlash started. The president visited the mosque at the Islamic Center of Washington, DC, on September 17 and warned against confusing terrorists with all Muslims. Occasional flare-ups of violence since 9/11 have led some critics to criticize the government by arguing that it should have repeated its message of tolerance with more consistency. Yet as soon as the backlash started, the government ordered the Civil Rights division of the U.S. Department of Justice to prosecute individuals for taking the law into their hands. Indeed, the FBI has been more diligent in investigating cases of suspected hate crimes since 9/11. In areas with large numbers of Arab and Muslim residents, the local police had pre-existing ties with Arab and Muslim leaders. While law enforcement officers were dispatched to protect sensitive sites, neighborhood officials and community representatives engaged in intense dialogue and negotiation. Together, they were instrumental in maintaining calm and cohesiveness among these diverse communities.

Following on the heels of the hate crimes and discrimination, the government set in motion a series of initiatives and policies that targeted the Middle Eastern and Asian communities and that profiled Arab and Muslim immigrant men in particular. Even though these directives were part of the "War on Terror" policies of the Bush Administration, they sent the reverse message. They institutionalized backlash by condoning ethnic and religious profiling of Middle Eastern or South Asian immigrant men. In other words, the series of government initiatives have become codified as formal procedures of the

President George W. Bush, standing with Muslim religious leaders at the Islamic Center of Washington, delivers a statement condemning rising anti-Muslim sentiment, September 16, 2001.

AP/Wide World Photos.

agencies involved in the nation's security and immigration. It is important to distinguish between two types of backlash. One consists of hate crimes and bias incidents, such as murder, arson, and acts of harassment, perpetrated by ordinary Americans against fellow citizens who are believed to be Middle Eastern. The second category encompasses various official directives, initiatives, and laws carried out by the U.S. government at the federal and/or local level, and has consequences for the Middle Eastern and South Asian American communities. The post–9/11 backlash is not one discrete event or action. The backlash is a phenomenon encompassing all these elements—that is, the hate crimes and bias incidents perpetrated by the public as well as the succession of official directives from the government.

Hate Crimes and Bias Incidents

There are conflicting reports on how many hate-motivated murders were committed as backlash in the week after the September 11 events. The FBI confirmed only four murders, though another seven cases are suspected of having been hate crimes. But in the post–9/11 era, hate-crime motivation must be ruled out in the murder investigation of any individual of Middle Eastern or South Asian origin, demonstrating the seriousness of the situation.

Overall, the toll from the hate crimes and discriminatory incidents from 9/11 was substantial. A September 19, 2001, *New York Times* article put it most succinctly: "Since the attacks, people who look Middle Eastern and South Asian, whatever their religion or nation of origin, have been singled out for harassment, threats and assaults." One organization—South Asian American Leaders of Tomorrow (SAALT)—tallied 645 incidents in just the week after September 11 from newspaper reports in cities across the United States. In its 2001 annual hate crimes report, the FBI discovered an increase of 1,600 percent in incidents against Muslim individuals, institutions, and businesses. There were 28 cases in 2000 compared with 481 in 2001. These data suffer from an undercount for a number of reasons. Some state and local law enforcement agencies do not keep records of hate crimes, do so inaccurately, or do not send them to the FBI. Moreover, ethnic origin and religious affiliation are not always reported or probed. Still, the FBI hate-crimes statistics are the most systematic for comparisons across time, if not across the country.

Hate crimes and bias incidents include hate speech, airline or airport discrimination, vandalism, assaults on individuals, employment discrimination, incidence of prejudice in public schools and murder. Most Arab and Muslim American organizations received threatening phone calls. The American-Arab Anti-Discrimination Committee has published some of the messages that were sent to them, including, "You F****** ARABS go to hell. You will pay . . . ," "ROT IN HELL FOREVER," "The only good Arab is a dead one," and "You people are animals. . . . I feel sick to my stomach to see an Arab." Several fundamentalist Christian evangelists, such as Pat Robertson and Franklin Graham (son of Billy Graham) have, since 9/11, voiced their anti-Muslim beliefs on television and other public venues. Their rhetoric has heightened tensions and distrust in the multireligious American society, even globally.

Airport and airline cases of discrimination were frequent after September 11, given the nature of the terrorist attacks. The costs of profiling Middle Eastern–looking individuals at airports are both psychological and monetary. In addition to being inconvenienced and humiliated in public, some individuals incurred expenses because of lost airline connections. Although careful inspections of all passengers are a legitimate procedure at airports and on airlines, singling out individuals with Arab/Muslim looks or names is unfair. These policies have been particularly harmful to members of the Sikh community. Their characteristic turban and beard have singled them out as Bin Laden look-a-likes. Even a year after 9/11, a flight attendant on Delta Airlines informed Hansdip Singh Bindra, a Sikh software consultant who was traveling from Newark (NJ) to Dayton (OH), that he and his fellow Middle Easterners should keep a low profile. When he tried to explain who he was, he was told to "shut up" and "stay seated" and "not to cause any problems." Sikh Mediawatch and Resource Task Force (SMART), and their counterparts in the Arab and Muslim American communities, have been helping victims of racial profiling to take their cases to court. More important, Sikhs have been actively educating the general public about who they are and what they believe in, while being prudent about the rights of Arabs and Muslims.

There have been numerous cases of physical assaults against Muslims and Arabs including vandalism; but women wearing the *hijab* (headscarf) have been particularly vulnerable to harassment. Some women who used to wear the veil before 9/11 have since removed their head covering, while others camouflaged their looks with hats and baseball caps. Veiled women were cursed, yelled at with racial slurs and death threats, spit at, hit with a stick, kicked, asked to remove the hijab in public, and prevented access to their destination. In spite of this, some Muslim women started to cover their hair with the hijab after 9/11 as an assertion of their religious identity.

Vandalism against mosques, religious schools, and Arab American community property was also common following the 9/11 attacks. The 2002 Council on American Islamic Relations (CAIR) Report includes a case in Bridgeport, Connecticut, on September 16, 2001, in which phone lines were cut and the words "You will die" were written on the mosque. There were also several cases of arson, such as the Molotov cocktail thrown at the Islamic Society of Denton, Texas, on November 17, 2001, and the suspicious fire at the Arab America Network, a social-service agency for Arab immigrants, in Chicago on December 3, 2001.

The Equal Employment Opportunity Commission (EEOC) has reported a marked increase in the number of job discrimination complaints filed by Arab and Muslim Americans since September 11, 2001, revealing another kind of fallout from the 9/11 attacks. In fiscal year 2000, there were 7,792 cases of discrimination based on national origin. This increased to 8,025 cases in 2001 and 9046 in 2002. Likewise, there was an increase in religious retaliation cases from 1,939 in 2000 to 2,127 in 2001 and 2,572 in 2002. Much of this growth is due to Arab and Muslim cases. More specifically, individuals have complained about workplace intimidation and ridicule by employers or coworkers, threats of being fired or job terminations for no valid reason, denial of hiring or promotion, and the refusal to accommodate religious requests such as prayer, fasting, and the accommodation of the veil for women and beard for men (and in the case of Sikhs, the turban). Other forms of discrimination, such as in obtaining mortgages or other bank loans, renting apartments, or seeking services of many kinds, have also increased.

The nation's public schools have been a fertile ground for perpetuating hate and bias. Students of Middle Eastern or South Asian origin were cursed, mocked, and called "terrorists" by their peers; boys whose name was Osama or Mohammad were particularly vulnerable. They were also spat at, kicked, and beaten. Instead of sowing seeds of tolerance, even some teachers, coaches, counselors, and other school staff singled out Arab and Muslim American students in a negative way. Many parents kept their children away from school for a few days or a week after 9/11, and several Muslim schools were closed because of threats.

The USA PATRIOT Act and Government Initiatives

Within a few weeks following the September 11 attacks, the Bush administration issued a series of initiatives and directives as part of its "War on Terrorism" policy. The USA PATRIOT Act is perhaps the most monumental piece of legislation to date that aims to insure the security of the land and its citizens. It was passed on October 25, 2001 by the Congress without many members reading it and with little debate or opposition, and signed into law the next day by President Bush. The USA PATRIOT Act, an acronym for the Uniting and Strengthening America by Providing Appropriate Tools Required to Intercept and Obstruct Terrorism Act, introduced sweeping changes in domestic law and intelligence agencies overseas, giving unprecedented powers to the government with little oversight from the courts. Due-process provisions, protections against unreasonable searches and seizures, detentions without hearings, probable cause and denial of bail are some of the issues that have concerned constitutional scholars and civil rights activists.

Detentions and deportations were the first of a series of initiatives issued by the U.S. attorney general in the effort to apprehend terrorists. Starting on September 17, 2001, immigrants from Middle Eastern and/or Islamic countries became subject to detention. If suspected of terrorism, detainees could be kept without charge for an extended period of time; hearings could be "secure," that is, closed to the public; bond could be denied; and attorney/client communication privilege could be disregarded. According to the "Report on the September 11 Detainees," issued April 2003 by the Inspector General of the U.S. Department of Justice, 762 illegal immigrant men from Arab and/or Muslim countries were detained, some for weeks and months, but none were charged with terrorism. Most of the arrests took place between September and December 2001, though arrests continued until summer 2002. Secrecy shrouded the entire process. Estimates on the number of detainees vary from 500 to over 1,200. Even Congress did not receive an answer when it questioned the Department of Justice about the detainees. The Inspector General's report was also critical of the physical and legal treatment of the detainees. Most were housed in the Metropolitan Detention Center in Brooklyn, New York, and the Passaic County Jail, in Paterson, New Jersey. Pakistanis made up the largest number of the detainees, followed by Egyptians, Turks, and Yemenis, suggesting that both Arabs and non-Arab Muslims were targeted.

The "absconder initiative" was named for the announcement made by INS commissioner James Ziglar on December 6, 2001, to publish the names of more than 300,000 aliens who were still in the United States in spite of deportation orders. This was followed on January 8, 2002, by an announcement by the Department of Justice to enter into the FBI database the names of about 6,000 male absconders, Arab and/or Muslim nationals, believed to be from Al Qaeda–harboring countries. These suspects were to be apprehended.

An important strategy in tracking terrorists is securing the nation's frontiers, since all the hijackers had managed to enter the country legally. The administration set in motion several measures to regulate the traffic of people, goods, and money across borders. The National Security Entry-Exit Registration System (NSEERS) obligates aliens from 25 predominantly Muslim countries (Afghanistan, Algeria, Bahrain, Djibouti, Egypt, Eritrea, Indonesia, Iran, Iraq, Jordan, Kuwait, Lebanon, Libya, Malaysia, Morocco, Oman, Pakistan, Qatar, Saudi Arabia, Somalia, Sudan, Syria, Tunisia, United Arab Emirates, and Yemen) to be registered, fingerprinted, and photographed upon arrival and periodically afterwards. NSEERS has been criticized for ethnic profiling, a violation of the equal-protection principle in U.S. law.

The Student and Exchange Visitor System (SEVIS) is a computer system that tracks all foreign student enrollments and as such is the only measure that is not limited to Muslim countries. Officials at institutions of higher education and U.S. embassies gather data on such details as start date of each semester, failure to enroll, full-time student status, disciplinary action by the institution, and early graduation. SEVIS became law on January 30, 2003, even though there were many glitches in the system that continued to create backlogs afterwards. Critics argue that these problems have contributed to the decrease in foreign students in U.S. colleges and universities, reversing a trend that showed a steady growth between 1948 and 2001. The dilemma is that the new restrictions imposed on foreign students may discourage from coming to the United States genuine students who are likely to become goodwill ambassadors for the United States when they return home.

Special registration is another legally problematic provision under NSEERS. Men older than age sixteen who were citizens of Iran, Iraq, Libya, Sudan, and Syria, allegedly terrorist-training countries, and who had entered the United States before September 10, 2002, and planned to remain at least until December 16, 2002, were required to register with the INS before December 16, 2002. On December 16, 2002, other countries were added to the list. Failure to report to the INS was cause for deportation. Ironically, many people who obeyed the order were deported anyway. Special registration increased the workload of an already strained INS staff. The men who complied with the orders complained of harsh treatment by INS staff and long waits without access to food or water. More seriously, the lives of many families were disrupted as husbands were detained and deported, leaving wives and children without any means of support and no opportunity to rejoin the men unless they return to his country of origin. More than eighty thousand men had registered by early May 2003.

Special registration resulted in the arrest of several hundred Iranians in Los Angeles who were deemed in violation of their visas. This order created unprecedented demonstrations and protests from the Iranian American population in Los Angeles, the largest such concentration in the United States. Having designated the Islamic Republic of Iran part of the "Axis of Evil," individuals bearing Iranian passports were denied visa issuance and subjected to Special Registration even though Iranians had nothing to do with the 9/11 attacks. In November 2003, almost coinciding with the first anniversary of the special registration, the government reversed its decision on requesting that men from a number of Arab and/or Muslim countries repeat this procedure annually, because this initiative did not lead to the apprehension of any terrorists.

The profiling of men from Arab and/or Muslim countries has been a persistent problem in many government initiatives after September 11, 2001. The supposedly voluntary interviews fall into this category. The attorney general ordered the FBI to interview some 5,000 men, ages eighteen to thirty-three, who had entered the United States between January 2000 and November 2001 from countries suspected of Al Qaeda presence or activity, once again targeting the Americans fitting the profile of the hijackers. On February 26, 2002, the *Final Report on Interview Project* was released. It revealed that out of the 5,000 Arab and/or Muslim men on the list, 2,261 were interviewed, but fewer than 20 were taken into custody—3 on criminal violations and the rest on immigration charges. In spite of the ineffectiveness of this policy as a means of finding terrorists, on March 19, 2002, the Department of Justice declared that it would conduct an additional 3,000 interviews. The results of this decision are not known. In November 2002, with the war in Iraq pending, more than 10,000 individuals born in Iraq were sought for questioning. Many were naturalized U.S. citizens, an exception to the detentions and special registration policies that previously only sought foreign nationals.

The government has been tightening controls of financial transactions internationally to dry up the sources of funding for terrorist organizations. To that end, in December 2001, the government froze the assets of three large Muslim charitable organizations—the Holy Land Foundation for Relief and Development, Benevolence International Foundation, and Global Relief Foundation—accusing them of money laundering. The government claimed that these organizations were funneling monies to terrorist organizations such as Hamas, a radical Islamic organization. These actions created fear and suspicion among the Middle Eastern and South Asian Americans and slowed down charitable contributions for a time. The Internal Revenue Service (IRS) continues to scrutinize the accounts of nonprofit organizations in these ethnic and religious communities more meticulously than before. Muslim Americans have been concerned with the government's interference in their religious obligation to pay *zakat* (alms). Another manifestation of this strategy was a raid in late March 2002 by the U.S. Customs Service, the IRS, other federal agencies, and local police on fourteen homes and businesses in northern Virginia alleged to be laundering money for terrorist organizations.

The "Homeland Security Act of 2002," signed into law on November 25, 2002, established the Department of Homeland Security and defined its mission and responsibilities. This new department, which employs 170,000 individuals, merged twenty-two federal agencies, including the USCIS, formerly known as the INS. Around the same time, President Bush also signed into law the Justice Department's Operation TIPS (Terrorism Information and Prevention System), which would enlist thousands of truck drivers, mail carriers, bus drivers, electricians, plumbers, and so on as "citizen observers." Because of heavy criticism from civil rights groups and the public, TIPS was not successful.

Assessment of Government Initiatives

In the end, the government's appropriation of unprecedented powers to catch terrorists within its borders has thus far not been successful. Perhaps the closest the FBI came to arresting anyone of Middle Eastern or South Asian origin remotely related to Al Qaeda was the capture on September 14, 2002, of six U.S. citizens of Yemeni descent in Lackawanna, New York. This is not to say, however, that some of the government initiatives in the aftermath of 9/11 were unnecessary. Indeed, many immigration procedures had been lax and flawed, and stricter border controls are a requirement in this age of global terrorism. However, the targeting and profiling of a specific population was unnecessary and unjust.

As the administration's critics often noted, searching for leads to terrorist cells requires the trust and collaboration of the very ethnic and religious communities that were angered and alienated by the presumption of guilt by association. Instead of winning the hearts and minds of Middle Eastern and South Asian Americans, the government's policies of singling them out had the opposite effect. The government initiatives enflamed the suspicions and stereotypes of the general public against Arabs and Muslims and heightened the climate of fear and insecurity. Clearly, Arab and Muslim Americans as a community could challenge individual hate crimes much more effectively than the government initiatives. In fact, they have walked a fine line between displaying loyalty to the United States and diplomatically challenging profiling. To do otherwise would have been un-American.

See also Al Qaeda; Arab/Muslim American Advocacy Organizations, Responding to the Backlash; Government Initiatives after the September 11, 2001, Attack on the United States; Hate Crimes; *Jihad*; Middle Easterners, Historical Precedents of Backlash against; Muslim Philanthropic Organizations, Closure of after September 11, 2001; Muslims, Terrorist Image of; September 11, 2001, Terrorism, Discriminatory Reactions to.

Mehdi Bozorgmehr and Anny Bakalian

Sharecropping

Sharecropping was a form of institutionalized labor widespread in the South after the ending of slavery in 1865. Land was rented out to sharecroppers, who farmed the land and in return would give landowners a portion of their yearly production. Sharecropping has come to be seen as a coercive and exploitative institution that left sharecroppers in a semipermanent, if not permanent, state of indentured servitude.

Sharecropping varied in form throughout the South. Landowners had differing policies regarding the rental of their property and the proportion of crop yields expected as payment. Also, if a sharecropper needed tools, machinery, or seed, these had to be borrowed against future production as well. Originally, sharecropping was seen as a potential form of economic development for former slaves. Through hard work, industrious sharecroppers and their families could apply their farming skills and agricultural knowledge to fund their own economic enrichment.

In practice, however, sharecropping rarely meant economic emancipation for former slaves and their immediate descendants. The sharecropping system overwhelmingly favored the economic interests of the landowner. Charges for rental of land, equipment, and seed were often exorbitant. Combined with the uncertainties of poor weather conditions, crop disease, and sometimes dubious accounting practices, this meant that sharecroppers rarely made even minimal profits from yearly production. Often, a sharecropper ended the year in debt to the owner, a situation usually resolved by the sharecropper agreeing to farm the owner's land again. This helped create a cycle of poverty in which sharecroppers and their families were locked into an indefinite period of indentured servitude. Many disillusioned sharecroppers fled the system and took part in the Great Migration to the cities of the North in the 1920s.

See also Civil War and the Abolition of Slavery; Emancipation Proclamation; Fourteenth Amendment; Freedmen's Bureau; Reconstruction Era.

Rebekah Lee

Shaw v. Hunt

Decided in 1996, *Shaw v. Hunt* was a U.S. Supreme Court case important in determining the constitutionality of the principle of redrawing congressional districts on the basis of race. When North Carolina gained an extra seat in the House of Representatives in 1990, it redrew district boundaries and created two irregularly shaped districts to include a majority of black voters. One of these was District 12, drawn with a distinctive "snake-like" shape to incorporate much of North Carolina's major urban centers. In essence, this redrawing created a "majority-minority" district in which historically underrepresented minorities became the majority constituency. In a series of cases between 1993 and 2001, including *Shaw v. Hunt*, the Supreme Court ruled on the constitutionality of such redrawings on the basis of race, also called "racial gerrymandering."

By a narrow 5-4 majority, the Supreme Court ruled in *Shaw v. Hunt* that the creation of District 12 was unconstitutional under the equal-protection clause of the Fourteenth Amendment. This upheld their previous ruling in *Shaw v. Reno* (1993), which said that race could not be the sole factor in the redrawing of congressional districts. The Shaw decisions resulted in the invalidation of irregularly shaped congressional districts in several states that were drawn primarily to increase the representation of black and Hispanic voters. However, in *Easley v. Cromartie* (2001), the Supreme Court revisited this issue and ruled that the creation of majority-minority districts could be constitutional provided that states use the criteria of "voting behavior" rather than race to draw district boundaries. This signaled a shift to a more flexible attitude on the part of the Court toward racial gerrymandering.

Shaw v. Hunt is significant because it highlights the legal and political complexities involved in attempting to address minority underrepresentation. African Americans were subject to racially discriminatory measures related to voting after they received the right to vote in 1870. Before the Voting Rights Act of 1965, discriminatory district drawing, literacy tests, and property requirements, particularly in the South, prevented blacks from achieving equal representation under the law. Racial gerrymandering is a controversial way in which states have attempted to undo the legacy of these discriminatory practices.

See also Gerrymandering, Racial; Redistricting; Voting Rights Act of 1965; Voting Rights Amendments of 1975.

Rebekah Lee

Shelley v. Kraemer

The U.S. Supreme Court, in 1948, considered an important housing discrimination question: whether state or local governments can enforce private contract agreements known as racially restrictive covenants. These covenants, common in the United States in the first half of the twentieth century, were initiated by owners of homes or buildings and stipulated that people of certain racial groups (usually "non-Caucasians") were not allowed to purchase, rent, own, or live in the homes or apartments on a certain block or in a neighborhood. In *Shelley v. Kraemer*, the Supreme Court ruled that the equal-protection clause of the Fourteenth Amendment to the U.S. Constitution legally prevents any governmental body from enforcing a racially restrictive covenant that denies individuals their right to acquire, enjoy, own, and dispose of property. While it did not declare racially restrictive covenants themselves unconstitutional, it did rule that no state or government authority or agent could enforce these racially discriminatory housing agreements, thus, from a legal perspective, restrictive covenants were null and void.

This case began in 1945 when an African American family (Shelley) tried to purchase a home on a section of Labadie Avenue in St. Louis that was covered by a restrictive covenant prohibiting any person "not of the Caucasian race" from occupying property on it. This clause was signed in 1911 by thirty out of thirty-nine property owners on part of Labadie Avenue, to remain in force for a period of fifty years (some of those who did not sign the agreement were black residents). The Supreme Court of Missouri respected the racially restrictive covenant and ordered that it be enforced, ruling that the Shelleys must move out. This decision was appealed to the U.S. Supreme Court, where a similar case from Detroit was joined to it. In reversing the Missouri court's ruling, the U.S. Supreme Court followed precedent in viewing the Fourteenth Amendment as prohibiting *government* from discriminating on the basis of race, but *not* prohibiting *private individuals or groups* from discriminating on the basis of race. It therefore said that a private racially restrictive covenant by itself is not a violation of the Fourteenth Amendment, but any action by the state to enforce that covenant *is* a violation of it. The Shelley family was allowed to purchase and occupy the house, and today the Shelley House is a National Historic Landmark.

See also Fourteenth Amendment; Restrictive Covenants.

Charles Jaret

Simpson, O. J. (1947–   )

Born on July 9, 1947, Orenthal James Simpson grew up in the ghettos of San Francisco, where he dabbled in petty crime and gang-related activity, until his skills as a football player made him a household name. He had a stellar career as a running back, earning the 1968 Heisman Trophy while playing for the University of Southern California and rushing for a remarkable 11,236 yards over the course of his National Football League career, with 2,003 yards coming in the 1973 season alone.

Simpson was able to parlay his success on the field into a second career as a television sports analyst. His popularity continued to grow and led him to an acting career that featured appearances in several high-profile television shows and theatrical films. Because of his high popularity and credibility with the public, he served as the celebrity spokesperson for the Hertz rental-car agency for many years.

Public admiration for Simpson gradually dissipated after 1994, when he was arrested and subsequently placed on trial for killing his ex-wife, Nicole Brown-Simpson, and her friend, Ronald Goldman. Despite Simpson's acquittal on Oc-

Pedestrians along a New York street react to the not guilty verdict at the O. J. Simpson trial, October 3, 1995.

AP/Wide World Photos.

tober 3, 1995, after a long and very public trial, many Americans remain convinced that "O. J. did it." These convictions were confirmed by the civil court ruling, which required Simpson to make financial reparations for the wrongful deaths of Brown-Simpson and Goldman.

The mere mention of the O. J. case evokes memories of a nation divided by race. Black and white Americans differed greatly in how they viewed the criminal trial proceedings and the verdict. The return of a not-guilty verdict largely was viewed by white Americans as a gross injustice, but many African Americans viewed the verdict as evidence that a person of color could get a fair trial in the United States.

See also Sports and Racism.

Romney S. Norwood

Sioux Outbreak of 1890

The Sioux "outbreak" in 1890 was in reality a rumor spread by ignorance and hysteria that resulted in the massacre of almost three hundred Native Americans at Wounded Knee, South Dakota. By 1890, the Sioux had experienced incredible deprivations as the result of broken promises by the U.S. government. Since 1825, the government had promised to protect the Sioux, and in 1868, both parties agreed to perpetual peace. With that mutual agreement, the government promised further to hold the Sioux reservation inviolate, permit Sioux hunting in the Bighorn Mountains, and acquire reservation land only with the approval of 75 percent of adult male Sioux on the reservation.

Congress violated this agreement only nine years later when it acted unilaterally to confiscate 7.3 million acres of reservation land in the Black Hills. This deprived the Sioux of their hunting lands, so in return, Congress declared it would provide them with rations and other assistance as long as necessary. The Sioux were also placed under the protection of U.S. law. Thus, the Sioux and other Native American groups were effectively placed under the military, which tried to enforce a policy of subjugation by disarming them and making them farmers. With the buffalo gone by the mid-1880s, the Native Americans claimed that the government had failed to appropriate enough funds to feed and support them. Interior Department inspectors, military officers, and missionaries all noted the government's failure in this regard.

In 1889, Congress again acted to acquire the reservation territory for white settlement, this time another 9 million acres. Contrary to the spirit of the 1868 agreement, Sioux reservation men were coerced into voting for Congress's proposal, and a number of illegal votes were cast for it. The law was passed without the required vote and signed by President Benjamin Harrison. What was left of the reservation was divided up into six smaller reservations. Rations were cut after the law was passed, leaving Indians on the reservations desperate for food, as there were widespread crop failures and an anthrax outbreak in the previous year. In fact, one military observer noted that the government had failed to provide required land titles, the required amount of seed and farm equipment, the required number of cattle, the required ration of food, or the required amount of annuity supplies—all things required by the treaty.

The Sioux became acquainted with the Ghost Dance after several Sioux men went to meet with Wovoka, its progenitor. The Ghost Dance religion, a mixture of Christianity and shamanism, promised the end of hostility, freedom from hunger, and freedom from white oppression. The time of this mystical transformation and rebirth of the earth could be quickened by the Ghost Dance. These dances, which lasted many nights, caught the attention of whites, and were interpreted incorrectly as war dances. Unfounded fears of a Sioux outbreak spread rapidly. In November 1890, President Harrison ordered the military to contain the Sioux on their reservations and to arrest the Sioux leaders until the Ghost Dancing had ceased.

December 1890 brought a series of tragedies in quick succession. A South Dakota militia, called the Home Guard, killed and scalped seventy-five Ghost Dancers at the Pine Ridge Reservation. On December 15, Sitting Bull and eight of his men were killed, allegedly because Sitting Bull had resisted arrest. With Sitting Bull gone, a warrant for the arrest of Chief Big Foot, his half-brother, went out. Wishing to avoid arrest and further conflagration, Big Foot, along with three hundred and fifty others, including some of Sitting Bull's followers who had fled the Standing Rock Reservation after the chief's death, set out on the long journey through the Badlands to the Pine Ridge Reservation. Chief Red Cloud had promised them food, shelter, and horses there. On December 28, however, the 7th Cavalry, George Armstrong Custer's old regiment, had surrounded the group. In spite of flying the white flag of surrender, Big Foot's group was forced to the bank of Wounded Knee Creek. Canons were perched above them.

A false rumor among the penned-in Indians that had them being removed to Indian Territory led to some agitation. When Colonel James Forsyth took over command with his five hundred reinforcements on the evening of December 28, the natives were disarmed and interrogated without sleep, which led to further agitation. Some began singing Ghost Dance songs. In the tension of the moment, a gun was fired, injuring no one, but the soldiers immediately began to shoot the unarmed Indians with pistols, and canon fire rained down upon them. Big Foot was killed. The few survivors of the massacre at Wounded Knee were hunted down as the soldiers sought revenge for the death of Custer and two hundred thirty-one soldiers who were killed at Little Big Horn.

While this incident has in the past been cited as the end of the Native American skirmishes with whites, it was in truth not a skirmish but a slaughter, an exclamation point to the long and sordid history of Euro-Americans' dealings with Native Americans. Long before the massacre at Wounded Knee, the natives' ability to mount an effective challenge to white dominance had ended.

See also Ghost Dance Religion; Indian Reservations; Native Americans, Conquest of; Native Americans, Forced Relocation of; Native Americans, Prejudice and Discrimination against; Noble Savage.

Further Reading

Brown, Dee Alexander. *Bury My Heart at Wounded Knee: An Indian History of the American West*, 30th anniversary ed. New York: Henry Holt, 2001.

Lazarus, Edward. *Black Hills/White Justice: The Sioux Nation versus the United States, 1775 to the Present*. New York: HarperCollins, 1991.

Ostler, Jeffrey. *The Plains Sioux and U.S. Colonialism from Lewis and Clark to Wounded Knee*. New York: Cambridge University Press, 2004.

Viola, Herman J. *Trail to Wounded Knee: Last Stand of the Plains Indians, 1860–1890*. Washington, DC: National Geographic Society, 2003.

Benamin F. Shearer

Sit-ins

Sit-ins, like boycotts, are a tactic that social movements and other groups use to put pressure on their opponents so that they will change laws, policies, or behaviors. This tactic involves gathering a group of people together and going to a place sensitive to the opponent, such as their place of business or a government facility, and occupying it until either the opponent agrees to negotiate or law enforcement arrives to break up the sit-in. This occupation can be very disruptive, preventing the facility from being used for the normal conduction of business, or it can be less disruptive and involve merely the occupation of space day and night. Sit-ins are attractive tactics to social movement groups because they are disruptive and draw attention to the movement without requiring financial input on the part of the group. However, because of law-enforcement responses, they can result in physical harm to participants, as well as arrests and jail time.

The most famous, and the first, incidence of a sit-in during the civil rights movement involved four students from the all-black Agricultural and Technical College sitting at the all-white lunch counter at the local Woolworth store in Greensboro, North Carolina. Sit-ins have also been popular among college and university students pushing for changes in curriculum and other policies by occupying university facilities, as part of the Third World movement and pan-ethnic movements.

An African American student sits at a lunch counter reserved for white customers during a sit-in to protest segregation in Nashville, Tennessee, March 25, 1960.

© Bettman/CORBIS.

See also Boycotts; Civil Rights Movement; Pan-ethnic Movements; "Third World Movement" of the 1960s.

Mikaila Mariel Lemonik Arthur

Skinheads

The skinheads are an international movement of white, largely male youth gangs associated with neo-Nazi and white-power ideologies. Neo-Nazi skinhead groups are among the most militant advocates of white supremacy and are believed responsible for the commission of numerous hate crimes since the 1970s.

Originating in the late 1960s and 1970s in the United Kingdom, skinheads presented themselves as working-class, antiestablishment radicals and developed a subcultural dress code of closely shaved heads, combat boots, combat fatigues, swastika tattoos, and suspenders. The 1970s British Skinheads were associated with punk subculture and punk music as well as Nazi-inspired fashion, and some skinheads today remain primarily focused on music and subcultural style. Neo-Nazi skinheads, however, are considered the foot soldiers of white supremacism and have created a white-power youth movement that has a global reach. By 1995, the Anti-Defamation League estimated that there

A neo-Nazi in Denver, Colorado.

© Marc Asnin/CORBIS SABA.

were approximately seventy thousand skinheads worldwide. The skinheads movement reached the United States in the mid-1980s. Although skinheads are generally only loosely organized, U.S. neo-Nazi skinheads are affiliated with a number of more organized groups, especially the White Aryan Resistance (WAR), a neo-Nazi hate group founded in 1983 by Tom Metzger. WAR and its skinhead youth wing, the Aryan Youth Movement, advocate for individual and small-cell guerilla terrorism and violence against immigrants and minorities as well as police and other officials. The Anti-Defamation League estimates that skinheads were responsible for at least forty-three hate-crime murders between 1990 and 1997.

See also Anti-Defamation League of B'nai Brith (ADL); Aryan Nations; Ku Klux Klan (KKK); Neo-Nazism; White-Supremacist Movement in the United States; White-Supremacist Underground.

Victoria Pitts

Slave Auctions

Slave auctions represented one of the most dehumanizing aspects of the institution of slavery. For a newly captured slave arriving from Africa, the slave auction was a chaotic, shaming introduction to the Americas. And for those slaves sold in the burgeoning interstate trade that developed once the international slave trade ended in the early nineteenth century, the auction block served to reemphasize their status as property. Slaves were chattel to be bought and sold with little regard to their humanity.

Slaves arrived at auctions in various ways. During the seventeenth and eighteenth centuries, auctions were held when slave ships arrived from the ports of West Africa or the Caribbean. In the nineteenth century, "professional" slave traders sought to cash in on the lucrative interstate trade market and were a regular presence at slave auctions, buying and selling large numbers of slaves.

However, slaves were also sold to pay off a landowner's debt or to settle a deceased owner's estate.

Slave auctions were designed to provide prospective buyers ample opportunity to consider their purchase. Concurrently, sellers generally tried to present their slaves in the best possible light, to maximize profits. These two factors meant that slaves were generally subject to a regimented series of dehumanizing experiences. Slaves were washed thoroughly. Sometimes, slaves were provided with fresh clothing. Large lots of slaves were divided by sex and arranged by height. They were admonished to "look smart" and behave

A slave auction in the South, circa 1861.

Courtesy Library of Congress.

well. Often, they were made to dance, so that potential buyers could observe their physical condition. Slaves were routinely physically handled by customers: hands, arms, bodies, mouths, and teeth were inspected. Customers could demand an even closer inspection, and then a slave was stripped. Slaves were sold with little, if any, regard for family or marriage bonds. Regardless of the humiliation suffered, slaves could utter no protest, for this was indicative of a rebellious spirit that would decrease their value.

See also Abolitionist Movement; Civil War and the Abolition of Slavery; Plantation System; Slave Codes; Slave Families; Slave Revolts and White Attacks on Black Slaves; Slave Trade; Slavery and American Indians; Slavery in the Antebellum South; Underground Railroad.

Rebekah Lee

Slave Codes

The slave codes represented a system of local and state laws that regulated the institution of slavery in the South. Developed over the course of two hundred years, the slave codes provided a legal basis for the continued subjugation of blacks as property and developed into a complex web of statutes covering every aspect of a slave's life. Laws governed issues such as slave mobility, racial classification, possession of alcohol, the sale of slaves, and criminal offenses. The laws' restrictiveness in the decades before the Civil War reflected growing Southern white fears of slave revolt.

Fundamental to the slave codes was the treatment of slaves as personal property. Because of this, a slave was legally and absolutely bound to the wishes of his master. A slave could be bought, sold, bequeathed, or used to pay off a debt. A slave could not acquire property of his own, was not deemed a competent witness in any trial, and could never file a suit in court. Slave marriages were not considered legally binding, since slaves could not enter into a contract of any kind. This provided the legal justification for the break up of slave marriages and the resultant separation of countless slave families.

Slave codes also helped white masters maintain discipline and quell the possibility of slave revolt. At all times, slaves were expected to respect whites and submit to the will of their masters, even if they were treated harshly. Slaves could only travel if given a written "pass" by their masters, and some Southern towns implemented curfews for slaves. Large gatherings of slaves without the presence of a white person were strictly forbidden. Slave codes also prohibited anyone from teaching slaves to read or write, giving slaves books or pamphlets, or harboring fugitive slaves.

See also Abolitionist Movement; Civil War and the Abolition of Slavery; Plantation System; Slave Auctions; Slave Families; Slave Revolts and White Attacks on Black Slaves; Slave Trade; Slavery and American Indians; Slavery in the Antebellum South; Underground Railroad.

Rebekah Lee

Slave Families

In Southern white society, the institution of the family revolved around a clear model of the ideal family type. Nuclear in structure, characterized by monogamous marriage, and bound by patriarchal privilege, this ideal was a fundamental base upon which a "civilized" patrician social order could be built. In contrast, slave families exhibited a large degree of variation in structure and composition. This diversity was partly the result of African cultural forms transplanted to the American context. However, the course and shape of black family life was also intimately bound to the exigencies of slavery itself.

Contemporary observers and slave narratives noted the presence of matrifocality (women headed households), polygamy, single-parent households, multigenerational extended households, and fictive kinship as part of slave-family structures. This represents to some degree the extent to which slave families deviated from the norm of the nuclear family espoused by whites. Though it is clear that wide variation existed, scholars generally agree that the extended-family structure and an emphasis on matrifocality were core features of most slave families.

Why was this the case? Some scholars argue that certain aspects of black family structure during slavery, such as extended kinship, polygamy and matrifocality, can be traced to slaves' African heritage. Although this may be correct, the institution of slavery itself must also be examined. It is evident that slavery mitigated against the formation of nuclear families and monogamous marriage bonds. Slave marriages were not binding because slaves could not legally enter into any contract. Their unions were also not recognized by the church. In addition, slaves' position as human property under the slave codes meant that husband, wife, and children could be separated and sold off with no notice at all. In practice, owners and slave traders did not balk at the prospect of separating spouses or family members. All familial obligations remained subordinate to a slave's primary obligation—that of unquestioning obedience to the owner.

The ramifications were manifold. Broken slave marriages became commonplace. Slave women were sometimes subject to sexual advances and rape from owners or members of their family. Slave children were socialized from an early age to expect their eventual separation from their parents. Children were often reared without the regular presence of their father because male slaves were frequently hired off to another work site or sold. If a father and mother belonged to different slave owners, restrictive slave codes prevented frequent visits. Furthermore, mothers and children were expected to retain their masters' surnames, which further erased the influence and identity of the father within the slave family. Childcare was the province of elderly or infirm slaves, although frequently children were left with little or no adult supervision. This left even the youngest children vulnerable to labor exploitation.

Many have pointed to these defining characteristics as evidence of the systematic and coercive breakdown of the African family during slavery. In this view, slavery perpetuated the dissolution of family life by eroding traditional marriage bonds, encouraging the rise of single-parent households, and contributing to male absenteeism within the family. Children of these broken families typically had low expectations and low self-esteem. Supporters of this view also contend that increased levels of crime, low educational attainment, and a host of other social ills today can be traced to this breakdown.

Detractors point out that certain features of slave family life, such as its matrifocality and emphasis on extended kinship networks, should not only be seen as unfortunate and deviant consequences of slavery. They should also be seen, and to some extent celebrated, as significant remnants of cultural forms brought from Africa and as successful adaptations by families to the limitations of slave existence.

See also Abolitionist Movement; Black Family Instability Thesis; Civil War and the Abolition of Slavery; *The Negro Family: The Case for National Action*; Plantation System; Slave Auctions; Slave Codes; Slave Revolts and White Attacks on Black Slaves; Slave Trade; Slavery and American Indians; Slavery in the Antebellum South; Underground Railroad.

Further Reading

Dunaway, Wilma. *African-American Family in Slavery and Emancipation*. Cambridge: Cambridge University Press, 2003.

Gutman, Herbert. *The Black Family in Slavery and Freedom, 1750–1925*. New York: Pantheon, 1976.

Stevenson, Brenda. *Life in Black and White: Family and Community in the Slave South*. New York: Oxford University Press, 1996.

Rebekah Lee

Slave Revolts and White Attacks on Black Slaves

Despite the fear that slave masters instilled in blacks to prevent rebellions and riots, slave revolts were widespread throughout the slavery era in the United States. From David Walker's appeal, which advocated the overthrow of slavery through violent means, to the Nat Turner uprising, slaves did their best to fight their masters and to resist a system that subjected human beings to the worst physical and mental degradation that existed in the modern world.

The fear of slave revolts and rebellions preoccupied the minds of slave masters throughout the South. In states and counties where slaves outnumbered whites, slaveholders enacted laws, created vigilante groups, and sought the assistance of other states to intimidate slaves from organizing any form of rebellion. Slaves began to rebel against their masters as soon as the institution became the primary mode of production in the colonies. In 1669, Virginia enacted a series of laws that made it a noncriminal act for slave owners to kill their slaves (Aptheker 1943). These laws were a reaction to various attempts by slaves to rebel against their conditions. Slave riots and rebellions in the South ranged from individual acts that took place daily on plantations to organized massive resistance.

As one of the richest territories of the colonies, Virginia had a fair share of slave revolts. For example, on August 30, 1800, more than one thousand slaves met outside Richmond and began to march on the city under the leadership of Gabriel Posser and Jack Bowler. A violent storm prevented them from reaching Richmond. As word had already circulated in Richmond that Posser and Bowler were fomenting a rebellion against their masters, scores of slaves in Richmond were arrested and thirty-five were summarily executed. Posser was captured a few months later and executed.

As news of slave revolts spread from one state to another, slave leaders in nearby states would organize their own rebellions. With the support of the newly black republic of Haiti, Denmark Vesey attempted to foment an insurrection against the slave masters in Charleston in 1822. When word leaked out to the slave masters, hundreds of slaves in Charleston were arrested. Several of them were killed to deter those who wanted to follow Vesey's leadership. In 1831, Nat Turner organized an insurrection against slave owners in Southhampton County, Virginia, which resulted in the death of sixty whites. The conspiracy of the slaves in Richmond, Virginia, prompted slave masters in North Carolina, Kentucky, and Louisiana to preemptively attack slaves who they suspected of rebellion. Fifteen slaves were hung in North Carolina for implication in conspiracies to foment riots after the Nat Turner rebellion (Franklin and Moss 1994). In December 1856, several slaves who were thought to be leaders of a failed rebellion were hung in Kentucky (Wish 1970, 31).

Murder was an act of last resort that slave owners would take against slaves who rebelled, because slaves produced wealth. By killing them, the masters would be deprived of a means to a good source of income. However, there were numerous other forms of attacks on slaves to prevent them from rioting against the system. Psychological manipulation, where masters attempted to convince slaves that they were innately inferior to whites, was one of the most effective forms of attack. The church and its theologians, schools, politicians, and the press played an important role in vulgarizing this form of attack on blacks. Humiliations, torture, branding, rape, the separation of slave families, and the frequent sale of slaves at auctions assured that bonding among members of the same family or slaves on the same plantation would never occur. Laws were enacted to regulate and restrict all conceivable activities of slaves, from public assembly to travel to possession of weapons to economic transactions. Slave masters organized militias to control and hunt runaway slaves. When all these forms of attacks could not control the slave population from rioting or rebelling, slaves were ultimately hung or summarily executed.

See also Abolitionist Movement; Civil War and the Abolition of Slavery; Plantation System; Slave Auctions; Slave Codes; Slave Families; Slave Trade; Slavery and American Indians; Slavery in the Antebellum South; Underground Railroad.

Further Reading

Aptheker, Herbert. *American Negro Slave Revolts*. New York: Columbia University Press, 1943.

Bracey, H. John, August Meier, and Elliott Rudwick. *American Slavery: The Question of Resistance*. Belmont, CA: Wadsworth Publishing, 1971.

Wish, Harvey. "American Slave Insurrections before 1861." *American Slavery: The Question of Resistance*, edited by John H. Bracey Jr., August Meier, and Elliot Rudwick. Belmont, CA: Wadsworth, 1970.

Francois Pierre-Louis

Slave Trade

Slave trade refers to the trafficking of human slaves both internationally and domestically. Of great significance to the course of slavery in the United States was the transatlantic slave trade, which spanned more than three hundred years and was controlled first by the Portuguese and then by the British. Though debate lingers over the exact number of slaves involved, it has recently been estimated that more than eleven million slaves were exported from Africa during this period. Generally, slaves were obtained along the western coast of Africa and bought from African leaders and traders in exchange for goods and guns, although slaves were also taken as a result of capture by Europeans themselves. The overwhelming majority of slaves were taken to Brazil, to colonies of the Spanish Empire, and to the Caribbean. It is estimated that approximately half a million slaves were imported to the British colonies in North America. The major destinations were South Carolina, which received about seventy thousand slaves between 1735 and 1775, and Virginia, which received about the same number between 1699 and 1775.

Initially, European slave traders attempted to kidnap Africans from their homes. This practice was met with violent resistance from Africans. Eventually, however, native Africans began a working relationship with the European shippers, developing various commercial networks for supplying slaves and moving them to the coast to trade with the Europeans for merchandise. The voyage from the African coast to the Americas was called the Middle Passage and lasted from twenty-five to sixty days. The slaves were shackled, overcrowded, and sometimes cruelly handled and driven to suicide. On average, 16 percent of the men, women, and children enslaved perished in transit.

In 1807, Britain abolished the slave trade within the British Empire. This affected the progression of slavery in the United States. After the abolition of the slave trade, slavery in America had to become a self-sustaining institution. In addition, the rise of the plantation economy in the late eighteenth century, particularly in the Deep South, necessitated the influx of a large number of slaves. To accommodate this need, a vigorous and profitable interstate slave trade developed. It is estimated that between 1790 and 1860, the Upper South exported almost one million slaves to the Deep South, which nearly quadrupled the slave population there. Virginia was a key exporter in this period. In addition, as new slave states were added to the west, the interstate slave trade ensured a regular flow of slaves into Arkansas, Texas, and Missouri. Slave trading represented another lucrative aspect of the institution of slavery.

Captives in an African village being sent into slavery.

Courtesy Library of Congress.

See also Abolitionist Movement; Civil War and the Abolition of Slavery; Plantation System; Slave Auctions; Slave Codes; Slave Families; Slave Revolts and White Attacks on Black Slaves; Slavery and American Indians; Slavery in the Antebellum South; Underground Railroad.

Rebekah Lee and Tracy Chu

Slavery and American Indians

American Indians have had a complex relationship with the institution of slavery since its introduction on the continent with the first wave of colonial settlers in the fifteenth and sixteenth centuries. American Indians have experienced slavery as both bondsman and master. Their position near, but not quite at, the bottom of the racial hierarchy during the antebellum period ensured a diverse response to slavery and to slaves themselves. Some groups of Indians actively took part in the slave trade and sought to emulate white-plantation-style agriculture, but other groups offered a safe haven for fugitive slaves and allowed escaped slaves a surprising degree of autonomy and integration into the Indian community. American Indians' historical involvement with, and resistance to, slavery necessarily challenges assumptions that slavery should be seen as relating only to the history of blacks and whites.

From the beginning of the colonial period, Indians were enslaved by Spanish, French, and British settlers. Enslavement was the by-product of colonial warfare and trade, and the result of slave-taking expeditions. For example, the Indian allies of a defeated colonial power would be vulnerable to enslavement. In addition, colonists exploited intertribal rivalries to gain more Indian captives, with the assistance of Indians themselves. By the beginning of the eighteenth century, American Indians made up a significant, if still minority, proportion of the slave population.

However, as plantation-style agriculture developed in the South, the need for a more coercive and racialized form of slavery arose. Indian slaves began to be seen as a liability because they could more easily escape bondage and blend into neighboring Native communities. Also, American Indians were perceived to be less adaptable to the harshness of the plantation labor regime, and their numbers declined dramatically because of exposure to epidemic diseases such as smallpox, against which they had little resistance. Slavery from the mid-eighteenth century onward thus lost its multiracial character (though evidence indicates that, particularly in Brazil and Mexico, the oppression of indigenous people continued to be fundamental to the maintenance of the plantation economy) and increasingly became a systematic form of *black* bondage.

Studies have revealed a wide variety of Indian responses to black slavery. Some Indian nations took part in the slave trade and helped capture and return fugitive slaves. Also, some Indians became slave owners themselves. Black slaves were seen as a strategic as well as an economic asset. Black slaves could serve as messengers, translators, and spies and were considered mobile "property," something that became increasingly important as Indians were systematically removed from their lands in the eighteenth and nineteenth centuries. As removal devastated the Indian population and economy, owning slaves may have become an important part of rebuilding Indian life in the new settlements of the West. Some groups, such as the Cherokee, sought to emulate Southern plantation ideals and economies and generally condoned the enslavement of blacks. A prominent Creek leader was known to have possessed more than fifty slaves on his holdings.

However, there was no uniform Indian position on slavery. Even within groups such as the Creek and Cherokee, internal divisions developed between supporters and detractors of slavery. These rifts only widened with the coming of the Civil War. Some groups, such as the Seminole Indians, formed a close alliance with blacks and were seen to provide a safe haven for both fugitive slaves and freed blacks. Black involvement was fundamental to Seminole military campaigns in the nineteenth century. Throughout the antebellum period, whites remained anxious of such alliances between Indians and slaves.

Relations between black slaves and Indians were similarly diverse. The Cherokee developed a slave code that echoed white Southern slave codes. For example, slaves were not allowed to be taught to read or write, and free blacks who helped slaves escape were subject to punishment. The property of free blacks who had no Cherokee blood could be seized. In contrast, blacks who lived among the Seminoles were allowed to accumulate property and were granted free mobility and the use of guns. Thus, in some Indian nations the boundary between "slave" and free became blurry and blacks were more completely integrated within Indian society. This integration was acknowledged in law in 1866, when the U.S. government made provision for the adoption of newly emancipated blacks into certain Indian nations. Under this law, the Seminoles granted blacks full and unconditional citizenship. However, groups such as the Cherokee, Creek, and Chickasaw delayed or gave only provisional citizenship with limited rights.

See also Abolitionist Movement; Civil War and the Abolition of Slavery; Native Americans, Conquest of; Native Americans, Forced Relocation of; Native Americans, Prejudice and Discrimination against; Plantation System; Slave Auctions; Slave Codes; Slave Families; Slave Revolts and White Attacks on Black Slaves; Slave Trade; Slavery in the Antebellum South; Underground Railroad.

Further Reading

Brooks, James, ed. *Confounding the Color Line: The Indian-Black Experience in North America*. Lincoln: University of Nebraska Press, 2002.

Littlefield, Daniel. *Africans and Creeks from the Colonial Period to the Civil War*. Westport, CT: Greenwood Press, 1979.

Perdue, Theda. *Slavery and the Evolution of Cherokee Society, 1540–1866*. Knoxville: University of Tennessee Press, 1979.

Porter, Kenneth. *Black Seminoles: History of a Freedom-Seeking People*. Gainesville: University of Florida Press, 1996.

Rebekah Lee

Slavery in the Antebellum South

The U.S. Constitution emphasizes freedom and equality for all, using the most powerful and most frequently cited clause that "all men are created equal." However, the document is also contradictory and hypocritical because it includes three clauses intended to protect slavery. Although black slavery existed in Africa, South America, the Caribbean Islands, and parts of North America, the most rigid form of slavery was established in the Antebellum South. Despite democratic and revolutionary ideals found in the Declaration of Independence and the U.S. Constitution, most of the Founding Fathers of the United States did not want to eliminate slavery from the new republic. In fact, most of them owned dozens or hundreds of black slaves. The contradictions and tensions between democratic ideals and the racial caste system have continued through the postemancipation segregation era to the contemporary period. The black-white racial hierarchy and boundary are still more rigid in the United States than in other multiracial societies.

Transatlantic Slave Trade

Modern slavery is usually said to have begun with the Portuguese explorations along the coast of Africa in the fifteenth century. Although some form of human bondage had been practiced in many parts of the world since ancient times, modern slavery is almost invariably associated with African or black labor. The first Africans captured off the West Coast of Africa were sent to Europe, where they worked primarily as domestic servants and laborers in port cities. With the opening up of the Americas in 1492 and burgeoning competition among the major European nations to exploit the natural resources of the newly found lands, the transatlantic traffic in African slaves rapidly became a major enterprise in the economic development and modernization of Europe.

The Portuguese initiated what would become the transatlantic slave trade in 1444. At first they kidnapped relatively small numbers of Africans in raids during their explorations of the African coast. After they made contact with African rulers in the interior, they began purchasing enemy captives from rival ethnic groups. Although African rulers participated in the slave trade, they usually did not sell their own kin. They shipped the first captives to Portugal and Spain, but after the beginning of the sixteenth century, they began shipping Africans to the Caribbean, Brazil, and other parts of the Americas. Between 1452 and 1494, a series of papal decrees and treaties granted Spain dominance over the territories of the New World, gave Portugal control over India and Brazil, and recognized the Portuguese monopoly over the slave trade.

After a failed attempt to exploit indigenous people for slave labor on the island of Hispaniola (present-day Haiti and the Dominican Republic), the first shipment of African slaves was brought to the Americas in 1502. The Portuguese continued to monopolize the slave trade until the middle of the seventeenth century, when other European nations began to compete for a share in the lucrative trade. The route of slave ships from Europe to Africa, then to the Americas, and back to Europe is often referred to as the triangular trade. The European traders carried goods from Europe to Africa, where they purchased slaves who would be transported across the Atlantic Ocean to the Americas. The final segment of the journey was the return to Europe with raw materials and other products, such as sugar, molasses, and rum. When the ship's destination was one of the Caribbean islands, there was often another stop in the North American colonies before heading back to Europe.

Slave captives were marched in chains from the African interior to the coast, where they were examined and branded by their purchasers. They were then held in cells or dungeons until a ship was ready to transport them to the Americas. Many slaves died of injuries and disease during the long march to the coast and during their wait at the slave-trading centers. The most arduous part of their journey was the transatlantic crossing, known as the Middle Passage. The slaves were crowded into the holds of the ships, where they were chained and often packed so tightly that they could hardly move. The unsanitary, crowded conditions aboard the ships exposed the captives to numerous illnesses and diseases. Many slaves committed suicide by starving themselves to death or jumping overboard. At its worst, the difficult journey across the ocean may have resulted in mortality rates as high as 40 percent. Most of the African captives were taken from West Africa, the Congo, and Angola; some were also taken from Mozambique and Madagascar. Of the estimated ten to twelve million Africans brought to the Americas during the transatlantic slave trade, about half a million were taken to the British colonies of North America.

Slaves and Bond Servants in Colonial America

Most historians of slavery in the Antebellum South emphasize the gradual, complex evolution of slavery as an institution from its earliest forms during the colonial period until the mid-nineteenth century. The first Africans brought to the North American English colonies arrived in Jamestown, Virginia, on a Dutch ship in 1619. There is some debate about the status of these first arrivals. Were they slaves or bond servants? The importance of this question lies in the fact that slavery had not yet received any legal recognition in the colonies. The early records of the period refer to Africans as "servants." Some historians believe they were indentured servants, but others point out the ambiguous use of the terms *servant* and *bond servant* in the seventeenth century. Bondage was common for whites brought to the colonies as debtors and convicts, and the historical records show that the status of blacks was similar to that of white indentured servants. The early colonists exploited unpaid labor wherever they could find it, whether that was among Native Americans, destitute whites, or captured Africans. Bondage was not yet synonymous with blackness, nor was it considered a permanent condition.

From the beginning, however, there were local and regional differences in how Africans brought to the colonies were treated. The greatest labor demands were in the Southern colonies, where tobacco, rice, and indigo were grown. The needs of the Mid-Atlantic and Northern colonies were met with less intensive labor. The economic activities of each region determined the need for bond servants or slaves. Differences in the relationship between slaves and slaveholders and differences in attitudes toward blacks also developed along local and regional lines. No matter how close the relationship might be, whether slave, indentured servant, or free, the black person was usually considered inferior. Whereas some argue that racial prejudice developed in direct relation to economic and historical circumstances, others maintain that Europeans were never race neutral.

The shift toward a hereditary system of slavery based on race began to develop in the middle of the seventeenth century. Massachusetts in 1641 and Connecticut in 1650 were the first colonies to pass legislation legalizing slavery. The New England Puritans had relatively little need for slave labor but became involved in the highly profitable slave trade, supplying slaves to the more labor-intensive, agricultural Southern colonies as well as conducting a lively trade with the West Indies. Virginia and Maryland were the first colonies to make slavery a permanent, hereditary condition determined by the status of the mother. By the middle of the eighteenth century, this new race-based slavery had been sanctioned by law throughout the colonies. The legal recognition of slavery was followed by increasingly restrictive statutes, or "slave codes," that limited the rights of slaves. Laws were passed forbidding intermarriage, literacy instruction, free assembly, and travel without written permission. These laws were intended to deter slave rebellions and to restrict the means by which a slave might gain freedom or participate in the daily life of the colonies. It was necessary to legalize the slave's *difference* from the rest of the population in every way, to such an extreme that the slave became less than fully human before the law. The idea of the innate inferiority of blacks became a necessary rationalization for the exploitation of slave labor.

Slavery and the American Revolution

As the economic and political conflicts between the colonies and England intensified, the contradictions between the revolutionary ideals espoused by the colonists and the status of blacks became ever more glaring. By the time that war broke out, the descendants of the Africans who had been arriving in ever-increasing numbers since 1619 were very much aware of the revolutionary ideas that were spreading throughout Europe, the Caribbean, and the rest of the Americas. Many of them saw the colonists' defiance of arbitrary rule as an opportunity to petition for their own freedoms. Some made appeals to local courts and colonial assemblies. Others, like Crispus Attucks, the seaman and fugitive slave who was killed by British troops in what came to be known as the Boston Massacre, gave their lives in defense of the American cause. Although blacks fought with the colonial militias in most of the early battles of the war, in late 1775, George Washington and the Continental Congress eventually decided to ban all blacks from the militias. There had always been fear of allowing blacks to bear arms and uneasiness about the inevitable demands for freedom that would come with their participation in the revolutionary struggle. Washington was forced to relax the ban and allow free blacks to enlist when the British governor of Virginia, Lord Dunmore, issued a proclamation offering freedom to any black who would fight on the side of the British. Washington, who owned some two hundred slaves, lost many of them to the Loyalist troops. An estimated five thousand free blacks served in the Continental army. But given the reluctance of the colonists to accept blacks' willingness to sacrifice their lives for the Revolutionary cause, just as many blacks decided to take their chances with the British.

Slavery and the restrictions placed on free blacks were a contradiction that the leaders of the American Revolution were in no hurry to resolve. The Philadelphia Quakers formed the first abolitionist society in 1775, on the eve of the Revolutionary War.

Slavery and Freedom: The Declaration of Independence and the Bill of Rights

Slavery continued to be a major inconsistency in both the Declaration of Independence (1776) and the Constitution of the United States (1787). The Declaration of Independence made no reference to slavery at all. In his original draft of the Declaration, Thomas Jefferson accused King George III of imposing the slave trade on the colonies and perpetuating an unjust system. This was an argument that had previously been made by the Virginia planters to justify levying taxes on the importation of slaves. This was not a humanitarian or antislavery measure. The planters wanted to be able to control the number of slaves coming into the colonies as a means of controlling levels of agricultural production and profits. They found themselves in the contradictory position of denouncing the inhumanity of the slave trade while at the same time insisting on their right to maintain a slave-labor system. Jefferson's reference to the slave trade in the initial draft of the Declaration was deleted when these same Southern planters objected to the strong antislavery implications of the charges made against the English king.

When the Constitutional Convention met in Philadelphia in 1787, the Northern delegates objected to any use of the word *slavery* in the laws that would govern the new nation. But since the Southern planters were determined to protect their economic interests, the Constitution refers indirectly to slaves as persons "held to service or labor." A further compromise had each slave counted as three-fifths of a person for purposes of representation and taxation in the new government. Although the earlier legislation in the same year excluded slavery from the Northwest Territory, three clauses intended to protect slavery were written into the Constitution. Existing states were given the right to continue importing slaves (i.e., those persons "held to service or labor"), and most problematic of all for the slave population, it was made a federal offense for any individual or state to aid or harbor a runaway slave. The Declaration of Independence held out the promise of freedom and equality for all, but the Constitution closed the door to any such possibility for slaves in the Southern states. These two founding documents are written evidence of the pattern of evasion, contradiction, and compromise that would undermine the avowed democratic principles of the new nation and ultimately divide the nation.

Plantation Slavery

After the American Revolution and the invention of the cotton gin in 1793, the institution of slavery underwent another major transformation. At the end of the eighteenth century there were nearly 700,000 slaves in the United States; by the middle of the nineteenth century their numbers had quadrupled, having reached some 3,953,760. For the most part the local slave population reproduced itself and was not dependent on the direct importation of

slaves from the Caribbean and Africa. Although the pattern of slave ownership and slave labor was never uniform and continued to vary from region to
region and household to household, most slaves worked as agricultural laborers on tobacco, rice, and cotton plantations. It is estimated that about
400,000 slaves worked in towns and cities as servants, skilled artisans, and
skilled and unskilled laborers. In both rural and urban areas, slaves were sometimes "hired out" to make money for their owners or, if they were more for-
tunate, to make money for themselves. Some slaves were even able to
purchase their own freedom this way. With the increase in the demand for
cotton in the European markets during the first half of the nineteenth century, more than half of the slave population of the United States became concentrated in the cotton-growing states of the lower Southern states, principally
Mississippi, Alabama, Louisiana, and Georgia.

Most slave owners operated small farms and plantations with fewer than
twenty slaves, but large cotton plantations usually required the labor of thirty
or more slaves. These plantations were organized like rural factories with a
highly regimented division of labor, which was intended to maintain high production levels. Most slave owners lived on their farms and plantations, but
those who operated a large plantation usually hired an overseer to help man-
age their property. The overseer was often assisted by a driver, a slave chosen
to keep up the work pace and help supervise the other slaves. Most slaves
were field workers engaged in relentless, backbreaking labor year-round from
dawn to dusk; the average field slave worked from ten to fourteen hours a day
and had very little time for socializing or recreation. Unlike the individual-task
system that was used in rice cultivation, the large cotton plantation used a
gang system, closely supervised groups of slaves working together at special-
ized tasks. Overseers and drivers used coercion and fear of physical punishment to extract the maximum work from the slaves; floggings were the most
common form of punishment. A smaller number of slaves worked as domestic servants and skilled laborers, such as mechanics and carpenters, who were
needed for the general upkeep of the estate. All slaves, whether they were
field workers or lived in the relative comfort of the house servant, were dependent on the goodwill of their owners.

By law, slave masters exercised total authority and control over their human
property. Yet slaves were able to sustain themselves emotionally and spiritu-
ally with their own belief systems, stories, songs, and rituals. Although plantations were usually isolated and there was little opportunity for the rituals of
courtship and marriage, slaves were able to form close relationships and family bonds. Most slave owners realized that strong family ties would ensure a
more willing and reliable work force.

As the antislavery sentiment grew and abolitionist propaganda intensified,
the slave owners felt compelled to protect the institution by creating ever-
more-stringent laws, called "slave codes," to control the movement and activities of their slaves. These laws were intended to keep slaves isolated and
dependent on their owners. Slaves were required to have written permission
to travel or leave the plantation; they were not allowed to socialize with free
blacks or assemble for any purpose without the presence of an authorized
white person. Antiliteracy laws were passed, forbidding anyone to teach slaves

how to read and write. Counties enlisted local volunteers called "patrollers" to control the movement of slaves, detect conspiracies, and put down rebellions. Even though these regulations and mechanisms for control became ever more repressive, the slaveholders continued to insist on the benevolence of the institution.

"A House Divided": Slavery and the Civil War

The acquisition of new territories in the first half of the nineteenth century as a result of the Louisiana Purchase and the Mexican-American War brought with it a debate over the expansion of slavery, which ultimately led to the crisis that almost split the new nation in two. When Missouri applied for statehood in 1819, the issue of slavery was at the center of a congressional struggle to maintain a balance in the conflicting economic and political interests of the Northern and Southern states. The irreconcilable nature of the differences between the free-labor industrial North and slave-labor agrarian South became increasingly evident in the series of failed legislative compromises that began with the Missouri Compromise of 1820. Missouri would be admitted as a state under the condition that slavery would be prohibited in the rest of the Louisiana Purchase territory north of its southern boundary.

Over the next three decades, the abolitionist campaign against slavery increased dramatically. White and black abolitionists alike became more radical and persistent in their attacks on the institution that lay at the heart of the Southern economy and way of life. The threat of slave insurrections, such as the Denmark Vesey conspiracy in Charleston, South Carolina, in 1822 and the Nat Turner rebellion in Southampton County, Virginia, in 1831, created fear among and harsh reprisals by the Southern slaveholders. Agitation by both abolitionist and proslavery forces and the acquisition of southwestern territories after the Mexican-American War resulted in the Compromise of 1850, which cobbled together a group of measures that failed to put an end to the controversy. Once again, the extension of slavery became the center of congressional debate. This compromise was far more complex than the earlier one and merely postponed the inevitable conflict over the status of slavery. Among other measures, California was admitted as a free state; Utah and New Mexico were granted legislative authority to decide for themselves, and the slave trade was prohibited in the District of Columbia. But the most contentious measure of all was the imposition of a more rigorous fugitive-slave law. Abolitionists openly defied the new fugitive slave law by organizing a rescue of slaves in the South by means of the Underground Railroad and often violent resistance to the efforts of slaveholders to force the return of slaves who found refuge in the North. Through newspapers, books, pamphlets, speeches, and continual lobbying, abolitionists kept slavery as a moral issue at the center of the power struggle between Northern and Southern states.

The Kansas-Nebraska Act of 1854 was the result of another bitter debate over the extension of slavery and in effect nullified the Missouri Compromise of 1820. Violent confrontations broke out between antislavery and proslavery factions in the new territories. The passage of this act had far-reaching consequences. The new Republican Party grew out of opposition to the bill, and the intensity of the conflict moved the nation closer to civil war. The end of all further compromise was signaled by the Dred Scott Decision in 1857, when the U.S. Supreme Court declared that the Missouri Compromise was unconstitutional and that Congress did not have the authority to ban slavery from any territories.

The national crisis reached the breaking point when the militant abolitionist John Brown led a raid on the federal arsenal at Harper's Ferry, Virginia, in 1859, and the Republican candidate, Abraham Lincoln, was elected to the presidency on an antislavery platform in 1860. After the Republican victory, seven Southern states immediately seceded, and four more joined them when Lincoln was forced to take action against the Confederate attack on Fort Sumter in Charleston, South Carolina, in 1861. Faced with the outbreak of the Civil War, Lincoln insisted on a policy of restoring national unity above all else. In an attempt to appease the four remaining slave states—Delaware, Maryland, Kentucky, and Missouri—Lincoln was exceedingly cautious about making this conflict a war against slavery. Despite his antislavery campaign, he refused to embrace the abolitionist cause.

Lincoln believed that slavery was unjust and morally wrong, but like Jefferson he had little faith in the ability of blacks to live among whites as equals. At the beginning of the war, following an all-too-familiar pattern, Lincoln prohibited blacks from participating as soldiers in the struggle against the Confederate army and vacillated about what to do with the thousands of slaves who sought refuge behind Union lines. Lincoln supported gradual, compensated emancipation, to be followed by the resettlement of as many blacks as possible in other parts of the world. He went so far as to invite a group of free blacks to the White House (the first meeting of its kind) to discuss this proposition. Some blacks were ready to leave, but most thought they had a right to stay and live as citizens in the nation they had helped build.

Since none of the Southern states, including the loyal border states agreed to Lincoln's plan of compensated emancipation, he was forced to issue an executive order proclaiming emancipation of all slaves in rebel-controlled territories. He conceived of this limited emancipation as a "military necessity" aimed at undermining the economic viability of the Confederate states. It was no longer possible, as the black abolitionist Frederick Douglass had forewarned, "to fight slaveholders, without fighting against slavery." After the battle of Antietam, on September 22, 1862, Lincoln announced that his emancipation proclamation would go into effect on January 1, 1863. As is often observed, Lincoln's proclamation did not free a single slave, since it only applied to the rebel states. It was not until two years later, after the Confederacy lost the war, that Congress passed the thirteenth amendment to the Constitution, abolishing slavery in all parts of the United States. The Civil War ended slavery but did not end racial discrimination, nor did emancipation result in full citizenship rights for former slaves.

See also Abolitionist Movement; Civil War and the Abolition of Slavery; Douglass, Frederick; Dred Scott Decision; Emancipation Proclamation; Fourteenth Amendment; Free Persons of Color in the Antebellum North; Lincoln, Abraham, and the Emancipation of Slaves; Manifest Destiny; Missouri Compromise; *The Peculiar Institution: Slavery in the Ante-bellum South*; Reconstruction Era; Slave

Auctions; Slave Codes; Slave Families; Slave Revolts and White Attacks on Black Slaves; Slave Trade; Slavery and American Indians; Underground Railroad.

Further Reading

Bennett, Lerone. *Before the Mayflower: A History of Black America*. New York: Penguin, 1993.

Berlin, Ira. *Many Thousands Gone: The First Two Centuries of Slavery in North America*. Cambridge, MA: Belknap Press, 1998.

Blassingame, John W. *The Slave Community: Plantation Life in the Antebellum South*. Rev. and enlarged ed. New York: Oxford University Press, 1979.

Curtin, Philip D. *The Atlantic Slave Trade: A Census*. Madison: University of Wisconsin Press, 1969.

Davis, David Brion. *The Problem of Slavery in Western Culture*. Ithaca, NY: Cornell University Press, 1966.

———. *The Problem of Slavery in the Age of Revolution*. Ithaca, NY: Cornell University Press, 1975.

Fields, Barbara J. "Slavery, Race and Ideology in the United States of America." *New Left Review* 181 (1990): 85–118.

Franklin, John Hope, and Alfred A. Moss, Jr. *From Slavery to Freedom: A History of African Americans*. 8th ed. New York: McGraw-Hill, 1999.

Genovese, Eugene. *Roll, Jordan, Roll: The World the Slaves Made*. New York: Vintage Books, 1972.

Heuman, Gad, and James Walvin, eds. *The Slavery Reader*. New York: Routledge, 2003.

Kelley, Robin D. G., and Earl Lewis, eds. *A History of African Americans*. New York: Oxford University Press, 2000.

Kolchin, Peter. *American Slavery, 1619–1877*. New York: Hill and Wang, 1993.

Stampp, Kenneth M. *The Peculiar Institution: Slavery in the Ante-Bellum South*. New York: Vintage Books, 1989.

Thomas, Hugh. *The Slave Trade: The Story of the Atlantic Slave Trade, 1440–1870*. Cambridge: Cambridge University Press, 1992.

White, Deborah Gray. *Ar'n't I a Woman? Female Slaves in the Plantation South*. New York: Norton, 1985.

Barbara J. Webb

SNCC

See Student Nonviolent Coordinating Committee (SNCC).

Social Construction of Whiteness

Until recently, the representation of whiteness—as an object of study—remained under the radar screen of most social scientists working in the area of race and race relations in America. Indeed, as has been pointed out by recent analyses of the social construction of whiteness, not only has the social construction of white identity eluded social criticism, it continues to operate as the invisible norm in American society as a whole. The invisibility of whiteness as the norm requires scrutiny, according to social critics, if American social policy is to successfully eliminate racial discrimination.

Earlier studies of race in the United States have been able to show, definitively, that race is not a biological entity but, rather, a sociocultural construction. Sociologists and geneticists have convincingly debunked the *ideology* of the biology of race, arguing that "race" has no empirical basis in reality, which in this case is genetics. The implications of demonstrating how race is a socially constructed phenomenon have opened up new ways of analyzing the sociohistorical construction of race and race relations. But most of the early studies focused on how blackness has been represented in the imagination of white society, or how white society implemented various practices of discrimination and exploitation of African Americans. Although these studies have proven indispensable in both providing a better understanding of race relations and as part of a project of creating the conditions for ending racial discrimination, recent studies on whiteness seek to show how race is not something that "happens" exclusively to people of color. White people are raced also, but because whiteness exists as an invisible norm, whites tend to position their identity as universal: they are just people, not black, Asian, Latino, and so forth, not named or seen in racial terms, but people in the general sense. Research on the mass media in the United States has repeatedly demonstrated that whites are disproportionately predominant in the various outlets of representation and as such become the standard, or norm. The implications are serious; the ubiquity of whiteness as norm, which leads to the assumption that white people are just people, is a few steps away from saying "colored" people are something else, *not* people.

For example, Richard Dyer, author of "The Matter of Whiteness" (2002) has pointed to many examples from everyday life where white people seem to escape race. Joke telling is one example. According to Dyer, "An old-style white comedian will often start a joke: 'There's this bloke walking down the street and he meets this black geezer,' never thinking to race the bloke as well as the geezer" (Dyer 1997, 2). It is often assumed that if someone says she is interested in issues of race, then that means she is interested in the issues facing people of "color," not "white" people. The methodological point to whiteness studies is to make whiteness seem strange, as a way to get a better understanding of it through asking questions like:"How was the white identity formed and why?" "How has history transformed whiteness?" "How did some ethnic groups, such as the Irish and the Jews, become white while others did not?" "How does pride in whiteness become white supremacy?" "What can whites who are concerned about racial inequality do about it?" These are some of the key questions that frame whiteness studies. To shift the analysis from nonwhites to whites is also a way to show how racism damages whites as much as nonwhites, although in different ways.

Whiteness, however, is not a monolithic category. Difference (especially class based and gender based) cuts across whiteness. Recent scholars in whiteness studies have argued that viewing all whites as the same, as part of a monolithic community, reproduces the same kinds of problems that emerge when whites view other races as all apart of one category: other. Getting at the problem of racial inequality requires an examination of class inequality and gender inequality, because race, class, and gender are all *lived* categories; all three are experienced simultaneously everyday. The authors of *White Trash: Race and Class in America*, for example, show how race and class are intimately bound together in American culture, and nowhere else are the two so connected as in the label "white trash." A close study of the creation of this label sheds light on the historical connection of racial and class discrimination in America and is important to examine because it reveals that not all whites enjoy the privilege of whiteness, but rather dominant whites exploit poor whites in part by representing them as something *not* exactly white: "trash." By shading poor whites as trash, or not white, dominant whites degrade poor whites by racializing them as trash. By examining the ways in which race and class mutually shape identities, it is thought that scholars can find novel ways to continue the project of ending racism. The study of whiteness continues to be one of the most exciting recent developments in the social sciences.

Further Reading

Delgado, Richard, and Jean Stephanic, eds. *Critical White Studies: Looking Behind the Mirror.* Philadelphia: Temple University Press, 1997.

Dyer, Richard. "The Matter of Whiteness," in *White Privilege: Essential Readings on the Other Side of Racism*, edited by Paula S. Rothenberg. New York: Worth, 2002.

———. *White.* New York: Routledge, 1997.

Wray, Matt, and Annalee Newitz, eds. *White Trash: Race and Class in America.* New York: Routledge, 1997.

Michael Roberts

Social Darwinism

Social theories are the product of a society. It is often perceived to serve the interests of certain groups of people and often generates both intended and unintended consequences. Social Darwinism is one of those idea systems created and used by people for different purposes. Social Darwinism is an ideology that claims that only the "fittest" in human society can survive and prosper just as in the natural world. According to its doctrine, the process of "natural" selection occurs in human societies as well as in the natural world.

It was Herbert Spencer (1820–1903) who applied natural scientist Charles Darwin's (1809–1882) theory of evolution to the human social world. Spencer, who lived in England, studied and was influenced by Darwin's work. Darwin's theory of biological evolution through the process of natural selection holds that a species changes physically over many generations as it adapts to the natural environment. Those species that adapt well to the natural environment will survive as the fittest. His theory of evolution, which was proposed in his 1859 book *The Origin of Species*, made a significant impact upon social scientists. Social thinkers of the nineteenth century who were investigating the alleged superiority and inferiority of different racial groups were heavily influenced by this theory. Applying the process of nat-ural selection to human society, they argued that superior human societies, classes, and races were the outcomes of this process of natural selection. These ideas became the basis of Social Darwinism, commonly known as "sur-vival of the fittest."

It was, in fact, Spencer, not Darwin, who coined the phrase "survival of the fittest." To Spencer, human society should ideally be modeled on nature. Think-ing of a parallel natural-selection process going on in the human social world, Spencer proposed that in the human social world one should never inten-tionally interfere with the "natural" process that selects only the fittest human beings for survival, prosperity, and dominance. This idea eventually led to a variety of beliefs and practices, such as Nordic racism created by social thinkers and later used by Nazi theoreticians. In this particular version of white racism, the Nordic race was believed to be superior to the shorter "Alpines" and the darker-skinned "Mediterraneans." It also led to eugenics, in which it was understood that the unfit transmitted their undesirable charac-teristics, so a breeding program was developed to cultivate a better society consisting of people with more desirable characteristics.

Social Darwinism also had a significant impact on American thought (Ban-nister 1979). As an ideology, it has been used to justify gross inequality in the capitalistic American society by such corporate leaders as John D. Rockefeller. According to the doctrine of Social Darwinism, the successful make a lot of money simply because they are innately superior to the unsuccessful. Those who are poor deserve to be poor because they are innately inferior. They are responsible for their own poverty. Government should not do anything to in-terfere in this process. This is the outcome of natural selection in human so-ciety.

Most important, Social Darwinism profoundly affected the emergence and strengthening of white racism. In the nineteenth century, when white Euro-peans left their own societies, exploring and contacting different peoples and colonizing them, they needed to justify the subsequent inequality between the colonizers and the indigenous people. Racism as a system of ideas became a tool for dominance during the colonization period, and white racism emerged as a dominant theory explaining the racial inequality. White racists believed that white Europeans became a superior race because they had evolved much faster than other races. That is, they were chosen to dominate. Social Darwinism contributed to the emergence of such racist ideas as these and popular usage of racist ideology in the nineteenth century. If white Amer-icans were the most powerful and successful, then this must be the result of innate characteristics of superiority formed through the process of natural se-lection in competition with other races. The belief that social achievement is essentially determined by human biological differences makes it simple and convenient to justify inequality among different groups of people who have physical differences. The idea was created and has been used to justify racial inequality in the United States and around the world.

See also Biological Racism; Eugenics Movement; Nordic Superiority; Spencer, Herbert.

Further Reading

Bannister, Robert C. *Social Darwinism: Science and Myth in Anglo-American Social Thought*. Philadelphia: Temple University Press, 1979.

Heon Cheol Lee

Social Distance

The concept of social distance is widely used in studies of ethnic and race relations, as well as in studies of class, gender, and status. Social distance refers to the extent to which members of a group are accepted or rejected by mainstream society. A high level of social distance between members of a group and the larger society indicates that they are not socially accepted, while a lower level of social distance indicates acceptance and closeness between the group and society.

Sociologist Emory Bogardus was the first person to create a scale measuring the concept of social distance. Developed in 1925, the Bogardus Social Distance Scale is based on willingness to allow any given group (e.g., based on race, ethnicity, or religion) within various degrees of intimacy. Respondents to the scale are asked to approve or disapprove of a range of relationships that a person from the selected group may have in relation to themselves, ranging from being a visitor to the country to being a fellow citizen, a neighbor, a close friend, a close kin by marriage, and so forth. Examples of questions from the Bogardus Social Distance Scale include, "Would you accept a [black] as a regular friend?" and "Would you accept a [black] as a speaking acquaintance?" Based on these items, scores on the Social Distance Scale run from a low of 1 (i.e., the respondent would marry a member of the group) to high of 7 (i.e., the respondent would restrict a member of that group from living in his or her country).

Results of studies using the Bogardus Social Distance Scale over the years reveal interesting trends in race relations in the United States, including how attitudes have remained fixed in regard to certain groups. Results from its original application in a 1926 national survey showed virtually no social distance (i.e., a high level of social acceptance) between respondents and those of British or Canadian descent. This finding was replicated in national studies in the 1940s, 1950s, and 1960s. In contrast, African Americans have consistently had the highest social distance score (i.e., the lowest level of acceptance). Historical analysis using the Bogardus Social Distance Scale also shows how attitudes toward certain racial or ethnic groups may be influenced by current political events and conflicts. For example, in the 1940s, there was a particularly high level of social distance between survey respondents and Japanese/Japanese American individuals, apparently in response to World War II.

Though the widespread use of the Bogardus Social Distance Scale has helped to make social distance an enduring concept in race relations, the intellectual legacy of social distance as a concept goes far beyond Bogardus. Bogardus's work is significant because he was the first to develop a scale to measure social distance. His concept of social distance was, however, based on the work of Robert Park, who in turn, had been influenced by the work of Georg Simmel. Simmel's original concept of social distance was a part of his larger work in the sociology of space, which looked at the relationship between meta-phoric, or social, space and geometric, or physical, space. Simmel pointed to the way that space may be subdivided for social purposes and framed in social boundaries that are distinct from physical or natural boundaries. In contrast to natural boundaries, the social boundaries are sociological facts that are formed spatially. Thus, the social boundary can precede the spatial reality—for example, when a sense of ethnic or religious solidarity leads to the drawing of physical boundaries between disparate groups of people. It is socially acceptable to converse at a closer distance at a dinner party then it is in the workplace. Although the physical distance may be the same in both instances, only in one case is it acceptable, because the social expectation differs.

Deriving his concept of social distance from Simmel's notion of social boundaries, Park believed that it had great importance for understanding race relations because the degree of intimacy between groups and individuals indicate the influence that each has over the other. The greater the social distance between individuals and groups, the less they influence each other reciprocally. In terms of relations between dominant and subordinated races or classes, as long as the subordinate in the relationship (i.e., a servant, or a racial minority) remains mindful of his or her place or distance, the dominant person in the relationship can enjoy a certain degree of personal warmth. For example, a person of wealth may confide in, and have a warm relationship with his or her servant. But this relationship is only viable as long as the servant keeps his or her "distance" from the employer; that is, as long as the servant does not step over the traditionally accepted social boundaries that predicate the relationship between servant and employer.

Further Reading

Bogardus, Emory S. *Social Distance*. Los Angeles: Antioch Press, 1959.

Marshall, Gordon. *A Dictionary of Sociology*. New York: Oxford University Press, 1998.

Owen, Carolyn, Howard C. Eisner, and Thomas McFaul. "A Half-Century of Social Distance Research: National Replication of the Bogardus Studies." *Sociology and Social Research* 66 (1981): 80–98.

Park, Robert E. "The Concept of Social Distance as Applied to the Study of Racial Attitudes and Racial Relations." *Journal of Applied Sociology* (later *Sociology and Social Research*) 8 (July/August 1924): 339–344.

Simmel, Georg, and Kurt H. Wolff. *The Sociology of Georg Simmel*. Glencoe, IL: Free Press, 1950.

Tracy Chu

South Asians, Ambiguity in Racial Identity among

Ambiguous racial identity is a common problem for South Asian Americans. Geographically, South Asia includes seven countries—India, Pakistan, Nepal, Bangladesh, Bhutan, Sri Lanka, and the Maldives. People from South Asia do not see themselves as being Asian because their features appear Caucasian and they have darker skin than most Asians. Other Asians, especially East Asians (Chinese, Japanese, and Koreans), do not think of South Asians as belonging to their racial category because South Asians are physically and culturally different from them. Thus, South Asians find themselves treated as racially ambiguous, inconsistently categorized nonwhites who do not belong to other major racial groups in the United States.

This ambiguity in racial identity among South Asian Americans results from complex historical processes in which both group self-definition and racial labeling have played a role. Like other ethnic groups, South Asian Americans view issues of racial identity in ways that are influenced by conceptions of race brought from their home countries. Common identity based on geography, however, is not easily found among these peoples: the classification "South Asian," while denoting the people who live in and originate from the South Asian countries, is a strained construct.

Even India, which covers three-quarters of the Indian subcontinent and contains three-quarters of its population, was politically united only in the face of foreign invaders/occupiers. Indians suffer from a subethnic division based on place of origin and religion. The religious division is a legacy of a long history of conflict between Hindus, the dominant religious group, and minority religious groups—Sihks, Muslims, Jains, and Parsis. Furthermore, each country's people may speak any of several provincial languages as well as the national language. For example, in Pakistan, people speak four dialects (Pashto, Punjabi, Sindhi, and Baluchi) and the national language, Urdu. Thus, South Asians usually see themselves in provincial, linguistic, and religious terms, defining themselves by a wide range of possible racial and ethnic terms.

American racial labeling further complicates South Asians' ambiguous racial identity. A fundamental dynamic of U.S. social systems is the dichotomous division of people into white and nonwhite. South Asian Americans are thus nonwhites. Their racial ambiguity, then, stems not from the question of whether they are white or not, but from the more complex question of who, exactly, they are as nonwhites. Those who lack clear-cut racial identities such as black, white, or Asian are likely to both feel and cause uncertainty about racial identity. South Asians, who do not fit well in any category, encounter a social dynamic that insists on classifying people. Thus, South Asians find themselves lumped in with Asians although they are so different from Asian Americans.

Differing political relationships between Asian countries and the United States have also affected patterns of immigration and identity formation. Specifically, immigrants from East/Southeast Asia (i.e., China, Taiwan, Korea, Japan, Vietnam, Laos, Cambodia, and the Philippines) show one pattern, while those from South Asia show another. East/Southeast Asians dominate the Asian American population numerically because of past alliances with America (as in the case of the Philippines, Korea, and Vietnam). This group has highly developed social and political structures within the American establishment. In contrast, South Asia and the United States have been far more distant associates. They have not been engaged in comparable military association or economic trade. All of these developments have contributed to the formation of South Asians' ambiguous racial identity.

Ambiguity in racial identity inevitably involves the risk of being ignored and invisible because ambiguous groups fail to fit into established racial schemes. Indeed, South Asians feel excluded from and marginalized in pan-Asian organizations or movements. Their sense of marginalization, physical affinity with other nonwhites, and the experience of white colonization may lead them to identify with blacks or other people of color. As the South Asian American population increases in the United States, the question of South Asians' inclusion with Asian Americans becomes increasingly problematic and the need to resolve questions of South Asian American identity more pressing.

See also Asian Americans, Discrimination against; Asian Americans, Perceptions of as Foreigners.

Further Reading

Kibria, Nazli. "Not Asian, Black or White? Reflections on South Asian American Racial Identity." *Amerasia Journal* 22, no. 2 (1996): 77–86.

Min, Pyoung Gap, and Rose Kim, eds. *Struggle for Ethnic Identity: Narratives by Asian American Professionals.* Walnut Creek, CA: AltaMira, 1999.

Shankar, Lavina Dhingra, and Rajini Srikanth. *Yet Apart: South Asians in Asian America.* Philadelphia: Temple University Press, 1998.

Sookhee Oh

Southern Christian Leadership Conference (SCLC)

The Southern Christian Leadership Conference (SCLC) was created in 1957 in New Orleans by a group of ministers, labor leaders, lawyers, and political activists who were concerned about the impact of segregation on their communities. Civil Rights leader Martin Luther King Jr. was the first president of the organization and remained so until his assassination in 1968. The SCLC played a critical role in the organization of marches, rallies, leadership-training programs, citizen-education projects, and voter-registration drives, which were held to bring attention to the consequences of segregation. These activities were organized throughout the South and in other border states. The leaders of the SCLC encouraged the members of their communities to use nonviolent tactics in their efforts to end racial discrimination and segregation. The SCLC played a central role in organizing the civil rights march on Washington, DC, in 1963.

After King's death, the SCLC was led by Rev. Ralph David Abernathy. The organization remained committed to fighting against discrimination through nonviolent methods, but the focus became more local in scope. The influence of the organization was further challenged due to internal strife, which led a key leader in the organization, Rev. Jesse L. Jackson, to depart and establish a new organization (Operation PUSH) along with his followers from Operation Breadbasket, an organization that focused on economic development.

Today, the SCLC is headquartered in Atlanta, and Martin Luther King III has served as president of the organization since 1997. His goal is to make the organization more modern by increasing membership through the use of the Internet. He also wants to build bridges between longtime SCLC members and young black America.

See also Civil Rights Movement; Jackson, Jesse; King, Martin Luther Jr.

Romney S. Norwood

Spanish-American War

The United States declared war on Spain on April 25, 1898, after the sinking of the battleship *Maine* in the Havana Harbor. On the surface, it seemed that the war was fought to free Cuba, Puerto Rico, the Philippine Islands, and other islands (including Guam) from Spanish control, but an underlying motive for the United States' entering the war was U.S. imperialist expansion. The United States won the war easily within a short period of time with a few thousand American lives sacrificed. Under the terms of the Treaty of Paris, the United States acquired Puerto Rico and Guam as its colonies from Spain and was allowed to occupy Manila, while Cuba became independent.

The Spanish Empire was once a great empire of the world. Spain was the first European nation to explore and claim westward territory across the Atlantic Ocean. In its prime, the empire extended from Virginia on the eastern coast of the United States south to Tierra del Fuego at the tip of South America and westward to California and Alaska. It also included the Philippines and other islands across the Pacific. By 1825, Spain had lost most of its colonies, with only Puerto Rico, Cuba, the Philippines, and a few Pacific islands left.

The United States' interest in the war began long before the war actually started. In 1884, the price of sugar began to drop dramatically in Cuba, and the country's "sugar nobility" began to lose the major role it had had in the island's economy and society. The United States took this opportunity to enter the Cuban sugar market. U.S. capitol, machinery, and technicians helped Cuban sugar mills to remain competitive with European beet sugar. By 1894, almost 90 percent of Cuba's export went to the United States, and 38 percent of Cuba's imports came from the United States. The United States had more than $50 million invested in Cuba, and annual trade was worth twice as much as it had been ten years earlier.

In 1895, the Cuban patriot Jose Martí began the Cuban fight for freedom that had been lost during the Ten Years' War (1868–1878), but Spain had a much greater number of troops than the Cubans. Cuban generals were forced to use guerilla warfare against the Spanish in hopes of exhausting their troops. Spain sent General Valeriano Weyler to pacify Cuba, but he began implementing a policy of reconcentration that moved the civilian population into central locations guarded by Spanish troops to deny the guerillas support in the countryside. President William McKinley, inaugurated on March 4, 1897, was anxious to become involved in the war. Two factors determined McKinley's decision to declare war. First, a letter written by Spanish foreign minister Enrique Dupuy de Lóme was published in the *New York Journal* criticizing McKinley. The second factor was the sinking of the U.S.S. *Maine* on February 15, 1898. After investigation by the U.S. Naval Court of Inquiry, it was found that a Spanish mine had blown up the ship. The Spanish government did everything to stop the war, yet less than one month after the investigation, the United States unjustifiably declared war. Martí, who had lived for many years in New York as an exile, knew about North American expansionism and that the United States always had its eye on Cuba. He feared that if the Cubans lost their fight for independence, it would lead to U.S. intervention and, ultimately, annexation of Cuba. He even believed that there was an "iniquitous plan to put pressure on the island and drive it to war [so] as to fabricate a pretext to intervene in its affairs and with the credit earned as guarantor and mediator keep it as its own."

After the declaration of war, the United States passed the Teller Amendment to emphasize that it had no intention of annexing Cuba. However, McKinley made it clear to Spain that his motive was not only to achieve independence for Cuba but the annexation of Puerto Rico and a Pacific island as well. The United States actually began fighting the war in Cuba when the marines captured Guantánamo Bay and 17,000 officers landed at Daquirí and Siboney, where Cuban revolutionaries joined them. U.S. troops attacked the San Juan Heights on July 1, 1898. Troops, including the African American 9th and 10th Cavalries and the 1st U.S. Volunteer Cavalry, commanded by Lt. Col. Theodore Roosevelt, moved up Kettle Hill while other forces led by Brig. Gen. Jacob Kent moved up San Juan Hill and pushed the Spanish forces inland, causing 1,700 deaths. On July 16, the Spanish surrendered their 23,500 soldiers around the city.

The Treaty of Paris was signed on December 10, 1898. Its contents included the independence of Cuba, transfer of Puerto Rico and Guam to the United States, and the transfer of the Philippines in return for $25 million to pay for Spanish property on the islands. To colonize the Philippines, the United States later fought a long and brutal war with the Philippines, which resulted in the killing of more than 200,000 Filipinos, mostly civilians. Although Cuba was granted independence, the Platt Amendment of 1902 limited its autonomy and created a dependent relationship with the United States. Some historians believe that the period 1895–1898 was only a transition period from Spanish Imperialism to American Imperialism. The Roosevelt Corollary of 1904 expanded on the idea of Manifest Destiny, which was the ideology claiming a god-given right to U.S. expansion across the western frontier.

See also Manifest Destiny; Philippine-American War.

Further Reading

Hernandez, Jose M. "Cuba Situation in 1898." Part 2. http://www.cubaheritage.com/articles.asp?cID=1&sID=9&ssID=6&offset=133.

"The Spanish American War: A gift from the gods." 2000. http://www.smplanet.com/imperialism/gift.html.

Trask, David. "The World of 1898: The Spanish-American War." 2002. http://www.loc.gov/rr/hispanic/1898/trask.html.

Tiffany Vélez

Spencer, Herbert (1820–1903)

Herbert Spencer was a British social philosopher in the Victorian era. Spencer argued that the evolutionary principle of "survival of the fittest," a phrase he coined, applied to people as well as to animal species. Although often referred to as a Social Darwinist, more accurately, Spencer brought the ideas of Jean-Baptiste Lamarck, a French naturalist of the early 1800s, to social philosophy. Lamarck had developed a theory of evolution positing that each generation inherited the traits acquired by its ancestors. As a result, Spencer was a strong proponent of competition in society. He believed that the "fittest" should be allowed to dominate to promote the evolution of a stronger society and more fit individuals. This idea became central in the eugenics movement, and critics have argued that Spencer's ideas have provided intellectual justification for extreme social stratification and even atrocities such as the Holocaust. Americans, notably Yale professor William Sumner (1872), enthusiastically took up Spencer's ideas. Herbert Spencer is often considered one of the founders of sociology because of his emphasis on looking at society as a part of nature and an organism in its own right. Most contemporary sociologists, however, reject his ideas on social hierarchy and the causes of inequality.

See also Social Darwinism.

Robin Roger-Dillon

Sports and Racism

In 1968, at the Olympic games in Mexico City, two sprinters, Tommie Smith (gold medallist) and Juan Carlos (Bronze medallist) participated in what was one of the most memorable and controversial victory ceremonies in modern Olympic history. As the

Herbert Spencer, a British social philosopher, argued that the "fittest" individuals should be allowed to dominate society.

Courtesy Thoemmes Continuum.

U.S. flag was raised and the national anthem played, Smith and Carlos raised their fists in a gesture of black-power protest. The two were part of a group called the Olympic Project for Human Rights (OPHR), which was organized by sociologist Harry Edwards. The original plan was for African Americans to boycott the Olympics as a way to point out that the civil rights movement had not gone far enough in eliminating racial injustices in society. The boycott never materialized, but the effectiveness of Smith and Carlos's protest endures. Although much progress had been made in eliminating racial injustices in sports by the 1968 Olympics, even today, almost forty years after Smith and Carlos's protest, serious problems remain. Racism in modern American sports began with segregation and continues today in the extreme underrepresentation of blacks in ownership and management position in an industry that thrives on the labor of black athletes. In many ways, sports is a microcosm of race relations in the broader American culture, reflecting the larger problems in a particular context.

The other famous moment in American sports that shined the spotlight on race relations in the United States took place twenty years before Smith and Carlos made their bold statement in Mexico City. In 1947, an African American baseball player named Jackie Robinson ran out onto the diamond at Ebbetts Field stadium in Brooklyn, New York, becoming the first black baseball player allowed to play in the major leagues. The color barrier in professional sports had finally fallen after almost a century of segregation and discrimination against African American baseball players. Before 1947, blacks had their own league, the Negro League, which is rich with history and accomplishment, but its history receives little attention in the mainstream media, a problem ball player Barry Bonds has spoken out about many times during his illustrious career. Today, African Americans are among the elite athletes in all the major professional sports in America: baseball, football, basketball, tennis, and golf, among others. Many point to Jackie Robinson as their hero, the icon of racial equality in sports.

Ironically, however, the Brooklyn Dodgers (now the Los Angeles Dodgers), the organization that hired Jackie Robinson, disgraced itself forty years later when an executive named Al Campinis was interviewed by news anchor Ted Koppel on ABC television in 1987. The interview is published in Kenneth Shropshire's book *In Black and White: Race and Sports in America* (1998).

> *Koppel*: Why are there no black managers, general managers or owners? . . . Is there still prejudice in baseball today?
> *Campinis*: No, I don't believe it's prejudice. I truly believe that they may not have some of the necessities to be, let's say a field manager, or a general manager.
> *Koppel*: Do you really believe that?
> *Campinis*: Well, I don't say all of them, but they certainly are short. How many quarterbacks do you have, how many pitchers do you have, that are black?
> *Koppel*: Yeah, but I have to tell you, that sounds like the same garbage we were hearing 40 years ago about players.
> *Campinis*: No, it's not garbage, Mr. Koppel, because I played on a college team, and the center fielder was black, and in the backfield at NYU with a fullback that was black. Never knew the difference if he was black or white. We were teammates. So it might just be, why are black men or black people not good swimmers? Because they don't have the buoyancy. [But they are] . . . God gifted people . . . gifted with great musculature and various other things. They are fleet of foot.

The Dodgers, after some hesitation, fired Campinis for these remarks, but Koppel had pointed out the *contemporary* racial barrier in sports: the color line between owners, management, and players. There are a few black coaches of professional and collegiate football and basketball teams, as well as a few black managers in professional baseball, but more than 95 percent of the three major professional sports franchises are white owned, and these are sports in which black athletes dominate. The problem of race and sports goes all the way down to the high-school level, where black and white kids are encouraged to have different aspirations and to take different directions. According to Shropshire, "A white kid tries to become President, and the skills and knowledge he picks up along the way can be used in a thousand different jobs. A black kid tries to become Willie Mays and all the tools he picks up are useless to him if he does not become Willie Mays." It remains to be seen if racial equality makes it up to the management and ownership of professional and collegiate sports in the United States.

See also Civil Rights Movement; Robinson, Jackie; Simpson, O. J.; Sports Mascots; Television and Racial Stereotypes.

Further Reading

Elias, Robert. *Baseball and the American Dream: Race, Class, Gender and the American Pastime*. Armonk, NY: M. E. Sharpe, 2001.

King, C. Richard, and Charles Fruehling Springwood. *Beyond the Cheers: Race as Spectacle in College Sports*. Albany: State University Press of New York, 2001.

Lapchick, Richard E. *Broken Promises: Racism in American Sports*. New York: St. Martin's Press, 1984.

Shropshire, Kenneth L., and Kellen Winslow. *In Black and White: Race and Sports in America*. New York: New York University Press, 1998.

Michael Roberts

Sports Mascots

Since the 1970s, American Indian activists in the American Indian Movement (AIM) and the National Coalition for Sports and Racism in the Media (NCRSM) have led a campaign to remove "Indian" mascots from collegiate and professional sports teams and replace them with something else, on the grounds that these particular mascots perpetuate racial stereotypes of American Indians. Professional sports franchises that use Indians for their names and mascots include the baseball teams the Atlanta Braves and the Cleveland Indians, and the football teams the Kansas City Chiefs and the Washington Redskins. There are also many college sports teams that use Indians for their mascots, although some schools have changed their mascots in recent years, indicating their sympathy and agreement with NCRSM that Indian mascots promote negative images of American Indians. The efforts of AIM and NCRSM have been successful in some cases, especially at the collegiate level, but professional sports teams have, for the most part, kept their Indian mascots.

According to AIM and NCSRM, the Indian mascots are as offensive to American Indians as the Sambo image was to African Americans or the "Frito Bandito" to Latino Americans. Particularly racist is the "Chief Wahoo" mascot for the Cleveland Indians. "Chief Wahoo" was designed by the team's management to have oversized buckteeth, red skin, and a big nose, exaggerated features that offend the American

A Cleveland Indians fan shows a "Chief Wahoo" sign during a game at Jacobs Field, 1997.

AP/Wide World Photos.

Indian community. For American Indians, the chief represents a position of respect, the highest and most politically powerful role in their society, but professional and collegiate sports have trivialized and degraded the image of the chief for mass entertainment. Indians have become something for sports fans to joke about. For example, in the 1998 American League playoffs between the New York Yankees and the Cleveland Indians, the *New York Post* ran a headline that read, "Take the Tribe and Scalp 'em." In Atlanta, the fans of the baseball team the Braves perform the "tomahawk chop" chant, in which fans are given styrofoam tomahawks to move up and down as they chant what is meant to represent sounds that Indians supposedly made when on the warpath. According to the American Indian community, the use of Indian sports mascots trivializes their people and their history. In short, American Indians, victims of genocide, have been reduced to objects for the entertainment of the American masses in a multibillion-dollar sports industry. In the words of NCRSM, "American Indians are a people, not mascots for other Americans' fun and games. We are human beings."

In school teams, however, progress has been made toward removing offensive sports mascots. In the 1970s, students at both Stanford University and Dartmouth College were able to pressure their administrations to change their school identities and sports mascots from Indians to other, race-neutral symbols. Stanford's team, for example, is now known as the Stanford Cardinal. In Los Angeles, California, the board of education voted to ban all images and reference to Indians in athletic and other venues at schools under their jurisdiction.

See also Native Americans, Prejudice and Discrimination against; Sports and Racism.

Further Reading

Berkhoffer, Robert F., Jr. *The White Man's Indian: Images of the American Indian from Columbus to the Present.* New York: Knopf, 1978.

Johnson, Bruce E. "Mascots: Honor Be Thy Name." *Native Americas* 18 (Spring 2001): 58–61.

United States Commission on Civil Rights. *Statement of the U.S. Commission on Civil Rights on the Use of Native American Images and Nicknames as Sports Symbols.* www.usccr.gov/nwsrel/archives/2001/041601st.htm.

Michael Roberts

St. Louis Riot of 1917

In terms of the property damage and injury caused, the St. Louis Riot was the worst riot in American history, but it was typical of white-on-black riots in that it was brought on by labor competition created by the migration of blacks from the South to Northern cities. Racial tensions had been brewing in St. Louis since 1906, when workers at Aluminum Ore, the largest producer of bauxite in the world, attempted to form a union. Refusing to accept the union movement, the company hired blacks with the intention of preventing future solidarity among workers. Across town in the packing houses, thirty-seven union organizers were fired after an attempt to force companies to recognize their union failed.

In May 1917, the rumor of a black man having killed a white man in a botched robbery, along with the false accusations of a white woman having been raped by a black man and two white girls having been shot by blacks, sparked several days of rioting as more than three thousand whites took to the streets vandalizing black neighborhoods and attacking black residents. The May riots were just a sign of worse things to come, as rumors continued to spread throughout the days of June that blacks were arming themselves for a revenge massacre that supposedly was to take place on July 4. On July 1, a car with four whites inside opened fire—without provocation—on black homes near seventeenth and Market streets. On the morning of July 2, speakers at a labor rally urged the crowd to arm itself and prepare for battle. As the crowd began to march up Broadway, they attacked and shot at every black person they encountered. As the fires raged, many African Americans found refuge in the homes of sympathetic whites but most fled town altogether. Some estimates claim that seven thousand blacks left town during the massacre. The rioting continued through the night, and the National Guard struggled to gain control of the situation. The next day it was discovered that more than two hundred black homes had been burned to the ground, and the newspapers reported two hundred deaths and scores of injuries.

See also Bellingham Riots; Los Angeles Riot of 1871; Memphis Race Riot of 1866; Race Riots.

Michael Roberts

Statistical Discrimination

Economists have sought to identify the causes of inequality in labor markets by defining discrimination. It is a fact, for example, that men earn more than women and whites make more than blacks for the same job. If an employer makes employment decisions based solely on race, sex, age, or any other factor that singles out a category protected by law, discrimination obviously has occurred. This kind of discrimination could produce workplaces that are all female, all white, all male, or all female, leaving employers to pay a premium for hiring decisions not based on worker productivity. Discrimination that affects worker earnings may also take place by customers and employees themselves. If customers want products made by a certain favored group of workers, the customers would pay a premium that may be reflected in the workers' earnings. Discrimination among employees themselves could negatively affect both earnings and productivity.

Statistical discrimination occurs when rational beliefs, expectations, and generalizations enter into economic decision making, as in the hiring process. If an employer has observed that whites seem to be more productive workers than blacks, he or she may hire a white candidate over a black one. In another case, the employer may have evidence that workers who graduated from a certain college are more productive than those who graduated from another, and chooses the candidate based on that generalization. Thus, statistical discrimination can lead to job crowding in some cases. Such generalizations are dangerous, however, because productivity has many causes that are unknown and unobservable. Therefore, the productivity of a group favored by discrimination should in theory eventually even out with that of a nonfavored group. Statistical discrimination, which has applications in many arenas, can have racial consequences. Racial profiling is one such example.

See also California Ballot Proposition 54; Hate Crimes Statistics Act (HCSA) of 1990.

Benjamin F. Shearer

Stereotypes

See Films and Racial Stereotypes; Middle Easterners, Stereotypes of; Muslims, Terrorist Image of; Television and Racial Stereotypes.

Strangers in the Land: Patterns of American Nativism, 1860–1925

Historians Leonard Dinnerstein and David Reimers praise John Higham's 1955 publication, *Strangers in the Land*, as "the most sophisticated analysis of American nativist thought ever penned by an American historian." Although this book focuses only on the period from 1860 to 1925, it remains a classic and a must-read for anyone interested in American attitudes toward immigrants. In studying nativism, Higham analyzed a set of ethnocentric attitudes that united two ideas: (a) defining and celebrating as "American" only what was considered to be white, Protestant, Anglo-Saxon culture and its associated social, political, and economic institutions; and (b) depicting immigrants as dangerous threats to the nation because they were religiously different (Catholic or Jewish), alleged to be political radicals, or deemed to be racially inferior.

Strangers in the Land begins in a period of mass open immigration to the

United States with no government regulation, and concludes in a time of very restrictive discriminatory nationality quotas imposed by Congress in 1917, 1921, and 1924. Higham analyzed the successes and failures of organizations that lobbied to reduce the number of immigrant "strangers" entering the United States, and described the actions of groups that tried to "Americanize" the newcomers. He shows fluctuations in the intensity, popularity, and content of Americans' beliefs and fears about foreigners by documenting opinions and attitudes of political, business, religious, scientific, editorial, and literary leaders as they shifted between an optimistic faith in the capacity of America to absorb large numbers of immigrants and create a better society, and a pessimistic belief that immigrants could not be absorbed and would weaken or destroy American society.

Strangers in the Land was one of the first books to delve into prejudice against immigrants. It was followed by many others and has been criticized for neglecting prejudiced attitudes toward Asians and Mexican "strangers," but it remains a monumental work of historical scholarship.

See also Immigrant Preference in Employment; Immigration Act of 1965; Immigrations Restriction League of 1894; National Origins Act of 1924; Nativism and the Anti-immigrant Movements; Naturalization Act of 1790; Undocuments Immigrants.

Further Reading

Higham, John. *Strangers in the Land: Patterns of American Nativism, 1860–1925.* New Brunswick, NJ: Rutgers University Press, 2002.

Charles Jaret

Student Nonviolent Coordinating Committee (SNCC)

The Student Nonviolent Coordinating Committee (SNCC) was founded in 1960 at Shaw University in Raleigh, North Carolina, to coordinate nonviolent protest actions, particularly sit-ins, across the South at lunch counters and other facilities with segregated or whites-only services. Throughout the first half of the 1960s, the organization was active in sponsoring and cosponsoring civil rights movement activities such as Freedom Rides, voter registration for African Americans, marches, and local community projects. The group also helped found the Mississippi Freedom Democratic Party, a political party organized to challenge white-dominated politics in Mississippi. It was organized in a radically democratic fashion, holding national leadership conferences for decision making, and it was ideologically pacifist. In 1966, Stokely Carmichael, an advocate of Black Power and Africanism, took over the leadership of SNCC and rejected the involvement of white students who had participated in the group since its inception. SNCC later changed its name to the Student National Coordinating Committee as its ideology moved away from its pacifist roots, which led to its disbandment in 1969.

See also Carmichael, Stokely; Civil Rights Movement; Freedom Riders.

Mikaila Mariel Lemonik Arthur

Symbolic Racism

Symbolic racism is a phenomenon of contemporary society whereby, despite putative acceptance of egalitarian principles and multicultural ideas, the content and form of old-fashioned racism are maintained through subtle ideations and "code words." In symbolic racism, views are expressed in a seemingly non-racist way and yet convey images and assumptions that are racist in nature. A person exhibiting symbolic racism may vociferously reject segregation and ethnocentrism, express sympathies for past injustices, and endorse egalitarianism and political correctness but also use geographic, economic, or professional references that ultimately represent racial distinctions between groups and convey subtle assumptions about the superiority or inferiority of certain racial groups.

Symbolic racism is described as being "symbolic" because it uses terms and ideas that are abstract and ideological—most often, terms that reflect whites' moral codes about how society should be (or is) organized. For example, individuals who would never use common racial slurs against African Americans as a group may use terms such as "criminal element" or "urban poor," or make geographic references to "South Central" (Los Angeles) or "Harlem"; a listener also socialized in the United States will know what the speaker is referring to, but neither speaker nor listener will have engaged in *explicitly* racist speech. Thus a symbolically racist speech, like an overtly racist speech, also has the effect of robbing people of color of their individuality and understanding them instead only as a part of their racial/ethnic group (Sears and Kinder 1971).

Cognitively, symbolic racism reflects the belief that racial discrimination is largely a thing of the past. Yet the origins of symbolic racism are in the "old-fashioned" stereotypes and symbols learned and internalized during childhood. In this respect, the modernization of racism has involved an increasing subtlety of reference, rather than a decreasing degree of fear, misunderstanding, or disrespect. This subtlety permits people to describe and discuss racial distinctions without "sounding racist."

With respect to African Americans, symbolic racism combines antiblack sentiment with modern manifestations of the traditional racialist idea that blacks violate traditional American values such as the work ethic, traditional morality, and respect for authority. Combined with the belief that "old-fashioned" racism is a thing of the past, it supports beliefs that one might confound with ideological conservatism: that if racial minorities just "worked harder" or "played by the rules" their disadvantages, too, would become a thing of the past. In this respect, symbolic racism feeds on its own unexpressed foundational ideas about the superiority of whites and the inferiority of blacks, Latinos, Asians, and Native Americans by refusing to acknowledge the continuing sociological effects of traditional racism.

Yet scholars have also characterized symbolic racism as "a new form of racism" that is independent of older racial and political attitudes. According to this perspective, the underlying psychological motive is to protect a dominant in-group's privileged position and suppress less powerful groups that aspire to equality. Symbolic racism is a considerably stronger political force in contemporary American society than are more traditional expressions of racial prejudice, both at the individual level (compared with the "overt racism" of slurs and explicit prejudice) and the institutional level (compared with "Jim Crow" racism).

See also Jim Crow Laws; Modern Racism.

Further Reading

Kinder, Donald R., and David O. Sears. "Prejudice and Politics: Symbolic Racism Versus Racial Threats to the Good Life." *Journal of Personality and Social Psychology* 40, no. 3 (1981): 414–431.

McConahay, J. B., and J. C. Hough. "Symbolic Racism." *Journal of Social Issues* 32 (1976): 23–45.

Sears, D. O. "Symbolic Racism." In *Eliminating Racism: Profiles in Controversy*, edited by P. A. Katz and D. A. Taylor, 53–84. New York: Plenum, 1988.

Khyati Joshi

T

Takao Ozawa v. United States (1922)

See Ozawa v. United States.

Television and Racial Stereotypes

Television was one of the most influential forms of media to emerge in the twentieth century. Television can serve as a reflection of the existing social norms and mores of a society. Because of its widespread accessibility and saturation in American culture, television can also act as a powerful socializing agent for both children and adults. It is an especially important socializing agent for race relations because, as a result of continued residential and school segregation, there is often very little meaningful interaction between races. Television depictions of minority members and interactions between whites and minority members can act as a vicarious racial experience for individuals who would rarely encounter minority members in everyday life. The issue of how race is portrayed on television is both a problem of large-scale exclusion of racial minorities and a problem of negative, or stereotypical, representation of those minority characters.

In terms of exclusion, top-rated shows (e.g., *Frasier*, *Friends*, and *Seinfeld*), which often take place in large metropolitan centers such as New York City, Seattle, and Los Angeles, offer only tertiary minority characters. Not only are these omissions untrue to the racial reality of the geographic location portrayed, but when minority groups are missing from the television curriculum, it implies to the viewer that they are inconsequential or unimportant. This underrepresentation of minorities, despite the reality of racially heterogeneous settings, reflects a social norm of exclusion in the consciousness of mainstream America.

With few exceptions, most of the television shows that do feature minority characters depict stereotypical representations of them. African Americans and Latino characters are limited to a set repertoire of roles, most often depicting criminals, servants, entertainers, or athletes. Latinos are often associated with criminal activity. Despite the overrepresentation of white-collar occupations on television in general, African Americans are most often depicted in menial, low-class, and service jobs. Young African American men are depicted as being unintelligent, clownish, and sex-crazed. African American women are often depicted as domineering and in a position of maternal dominance, where they act as sole holders of power in a family and habitually belittle men.

Though minority characters of many different races may appear sporadically in various genres of television programming (e.g., dramas, comedies, reality programming), a limited number of television shows feature a large proportion of minority characters in their permanent cast. Most of these shows fall within the specific genre of African American situational comedies. The fact that the only television shows with large African American casts are almost exclusively comedic in nature indicates a one-dimensional or superficial interest in the depiction of African American life. Further, these comedies are almost always racially homogeneous and, in recent years, are often segregated to specific "niche" television networks, often on particular nights. This isolation further asserts a sense of racial segregation.

Given the limited portrayal of racial minorities on television, the opportunities to view intergroup interaction are extremely rare. When intergroup interactions are presented on television, they tend to be portrayed as neutral or positive. Minority characters tend to either appear as their "stock" stereotypical character (e.g., the criminal, the athlete, the entertainer), or they exist as "background" characters and are woven into a peer group in a public setting. Situations of racial unease or overt acts of prejudice in these interactions are rarely portrayed, thus there are few opportunities to model how to handle these types of situations.

See also Films and Racial Stereotypes; Hollywood and Minority Actors; Music Industry, Racism in; Sports and Racism; Television Drama and Racism.

Further Reading

Baptiste, David A. "The Image of the Black Family Portrayed by Television: A Critical Commentary." *Marriage and Family Review* 10 (April 1996): 41–63.

Graves, Sherryl Browne. "Television and Prejudice Reduction: When Does Television as a Vicarious Experience Make a Difference?" *Journal of Social Issues* 55, no. 4 (1999): 707–727.

Tracy Chu

Television Drama and Racism

The representation of black people on American television has come a long way since the days of shows like *Amos and Andy* and the *Jack Benny Show*, in which blacks were portrayed in ways that reinforced white beliefs in the inherent servitude of African Americans. In the early days of television, there

were no black characters cast in leading roles, and most of the black characters reinforced the worst racial stereotypes prevalent in the pre-civil rights
era of television. Today, however, some popular television shows not only have
black characters in leading roles, but in a few cases—especially drama—TV
shows depict blacks in positions of authority *over* whites. But serious problems remain. Despite the increasing numbers of blacks cast in leading roles,
television remains a segregated medium, and for all the positive images of
African Americans displayed on television today, negative stereotypes of black
people continue to dominate the medium. Mass media, in short, continues to
represent blacks as fundamentally different from whites, and blacks are consistently misrepresented by contradictory images on television that portray
blacks disproportionately as either unusually gifted athletes or deviant drug
dealers.

Media both reflect and shape the world, including the complicated network
of race relations in America. In some ways, the positive images of blacks on television reflect the real-world material gains made by African Americans since
the civil rights era. On the other hand, the major networks still push most of
the black characters to the margins, just as in "real-world" America, blacks and
whites live segregated private lives. The only place in the world of television
where blacks *are consistently* cast in the leading roles is the nightly news,
where images of chaos and crime bombard the audience each evening, satu-
rating the mostly white audience with negative images of African Americans.

In early 2000, the National Association for the Advancement of Colored
People (NAACP) threatened to boycott the major broadcast networks—ABC,
CBS, NBC, and Fox—if they did not agree to feature more prominent black
actors on primetime television. Critics pointed to the most popular shows,
like *Beverly Hills 90210* on Fox, *ER* on NBC, *Friends* on NBC, *Party of Five*
on Fox, and *Will & Grace* on NBC: among all these shows only two blacks,
two Asians, and one Latino were cast in lead roles—as evidence that television continues to discriminate against racial and ethnic minorities.

The first prime-time drama series to air on network television that had a
predominantly black cast was the CBS series *City of Angels*. The show was
produced by Steven Bochco, who had a string of drama series hits, including
Hill Street Blues, *L.A. Law*, and *NYPD Blue*. Producers hoped that *City of Angels* would have crossover appeal in the white audience because Bochco's previous productions were so popular. Unfortunately for the cast of *City of
Angels*, the show never made it past the first season, suggesting that a drama
series with a black cast has yet to cross over to a white audience. In some
ways, the increasing fragmentation of television into more and more niche
markets makes it more difficult to produce a series with crossover appeal.
There are a few successful crossover drama series that cast African Americans
in leading roles, but none with a predominantly black cast.

For example, *ER*, a hit series consistently in the top-twenty ratings for both
white and black audiences, had a black lead character, Dr. Benson, played by
Eriq LaSalle. Dr. Benson became one of the most popular characters on *ER*,
but it took more than five seasons for the producers to build an episode
around him, whereas the other principal actors had many episodes that featured their characters. But what makes *ER* stand out as a particularly sharp

representation of race relations in America is the romance that developed between Dr. Benton and a white British doctor, played by actress Alex Kingston. LaSalle asked that the producers end Dr. Benson's relationship with the white doctor because he felt it sent a message that black men can only have stable relationships with *white* women. All of Dr. Benson's previous relationships had been with black women, and all failed. LaSalle told the Washington Post, "We have to take care of the message that we are sending as African Americans . . . that we have the same type of exchanges with our mates that we get to see our White counterparts have" (April 9, 1999). Fans of the show were upset that the producers ended the romance between the characters, but the producers were aware of the far-reaching implications a show as popular as theirs has in U.S. society.

The producers of television drama series are increasingly under pressure from their network bosses to present images that appeal to affluent—which in their minds means *white*—audiences, as a way to appease the corporate sponsors who have the power to pull the plug on "controversial" drama series. In the words of one producer at Fox television, "I don't think anyone's crying out for integrated shows. By pursuing advertisers and demographics rather than a mass audience, the networks have declared they don't need Blacks in their audience" (quoted in Entman and Rojecki, 161). If integration remains a goal of public policy in the United States, then one necessary step in that direction is to integrate television, especially popular drama series, as those shows already have black and white audiences. Perhaps in the not-so-distant future, a character like Dr. Benson on *ER* will be able to have an intimate, romantic relationship with a character not of his "race."

See also Films and Racial Stereotypes; Hollywood and Minority Actors; Music Industry, Racism in; Sports and Racism; Television and Racial Stereotypes.

Further Reading

Entman, Robert M., and Andrew Rojecki. *The Black Image in the White Mind: Media and Race in America*. Chicago: The University of Chicago Press, 2001.

Michael Roberts

Terman, Lewis (1877–1956)

Lewis Terman, a psychologist at Stanford University, was notorious for arguing in favor of hereditary differences in IQ scores among different racial groups. In 1916, Terman and his associates developed the Stanford-Binet scale of intelligence. Based on his research on intelligence tests, Terman claimed that a low level of intelligence is common among Spanish-Indian and Mexican families in the Southwest as well as among Negroes. He believed that many of the children from these families were uneducable beyond basic training and that education could improve their intelligence to the level that would allow them to be intelligent voters or capable citizens.

Terman is therefore one of the major scholars in the United States in the laying of the groundwork for biological racism, the view that racial minority groups have low levels of intelligence influenced by genetic differences.

See also Biological Racism; Goddard, Henry H.; Jensen, Arthur.

Further Reading

T. F. Gosset. *Race: A History of an Idea in America*. New York: Schocken Books, 1965.

Pyong Gap Min

Texas, Annexation of

When Mexico gained its independence from Spain in 1810, its territory encompassed an area as far north as what is today Colorado. Most of this northern Mexico region was inhabited by Indians and a smaller number of Mexicans. To populate this vast area, the Mexican government granted permission for foreigners—mainly white Americans—to settle in the area in 1821. As more Anglos settled in the area, which is Texas today, they became a numerical majority. In 1835–1836, the colony revolted and established itself as an independent republic. Mexico never recognized the independence of Texas. When it became clear that the United States favored annexation of the territory, much friction was created between the American and Mexican governments. The actual annexation of Texas in 1845 resulted in war in 1846. The Mexican-American War was devastating to Mexico. Under the terms of the treaty of 1848 after the end of the war, Mexico was forced to cede more than half of its territory to the United States. The United States acquired what are today the states of California, Colorado, New Mexico, Nevada, Utah, and most of Arizona, in addition to Texas.

The annexation of Texas in 1845 and the ensuing war fundamentally altered the nature of the relations between Mexicans and Anglos in the Southwest. The war and overt conflict intensified their negative feelings toward each other for many generations to come. Although their property rights and political rights were guaranteed by the Treaty of Guadalupe Hidalgo, Mexicans in the newly acquired American territory found themselves increasingly displaced by Anglos. Anglos firmly established themselves in economic and political power. Mexicans in the region had become racial minorities in their own land and have been discriminated against ever since.

See also Guadalupe Hidalgo, Treaty of; Manifest Destiny; Mexican-American War; Texas Rangers; Texas Rebellion.

Further Reading

Singletary, Otis. *The Mexican War*. New York: Oxford University Press, 1960.

Heon Cheol Lee

Texas Rangers

The Texas Rangers are an elite state law-enforcement agency that can trace its history back to the year 1823. At that time, Stephen F. Austin, who settled the first Anglo-American families in Texas (he is often referred to as the "Father of Texas"), called a group of citizens who protected others "Rangers." The Texas

Rangers during this early period had a variety of duties such as frontier patrol (with Mexico), battling Indians, and protecting trains. The familiar Texas Rangers of today were founded on September 1, 1935. At that time, the Texas Legislature created the Department of Public Safety, and the Rangers as well as the Highway Patrol became members of that agency.

The Texas Ranger Division currently consists of 118 sworn officers who have statewide jurisdiction. The Division has six companies—"A" through "F"— that cover the entire state. The Rangers' duties and responsibilities, similar to those of other elite law-enforcement units, include conducting investigations, apprehending criminals, protecting dignitaries, and assisting other agencies. In 2002, for example, the Rangers made 1,805 felony arrests.

One area of controversy for the Rangers is their handling of migrant farm workers, particularly in 1967. The Rangers were accused of brutality and violating the workers' civil rights. Hearings into these allegations were conducted in Rio Grande City by the Texas Advisory Committee to the U.S. Civil Rights Commission on May 25–26, 1967. As a result of many civil rights lawsuits against them, Texas Ranger policy was eventually changed to prevent their deployment in labor disputes.

See also Guadalupe Hidalgo, Treaty of; Manifest Destiny; Mexican-American War; Texas, Annexation of; Texas Rebellion.

John Eterno

Texas Rebellion

The Texas Rebellion began in 1835 when the residents of Gonzales, east San Antonio, Texas, expelled Mexican forces in rebellion, and eventually led in 1836 to Texas's independence from Mexico. In the 1820s, the Mexican government allowed U.S. citizens to immigrate into Texas under the conditions that they be loyal to the Mexican government, learn Spanish, and become Roman Catholics. But the remoteness of the area made the government's control ineffectual. By the early 1830s, new settlers outnumbered the Tejanos and found themselves at odds with the Mexican government, which tried to regain its control over the territory. Many settlers were slave owners, who engaged in cotton production, and Mexico's abolition of slavery in 1831 would have undermined their existence, if consistently enforced. Slave owners turned to the United States, which tolerated slavery.

To secure its power over Texas, the Mexican government stopped immigration and imposed heavy duty on imports. In 1833, General Antonio López de Santa Anna launched his effort to strengthen national unity. Disgruntled settlers rebelled against the Mexican forces with the help of the United States. Santa Anna's army prevailed at first and killed hundreds of settlers at Alamo and Goliad. But Santa Anna was captured in the Battle of San Jacinto and released only upon concessions of Texan independence and movement of the border southward, at the Rio Grande. In 1836, Samuel Houston, newly inaugurated president of the Republic of Texas, sent a representative to Washington and repealed the prohibition on slavery. Texas was not annexed until the Treaty of Guadalupe Hidalgo (1848).

See also Guadalupe Hidalgo, Treaty of; Manifest Destiny; Mexican-American War; Texas, Annexation of; Texas Rangers.

Dong-Ho Cho

Thind v. United States

See United States v. Thind.

Third World Movement of the 1960s

Through their participation in other social movements of the 1960s (for instance, the civil rights movement and the peace movement), African American, Asian American, Latino/a, and Native American individuals started to develop an awareness of their ties with one another and with the conditions of racism and oppression operating in their lives and on their college campuses. Starting at campuses such as the University of California, Berkeley, and San Francisco State University and spreading across the country, so-called Third World people joined together in coalitions to fight for recognition of their existence and their needs, as well as those of people actually living in the Third World. They called attention to the persistence of structural racism even after the passage of landmark civil rights legislation earlier in the decade, to the racist elements of U.S. foreign policy and the Vietnam War, and to the particular needs of Third World students at colleges and universities. One issue of particular interest to the movement was that a disproportionate number of the young men sent to fight and die in Vietnam were people of color.

On campus, the students demanded cultural centers, admissions policies taking their backgrounds into account, and course work relevant to their experiences. Campus-wide strikes of students of color precipitated the formation of the first departments of ethnic studies between 1968 and 1971, primarily in California. Other developments included affirmative action policies, cultural centers, and support services. The Third World Student Strike at San Francisco State, the moment at which the movement coalesced, began on November 6, 1968, and ended on March 21 of the following year. It was led by a coalition of students of color who demanded the creation of black and ethnic studies courses, the hiring of faculty of color, a special admissions process for applicants of color who were not prepared to meet college entrance requirements, the reinstatement of various personnel who had been fired for race-related reasons, and the development of new financial-aid policies more favorable to students of color. Many of these demands were agreed to, though it took significant time for them to be fully implemented by the college administration.

It is important to remember, however, that this movement was not confined to California. Indeed, it was not confined to the United States. Activists from Third World countries on disparate continents have worked since the 1960s to join in common cause in resisting the dominance of the United States and Europe in international affairs, particularly in terms of trade and environmental treaties that do not take the best interests of Third World countries into account. The effect of these coalitions can still be seen today in the opposition to the World Trade Organization and the World Bank.

In all of its incarnations, the Third World movement has drawn attention to the importance of looking beyond pure economic motivations in choosing policies and to the necessity of participatory and democratic governance systems that take into account the diverse needs and experiences of all. The continuing effects of this movement on college campuses across the country have been significant: many universities now have a variety of ethnic-studies programs, and cultural centers and various race-specific scholarships have been developed and funded. But as the continuing struggles over affirmative action show, the problems that the Third World movement aimed to address have not vanished. Students of color are still underrepresented at many colleges and universities. A significant number continue to offer few support services or ethnic studies courses to their student bodies. Students have continued to mobilize for these kinds of reasons up until the present, and there is every reason to believe that they will continue to do so in the future. In addition, people of color in the United States today are still working to develop international ties with Third World peoples across the globe as they struggle to combat similar problems, such as poverty, environmental degradation, and oppression.

See also Multiculturalism; Pan-Asian Solidarity; Pan-ethnic Movements.

Further Reading

Barlow, William, and Peter Shapiro. *An End to Silence: The San Francisco State College Student Movement in the '60s*. New York: Pegasus, 1971.

Mikaila Mariel Lemonik Arthur

Thomas, Clarence (1948–   )

Since his appointment in 1991, Clarence Thomas, an African American, has been considered by some to be the most conservative member of the U.S. Supreme Court. He was born on June 28, 1948, in Pinpoint, Georgia. Thomas earned an associates degree from Holy Cross College, received a JD degree in 1974 from Yale Law School, and was admitted to practice in Missouri that same year. Thomas has held various high-ranking governmental positions, serving as assistant attorney general of Missouri (1974–1977) and chairman of the U.S. Equal Employment Opportunity Commission (EEOC) (1982–1990) during the Reagan Administration. In the latter post, he often came into conflict with civil rights organizations over the merits of affirmative action because he questioned the existence of systemic forms of racial discrimination and focused his efforts at the EEOC on cases for individual claimants rather than working to bring about societal-level change. Because of his conservative political and ideological stance as a black person, Thomas gained attention in the Republican Party and was nominated to the U.S. Court of Appeals for the District of Columbia Circuit by President George H. W. Bush in 1990. This position is commonly considered a stepping-stone for a Supreme Court appointment, and President Bush later nominated Thomas for this post. Although his candidacy was tainted by the allegations of sexual harassment made by colleague Anita

U.S. Supreme Court nominee Judge Clarence Thomas denounces sexual harassment allegations before the Senate Judiciary Committee, October 1991.

AP/Wide World Photos.

Hill, Thomas was sworn in as an associate justice of the U.S. Supreme Court on October 23, 1991, by a 52–48 vote margin: the smallest margin by which any justice has been confirmed in this century. Thomas has gained a reputation as a black conservative with a history of distancing himself from controversial issues, especially those dealing with race.

See also Black Conservatives.

Sandra L. Barnes

Thurmond, Strom (1902–2003)

Strom Thurmond was a controversial figure in American politics. Thurmond served as a U.S. Senator from South Carolina from 1954 to 2002. Before becoming a senator, Thurmond served as the governor of South Carolina. Thurmond was an outspoken segregationist and fought to maintain laws separating blacks and whites. He ran for the presidency of the United States in 1948 on a segregationist platform. As a senator, Thurmond filibustered civil rights legislation. In an apparent change of heart, Thurmond later went on to support civil rights legislation, including the 1982 extension of the civil rights act and making Martin Luther King Jr.'s birthday a national holiday. For some, Thur-

South Carolina governor Strom Thurmond responds to applause at the Dixiecrats State's Rights Convention, Birmingham, Alabama, July 1948. The Dixiecrats have just nominated him for president of the United States.

AP/Wide World Photos.

mond's story parallels the evolution of the segregationist "Old South" into a more inclusive "New South." For others, Thurmond remained a symbol of racial intolerance.

Few segregationists remained in the public eye for so long. Thurmond's continued political role made him a focal point for racial issues. In 2002, Senator Trent Lott (R-Mississippi) was forced to step down from his majority leadership position in the Senate after suggesting, at Thurmond's one-hundredth-birthday celebration, that the country would have been better off had it followed Thurmond's lead. Lott's remark was widely interpreted as support for Thurmond's segregationist past. The swift public response to Lott highlighted that in the year 2002, Thurmond remained a symbol of racial division and intolerance in the United States. Thurmond died on June 26, 2003.

See also Civil Rights Movement; King, Martin Luther, Jr.; Race Card in Political Campaigns; Religious Right.

Robin Roger-Dillon

Tijerina, Reies Lopez (1926–)

Reies Lopez Tijerina was one of the prominent leaders of the radical Chicano movement in the 1960s that had its base in New Mexico. He was born to a family of sharecroppers on September 21, 1926, in Fall City, Texas. After graduating from Assembly of God Bible Institute, he became an itinerant preacher. In 1956, he stopped preaching and participated in building a commune in Arizona called The Valley of Peace. He was troubled by the fact that many Mexican Americans had been cheated out of their rights to ancestral land that the Treaty of Guadalupe Hidalgo (1848) guaranteed. Tijerina founded the Alianza Federal de Pueblos Libres (Federal Alliance of Land Grants) in 1963 to reclaim Spanish and Mexican land grants held by Mexicans and Native Americans before the Mexican-American War.

At the beginning, the Alianza was a moderate pressure group. Later, it adopted more militant protest strategies, including a massive march to the state capitol in 1965, the occupation of the Echo Amphitheater in 1966, and the notorious Tierra Amarrilla Courthouse Raid in 1967. The armed raid on the county courthouse brought national attention to the land-grant issue and added vigor to the already unfolding Chicano movement. In 1968, Tijerina formed the People's Constitutional Party to take the land-grant struggle into the political arena. The party failed in its electoral bid but provided abundant opportunity to educate the voters about the land-grant issue and demonstrate the incapability of the two major parties to address the issue. Tijerina's imprisonment from 1969 to 1971 eventually led to the dissolution of the Alianza.

See also Chicano Movement.

Dong-Ho Cho

Timid Bigots

See Bigots, Types of.

Tokenism

Tokenism is a modern form of racism involving a symbolic but empty gesture of support for diversity. It can be classified as racism because it helps to maintain certain stereotypes and keeps the structure of racist institutions intact. Although clothed with the language and image of egalitarianism and "political correctness," tokenism is only a superficial attempt to embrace multiculturalism; it rarely results in the outcomes it purports to advance. Tokenism can exist in virtually any social context, from the workplace to educational settings to social situations. It diminishes the persons of color involved by attaching the value of their presence to their race or ethnicity rather than to their contribution or performance, which has the effect both of isolating them and of robbing them of their individuality by placing them in the position of representative and spokesperson for their racial or ethnic group.

The quintessential example of tokenism is the practice of hiring or appointing a person from an underrepresented group to a position of visibility and, by appearances, of substantial responsibility. Such a step is often under-taken in response to past criticism or to avoid future criticism of an orga-nization's lack of diversity. The person's differences are highlighted, and his or her role more often than not is prescribed and limited in power, with real decision-making power remaining in another person or in the organization's majority group. The situation is therefore robbed of its opportunity to foment change because the "token" is not enabled or permitted to undertake the ad-vances in diversity that are his or her putative role in the organization.

See also Political Correctness (P.C.).

Khyati Joshi

Toxic Neighborhoods

A report issued in 1987 by the Commission for Racial Justice found that aban-doned toxic waste sites and waste landfills were more likely surrounded by black than by white neighborhoods. A Government Accounting Office report in 2000 found likewise that in nine Southern states studied, all the hazardous waste landfills were in majority-black neighborhoods. There are serious con-sequences for those who live in these neighborhoods. The Centers for Disease Control has noted that as a result of high air-pollution levels in these neigh-borhoods, blacks are more likely than whites to experience blood and respi-ratory problems.

Toxic neighborhoods have been created by a complex combination of eco-nomic factors. Polluting industries have been induced by favorable tax treat-ment to locate in underdeveloped neighborhoods that governments want to build up. In many cases, environmental concerns took backstage to develop-ment goals and in some cases, environmental regulations were simply waived. The industries had little to fear from its disenfranchised and impoverished neighbors, who tended to have no political power. The choice was between jobs and pollution. These factors, combined with the discriminatory practice of redlining neighborhoods to limit access to housing funds, have left the country littered with toxic waste sites next to poor, minority neighborhoods.

The federal government became involved when President Bill Clinton signed Executive Order 12898 in 1994. The Environmental Protection Agency (EPA) developed its Environmental Justice Strategy, defining environmental justice as the "fair treatment for all people of all races, cultures, and incomes, regarding the development of environmental laws, regulations, and policies." The EPA also developed the Toxic Release Inventory, which is available in a Web-based database and contains information on toxic chemical releases in neighborhoods, organized by zip code.

See also Environmental Racism.

Further Reading.

Environmental Protection Agency, http://www.epa.gov/tri.

Benjamin F. Shearer

Tracking

Tracking is an educational system that places high-achieving students in classes that separate them from average students and students who are not performing well. Within this tracking system, the high-performing students are offered special classes that provide opportunities for advancement, while the students who perform less well or who are perceived as low achievers are offered courses that are less challenging academically and feature a significant amount of remedial course work.

Recent evidence suggests that this form of tracking has become the new, subtle (de facto) form of segregating schools based on race since blatant forms of racial segregation were prohibited by the Supreme Court ruling in *Brown v. Board of Education of Topeka* (1954). Rather than having separate schools for whites and nonwhites, separate curricula are offered. These separate "tracks" are justified by placing students in courses based on past achievement and performance on intelligence quotient (IQ) tests and other standardized academic tests.

The high-performing classes tend to have higher proportions of whites, while the low-performing classes have higher proportions of racial minorities. Tracking students in this manner perpetuates racial inequality because many minority students have received an inferior education in the past and are now being further penalized for these past disparities, since economic well being and level of career attainment is dependent on one's education. Some argue that the creation of this tracking system promotes the emergence of an educational culture that accepts that minority students are inherently less capable of succeeding than white students and therefore should be placed into courses based on this assumption.

See also Education and Racial Discrimination; Intelligence Tests and Racism.

Romney S. Norwood

Tuskegee Syphilis Experiment

The Tuskegee Study of Untreated Syphilis in the Negro Male was conducted from 1932 to 1972 in Macon County, Alabama. This study, which exploited and misled hundreds of African American men in the name of science, was condoned and funded by the U.S. Public Health Service. Beginning in 1932, the U.S. Public Health Service contracted the Tuskegee Institute to document the natural history of syphilis as part of a plan to justify creating treatment programs for blacks. A total of 600 black men participated in the study: 399 with syphilis and 201 without the disease. The participants received free medical exams, meals, and burial insurance for their participation in the study. Throughout the study, the men received absolutely no treatment for syphilis. Although the study was originally scheduled to last for only six months, it continued for forty years.

A story about the study sparked public outrage in 1972 when it was published in the *New York Times* and led to the appointment of a nine-member panel, with representatives from various professional disciplines to review the study. The panel concluded that the researchers misled the participants and failed to provide them with sufficient information about the study, making it impossible for the participants to provide informed consent. The panel also determined that the researchers were negligent in providing adequate medical assistance, because they failed to offer penicillin to the study subjects once it became the recommended course of treatment for syphilis in 1947. This permanent stain on the medical research community has very specific implications for the African American community. The study contributed to a pervasive distrust of federal authorities and the medical community among African Americans, which continues to impact the quality of health care African Americans, particularly men, receive.

Romney S. Norwood

U

UFW

See United Farm Workers (UFW).

Underground Railroad

Borrowing from the nomenclature of the expanding railroads, the Underground Railroad was not a railroad but a loose organization of like-minded men and women who conducted fugitive slaves through woods, over mountains, and up rivers from station to station (safe houses) to freedom in the North. It is thought to have begun with the efforts of Pennsylvania and New Jersey Quakers late in the eighteenth century. "Conductors" would head south to assist small groups and individuals find their way through the maze of secret routes that were the tracks of this railroad. These tracks or paths extended through fourteen Northern states and Canada. The stations, homes, and businesses where they could be pirated away during daylight hours, were about twenty miles from each other. Homeowners provided the runaways, "passengers" on the railroad, not only with shelter, but also with food and money.

The number of people involved in the Railroad and the number of fugitive slaves led to freedom can only be estimated because of the informality of the system. Approximately three thousand people are estimated to have been involved in Railroad activities by 1850, and about fifty thousand slaves are thought to have used the Railroad in their journey northward. A number of notable figures were involved in the Railroad's activities, including Harriet Tubman, herself a runaway slave, ex-slave and famous abolitionist and orator Frederick Douglass, naturalist Henry David Thoreau, and feminist Susan B. Anthony. Certainly the Railroad played a role in the complaints of slave owners who

Fugitive slaves escaping from the eastern shore of Maryland.

Courtesy Library of Congress.

clamored for a strict law to safeguard their "property." Congress gave it to them with the 1850 Fugitive Slave Act, which provided for fining federal marshals $1000 if they failed to arrest a runaway slave and for fining those who aided runaways that same amount, along with six months in prison.

See also Douglass, Frederick; Slave Codes; Slave Families; Slavery in the Antebellum South.

Further Reading

Blockson, Charles L. *The Underground Railroad*. New York: Prentice Hall, 1987.

Benjamin F. Shearer

Undocumented Immigrants

An undocumented immigrant (also undocumented worker, illegal immigrant, or illegal alien) refers to a foreign-born individual residing in the United States without legal authorization. The United States did not have undocumented immigrants until 1875, when the nation passed its first immigrant-exclusion law, which targeted prostitutes and convicts. Today, the flow of undocumented immigrants to the United States is increasing in volume and complexity, spanning a wider variety of sending countries, methods of entry, and settlement patterns upon arrival. Despite federal legislation in 1986 and 1996 designed to reduce the number of undocumented immigrants entering and staying in the United States, current estimates range from eight million to fourteen million. Entry is gained in two primary ways, either by crossing the border without authorization, or by entering with a valid temporary visa and overstaying or otherwise violating its terms. Unauthorized entries account for just over half of the undocumented immigrants in the United States. The remainder are tourists, students, and businesspeople who stay beyond their visa limits or change status without authorization; for instance, students or tourists may take a job. Today, Mexicans make up more than 50 percent of undocumented immigrants to the United States, but in recent years, other countries have increased their share. El Salvador, Guatemala, Canada, Haiti, the Philippines, Honduras, Poland, Nicaragua, and the Bahamas rounded out the top-ten countries of origin for undocumented immigrants in the 1990s. California, New York, Texas, and Washington, DC, remain primary U.S. destinations, although settlement patterns continue to diversify.

Anti-immigrant sentiment, particularly directed at undocumented workers, ebbs and flows in the United States. At times, popular opinion and media coverage portray an "alien invasion" flooding the country, overwhelming its borders and taking jobs. In response, the U.S. government passed the Immigrant Reform and Control Act of 1986 (IRCA), which required employers to verify the legal status of every employee and imposed sanctions on employers who knowingly hired undocumented workers. IRCA also provided a one-time amnesty to 3.1 million undocumented immigrants and significantly increased funding for enforcement along the U.S.-Mexico border to stop future illegal crossings. Initially, undocumented immigration dropped sharply, but numbers began to increase again steadily, a result attributed by some authorities to IRCA itself.

Congress passed two bills in 1996 that affected undocumented workers. The Personal Responsibility and Work Opportunity Reconciliation Act (also known as the Welfare Reform Act) established new limits on social services and welfare benefits for noncitizens and differentiated between refugees, legal immigrants, and undocumented immigrants for benefit eligibility. Also passed in 1996, the Illegal Immigration Reform and Immigrant Responsibility Act (IIRIRA) raised the family income threshold for those wishing to sponsor members for immigration to 25 percent above federal poverty levels and again dramatically increased funding for enforcement, including hiring more Border Patrol officers, introducing sophisticated technology, building border fences, and fining immigrants for illegal entry. Despite these efforts, increased interdiction of illegal border crossings has not stopped the immigrant flow but has made it more expensive and more dangerous. Militarization of the U.S. borders has forced immigrants and their smugglers to choose more remote and dangerous entry roots and led to an increase in deaths, now tracked at one each day. International human smuggling has become a $5 billion industry annually.

Legislation to limit undocumented immigration also has emerged at the state level, most notably in California's November 1994 ballot initiative, Proposition 187, which passed with 59 percent of the vote. The law required California State employees to verify the immigrant status of the individuals they served, report undocumented immigrants to state and federal officials, and deny health care, social services, and education to those found to be undocumented. Civil rights groups quickly challenged the constitutionality of a state usurping the federal government's exclusive authority to regulate immigration. Within a week, a California court had issued a temporary restraining order, and in March 1998 key components of the bill were declared unconstitutional in federal court.

Since the mid-1980s, the U.S. economy has expanded steadily, and businesses, demanding cheap labor, have relied heavily on undocumented workers. These immigrants now play a significant role in major U.S. economic sectors, including agriculture, restaurants, garment factories, hotels, and meat processing. With wage differentials so stark between the United States and developing countries, the lack of opportunities drives the most resourceful to consider immigration as an economic strategy for themselves and their families. Undocumented immigration also results from people fleeing civil war and strife in their home countries, often perpetrated and funded by U.S. policies, as was the case in El Salvador. In light of this, what some perceive as an alien invasion is perhaps more aptly described as mostly an international response to the U.S. economy's ravenous demand for low-wage workers.

See also California Ballot Proposition 187; Nativism and the Anti-immigrant Movements.

Further Reading

Kwong, Peter. *Forbidden Workers: Illegal Chinese Immigrants and American Labor.* New York: The New Press, 1997.

Portes, Alejandro, and Ruben Rumbaut. *Immigrant America: A Portrait.* Berkeley: University of California Press, 1996.

Kenneth J. Guest

United Farm Workers (UFW)

The United Farm Workers (UFW) was a union representing mostly Chicago farm workers in California and Arizona that was cofounded and led by the charismatic labor activist Cesar Chavez. The union was formed in 1971 from the merger of two separate unions—the Agricultural Workers Organizing Committee, founded by the AFL-CIO in 1959 but which was an outgrowth of the Agricultural Workers Association founded earlier by Dolores Huerta, and the National Farmworkers Association (NFWA), cofounded by Chavez and Huerta in 1962. At the time of its founding, the working conditions of migrant farm workers were atrocious; workers earned an average of 90 cents an hour and often lived in rented, unheated shacks, segregated by race and lacking basic amenities, such as indoor plumbing or kitchens. Starting around 1965, the NFWA grew significantly in power after a successful strike against grape growers around Delano, a farm town in central California. The strike involved more than thirty farms and several thousand workers. Under Chavez's leadership, the strike utilized nonviolent tactics, such as a rotating system of picketing farms and also undertaking a 340-mile protest march to Sacramento, the state's capital. The union additionally sought public support through creating awareness of the farmworkers' difficult living and working conditions. It was aided by the millions of consumers who heeded the call to stop buying grapes that lacked a union label.

By 1970, most grape growers accepted collectively bargained union contracts. The first contracts included restrictions on the use of dangerous pesticides, agreements on parental leave and profit sharing, access to state coverage for unemployment, disability, and workers' compensation, and a ban on discrimination or sexual harassment of women. By then, the union also had grown to include a union-run hiring hall, a health clinic, and a credit union, as well as higher wages. Today, the UFW continues to fight for the improvement of working conditions, benefits for farm workers, and extending legal immigration status to undocumented agricultural workers and their families.

See also Chavez, Cesar; Mexican Illegals, Labor Exploitation of.

Rose Kim

United States v. Thind

United States v. Thind was argued before the Supreme Court of the United States in the winter of 1923. At issue were whether a "high-caste Hindu of full Indian blood" qualified as a white person and whether the Immigration Act of 1917 disqualified Hindus from citizenship who would have been eligible before the passage of that law. The case also aimed to clarify a question left unanswered in *Ozawa v. United States* (1922), which was what the boundaries of whiteness were. The applicant for citizenship in this case claimed that he was white on the basis of his northern Indian Aryan/Caucasian background. The Court came to the conclusion that Aryan was a linguistic rather than a racial category and that Caucasian is a category too broad to be used in determining race. The Court followed this determination by stating that Indians, on the basis of their physical characteristics, which are distinct from those of Europeans', could not be contained within the group delineated as "free white persons eligible for citizenship." Additionally, the Court made the point that Congress would not have wanted to render a class of people eligible for citizenship who were not considered eligible for immigration (no Asian was able to immigrate at this time). The Court was careful to make the point that they were not suggesting racial superiority or inferiority, merely racial difference— and that this difference was sufficient to disallow citizenship.

The consequence of this decision was that only individuals considered to be of European or African descent were allowed to become citizens of the United States. Citizenship brings with it not only the right to vote and hold elected office but freedom from certain kinds of political and criminal persecution. Additionally, at the time that this case was argued, immigrants not eligible for citizenship were not allowed to own property or engage in certain occupations. This case, therefore, relegated Asian Americans to a subservient position in U.S. society, regardless of their education or income, until legislation began to repeal its effects, starting in 1943 when Chinese Americans were granted the right of naturalization. Filipinos and South Asians gained naturalization rights in 1946, but Japanese and Korean Americans had to wait until 1952.

See also Asian Americans, Discrimination against; *Ozawa v. United States*.

Mikaila Mariel Lemonik Arthur

U.S. Border Patrol

The Border Patrol is an agency of the federal government in the Bureau of Citizenship and Immigration Services that has recently been placed under the Department of Homeland Security. The Border Patrol was established in 1924. Its primary mission is to detect and prevent the illegal entry of aliens into the United States, and it is most visible patrolling the more than eight thousand miles of international boundaries. In Fiscal Year (FY) 2001 (October 1, 2000, to September 30, 2001), Border Patrol agents apprehended almost 1.2 million persons nationwide for illegally entering the country. The area near San Diego accounts for nearly half of these apprehensions.

The Border Patrol has also worked in conjunction with other agencies, including the military, especially with respect to the "war on drugs." In FY 2001, Border Patrol Agents seized more than 18,500 pounds of cocaine and more than 1.1 million pounds of marijuana. The estimated street value of the total drugs seized in FY 2001 was approximately 1.4 billion dollars.

There have been claims, especially from organizations representing human rights and indigenous Americans, that the U.S. Border Patrol has a double stan-

U.S. Border Patrol agents apprehend suspected illegal immigrants in Jamul, California, 1996.

AP/Wide World Photos.

dard, treating those who have darker skin with suspicion. The Border Patrol has also been criticized for alleged overly aggressive behavior toward illegal aliens. Lastly, collaborative enforcement efforts between the military and the Border Patrol to shut down illegal-drug operations have caused concern with respect to protecting basic human rights.

See also Undocumented Immigrants.

John Eterno

USCCR

See U.S. Commission on Civil Rights (USCCR).

U.S. Commission on Civil Rights (USCCR)

The U.S. Commission on Civil Rights (USCCR) was founded in 1957 as part of the Civil Rights Act of 1957 as an independent, fact-finding arm of the federal government. Its mission consists of investigating complaints about, collecting information related to, appraising federal laws and policies with regard to, making reports on, and issuing public-service announcements about discrimination based on race, color, religion, sex, age, disability, national origin and in the administration of justice. The USCCR can hold hearings, issue advisories, and consult with both governmental officials and private organizations, but it does not have any enforcement powers. In 1983, the legislation establishing it was renewed.

The major aim of the civil rights legislation founding the USCCR was to increase the number of African Americans who were registered to vote (other provisions of the law made it a crime to interfere with a citizen's right to vote, though enforcement was weak); thus, much of its early work focused on voting rights. Other early issues included school desegregation, employment opportunities, and property rights. It held hearings on these issues and issued reports aimed at both government policymakers and the general public. In the 1970s, it began to investigate issues of concern to Asian Americans, Native Americans, and Latino/a migrant workers and issued its first Spanish-language report (on the Equal Rights Amendment). Other issues addressed throughout the 1980s and 1990s include domestic violence, housing equality, immigration, Hawaiian homelands, girls' sports, and the economic status of various ethnic groups. The USCCR also issued reports on discrimination and governmental relations in particular states and localities. Some of the most recent reports have addressed police brutality, voting irregularities in the 2000 U.S. presidential election, bioterrorism, health care, the Americans with Disabilities Act, Affirmative Action, and asylum seekers.

The USCCR also advises individuals on filing civil rights complaints, particularly in cases where citizenship rights might be limited (as in the case of prison inmates, military personnel, and Native Americans living on reservations). Regional offices and state advisory committees deal with issues in specific localities. The USCCR meets monthly at a time and place announced in advance. Additionally, the USCCR maintains the Robert S. Rankin Civil Rights Library in Washington, DC. This library is accessible to the general public and maintains a collection of the USCCR's own publications, along with books, journals, magazines, and electronic resources addressing such subjects as campus tension, disabilities, discrimination, education, the elderly, housing, racism, and women's issues.

Since the USCCR has no enforcement power, its ability to have a significant impact on the civil rights of Americans has been somewhat limited, though not nonexistent. It has played an important role in educating Americans about their civil rights and helping individuals learn how to file complaints of civil rights violations. The fact that it is required by law to contain an equal number of Republicans and Democrats has helped it serve as a nonpartisan force that brings agreement on important issues. The reports issued by the USCCR have been extremely useful for nongovernmental civil rights organizations in their struggles for legislative, judicial, and policy changes, especially because an authoritative governmental body has prepared them.

Further Reading

Thurgood Marshall Law Library of the University of Maryland. "Historical Publications of the United States Commission on Civil Rights." http://www.law.umaryland.edu/ edocs/USCCR/html%20files/usccrhp.asp.

Mikaila Mariel Lemonik Arthur

U.S. Department of Housing and Urban Development (HUD)

The Department of Housing and Urban Development (HUD) is the federal agency created in 1965 with the mission of handling housing issues and community-supportive services. HUD evolved from the Federal Housing Administration (FHA), which was established in 1934. It served as a review committee for banks and other loan institutions to make loans available to low-income families as a part of President Lyndon B. Johnson's War on Poverty in 1964.

One of the essential missions of HUD since its creation has been to use all of its programs and the direct authority given by civil rights legislation to eliminate racial discrimination in housing and to promote integration of the races. HUD's responsibilities and authority derive from a series of executive orders and laws that have become progressively broader in scope. The first was President John F. Kennedy's Executive Order of 1962, which prohibited racial discrimination in housing financed by FHA-insured or Veterans Affairs (VA)–insured mortgages and in federally assisted public housing. The Kennedy action was, therefore, limited; the great bulk of housing was conventionally financed; that is, non-FHA or non-VA. Moreover, FHA and VA housing was affected only if it was financed after the executive order was initiated.

Two years later, the Civil Rights Act of 1964 was passed. Title VI of this law prohibited racial discrimination in housing or in any other construction receiving federal financial assistance. The law extended to housing constructed in urban-renewal areas and to all public housing, no matter when it was initiated. However, most financing of housing in the country remained unaffected.

Finally, the Fair Housing Act of 1968 (Title VIII of the Civil Rights Act) prohibited racial discrimination based on race, color, religion, sex, national origin, handicap, or familial status in the sale, rental, and use of nearly all housing (about 80 percent), as well as in mortgage lending, sales, and advertising practices. The act provided the secretary of HUD with investigation and enforcement responsibility for curbing discriminatory practices. The Housing and Community Development Act of 1974 added more responsibility for reducing the isolation of income groups and promoting diversity within neighborhoods. In this respect, HUD played a leading role in administering the Fair Housing Act to eliminate racial discrimination in housing.

HUD's efforts, however, encountered three limitations. First, HUD's power to control various forms of housing discrimination rested on its authority to investigate complaints from persons who claimed they had been discriminated against on racial grounds. It could not initiate a court action itself. Many cases that did not lack merit remained unresolved and were frequently transferred to the U.S. Civil Rights Commission (USCCR). This recognition led to

1988 amendments that greatly increased the department's enforcement role by allowing it to investigate, conciliate, and prosecute complaints.

Second, HUD was far from an effectual organization. For example, according to the USCCR, which studied nearly two thousand complaints received by HUD during 1972 and 1973, HUD had not effectively pursued many of the complaints it had received. More than 20 percent of these complaints reached the conciliation stage, and 80 percent were dropped without any relief to the complaintants. Furthermore, many of the unpursued complaints were simply neglected. About twenty-five years later, the 2000 HUD fact sheet reported that HUD handled over 12,000 inquires and about 6,300 complaints (53 percent) were filed in 1999. Of those, 39 percent were settled, and in 5 percent of the cases, findings of discrimination were issued.

Third, it has been noted that HUD's efforts have had minimal impact on preventing or eliminating housing discrimination not only because of legal limitations in its enforcement power and administration, but also because of de facto racial discrimination, which is subtle, hard to discover, and harder to monitor. For example, suburban zoning commissions, to increase tax revenues, often zone residential land in such a way that all but the most expensive homes are barred. This zoning can effectively restrict most blacks.

In the purchase and sale of new and existing homes, real estate agents and the mortgage lending institutions also practice subtle forms of discrimination by dealing personally with both buyers and sellers. Redlining around certain run-down city neighborhoods is another form of racial discrimination practiced by lenders. Even if its motive seems economic, the effect is to make it hard or impossible for even reliable individual residents of the redlined communities to get a loan to sell or improve their houses. For these and other reasons, the enforcement of antidiscrimination laws by HUD in housing is much more challenging than in public transportation, education, and jobs.

See also Fair Housing Act of 1968; Fair Housing Amendments Act of 1988; Federal Housing Administration (FHA); Housing Discrimination; Redlining; Residential Segregation.

Further Reading

HUD. *Fair Housing Laws and Presidential Executive Orders.* http://www.hud.gov/offices/fheo/FHLaws/index.cfm.

Mayer, Neil. "HUD's First 30 years: Big Steps Down a Longer Road." *Cityscape: A Journal of Policy Development and Research* 1, no. 3 (1995): 1–29.

McFarland, Carter. *Federal Government and Urban Problems: HUD: Successes, Failures, and the Fate of Our Cities.* Denver, CO: Westview Press, 1978.

Sookhee Oh

V

Violence

See Non-Judeo-Christian Immigrant Groups, Violence against.

Voluntary Minorities

See Colonized versus Immigrant Minorities.

Voluntary Segregation

See Segregation, Voluntary versus Involuntary.

Voting Rights Act of 1965

Despite the fifteenth and nineteenth amendments to the U.S. Constitution, which enfranchised black men and women, Southern voter registration boards used poll taxes, literacy tests, and other bureaucratic impediments to deny African Americans their legal right to vote. Southern blacks also risked harassment, intimidation, economic reprisals, and physical violence when they tried to register or vote. As a result, until the early 1960s African Americans had little, if any, political power, either locally or nationally. Participants and activists in the civil rights movement, under the guidance of the Rev. Dr. Martin Luther King Jr. and the Southern Christian Leadership Conference (SCLC), staged non-violent demonstrations in Albany, Georgia, and Birmingham, Alabama, partly to protest the systematic disenfranchisement of African Americans.

Adopted on August 6, 1965, the Voting Rights Act was extended in 1970, 1975, and 1982, and is considered the most successful piece of civil rights legislation adopted by the U.S. Congress. The act codified the fifteenth Amendment's permanent guarantee that no person shall be denied the right to vote on account of race or color. The act contains several special provisions that impose even more stringent requirements on "covered" jurisdictions in certain areas of the country, meaning that no voting changes were legally enforceable until approved by a three-judge court in the District of Columbia or by the attorney general of the United States. The requirement that certain state and local governments obtain federal approval prior to implementing any changes to their voting procedures is known as "preclearance." This far-reaching statute was a response to the compelling evidence of continuing interference with attempts by African American citizens to exercise their right to vote. The following states (or parts of the state) that are subject to preclearance are Alabama, Mississippi, Alaska, New Hampshire, Arizona, New York, California, North Carolina, South Carolina, Florida, Georgia, South Dakota, Louisiana, Texas, Michigan, and Virginia.

At the time the act was first adopted, only one-third of all African Americans of voting age were on the registration rolls in the specially covered states, while two-thirds of eligible whites were registered. Now black voter registration rates are approaching parity with those of whites in many areas, and Hispanic voters in jurisdictions added in 1975 to the list of those specially covered by the act are not far behind. Enforcement of the act has also increased the opportunity of black and Latino voters to elect representatives of their choice by providing a vehicle for challenging discriminatory election methods, such as racially gerrymandered districting plans or at-large elections that may dilute minority groups' voting strength. Virtually excluded from all public offices in the South in 1965, black and Hispanic voters are now substantially represented in the state legislatures and local governing bodies throughout the region.

The 1965 Voting Rights Act serves as a cornerstone piece of legislation that ensures all racial minorities have fair access to casting a ballot and fair opportunities for their votes to be meaningful. This law also protects the voting rights of many people who have limited English language proficiency. Section 203 of the Voting Rights Act protects the voting rights of linguistic-minority groups by requiring that particular jurisdictions print ballots and other election materials in the minority language as well as in English and provide oral translation at the polls.

See also Black Political Disenfranchisement; Fourteenth Amendment; Literacy Test; Poll Tax; Voting Rights Amendments of 1975.

Further Reading

Asian American Legal Defense and Education Fund. "Asian American Access to Democracy in the 2002 Elections in New York City." 2003.

Tarry Hum

Voting Rights Amendments of 1975

In 1975 the U.S. Congress amended the Voting Rights Act of 1965 (sections 4 and 203) to protect the voting rights of citizens of certain ethnic groups whose language is other than English. The amendment was partly the result of the Mexican American Defense and Educational Fund's argument before Congress that English-only elections in Texas had the same effects as the literacy requirements, (which were abolished by the 1965 Voting Rights Act). The language provision of the 1975 act was therefore intended to enable members of linguistic minorities—Spanish-speaking groups, American Indians, Asian Americans, and Alaskan Natives—to participate effectively in the electoral process. It required states and political subdivisions to conduct elections in the language of the named minority groups when more than 5 percent (a minimum of 10,000 voters) of the voting-age citizens of a given jurisdiction are members of a single linguistic-minority group, and either the English literacy rate was below the national average or the voter turnout in the last English-only election was less than 50 percent of the voting-age population of that jurisdiction. The act required that written election materials in the language of the minority groups be offered, and for American Indians and Alaskan Natives, whose languages are oral languages only, verbal assistance and publicity. Implementation of the act was left to the state legislatures.

See also Black Political Disenfranchisement; Fourteenth Amendment; Literacy Test; Poll Tax; Voting Rights Act of 1965.

Carmenza Gallo

W

Wagner Act

The Wagner Act, also known as the National Labor Relations Act (NLRA), was sponsored by Senator Robert Wagner of New York, and passed in 1935. The Wagner Act is seen by most as a great victory for workers' rights, because workers in the United States were given the right, under section 7(a), to have independent, union representation for purposes of collective bargaining with their employers. Before the Wagner Act, employers routinely fired—with impunity—their employees for joining or organizing labor unions at their workplace. Today, employers are obliged by law to recognize unions when their workers vote in favor of union representation.

Not all workers benefited from the gains of the Wagner Act, because the Wagner Act did nothing to prevent racial discrimination by either employers or unions. In fact, the Wagner Act allowed race-based discrimination to be included in labor contracts created by the collective bargaining between unions and employers. Furthermore, the Wagner Act was unable to prevent unions from excluding potential members because of their race. Some have argued that it was because of this that the Labor Department and the National Labor Relations Board, which were both created by the NLRA to look after the interests of unions, turned a blind eye toward unions who discriminated against blacks.

In 1944, the U.S. Supreme Court addressed the issue in the case *Steele v. Louisville and Nashville Railroad*. In that case, the Supreme Court ruled that because unions have been given the right by the NLRA to be the exclusive representatives of workers in the process of collective bargaining, they must do so fairly, without discrimination. The Court reasoned that if the federal government gave unions the right to bargain for workers, and if unions discriminated against certain workers, then by default, the government was condoning discrimination, which was a violation of the Constitution. The federal government finally ended the practice of racial discrimination among unions when it passed the Civil Rights Act in 1964, which forced unions to integrate.

See also Civil Rights Act of 1964; Labor Movement, Racism in.

Michael Roberts

Wallace, George (1919–1998)

George Corley Wallace, born in Clio, Alabama, on August 25, 1919, was a politician in the Democratic Party who is closely associated with segregation and white supremacy in the South. From 1946 to 1958, he served variously as assistant state attorney, a member of the state legislature, and a judge in the Third Judicial Circuit of Alabama. He was also governor of Alabama for four terms, elected in 1962, 1970, 1974, and 1982.

Governor George Wallace with President Richard Nixon at the Southern Regional Media Conference in Alabama, May 1971.

Courtesy National Archives.

His Alabama political career was based on racist attitudes. In 1958, he lost an election for governor by running a campaign for better roads, education, and industrial recruitment. He lost to General John Patterson, a staunch segregationist who was backed by the Ku Klux Klan. At the end of this election Wallace stated, "I'll never be out-niggered again." The remainder of his career, in the 1960s and 1970s, was associated with racism at its worst. After winning the governorship in 1962 he made extreme attempts to prevent integration in the state. Indeed, in his inaugural speech, he stated, "Segregation today, segregation tomorrow, and segregation forever!" Wallace even tried to prevent the enrollment of two blacks at the University of Alabama by standing in front of the auditorium; eventually, however, he succumbed to the power of the National Guard. He is also known for using troops to attempt to prevent integration.

Wallace also tried to run for the Presidency, but while campaigning for the Democratic Party's nomination, he was shot by Arthur Herman Bremer. The bullet lodged in his spine, so he was partially paralyzed from the waist down and remained so for the rest of his life. After the assassination attempt, Wallace seemed to have at least tried to change. A coalition of blacks and whites did allow him to win another term as governor of Alabama in 1982. Some believe that Wallace was truly changed in his later years, but most still associate his name with racial hatred and white supremacy in the Deep South. Wallace died on September 13, 1998, of cardiac arrest from complications of his paralysis and Parkinson's disease.

See also Civil Right Movement; Ku Klux Klan (KKK).

John Eterno

War and Racial Inequality

Minorities have fought in all the wars of the United States. During the Revolutionary War, about 5,000 African Americans fought for American independence. During the War of 1812, blacks served in the U.S. Navy as well as in both mixed and segregated regiments in the U.S. Army. During the Mexican-American War, numerous free blacks answered the call of Congress for 50,000 volunteers. After Congress permitted black recruits into the military in 1862 and the Emancipation Proclamation took effect on January 1, 1863, the War Department created the Bureau of Colored Troops. The Bureau developed 149 segregated units commanded by white officers, many of whom were unenthusiastic about leading armed blacks into battle. About 186,000 blacks served in the army, and another 30,000 in the navy, during the Civil War. When the war ended, Congress institutionalized segregated military units when it authorized the all-black 9th and 10th Cavalry, which became known as the Buffalo Soldiers, and the 24th and 25th Infantry.

Maintaining a standing army was a long-held American fear stemming from Revolutionary War days. Thus, when war came on the horizon, the government scurried to put military forces together, and the issue of race became secondary to recruitment. That remained so after the Civil War. A total of 10,000 blacks volunteered in army service during the Spanish-American War, and 404,000 blacks served in the army during World War I, almost 11 percent of the total force and separately recruited from whites. Curiously, however, the navy remained an integrated force up until 1900. The prevailing belief among military leaders was that with white direction, all-black units could work effectively, even though many blacks were assigned to menial tasks.

The Selective Service Act of 1940 took the factor of race out of military recruitment in law, but not in practice. President Franklin D. Roosevelt resisted the entreaties of civil rights leaders to integrate the military, although some progress was made in improving the assignments of black soldiers. During World War II, one million blacks served in the military, mostly in the army, but 145,000 served in the U.S. Air Force and another 150,000 in the navy. In 1942, the U.S. Marines permitted its first black recruit. The military forces remained segregated until President Harry S. Truman required their integration on July 26, 1948, in Executive Order 9981. By the end of 1954, 300 all-black units had been integrated into the services, and the legacy of a physically segregated military ended.

Integration came to be seen as a military imperative that would assure combat readiness and efficiency. During the Korean War, military planners discovered that integrated forces resulted in significant efficiencies because the race element was eliminated from the tasks of procurement, assignment, and training. Race came to be seen as another factor in every equation that simply produced more work rather than better work. Training, for example, could be more effective if based on individual talent rather than race. Yet in the time up to and including the Vietnam War, the military services found themselves embroiled in racial problems that nearly brought them to a standstill. Racial violence among military personnel became commonplace. White officers were for the most part unaware of black issues and tended to perceive dissatisfaction as disrespect.

Among the many hard-learned lessons of Vietnam was that racism was so powerful as to render a fighting force useless. If commanders could not communicate with their troops and vice versa, if respect on both sides was completely lacking, the enemy was within. Indeed, it became very clear that racism remained in the integrated military. In the early days of the Vietnam War, black combat deaths had mounted to more than 20 percent of all casualties, nearly twice the percentage of black youths in the total U.S. population. This prompted President Lyndon B. Johnson, at the behest of civil rights leaders, to decrease the number of blacks in combat. Yet by the end of the war, the casualties of black enlisted men were still over 14 percent of all casualties. Data on Latinos was not maintained.

The full integration of the military forces would never be possible until all the vestiges of racism in the form of white supremacy were removed. Excessive minority casualties could not be avoided, and battle-ready, effective fighting forces achieved, without opening up the officer ranks to minorities. When the all-volunteer force came into being in 1973, only 2.8 percent of all military officers were black. Twenty years later, about 19 percent of active military officers were minorities: 8.8 percent black; 4 percent Hispanic; 3.2 percent Asian-American; and .6 percent Native-American. Yet the minorities made up nearly 40 percent of all enlisted personnel: 21.7 percent black; 9.6 percent Hispanic; 4 percent Asian American; and 1.2 percent Native American.

Beliefs in racial inequality formed American experience in war. Who would lead, who would follow, who would die: all were determined in part by beliefs tainted with racism. Abolitionist Frederick Douglass urged blacks to enter into military service during the Civil War because he thought that fighting for the Union would bring all the benefits of full citizenship to them. He could not have imagined that he spoke more than a hundred years too soon.

See also Civil War and the Abolition of Slavery; Douglass, Frederick; Executive Order 9981; Gulf War; Japanese American Internment; Mexican-American War; Spanish-American War; War Relocation Authority (WRA).

Further Reading

Buckley, Gail Lumet. *American Patriots: The Story of Blacks in the Military from the Revolution to Desert Storm*. New York: Random House, 2001.

Moskos, Charles C., and John Sibley Butler. *All That We Can Be: Black Leadership and Racial Integration the Army Way*. New York: Basic Books, 1996.

Benjamin F. Shearer

War on Poverty and the Great Society

In the early 1960s, President John F. Kennedy brought new attention and energy to America's social problems, particularly poverty. In 1962, Michael Harrington's influential book *The Other America*, which detailed the prevalence of poverty in affluent America was published and caught the attention of President Kennedy and other politicians. Harrington's accessible and persuasive book helped to popularize the movement to end poverty in the United States. Kennedy initially looked toward improved social work as the best method for eliminating poverty. He hoped that strong social services could help poor families make better choices and improve their lives. But Kennedy quickly changed his views on the causes of poverty and began to understand poverty as a social and structural problem rather than a problem of individual pathology.

After President Kennedy was assassinated, Lyndon B. Johnson increased the policy emphasis on structural opportunities in the War on Poverty and Great Society programs. On March 16, 1964, Johnson proposed to begin a "war on poverty." One of the hallmarks of the War on Poverty was its ambitious attempt to end poverty by creating a more just society. The central legislation of this proposal was the Economic Opportunity Act of 1964. The antipoverty programs of the 1960s were far more complex than those of the New Deal. They aimed, in President Johnson's words, "at the causes, not just the consequences of poverty." Johnson wanted to create new opportunities for whole groups of people who had formerly been left out of many mainstream social and economic opportunities. The Great Society programs were extremely ambitious. They attempted to increase job opportunities and education for the young and to empower the disenfranchised.

Social-science research had played a significant role in motivating the War on Poverty. In addition to Harrington, economist Robert Lampman provided evidence that economic growth was no longer affecting poverty as it once had. This seemed to suggest that the poor were becoming detached from the larger American society. Sociologist Leonard Cottrell brought his research on the ecology of neighborhoods to the discussions of community development as a solution to poverty. Sociologists Lloyd Ohlin and Richard Cloward developed sophisticated structural models to explain poverty and delinquency and to identify target areas for government reform. Before this awakening of interest in poverty, there had been remarkably little government or academic research on the subject. In the early 1960s, a comprehensive bibliography on poverty did not fill two typewritten pages. The first official statistics on poverty in the United States were not released until 1965.

What happened to the war on poverty and the ambitions of the great society is controversial. One argument is that the war in Vietnam took attention and resources away from the war on poverty. Undoubtedly, there is truth in this argument. The war and the social changes of the late 1960s changed the political context. In the early 1960s, Harrington's argument that poverty was pulling people away from an otherwise cohesive society had resonance. The United States seemed affluent and stable. It did not seem unreasonably ambitious to think that it could solve the problem of poverty. By the late 1960s, the Vietnam War, race riots, and social unrest drained away the focus and ambition of the War on Poverty.

Other factors have also been noted for the failure of the War on Poverty. Many of the ambitious programs were never fully funded or permitted to develop. It was also hard to measure the successes of the programs. Since the programs aimed not only to reduce poverty but also to create a more just and equitable society, it was difficult to produce evidence of their success. Arguably, racial tensions also undermined support for the programs among white Americans. The themes of empowerment and community participation were perhaps more threatening in the volatile context of racial politics in the late 1960s. Some conservative critics have argued that the premise of the War on Poverty was misguided. The state, they argue, cannot reduce poverty by creating government programs.

Since the 1960s, Americans have become skeptical about the positive impact that government can have on poverty. Welfare reform in 1996 was largely premised on the idea that the less involved government was in poor families' lives, the better off they would be. Nonetheless, there have been some clear successes in reducing poverty in the United States. Most notably, before the Social Security system was established, the elderly were among the poorest Americans. Now they are among the most affluent. The War on Poverty and the Great Society programs represent a brief moment of optimism that researchers and government could create a partnership to improve society and eliminate, or at least reduce, poverty. Whether those ambitions could have been achieved with a greater social commitment remains an open question.

See also Civil Rights Movement; Racial Differences in Poverty Rate.

Further Reading

Aaron, Henry J. *Politics and the Professors*. Washington, DC: Brookings Institution Press, 1978.

Harrington, Michael. *The Other America*. Baltimore: Penguin, 1981.

Patterson, James. *America's Struggle against Poverty*. Cambridge, MA: Harvard University Press, 1986.

Robin Roger-Dillon

War Relocation Authority (WRA)

The War Relocation Authority (WRA) was established by President Franklin D. Roosevelt in 1942 by executive order. This department of the federal government was charged with removing persons believed to be threats to national security from "designated areas" and supervising the evacuees with regard to security and gainful employment. The WRA established ten relocation centers, primarily in the inland western part of the United States (California, Arizona,

Idaho, Wyoming, Colorado, and Utah, as well as Arkansas). Within eighteen months after the executive order establishing the WRA was issued, about 120,000 individuals of Japanese descent—including U.S.-born citizens—who had been living on the Pacific coast were relocated.

Many of these individuals remained imprisoned in these facilities, which have come to be known as internment camps, until the end of World War II. Some, however, were able to gain their freedom by signing an oath of loyalty to the United States and agreeing to be relocated to the eastern part of the country, attend college outside of the Pacific zone, or serve in the U.S. armed forces. In 1943, the Tule Lake Relocation Center was designated as the special facility to which those who would not sign the loyalty oath or were otherwise perceived as being more loyal to Japan than to the United States were moved. These individuals eventually numbered approximately eighteen thousand. By November 1945, four months after Japan's surrender, all of the camps besides Tule Lake were closed. Tule Lake remained in operation until March of 1946, and President Harry S. Truman disbanded the WRA on June 26, 1946.

It is important to note that although the United States was at war not only against Japan but also against Germany in World War II, descendants of German immigrants were never subject to such relocation and internment. While the federal government did eventually provide $38 million to settle claims for property and other loss by the internees, the claims themselves totaled well over $100 million. In 1987, a provision was made for the payment of $20,000 for each surviving Japanese American as "redress" for the wrongs they suffered. However, these monetary payments could not make up for the disruptions in the lives of Pacific Coast Japanese Americans (the bulk of all Japanese Americans at the time) or the difficulty they had finding jobs, homes, and new lives after the war.

See also Executive Order 9066; Japanese American Internment; Japanese Americans, Redress Movement for.

Mikaila Mariel Lemonik Arthur

Washington, Booker T. (1856–1915)

Born a slave in Virginia, Booker Taliaferro Washington rose to become a dominant voice in race relations and black affairs in the late nineteenth and early twentieth centuries. An educator, fund-raiser, public speaker, and presidential advisor, Washington's influence was felt across racial, geographic, and economic divides. His accommodationist viewpoint garnered considerable criticism from the black community, particularly later in his life. Yet, he remains known for his passionate advocacy of education and moral training as fundamental to the advancement of blacks in the South.

As recalled in his autobiographical account *Up from Slavery*, published in 1901, education enabled Washington to escape hard labor in the salt mines of West Virginia, where his family had settled upon emancipation. Washington received his secondary education at the Hampton Normal and Agricultural Institute in Virginia. He was later appointed to be the first principal of a fledgling institute modeled on Hampton, in a small town called Tuskegee in Alabama. Under Washington's leadership, Tuskegee Institute, established in

Booker T. Washington, a former slave, promoted black advancement through common industrial and agricultural labor, rather than through political protest.

Courtesy Library of Congress.

1880 through an act of the Alabama State Legislature, came to be both a moral and an educational force in the South. Tuskegee offered vocational training in the areas of agriculture, crafts, and trade, with a strong emphasis on Christian moral education. Washington was instrumental in attracting Northern donations to Tuskegee, and it soon established its reputation as the premier vocational institute for blacks in the South.

Though committed to black economic and educational development, Washington remained politically conservative, at least outwardly, throughout his life. In 1895, at the Cotton States and International Exposition in Atlanta, he delivered a speech that came to be known as the "Atlanta Compromise." In this speech, Washington reassured white listeners anxious about growing racial tension in the South that the key to black advancement was through common labor in agriculture and industry, rather than political agitation. Washington faced mounting opposition within the black community, most notably from W.E.B. Du Bois, who saw Washington's accommodationist positions as untenable in an age of lynchings and disregard for black civil rights. Also, Washington's emphasis on agricultural and crafts training was increasingly undermined in the early decades of the twentieth century by the mass migration to Northern cities of blacks in search of employment. Nevertheless, Washington remained a strong force in political and educational circles and served as the chief advisor for black affairs to both Presidents Theodore Roosevelt and William Taft.

See also Du Bois, W.E.B.; Lynching.

Rebekah Lee

WASPs

WASP, an acronym standing for White Anglo-Saxon Protestant, is sometimes used disparagingly to refer to whites in general, but it is also used to refer to the dominant ethnic group in the United States. Before 1830, the U.S. population was a relatively homogenous group (in terms of shared culture values), since the indigenous population had been devastated by disease introduced by Europeans, war, conquest, and famine, and peoples of African descent were subordinated by the system of slave labor in the South. As a result, the dominant ethnic group comprised people from an English and Protestant background. WASPs were able to force subsequent ethnic groups to adapt to their cultural paradigm. In their book, *Beyond the Melting Pot: The Negroes, Puerto Ricans, Jews, Italians, and Irish of New York City* (1970), Nathan Glazer and Daniel P. Moynihan wrote, "These original [sic] Americans already had a frame in their minds, which became a frame in reality, that placed and ordered those who came after them. It was important to be white, of British origin, and Protestant. If one was all three, then even if one was an immigrant, one was really not an immigrant, of not for long" (15). WASPs, as the dominant ethnic group, see themselves as the "old" Americans, or "old stock." The Anglo group has not been able to exert total dominance, however, because other racial and ethnic groups have contributed to the cultural "frame of mind" in the United States. Yet, WASPs have virtually been able to monopolize most positions of power in the economy and polity to this day. Minority groups continue to increase their influence in American culture and society, but WASPs still are over-represented in positions of power in the United States.

See also Melting Pot.

Further Reading

Glazer, Nathan, and Daniel Patrick Moynihan. *Beyond the Melting Pot: The Negroes, Puerto Ricans, Jews, Italians, and Irish of New York City.*

Michael Roberts

Welfare Dependency

Before 1996, Aid to Families with Dependent Children (AFDC) was the major American welfare program. This program provided money to poor families, primarily those headed by single mothers with children. In 1996, AFDC was replaced by Temporary Assistance for Needy Families (TANF), a program that provides short-term benefits and requires that most recipients work. This change was widely known as welfare reform. While the term *welfare* has been used extensively to refer to AFDC and TANF, it can be used to refer to any number of programs. For example, in the mid-1990s, a survey found that Americans identified numerous programs, from school lunches to Medicare to Food Stamps, as constituting welfare. Some social critics also call tax breaks for corporations corporate welfare. Therefore, it is important to specify which social programs are being discussed when either welfare and welfare dependency is referred to.

Proponents of welfare reform argued that AFDC acted as a kind of narcotic, creating a destructive dependency on the state. Some critics, such as sociologist Charles Murray, argued that AFDC encouraged the formation of single-parent families and fostered socially undesirable behavior among recipients and their children. Other critics note that charges of "welfare dependency" tend to be leveled against African American women and their families more often than at white women. Feminist scholars such as Nancy Fraser and Linda Gordon further argued that dependency is, in fact, the normal human condition—everyone is in some way dependent on the labor of others. Why should dependency, then, be stigmatized for poor women?

Before the 1960s, minorities, particularly black women, were disproportionately denied welfare benefits. Through a series of court rulings and social movements, welfare eligibility became more open and black women—who are disproportionately poor—began to receive a larger share of welfare benefits. As welfare became associated with black women, public support for the program declined. By the 1980s and early 1990s, phrases such as "Welfare Queen" and "welfare dependency" carried strong racial overtones. In 1996, the entitlement to welfare was eliminated.

See also Losing Ground: American Social Policy, 1950–1980.

Further Reading

Murray, Charles. *Losing Ground: American Social Policy, 1950–1980.* New York: Basic Books, 1984.

Robin Roger-Dillon

West Side Story

Originally a highly acclaimed Broadway musical, with memorable music by Leonard Bernstein, *West Side Story* is a 1961 film based on William Shakespeare's play *Romeo and Juliet.* The story was conceived by Jerome Robbins, who also directed and choreographed the original Broadway production. The film received many accolades and awards, including an Academy of Motion Picture Arts and Sciences Award for best picture and best supporting actress (Rita Moreno) and actor (George Chakiris). *West Side Story* is the story of young lovers who must face tremendous odds to be together. The story takes place in New York City, where rival gangs, the Jets and Sharks, battle for turf rights and respect. Puerto Rican American Maria and Polish American Tony discover a mutual attraction, only to realize that their union would be quite controversial, because they are enemies due to their affiliation with rival gangs.

West Side Story, an instant classic, is often praised for presenting characters from a variety of racial and ethnic backgrounds. The United States was in the early stages of adapting to racial integration when the film was released in 1961. *West Side Story* served as a microcosm of the state of race relations in the United States. Despite the popularity of the film and the diversity of the cast, it has been criticized for its stereotypical depiction of Puerto Ricans. Puerto Ricans were depicted as American newcomers who were anxious to take advantage of the resources available in the United States, even if through violent means. There were few prominent images of Puerto Ricans before the release of *West Side Story*, so the film perpetuated the notion that all Puerto

Ricans live in economically disadvantaged barrios, where gang membership is standard practice. Ultimately, the gang warfare between the Jets and the Sharks in the film sent the message that America was not quite ready for interethnic/interracial relations. Only after Tony is killed do the two opposing groups seriously contemplate trying to bridge the racial/ethnic divide between them.

See also Hispanics, Prejudice and Discrimination against; Films and Racial Stereotypes; Hollywood and Minority Actors; Music Industry, Racism in.

Romney S. Norwood

Wheeler-Howard Act

See Indian Reorganization Act of 1934 (IRA).

White Attacks on Black Slaves

See Slave Revolts and White Attacks on Black Slaves.

White Flight

The term *White flight* is used to describe the process of whites leaving central city areas for suburban residences. This flight is often described as a response to minorities' movement into predominantly white neighborhoods after the passage of key civil rights laws and the 1968 Fair Housing Act. But the reality is that much of the population shift occurred well before these laws were passed. Directly after World War II, a tremendous amount of financial resources were invested in housing construction, and most of this new construction occurred in suburban areas. White Americans were poised to take advantage of this new construction.

Another process, one of ethnic succession, was taking place in central cities. As whites were moving to the suburbs to the newly constructed homes, the older housing stock left behind in the central cities was beginning to be occupied by nonwhites who had lower incomes. Still, the fact that very few families of color with similar income levels were present in the new suburban communities suggests that white flight was racially motivated, at least in part. Recent research indicates that it is motivated by concerns about property values, crime, graffiti, and drug use in communities that are experiencing an increase in racial diversity.

See also Fair Housing Act of 1968; Housing Discrimination; Residential Segregation.

Romney S. Norwood

White-Supremacist Movement in the United States

The white-supremacist movement in the United States is composed of a variety of hate groups whose common ideology is that whites, as a race, are superior. Supremacists vehemently argue against well-documented and scientifically grounded facts indicating that differences between races are based on what sociologists call a "social construct." That is, the meaning attached to physical differences between races is socially, not biologically, determined. For example, there are many differences between people: hair color, eye color, skin color, and so forth. These color differences, however, are essentially meaningless. The rules and norms that a society or culture associates with any differences are the key to understanding how people in that particular society or culture will behave toward the group identified as being different. Thus, each society decides which differences are important and which will be ignored.

White supremacists attach extreme significance to differences in skin color. They make the claim that the white race is superior. In making their arguments, supremacists try to associate skin color with other qualities of people, such as intelligence, beauty, and evil. There is no scientific evidence, biological or otherwise, for any of these claims. For example, supremacists argue that "pure" whites are always more intelligent, more beautiful, and the essence of good. Regardless of their views, there are no pure races. Indeed, it is scientifically impossible to describe one racial group to the exclusion of all others. One cannot use physical characteristics such as eye color, hair color, or skin color to describe one race that eliminates all others. As previously stated, race is a socially constructed term, not a biologically derived term. Additionally, difficulties arise in trying to racially categorize the offspring of interracial couples.

White supremacists have great difficulty in distinguishing among races. This was an issue as far back as the 1700s for slave owners in the South. By the beginning of the 1700s, many Southern states adopted what is called the "one-drop rule" still found in the rhetoric of supremacists today. This rule meant that any person with one drop of black blood would be considered black regardless of how that person looks. While this may appear easy to follow, in practice, even with today's advanced science, it is literally impossible to differentiate races using blood (Schaefer 2001, 258–259).

While the dominance of the white race is essential to understanding supremacists, they also argue that Jews are the ultimate threat. They see the Jewish people as having taken control of every aspect of society. This includes the government, the media, and economic systems. Indeed, they often refer to the United States as the Zionist Occupied Government. This supposed control that Jews have is also seen as somehow being a direct threat to the white race.

Although there are no well-accepted figures on the number of white-supremacist groups, some research has identified about 330 white-supremacist groups in the United States, with a combined active membership of approximately 40,000 people. However, other figures are widely cited as well. For example, the Southern Poverty Law Center has recently identified about 500 groups that could be classified as white supremacist. In addition, countless other people may be sympathetic to supremacists' arguments: reading their literature, listening to their music, supporting their efforts through donations, viewing their Internet sites, and so forth. Regardless, they all have a common theme of promoting hate for anyone who does not fit their idea of the world. Many of these groups are exceedingly violent or have been in the past.

Classification of White-Supremacist Groups

Typically, white supremacist groups are divided into four categories: the Ku Klux Klan, neo-Nazis, the Christian Identity Church movement, and the militia movement.

Ku Klux Klan (KKK). The KKK is the oldest and most well known white-supremacist organization in the United States. Its roots can be traced to the Reconstruction period just after the Civil War. The KKK was very violent at that time. They mercilessly lynched and terrorized blacks during what are known as night rides. The KKK, however, soon became extinct, since the purpose of the Klan was being served by the widespread Jim Crow segregation laws that institutionalized racism and kept whites in power. During the early 1920s, the KKK reached its high point, with having more than five million members. This is partially due to the immense popularity of the film *Birth of a Nation* (1915) (a historically distorted film on the KKK during Reconstruction) and on an image of the Klan as a fraternal organization. However, by the end of the 1920s, the group dwindled to a membership of 350,000 because of the Depression, internal squabbling, and financial scandals.

The civil rights movement of the 1950s and 1960s continued to have an adverse affect on Klan membership. It is estimated that in 1965 there were 65,000 members of the KKK. However, as the KKK continued its terrorizing, their membership drastically decreased. The following are three examples of the terrorist acts for which the KKK was responsible in the 1960s. First, the KKK was implicated in the murders of three young men (one black) who went to Mississippi in an attempt to increase black voter registration. Second, the KKK was directly linked to a bombing of a church in which four young black girls were killed. Last, the KKK was responsible for assaults on freedom riders, groups of blacks and whites who defied Jim Crow segregation laws by illegally riding together on segregated buses in Southern states. By the 1970s, the Klan had dropped to a low of approximately 1,500 members.

Recently, the Klan has tried to change its image from one of a terrorist group based on hatred to that of a more clean-cut, law-abiding mainstream organization. David Duke, who was elected to the Louisiana legislature, in 1989 personifies this image, but Duke's 2004 arrest for mail fraud and tax charges will likely have a negative influence on the Klan. Current membership is said to be about 6,000.

Neo-Nazis. George Lincoln Rockwell founded the American Nazi party in 1958. Rockwell was assassinated in 1967, and the party broke off into various branches. The New Order, formerly the National Socialist White People's Party, is the offshoot of the earlier Nazi party. Matthias Koehl is currently leading the party, and "the organization remains the most strictly committed to Nazi ideals, has new members pledge their loyalty to a statue of Hitler, and maintains international contacts through the World Union of National Socialists" (Ferber 1999, 349).

Another active neo-Nazi group is National Alliance, formerly headed by William Pierce. Pierce's novel, *The Turner Diaries*, written under the name Andrew MacDonald, was read by domestic terrorist Timothy McVeigh, who was responsible for the bombing of the federal building in Oklahoma City in 1995. The novel portrays white supremacists as exceedingly agitated over federal gun-control legislation, leading them to blow up FBI Headquarters. A copy of one page of this book was found on McVeigh when he was arrested for the bombing. Pierce, who has recently died, denied any involvement with the bombing.

Another branch of the neo-Nazi movement is the skinheads. They first became known in England in the early 1970s. Skinheads have since expanded to continental Europe, the United States, and Australia. In the United States, the movement began in the early 1980s. Skinheads are generally associated with extreme violence: "Skinheads have been responsible for dozens of murders in the United States, most recently the murder of a police officer and a West African man in two separate incidents in Denver, Colorado" (Ferber 1999, 349). The outward appearance of skinheads is generally quite obvious, owing to their outlandish styles, including shaved heads, combat boots, and tattoos of Nazi symbols. However, they are most noted for their hate music known as "oi." They are also quite active on the Internet. There are approximately 70,000 active members worldwide and approximately 3,500 racist skinheads in the United States. Spinoff groups such as Hammerskin Nation are also associated with skinheads and the white-supremacist movement.

Another quality of neo-Nazi groups is that they generally do not accept exceedingly well documented facts about the Holocaust. They argue that either the Holocaust did not occur or that its horrors are drastically overstated. Often they argue that the Holocaust was a myth or some sort of gross exaggeration used to gain sympathy for Jews.

The Christian Identity Church Movement. This movement, just like the neo-Nazis' revisionist ideas of the Holocaust, drastically alters historical facts and the interpretation of those facts. They reconstruct Christian doctrine and history to conform to the ideology of the white-supremacist movement. Indeed, the Christian Identity Church movement completely changes the essence of Christian theology to its polar opposite—from a message of love to a message of hate. Christian Identity essentially argues that white Europeans are God's chosen and will lead the Aryan nations against the Satanic Jews. They also teach that nonwhites are "pre-adamic mud people" without souls.

The Christian Identity Church movement was organized in the late 1970s, although some identity doctrine can be traced to earlier times. One anti-Semitic group based in Hayden Lake, Aryan Nations, a paramilitary organization with a few hundred members, has been led by Richard Butler. Recently, however, Butler named a successor, Harold Ray Redfaeirn of Ohio's white-supremacist Church of the Sons of YHVH. Redfaeirn is exceedingly violent and served six years in prison after being convicted of aggravated robbery and attempted aggravated murder in the shooting of a Dayton police officer in 1985. Also, on the Web, he shows sympathy for Islamic terrorist organizations Hamas and Islamic Jihad.

One important event often used by white supremacists to justify violence can be traced to Christian Identity member Randy Weaver. In 1992, he sold an illegal firearm to Bureau of Alcohol, Tobacco, and Firearm agents. Weaver later refused to be arrested and took his family to a cabin in Ruby Ridge, Idaho.

In a standoff with federal agents, his fourteen-year-old son and a federal agent were killed. Weaver surrendered the next day, but not before his pregnant wife was killed by a federal sniper.

The Militia Movement. The militia movement includes a network of groups who refuse to accept the government of the United States as sovereign. There are at least fifteen thousand members in these militias spread out among forty states. They vehemently argue against gun control and are, in general, preparing for a showdown with the federal government. These militias are paramilitary in organization and are essentially vigilante groups. They see the local sheriff as the only authority. While not all militias are associated with the white-supremacist movement, many are. As Ferber (1999, 350) states, "Militias are the direct descendants of the Posse Comitatus, a group of activists who embrace Christian Identity doctrine with an antigovernment agenda. . . . Some militia organizations, such as the Montana Freemen, believe that the true Constitution protects only whites, and they do not recognize the Thirteenth and Fourteenth Amendments."

Recent Studies

Overall, white supremacists attempt to construct an entirely different view of the world based on their hate ideology. These views force them to twist basic historical facts to fit their vision of the world. This can easily be seen in a variety of social-research studies focusing on supremacist groups. These studies often examine supremacist literature, media appearances, or Internet site information (i.e., content analysis).

One study was conducted by Berbrier (2000), who examined hundreds of archival records, several white-supremacist periodicals, transcripts from media appearances, and discourse in mainstream media. His work shows how supremacists attempt to portray themselves as victims. First, supremacists argue that whites, not blacks, are the oppressed victims of discrimination; for example, whites are seen as being subjected to a double standard, and their survival is at issue. Documentary evidence about the oppression of minorities is discarded and replaced with the revisionist ideology that it is actually whites who are oppressed. David Duke, for example, created an organization called the National Association for the Advancement of White People (NAAWP) with an obvious and admitted association with the National Association for the Advancement of Colored People (NAACP). According to Mitch Berbrier (2000, 180) Duke claimed that "gains won by this organization [NAACP] on behalf of African Americans came at the expense of Whites and that the NAACP is actively 'seeking discriminatory policies' while the NAAWP seeks 'greater racial understanding and goodwill.' "

White-supremacist groups also argue that the United States is taking away the rights of white people and that whites are being denied the right to have their own culture. Berbrier (2000, 180) quotes Thom Robb (leader of the KKK), from his appearance on the television show *Geraldo*, "The issue isn't who's superior. . . . Even if we [whites] were nothing but a race of cave men, we still have a right to preserve our heritage and culture and give that to our children. Nobody has the right to deny that from us. And that is the attempt that's being done today."

Another way in which these groups try to portray themselves as victims is the claim that they are "excluded from pride; stigmatized and shamed." Berbrier (2000, 182) cites an example in a white-supremacist periodical, *The Populist Observer*: "Blacks, Orientals, Indians and Hispanics are taught to love their history, while Whites are being taught to hate their own." White supremacists further the image by insisting that this leads to low self-esteem and eventually will threaten the survival of the white race.

Such verbiage is carefully constructed to emphasize that the white race is victimized, but it clearly fails to acknowledge the true message behind these views—a message of intolerance and hatred. As Berbrier (2000, 182) states, "White supremacist literature is designed precisely to speak very abstractly about pride and heritage preservation, and as little as possible concretely about hatred for others or discomfort with difference."

Another way to study the vision of white supremacists is through their Internet sites. White-supremacist groups have been active on the Internet. One study uses an innovative methodology to study white-supremacist groups. Burris et al. (2000) examined the character and frequency of links from supremacist Web sites to other Web sites. They found that four sites were most "central": Stormfront, Zundelsite, Resistance Records, and National Alliance. Stormfront is run by the successor to David Duke, Don Black. He, like Duke, tries to present a different, cleaner image. Zundelsite is run by a German-born Canadian, Ernst Zundel, who is an outspoken Nazi sympathizer and denies the existence of the Holocaust. Resistance Records is the site for the leading producer of white-power "oi" music. National Alliance is a white supremacist organization founded by William Pierce and is based in West Virginia. These sites, which have the most links to them from other supremacist sites, offer the typical messages of hate. While the Internet offers these groups some freedom to spread their messages of hate, it also offers an opportunity for social scientists' careful study of those messages and oversight by law enforcement to ensure their activities do not go beyond the boundaries of the law. Whether the message is overtly stated or carefully hidden, messages of bigotry and hatred based on racial and ethnic prejudice are the basis of these organizations.

See also Anti-Semitism in the United States; Duke, David; Hate Crimes; Ku Klux Klan (KKK); Oklahoma City Federal Building Bombing; Neo-Nazism; Skinheads; White-Supremacist Underground; Zionist Occupied Government (ZOG).

Further Reading

Berbrier, Mitch. "The Victim Ideology of White Supremacists and White Separatists in the United States." *Sociological Focus* 33, no. 2 (2000): 175–191.

Burris, Val, Emery Smith, and Ann Strahm. "White Supremacist Networks on the Internet." *Sociological Focus* 33, no. 2 (2000): 215–235.

Daniels, Jesse. *White Lies: Race, Class, Gender, and Sexuality in White Supremacist Discourse.* New York: Routledge, 1997.

Ferber, Abby L. "The White Supremacist Movement in the United States Today." In *Race and Ethnic Conflict: Contending Views on Prejudice, Discrimination, and Eth-*

noviolence. 2nd ed., edited by Fred L. Pincus and Howard J. Ehrlich. Boulder, CO: Westview, 1999.

Ferber, Amy. *White Man Falling: Race, Gender, and White Supremacy.* New York: Rowman & Littlefield, 1998.

Knickerbocker, Brad. "Setbacks for White-Supremacist Groups." *The Christian Science Monitor* 10 (January 2003): 2.

Schaefer, Richard T. *Sociology.* 7th ed. New York: McGraw-Hill, 2001.

John Eterno

White-Supremacist Underground

In the United States, the white-supremacist underground is widespread and made up of dozens of hate groups that undertake secret or covert activities and operations, whether on their own or in alliance with other groups, to advance their political and social agendas. Some of the most well known of these are Aryan Nation and its prison organization, Aryan Brotherhood; White Aryan Resistance (WAR) and its youth wing, Aryan Youth Movement; the Order; the Montana Militia; the National Alliance; the Klu Klux Klan; and Skinheads, who form a loosely affiliated network of youth gangs. The white-supremacist movement is motivated by a wide range of racist and anti-Semitic ideologies, including white power and white separatism, National Socialism, and Christian Identity. The underground promotes itself by holding annual conferences and festivals, organizing domestic-terrorist training camps, maintaining telephone hotlines, publishing books and newsletters, sponsoring youth- and prison-outreach programs, maintaining Internet Web sites, and promoting white-power culture, including white-power rock music.

The white-supremacist underground has been influential in far-right political culture. The Christian Identity movement, which argues that whites are God's chosen people, has created links between white supremacists and some far-right Christian extremists. In addition, some leaders, such as David Duke, once a Grand Wizard of the Klan and later a member of Congress, advocate for the mainstreaming of white supremacism. However, according to the Anti-Defamation League, the largest and most organized white-supremacist group in recent years has been the underground group the National Alliance, founded by William Pierce (1933–2002), the author of *The Turner Diaries*, an apocalyptic novel that depicts an Aryan revolution. This novel is said to have inspired Timothy McVeigh to bomb the federal building in Oklahoma City in 1995. A number of other groups, including the Klan, Aryan Nation, WAR, the National Alliance and the Montana Militia, have advocated antigovernment action. The underground has also created criminal gang networks, such as the Nazi Low Riders, which is affiliated with the prison group the Aryan Brotherhood. The white-supremacist underground has inspired countless hate crimes against African Americans, Jews, immigrants, gays, and many other groups.

See also Anti-Semitism in the United States; Duke, David; Hate Crimes; Ku Klux Klan (KKK); Oklahoma City Federal Building Bombing; Neo-Nazism;

Skinheads; White-Supremacist Movement in the United States; Zionist Occupied Government (ZOG).

Victoria Pitts

Wovoka

See Ghost Dance Religion; Sioux Outbreak of 1890.

WRA

See War Relocation Authority (WRA).

Y

Yellow Peril

The Yellow Peril is one of the most sinister stereotypes of Asians and Asian Americans. The Yellow Peril may have originated from a painting completed in 1895 by Kaiser Wilhelm II of Germany that depicted the menace to nations of Europe and their holiest possessions—civilizations and Christianity—by heathen of the Orient. But the origins of the idea of the Yellow Peril can be traced to the European imagination long before Wilhelm II's articulation, perhaps as early as the fifth century B.C., arising from the Greek-Persian conflict, or in the thirteenth century A.D., when Mongols devastated portions of Europe. The Yellow Peril was a means of defining European identity and a justification of European expansion and colonization.

In the American context, the notion of Yellow Peril suggests that Asians were seen as a threat to white-dominated society. Such a threat takes the material form of physical danger, economic competition with white labor, moral degeneracy, and sexual conquest. It signifies the irrational fear of Oriental conquest, with its racial and sex fantasy overtones. While not the first Yellow Peril character, the literary and cinematic character the diabolic Dr. Fu Manchu, created by British author "Sax Rohmer" (a.k.a. Arthur Sarsfield Ward) in *The Mystery of Fu Manchu* (1913; American title, *The Insidious Dr. Fu Manchu*), is the archetype of the Yellow Peril image. The Yellow Peril is created to demarcate racial lines, to reinforce white supremacy, and to alert against Asian invasion of white culture and society.

See also Alien Land Laws on the West Coast; Chinese Exclusion Act of 1882; Fu Manchu.

Philip Yang

Yellows

"Yellows" or "High Yellows" were terms used to describe light-skinned mulattos, people of both black and white racial heritage, who might be able to pass for white only. The United States is a nation of individuals from a wide variety of racial and ethnic backgrounds. Reflecting this diversity, classification of individuals along socially constructed racial groups has been prevalent, and the history of such classification systems informs on the historical pathways of intercultural relations. Before the twentieth century, Southern legislatures typically clarified race dichotomously as black and white, based on visible physical appearances. The mulattos were considered white when they had light skin, while those who had darker skins were classified as black. However, a concern was raised, as the population of mulattos grew, that many mixed people were "passing" as whites. To address this concern, many Southern states adopted the "one-drop" rule, in which blacks were defined as individuals with any black blood at all; hence, all mulattos were considered black under this rule. Other states defined blackness in terms of the percentage of black blood in an individual's heritage.

Still, the variability in physical attributes among those defined as "black" continued to be acknowledged. The light-skinned mulattos designated as "Yellows" were frequently preferred over their darker-skinned counterparts in urban service industries. However, they were also associated with the sin of miscegenation, which was perceived to selectively breed the weaknesses of both races. Yellows, therefore, were unwelcome in both black and white communities.

See also Mulatto; One-Drop Rule.

Daisuke Akiba

Z

Zionist Occupied Government (ZOG)

Since 1980, proponents of ideologies espousing white supremacy, separatism, and dominance have formed new groups and reorganized existing white racist associations. Their meetings, publications, and Web sites are filled with calls for action to stop the advance of the allegedly "inferior" races (defined as "non-Aryans," "coloreds and Jews," and non-Europeans) who no longer "know their place" and are "taking over" American society and allegedly destroying white people's culture or civilization and plotting genocide against whites. Two central contentions in these "white-power" groups' belief system are that (1) two "races"—Aryans and Jews—are enemies locked in a long mortal combat, with Jews trying to destroy Aryans; and (2) the Jews now have gotten the upper hand in the struggle by secretly gaining control over the government of the United States and a few other countries. In fact, white racist organizations like the Aryan Nations or National Alliance often use the acronym "ZOG," which stands for "Zionist (Jewish) Occupied Government" when they refer to the federal government or Washington, DC. They urge their followers to resist or fight all U.S. government agencies, policies, and politicians that they believe Jews have corrupted or manipulated to harm whites. Their goal is to "take back" the reigns of power and governmental control from the Jews and others seeking racial equality and integration and to reinstitute white dominance. Conspiracy theories about Jews allegedly trying to gain control over a nation, or even the whole world, have a long history. Claims about "ZOG" are an update and recycling of false charges against Jews from an old anti-Semitic forged document know as "The Protocols of the Elders of Zion" and from the propaganda circulated in Nazi-era Europe. By pointing to some Jews (or people of Jewish ancestry) who are influential politically or outspoken on civil rights, white supremacists try to make it appear that a "Jewish race" is the enemy of white people.

See also Anti-Semitism in the United States; White-Supremacist Movement in the United States.

Charles Jaret

ZOG

See Zionist Occupied Government (ZOG).

Zoot Suit Riots

The Zoot Suit riots, the most important twentieth-century example of white violence against Mexican Americans, occurred in 1943 in Los Angeles, the city with the largest Mexican population in the United States. The riots were so named because their victims, young Mexican American males, followed the fad of wearing long, loose-fitting jackets with wide shoulders, baggy trousers, and flat-topped hats. On June 3, 1943, two incidents precipitated the riots. Some Mexican boys, on their way home from a police-sponsored club meeting, were attacked by a group of white hoodlums in a Los Angeles neighbor-

Two young victims of the four-day Zoot Suit riot, June 20, 1943.

AP/Wide World Photos.

hood. Second, the same evening, eleven white sailors on leave were attacked, and one of them hurt badly, by assailants whom the victims identified as Mexican youths. When the police found no one to arrest as suspects, in retaliation, about two hundred white marines, soldiers, and sailors drove through the Mexican area in taxis and randomly attacked Mexican young men on the streets. Cars passing on the streets were stopped, and Filipino and black riders as well as Mexicans were pushed out and punched at random. Some Mexican men were stripped of their clothes, left cowering on the pavements and bleeding, surrounded by mobs of men. But the police did nothing to stop it. Instead, they arrested the Mexican victims. The media incited the riots by emphasizing a mass retaliation by Mexican zoot-suiters. As a result, the bloody attacks lasted four days.

Although an incident involving white sailors and Mexican young men triggered the riots, Anglos' deep-seated prejudice against Mexicans contributed to the racial aggressions. Also, the Los Angeles media's sensational accounts of Mexican young gangs in the previous years contributed to the riots.

See also Hispanics, Prejudice and Discrimination against; Mexican Americans, Prejudice and Discrimination against; Mexican Americans, Violence against; Race Riots.

Further Reading

Garcia, F. Chris, and Rudolph P. de la Garza. *The Chicano Political Experiences: Three Perspectives*. North Scituate, MA: Duxbuy, 1977.

McWilliams, Carey. *North from Mexico: Spanish-Speaking People in the United States*. New York: Greenwood Press, 1968.

Pyong Gap Min

APPENDIX

PRIMARY DOCUMENTS

1. Slave Codes of the State of Georgia, 1848
2. Excerpts from Treaty of Guadalupe Hidalgo (1848)
3. The Emancipation Proclamation (1863)
4. Fourteenth Amendment (June 1866)
5. The Chinese Exclusion Act of 1882
6. Excerpt from the Indian Allotment Act (1887)
7. *Plessy v. Ferguson* (1896)
8. The National Origins Act of 1924 (Johnson-Reed Act)
9. Executive Order 9066 (February 1942)
10. *Brown v. Board of Education* (May 1954)
11. The Civil Rights Act of 1964
12. Excerpt from the Immigration and Naturalization Act of 1965
13. Voting Rights Act of 1965
14. Executive Order 11246 (1965), as Amended
15. Excerpt from the Kerner Commission Report (1968)

ORIGINAL WRITINGS

16. Excerpt from President Abraham Lincoln's "Letter to James C. Conkling" (August 26, 1863)
17. Excerpt from W.E.B. Du Bois's *The Souls of Black Folk* (1903)
18. Excerpts from Madison Grant's *The Passing of the Great Race* (1916)

19. Excerpt from Gunnar Myrdal's *An American Dilemma: The Negro Problem and Modern Democracy* (1944)

20. Excerpt from Martin Luther King Jr.'s "Letter from a Birmingham Jail" (1963)

21. Excerpt from Martin Luther King Jr.'s "I Have a Dream" Speech (1963)

22. Excerpt from Malcolm X's *The Autobiography of Malcolm X* (1965)

23. Excerpt from James Mooney's *The Ghost-Dance Religion and the Sioux Outbreak of 1890* (1965)

24. Excerpt from the Aryan Nations Platform

25. Excerpt from the American Sociological Association's "The Importance of Collecting Data and Doing Social Scientific Research on Race" (2003)

26. Poem by Haunani-Kay Trask, "Settlers, Not Immigrants" (2000)

PRIMARY DOCUMENTS

1. Slave Codes of the State of Georgia, 1848

Africans were brought to North America from the early sixteenth century as indentured servants or "bondservants." In the middle of the seventeenth century, Southern colonies began to develop a hereditary system of slavery based on race, to tie African workers to permanent bondage. By the middle of the eighteenth century, all Southern colonies had established this new race-based slavery system. They further developed increasingly restrictive statues, known as slave codes, that limited the rights of slaves.

SEC. I. CAPITAL OFFENCES.

1. Capital crimes when punished with death.

The following shall be considered as capital offences, when committed by a slave or free person of color: insurrection, or an attempt to excite it; committing a rape, or attempting it on a free white female; murder of a free white person, or murder of a slave or free person of color, or poisoning of a human being; every and each of these offences shall, on conviction, be punished with death.

2. When punished by death, or at discretion of the court.

And the following, also, shall be considered as capital offences, when committed by a slave or free person of color: assaulting a free white person with intent to murder, or with a weapon likely to produce death; maiming a free white person; burglary, or arson of any description; also, any attempt to poison a human being; every and each of these offences shall, on conviction, be punished with death, or such other punishment as the court in their judgement shall think most proportionate to the offence, and best promote the object of the law, and operate as a preventive for like offences in future.

3. Punishment for manslaughter.

And in case a verdict of manslaughter shall be found by the jury, the punishment shall be by whipping, at the discretion of the court, and branded on the cheek with the letter M.

4. Punishment of slaves for striking white persons.

If any slave shall presume to strike any white person, such slave upon trial and conviction before the justice or justices, according to the direction of this act, shall for the first offence suffer such punishment as the said justice or justices shall in his or their discretion think fit, not extending to life or limb; and for the second offence, suffer death: but in case any such slave shall grievously wound, maim, or bruise any white person, though it shall be only the first offence, such slave shall suffer death.

5. When the striking a white person justifiable.

Provided always, that such striking, wounding, maiming, or bruising, be not done by the command, and in defense of the person or property of the owner or other person have the care and government of such slave, in which case the slave shall be wholly excused, and the owner or other person having the care and government of such slave, shall be answerable, as if the act has been committed by himself.

6. Punishment for burning or attempting to burn houses in a town.

The willful and malicious burning or setting fire to, or attempting to burn a house in a city, town, or village, when committed by a slave or free person of color, shall be punished with death.

7. Punishment for burning or attempting to burden houses in the country.

The willful and malicious burning a dwelling house on a farm or plantation, or elsewhere, (not in a city, town or village) or the setting fire thereto, in the nighttime, when the said house is actually occupied by a person or persons, with the intent to burn the same, when committed by a slave or free person of color, shall be punished by death.

8. Trials of offenders for arson.

The trial of offenders against the provisions of this act, shall be had in the same courts, and conducted in the same manner, and under the same rules and regulations as are provided by the several acts now in force in this state for the trial of capital offences, when committed by a slave or free person of color.

9. Punishment of free persons of color for inveigling slaves.

If any free person of color commits the offence of inveigling or enticing away any slave or slaves, for the purpose of, and with the intention to aid and assist such slave or slaves leaving the service of his or their owner or owners, or in going to another state, such person so offending shall, for each and every such offence, on conviction, be confined in the penitentiary at hard labor for one.

10. Punishment for circulating incendiary documents.

If any slave, Negro, mustizoe, or free person of color, or any other person, shall circulate, bring, or cause to be circulated or brought into this state, or aid or assist in any manner, or be instrumental in aiding or assisting in the circulation or bringing into this state, or in any manner concerned in any written or printed pamphlet, paper, or circular, for the purpose of exciting to insurrection, conspiracy, or resistance among the slaves, Negroes, or free persons of color of this state, against their owners or the citizens of this state, the said person or persons offending against this section of this act, shall be punished with death.

SEC. II. MINOR OFFENCES.

11. Punishment for teaching slaves or free persons of color to read.

If any slave, Negro, or free person of color, or any white person, shall teach any other slave, Negro, or free person of color, to read or write either written or printed characters, the said free person of color or slave shall be punished by fine and whipping, or fine or whipping, at the discretion of the court.

12. Punishment of free persons of color for trading with slaves.

If any slave or slaves, or free persons of color shall purchase or buy any of the aforesaid commodities from any slave or slaves, he, she, or they, on conviction thereof, before any justice of the peace, contrary to the true intent and meaning of this act, shall receive on his, her, or their bare back or backs, thirty-nine lashes, to be well laid on by a constable of said county, or other person appointed by the justice of the peace for that purpose: Provided, that nothing herein contained shall prevent any slave or slaves from selling poultry at any time without a ticket, in the counties of Liberty, McIntosh, Camden, Glynn, and Wayne.

13. Punishment of slaves for harboring slaves.

If any free person or any slave shall harbor, conceal, or entertain any slave that shall run away, or shall be charged or accused of any criminal matter, every free Negro, mulatto, and mustizoe, and every slave that shall harbor, conceal, or entertain any such slave, being duly convicted thereof according to the direction of this act, if a slave, shall suffer such corporeal punishment, not extending to life or limb, as the justice or justices who shall try such slave shall in his or their discretion think fit; and if a free person, shall forfeit the sum of thirty shillings for the first day, and three shillings for every day such slave shall have been absent from his or her owner or employer, to be recovered and applied as in this act hereafter directed.

14. Punishment of free persons of color for harboring slaves.

All free persons of color within this state, who shall harbor, conceal, or entertain a slave or slaves who shall be charged or accused or any criminal matter, or shall be a runaway, shall, upon conviction (in addition to the penalty already provided for in said section), be subject to the same punishment as slaves are under said section of the above recited act.

15. Constables authorized to search suspected premises for fugitive slaves.

Any lawful constable having reason to suspect that runaway slaves, or such Negroes who may be charged or accused of any criminal offence, are harbored, concealed, or entertained in the house or houses of such slaves or free persons of color, they or any of them are authorized to enter such houses, and make search for the said runaway or runaways, or accused criminal or criminals.

16. Persons of color not allowed to preach or exhort without written license.

No person of color, whether free or slave, shall be allowed to preach to, exhort, or join in any religious exercise with any persons of color, either free or slave, there being more that seven persons of color present. They shall first obtain a written certificate from three ordained ministers of the gospel of their own order, in which certificate shall be set forth the good moral character of the applicant, his pious deportment, and his ability to teach the gospel; having a due respect to the character of those persons to whom he is to be licensed to preach, said ministers to be members of the conference, presbytery, synod, or association to which the churches belong in which said colored preachers may be licensed to preach, and also the written permission of the justices of the inferior court of the county, and in counties in which the county town is incorporated, in addition thereto the permission of the mayor, or chief officer, or commissioners of such incorporation; such license not to be for a longer term than six months, and to be revocable at any time by the person granting it.

17. Punishment for preaching or exhorting without license.

Any free person of color offending against this provision, to be liable on conviction, for the first offence, to imprisonment at the discretion of the court, and to a penalty not exceeding five hundred dollars, to be levied on the property of the person of color; if this is insufficient, he shall be sentenced to be whipped and imprisoned at the discretion of the court: Provided, such imprisonment shall not exceed six months, and no whipping shall exceed thirty-nine lashes.

18. Prosecution by indictment.

Each offence under this act may be prosecuted by indictment in the superior court of the county in which the same shall have been committed, and the penalties shall be recoverable by qui tam action in the superior or inferior court, one half to the use of the informer, and the other to the use of the county academy.

19. Slaves giving information of design to poison, how rewarded.

Every Negro, mulatto, or mustizoe, who shall hereafter give information of the intention of any other slave to poison any person, or of any slave that hath furnished, procured or conveyed any poison to be administered to any persons, shall, upon conviction of the offender or offenders, be entitled to and receive from the public of this province, a reward of twenty shillings, to be paid him or her by the treasurer yearly and every year, during the abode of such Negro, mulatto, mustizoe in this province, on the day that such discovery was made, and shall also be exempted from the labor of his or her master on that day; and every justice before whom such information and conviction is made, is hereby required to give a certificate of every such information, which certificate shall entitle the informant to the reward aforesaid: Provide always, nevertheless, that no slave be convicted upon the bare information of any other slave, unless some circumstances or overt act appear, by which such information shall be corroborated to the satisfaction of the said justices and jury.

20. Punishment for giving false information.

In cases any slaves shall be convicted of having given false information, whereby any other slave may have suffered wrongfully, every such false informer shall be liable to, and suffer the same punishment as was inflicted upon the party accused.

21. Punishment of slaves for teaching other to poison.

In case any slave shall teach and instruct another slave in the knowledge of any poisonous root, plant, herb, or other sort of a poison whatever, he or she offending shall, upon conviction thereof, suffer death as a felon; and the slave or slaves so taught or instructed, shall suffer such punishment, not extending to life or limb, as shall be adjudged and determined by the justices and jury before whom such slave or slaves shall be tried.

22. Punishment of slaves for killing, marking, or branding cattle.

In case any slave or slaves shall be found killing, marking, branding, or driving any horse or neat cattle, contrary to the directions of this act, every such slave or slaves, being convicted thereof by the evidence of a white person, or of a slave, shall be punished by whipping on the bare back, not exceeding thirty-nine lashes, by order or warrant of any justice of the peace before whom the fact shall be proved.

23. Offences not defined, how punished.

All other offences committed by a slave or free person of color, either against persons or property, or against another slave or person of color, shall be punished at the discretion of the court before whom such slave or person of color shall be tried, such court having in view the principles of humanity in passing sentence, and in no case shall the same extend to life or limb.

ART. II. PROSECUTION OF OFFENCES.

SEC. I. COMMENCEMENT OF PROSECUTION.

24. Tribunal for the trial of free persons of color.

An act passed at Milledgeville on the sixteenth day of December, eighteen hundred and eleven, entitled an act to establish a tribunal for the trial of slaves within this state; the court therein established is hereby made a tribunal for offences committed by free persons of color, to all intents and purposes, as if the words free persons of color had been inserted in the caption, and every section of the said act to establish a tribunal for the trial of slaves within this state.

25. Arrests and trial of slaves and free persons of color.

Every slave or free person of color, charged with any offence contained in this act, shall be arrested and tried, pursuant to an act entitled, "An act to establish a tribunal for the trial of slaves within this state," passed the sixteenth day of December, eighteen hundred and eleven, and the seventh, eighth and ninth sections of this act, and shall receive sentence agreeably to the requisitions contained in this act.

26. Offences, how prosecuted.

Upon complaint being made to, or information received upon oath, by any justice of the peace, of any crime having been committed by any slave or slaves within the county where such justice is empowered to act, such justice shall, by warrant from under his hand, cause such slave or slaves to be brought before him, and give notice thereof, in writing, to any two or more of the nearest justices of the peace of said county, to associate with him on a particular day, in said notice to be specified, not exceeding three days from the date of said notice, for the trial of such slave or slaves; and the justices so assembled, shall forthwith proceed to the examination of a witness or witnesses, and other evidence, and in case the offender or offenders shall be convicted of any crime not capital, the said justices, or a majority of them, shall give judgement for the inflicting any corporeal punishment, not extending to the taking away life or member, as in their discretion may seem reasonable and just, and shall award and cause execution to be done accordingly; and in case it should appear to them, after investigation, that the crime or crimes wherewith such slave or slaves stand or stands charged, is a crime or crimes for which he, she, or they ought to suffer death, such slave or slaves shall immediately be committed to the public jail of said county, if any, provided it should be sufficient, or to the custody of the sheriff or said county, or to the nearest sufficient jail thereto.

27. Inferior court to be notified.

The said justices shall, within three days next thereafter, give notice, in writing, to one of the justices of the inferior court of said county, of such commitment, with the names of the witness or witnesses, and such justice of the inferior court shall, within three days after the receipt thereof, direct the sheriff of said county, whose duty it shall be to summon a jury of twelve free white persons of said county, to be drawn in the manner hereinafter pointed out, to attend in like manner.

28. Duty of justice notified.

When any justice of the inferior court shall have received notice of the commitment of any slave or slaves, or free person or persons of color, (under the description of a free Negro or Negroes, mulatto, or mustizoe), to jail, in pursuance of the second section of an act entitled, "An act to establish a tribunal for the trial of slaves in this state," passed the sixteenth day of December, eighteen hundred and eleven, it shall be the duty of the said justice of the inferior court, within three days after the receipt thereof, to give notice, in writing, of such commitment, to the justices of the inferior court, or a majority of them, together with the clerk of said court, requiring their attendance at the court house of said county, where such slave or slaves, or person or persons of color, as aforesaid, may have been committed, on a particular day, in said notice to be specified in writing, not exceeding ten days from the date of said notice.

29. Continuance may be granted for cause.

The said court, so constituted as a aforesaid, shall immediately proceed to such trial, unless it should appear necessary for the said court, either for the want of sufficient proof, or any other sufficient reason, to delay the same, as in their judgement may seem for the furtherance of justice.

30. Clerk of inferior court to act as prosecuting officer.

In all prosecutions for a capital offence against any slave or free person of color, the clerk of the inferior court shall act as the prosecuting officer in behalf of the sate.

31. Accusation to be preferred by clerk in writing.

It shall be the duty of such justices, clerk, and jurors, to attend accordingly, and the said court, when so assembled, shall cause the clerk of said court to commit the charge or accusation alleged against such slave or slaves in writing, therein particularly setting forth the time and place of the offence, and the nature thereof.

32. Record of proceedings, subpoenas for witnesses, rules of evidence.

It shall be the duty of the clerk to make a record of the proceedings against such slave or slaves, separated and distinct from other records of his office, and he shall also issue subpoenas and other writs necessary to procure the attendance of a witness or witnesses, at the instance of either party, and that in all cases respecting the admission of evidence against people of color, the rules shall be the same as heretofore practiced in this state.

SEC. II. TRIAL.

33. Jurors, how drawn and summoned.

The justices of the inferior court, at their regular terms, shall draw, in the manner pointed out by law, not more than thirty-six, nor less than twenty-six jurors, twenty-four of whom shall be directed by such justices of the court to be summoned as aforesaid, to attend at the day and place pointed out for the trial of such slave or slaves, in manner aforesaid; and in case a sufficient number of those summoned should not attend, the said court shall direct the panel to be made up by talesmen, and all defaulting jurors so summoned in the manner pointed out by this act, shall be fined as in other cases pointed out by law.

34. At what time jurors to be drawn.

So much of the eighth section of the before recited act, as requires, the justices of the inferior courts in this state to draw a jury of thirty-six, at their regular terms, for the trial of such slave or slaves, person or persons of color, as aforesaid, shall be, and the same is hereby repealed; and in lieu of such regular drawing of jurors, it shall be the duty of such justices, or a majority of the, forthwith after being notified of such commitment as aforesaid, to cause to be drawn fairly and impartially from the jury box the names of persons subject to serve as jurors, not less than twenty-six nor more than thirty-six jurors, who shall be summoned according to the requisitions of the before-recited act, to attend at the time and place pointed out for the trial of such slave or slaves, or person or persons of color, by the said justices of the inferior court.

35. Challenging jurors; number allowed state and defendant.

The owner or manager of such slave or slaves, shall have the right of challenging seven of the said number summoned, and the said court five on the part of the sate, and the remaining twelve shall proceed to the trial of such slave or slaves.

36. Oath of jurors.

As soon as the justices and jury shall be assembled, as aforesaid, in pursuance of the direction of this act, the said jury shall take the following oath:"I, A. B., do solemnly swear, in the presence of Almighty God, that I will truly and impartially try the prisoner or prisoners, brought upon his, her, or their trial, and a true verdict give according to evidence, to the best of my knowledge; so help me God."

37. Trial by jury.

The said court shall cause twelve persons of those summoned, to be empaneled and sworn (the usual oath on such occasions made and provided) as jurors, to whom the said charge or accusation, in writing, and the evidence, shall be submitted.

38. Jury failing to render verdict, proceedings.

If [in] any court held hereafter, within this state, for the trial of a slave or slaves, or free person or persons of color, the jury empaneled and sworn for such trial, shall, from any cause, fail to render a verdict, it shall and may be lawful for said court to adjourn to a succeeding day, not exceeding thirty days from the day of adjournment; and at the time of its adjournment, and before is shall adjourn, said court shall draw, agreeable to the provisions of the before-recited act, not less than twenty-six, and not more than thirty-six jurors, who shall be summoned to attend said adjournment, in the mode prescribed in the acts aforesaid; and the proceedings of said adjournment shall be in all respects the same as those pointed out in the before-recited acts.

39. Jury may be completed by talesman.

In all cases where a sufficient number of the jurors summoned shall fail to attend, it shall be lawful for the court to complete the requisite number by summoning talesmen.

SEC. III. EVIDENCE.

40. Persons considered competent witnesses.

On the trial of a slave or free person of color, any witness shall be sworn who believes in God and a future state of rewards and punishments.

41. Slaves, when competent witnesses.

The evidence of any free Indians, mulattoes, mustizoes, Negroes, or slaves, shall be allowed and admitted in all cases whatsoever, for or against another slave, accused of any crime or offence whatsoever, the weight of which evidence, being seriously considered and compared with all other circumstances attending the case, shall be left to the justices and jury.

42. Justices may compel the appearance and answer of witnesses.

The said justices, or any of them, are hereby authorized, empowered, and required, to summon and compel all persons whatsoever, to appear and give evidence upon the trial of any slave, and if any person shall neglect or refuse to appear, or appearing shall refuse to give evidence, or if any master or other person, who has the care and government of any slave, shall prevent and hinder any slave under his charge and government, from appearing and giving evidence in any matter depending before the justices and jury aforesaid, the said justices may, and they are hereby fully empowered and required, upon due proof made of such summons being served, to bind every such person offending as aforesaid, by recognizance, with one or more sufficient sureties, to appear at the next general court, to answer such their offence, and contempt, and for default of finding sureties to commit such offenders to prison, for any term not exceeding the space of two months.

SEC. IV. VERDICT, JUDGEMENT, AND SENTENCE.

43. Verdict and judgement.

The said jurors by their verdict shall say whether such slave or slaves are guilty or not guilty, and if a verdict of guilty should be returned by such jury, the court shall immediately pronounce the sentence of death by hanging, or some other punishment not amounting to death.

44. Sentence of death.

Whenever a slave or free person of color is brought before the inferior court to be tried for an offence deemed capital, it shall be the duty of said court to pass such sentence as may be pointed out by law for the offence of which slave or free person of color may be guilty.

45. Punishment to be proportionate to the offence.

In all cases where the jury, on the trial of any slave or free person of color, shall return a verdict of guilty, the court shall pass the sentence of death on such slave or free person of color, agreeably to the requisitions and subject to the same restrictions as are required by the before-recited act, or proceed to inflict such other punishment as in their judgement will be most proportionate to the offence, and best promote the object of the law, and operate as a preventive for [of] like offences in future.

46. Suspension of sentence in minor offences.

Where any jury shall find a verdict of guilty against any such slave or slaves, or person or persons of color as aforesaid, in pursuance of the fifth section of the act referred to in the preceding section, it shall and may be lawful for the said court to suspend the passing sentence against such slave or slaves, or person or persons of color as aforesaid, for any term of time not exceeding two day.

ART. III. CORRECTION OF ERRORS, PARDON, EXECUTIONS, AND COSTS.

SEC. I. CORRECTION OF ERRORS.

47. Exceptions may be taken; proceedings.

In all trials and proceedings before justices of the peace and justices of the interior courts, under any by virtue of the act passed on the sixteenth day of December, eighteen hundred and eleven, and of the act passed on the nineteenth day of December, eighteen hundred and sixteen, in relation to slaves and free persons of color, and of any acts amendatory thereof, when either party shall be dissatisfied with any decision of the court before whom such trial and proceedings may be had, affecting the real merits thereof, such party shall and may offer exceptions in writing to such decisions, which shall be signed by such party, or his or her attorney; and if the same shall be overruled by said court, the party making the exceptions may or twenty days' notice to the opposite party, or his or her attorney, apply to one of the judges of the superior court, and if such judge shall deem the exceptions sufficient, he shall forthwith issue a writ of certiorari to said justices, or to the clerk of the inferior court, as the case may be, requiring the proceedings in said matter to be certified and sent to the superior court next to be held in and for the county in which said proceedings or trial may have been had; and at the term of the court to which such proceedings shall be certified, said superior court shall determine thereon, and make such order, judgement and decisions, as shall be agreeable to law and justice.

48. When execution may be suspended.

When exceptions shall be offered in manner aforesaid, the said justices before whom said trials or proceedings may be, shall suspend the execution of their judgement and sentence for forty days; and when a certiorari shall be sanctioned in manner aforesaid, the judge issuing the same shall order the said judgement and sentence to be suspended until the final order and decision of said superior court shall be had in the cause.

49. When judge of superior court may fix day of execution.

Whenever a certiorari shall be granted agreeable to the provisions of the before-mentioned act, passed on the twenty-second day of December, eighteen hundred and twenty-nine, if sentence shall have been passed and a day fixed when the same shall be carried into effect by the inferior court before whom the slave or slaves, or free person or persons of color, were had and convicted; and if, after considering said certiorari, the judge of the superior court before whom the same may be, shall be of the opinion that the sentence of the inferior court should not be altered or disturbed, he is hereby authorized and directed to order the execution of said sentence on some other day than that fixed by said inferior court shall have passed before the final hearing and discussion of said certiorari.

50. When new trial may be granted; proceedings.

If the judge of the superior court before whom any *certiorari*, as contemplated by the before-recited act, passed on the twenty-second of December, eighteen hundred and twenty-nine, shall be argued and considered, shall, after considering the same, be of opinion that error has been committed in the court before, and that a new trial should be had, he shall pass such order as may be necessary to effect this object; and the inferior court to whom said order may be directed shall obey the same; and whenever a new trial shall be ordered, said inferior court shall assemble on the day to be specified in said order, shall draw a jury, have them summoned in the manner prescribed by the before-recited acts, and in all cases of a new trial, the presenting shall in all cases be the same as those presented in the before-mentioned acts.

51. Pardon of capital offences.

In every case of conviction, for a capital felony, the owner of the slave, or guardian of the free person of color convicted, may apply to the court before which the conviction shall have taken place, and obtain a suspension of the execution of the sentence, for the purpose of applying to the governor for a pardon, and it shall be in the power of the governor to grant said pardon.

52. Offences not capital, court may grant time to obtain pardon.

On a conviction for any other offence not punishable by death, the court may, at its discretion, grant a suspension of the execution of the sentence for the purpose of enabling the owner of a slave, or guardian of a free person of color, to apply to the governor for a pardon, or commutation of the punishment in such manner, and upon such terms and conditions as he may think proper to direct.

SEC. III. EXECUTIONS AND COSTS.

53. Execution of sentence.

All and every the constable and constables in the several parishes within this province, where any slave shall be sentenced to suffer death, or other punishment, shall cause execution to be done of all the orders, warrants, precepts, and judgements of the justices hereby appointed to try such slaves, for the charge and trouble of which the said constable or constables respectively shall be paid by the public, unless in such cases as shall appear to the said justice or justices to be malicious or groundless prosecutions, in which cases the said charges shall be paid by the prosecutors.

54. Officer may press slaves to aid in executing sentence.

And that no delay may happen in causing execution to be done upon such offending slave or slaves, the constable who shall be directed to cause execution to be done, shall be, and he is hereby empowered to press one or more slave or slaves in or near the place where such whipping or other corporeal punishment shall be inflicted, to whip or inflict such other corporeal punishment upon the offender or offenders; and such slave or slaves so pressed shall be obedient to, and observe all the orders and directions of the constable in and about the premises, upon pain of being punished by the said constable by whipping on the bare back not exceeding twenty lashes, which punishment the said constable is hereby authorized and empowered to inflict; and the constable shall, if he presses a Negro, pay the owner of the said Negro two shillings out of his fee for doing the said execution: and in cases capital, shall pay to the Negro doing the said execution the sum of two shillings, over and above the said fee to his owner.

55. State not liable to owner for slave executed.

The state shall in no instance be answerable for, or liable to pay the owner whatever for any Negro slave or slaves who may laws of this state.

56. Expenses of prosecution, when paid by master.

All expenses and fees chargeable by any of the public officers, for prosecuting any Negro slave or slaves, convicted of any crime, not capital, against the laws of this state, shall be paid by the owner or owners of such slave or slaves.

57. When paid by the count.

But in all cases where any slave shall be convicted of any crime whereby he, she, or they may suffer death, the expenses attending the trial and execution of such slave or slaves shall be paid by the county where they shall be executed.

58. Fee of officer executing sentence.

For whipping or other corporeal punishments not extending to life, the sum of five shillings; and for any punishment extending to life, the sum of fifteen shillings; and such other charges for keeping and maintaining such slaves, as are by the act for erecting the workhouse appointed; for levying of which charges against the prosecutor, the justices are hereby empowered to issue their warrant.

59. Clerk and sheriff's fees.

The following shall be the fees of the clerk in such cases, to wit:
Clerk's Fees.

For attending the court to draw jury	$1.25
For drawing up specifications of the charge	2.00
For attending each trial	1.25
For recording the proceedings of trial	87½
For copying order, or sentence, and delivering the same to the sheriff	50

And the following shall be the fees of sheriffs in such cases, to wit:
Sheriff's Fees.

For summoning jury	4.00
For attending each trial	1.25
For executing order of sentence of the court the same as contained in the general fee bill.	

2. Excerpts from Treaty of Guadalupe Hidalgo (1848)

The settlement of Anglos in Texas, Mexico, led to the independence of Texas from Mexico and then its annexation by the United States in 1845. The U.S. annexation of Texas led to the breakout of the Mexican-American War in May 1846. The war was closed by the Treaty of Guadalupe Hidalgo, by which the United States gained not only Texas but New Mexico and upper California.

Treaty of Peace, Friendship, Limits, and Settlement between the United States of America and the United Mexican States Concluded at Guadalupe Hidalgo, February 2, 1848; Ratification Advised by senate, with Amendments, March 10, 1848; Ratified by President, March 16, 1848; Ratifications Exchanged at Queretaro, May 30, 1848; Proclaimed, July 4, 1848.

In the Name of Almighty God:

The United States of America and the United Mexican States, animated by a sincere desire to put an end to the calamities of the war which unhappily exists between the two republics and to establish upon a solid basis relations of peace and friendship, which shall confer reciprocal benefits upon the citizens of both, and assure the concord, harmony, and mutual confidence wherein the two people should live, as good neighbors have for that purpose appointed their respective plenipotentiaries—that is to say, The President of the United States has appointed Nicholas P Trist, a citizen of the United States, and the President of the Mexican Republic has appointed Don Luis Gonzaga Cuevas, Don Bernardo Couto, and Don Miguel Atristain, citizens of the said republic, who, after a reciprocal communication of their respective full powers, have, under the protection of Almighty God, the author of peace, arranged, agreed upon, and signed the following:

Treaty of Peace, Friendship, Limits, and Settlement between the United States of America and the Mexican Republic.

. . .

ARTICLE VIII

Mexicans now established in territories previously belonging to Mexico, and which remain for the future within the limits of the United States, as defined by the present treaty, shall be free to continue where they now reside, or to remove at any time to the Mexican republic, retaining the property which they possess in the said territories, or disposing thereof, and removing the proceeds wherever they please, without their being subjected, on this account, to any contribution, tax, or charge whatever.

Those who shall prefer to remain in the said territories, may either retain the title and rights of Mexican citizens, or acquire those of citizens of the United States. But they shall be under the obligation to make their election within one year from the date of the exchange of ratifications of this treaty; and those who shall remain in the said territories after the expiration of that year, without having declared their intention to retain the character of Mexicans, shall be considered to have elected to become citizens of the United States.

In the said territories, property of every kind, now belonging to Mexicans not established there, shall be inviolably respected. The present owners, the heirs of these, and all Mexicans who may hereafter acquire said property by contract, shall enjoy with respect to it guarantees equally ample as if the same belonged to citizens of the United States.

ARTICLE IX

The Mexicans who, in the territories aforesaid, shall not preserve the character of citizens of the Mexican republic, conformably with what is stipulated in the preceding article, shall be incorporated into the Union of the United States, and be admitted at the proper time (to be judged of by the Congress of the United States) to the enjoyment of all the rights of citizens of the United States, according to the principles of the Constitution; and in the mean time shall be maintained and protected in the free enjoyment of their liberty and property, and secured in the free exercise of their religion without restriction.

ARTICLE X

[Stricken out by the U.S. Amendments]

ARTICLE XI

Considering that a great part of the territories which, by the present treaty, are to be comprehended for the future within the limits of the United States, is now occupied by savage tribes, who will hereafter be under the exclusive control of the government of the United States, and whose incursions within the territory of Mexico would be prejudicial in the extreme, it is solemnly agreed that all such incursions shall be forcibly restrained by the government of the United States whensoever this may be necessary; and that when they cannot be prevented, they shall be punished by the said government, and satisfaction for the same shall be exacted—all in the same way, and with equal diligence and energy, as if the same incursions were meditated or committed within its own territory, against its own citizens.

It shall not be lawful, under any pretext whatever, for any inhabitant of the United States to purchase or acquire any Mexican, or any foreigner residing in Mexico, who may have been captured by Indians inhabiting the territory of either of the two republics, nor to purchase or acquire horses, mules, cattle, or property of any kind, stolen within Mexican territory by such Indians.

And in the event of any person or persons, captured within Mexican territory by Indians, being carried into the territory of the United States, the government of the latter engages and binds itself, in the most solemn manner, so soon as it shall know of such captives being within its territory, and shall be able so to do, through the faithful exercise of its influence and power, to rescue them and return them to their country. or deliver them to the agent or representative of the Mexican government. The Mexican authorities will, as far as practicable, give to the government of the United States notice of such captures; and its agents shall pay the expenses incurred in the maintenance and transmission of the rescued captives; who, in the mean time, shall be treated with the utmost hospitality by the American authorities at the place where they may be. But if the government of the United States, before receiving such notice from Mexico, should obtain intelligence, through any other channel, of the existence of Mexican captives within its territory, it will proceed forthwith to effect their release and delivery to the Mexican agent, as above stipulated.

For the purpose of giving to these stipulations the fullest possible efficacy, thereby affording the security and redress demanded by their true spirit and intent, the government of the United States will now and hereafter pass, without unnecessary delay, and always vigilantly enforce, such laws as the nature of the subject may require. And, finally, the sacredness of this obligation shall never be lost sight of by the said government, when providing for the removal of the Indians from any portion of the said territories, or for its being settled by citizens of the United States; but, on the contrary, special care shall then be taken not to place its Indian occupants under the necessity of seeking new homes, by committing those invasions which the United States have solemnly obliged themselves to restrain.

ARTICLE XII

In consideration of the extension acquired by the boundaries of the United States, as defined in the fifth article of the present treaty, the government of the United States engages to pay to that of the Mexican Republic the sum of fifteen millions of dollars.

Immediately after the treaty shall have been duly ratified by the government of the Mexican republic, the sum of three millions of dollars shall be paid to the said government by that of the United States, at the city of Mexico, in the gold or silver coin of Mexico. The remaining twelve millions of dollars shall be paid at the same place, and in the same coin, in annual installments of three millions of dollars each, together with interest on the same at the rate of six per centum per annum. This interest shall begin to run upon the whole sum of twelve millions from the day of the ratification of the present treaty by—the Mexican government, and the first of the installments shall be paid at the expiration of one year from the same day. Together with each annual installment, as it falls due, the whole interest accruing on such installment from the beginning shall also be paid.

. . .

A. H. Sevier
Nathan Clifford
Luis de la Rosa

3. The Emancipation Proclamation (1863)

In September 1862, President Abraham Lincoln issued the Emancipation Proclamation, according to which, all slaves within states or parts of states in rebellion against the United States would be free effective on January 1, 1863. Black slaves in other states were not influenced by the Emancipation Proclamation. Moreover, it did not set free even those slaves within Confederate-controlled areas, as those state governments did not heed it. But it led many black slaves in Confederate states to flee to northern states, with nearly 200,000 freed slaves joining the Union army to fight against Confederate states. Giving black slaves the motive to fight for the Union army was important to President Lincoln's timing in proclaiming their emancipation. It was the Thirteenth Amendment, passed in December 1865, that abolished slavery in the entire United States.

BY THE PRESIDENT OF THE UNITED STATES OF AMERICA: A PROCLAMATION

Whereas, on the twenty-second day of September, in the year of our Lord one thousand eight hundred and sixty-two, a proclamation was issued by the President of the United States, containing, among other things, the following, to wit: "That on the first day of January, in the year of our Lord one thousand eight hundred and sixty-three, all persons held as slaves within any State or designated part of a State, the people whereof shall then be in rebellion against the United States, shall be then, thenceforward, and forever free; and the Executive Government of the United States, including the military and naval authority thereof, will recognize and maintain the freedom of such persons and will do no act or acts to repress such persons, or any of them, in any efforts they may make for their actual freedom.

"That the Executive will on the first day of January aforesaid, by proclamation, designate the States and parts of States, if any, in which the people thereof, respectively, shall then be in rebellion against the United States; and the fact that any State or the people thereof shall on that day be, in good faith, represented in the Congress of the United States by members chosen thereto at elections wherein a majority of the qualified voters of such States shall have participated, shall, in the absence of strong countervailing testimony, be deemed conclusive evidence that such State and the people thereof are not then in rebellion against the United States."

Now, therefore, I, Abraham Lincoln, President of the United States, by virtue of the power in me vested as Commander-In-Chief, of the Army and Navy of the United States in time of actual armed rebellion against the authority and government of the United States, and as a fit and necessary war measure for suppressing said rebellion, do, on this first day of January, in the year of our Lord one thousand eight hundred and sixty-three, and in accordance with my purpose so to do publicly proclaimed for the full period of one hundred days from the day first above mentioned, order and designate as the States and parts of States wherein the people thereof, respectively, are this day in rebellion against the United States the following, to wit:

Arkansas, Texas, Louisiana (except the Parishes of St. Bernard, Plaquemines, Jefferson, St. John, St. Charles, St. James, Ascension, Assumption, Terrebone, Lafourche, St. Mary, St. Martin, and Orleans, including the city of New Orleans), Mississippi, Alabama, Florida, Georgia, South Carolina, North Carolina, and Virginia (except the forty-eight counties designated as West Virginia, and also the counties of Berkely, Accomac, Northhampton, Elizabeth City, York, Princess Ann, and Norfolk, including the cities of Norfolk and Portsmouth[)], and which excepted parts, are for the present, left precisely as if this proclamation were not issued.

And by virtue of the power and for the purpose aforesaid, I do order and declare that all persons held as slaves within said designated States, and parts of States, are, and henceforward shall be free; and that the Executive Government of the United States, including the military and naval authorities thereof, will recognize and maintain the freedom of said persons.

And I hereby enjoin upon the people so declared to be free to abstain from all violence, unless in necessary self-defence; and I recommend to them that, in all case when allowed, they labor faithfully for reasonable wages.

And I further declare and make known that such persons of suitable condition, will be received into the armed service of the United States to garrison forts, positions, stations, and other places, and to man vessels of all sorts in said service.

And upon this act, sincerely believed to be an act of justice, warranted by the Constitution upon military necessity, I invoke the considerate judgment of mankind, and the gracious favor of Almighty God.

In witness whereof, I have hereunto set my hand and caused the seal of the United States to be affixed.

Done at the City of Washington, this first day of January, in the year of our Lord one thousand eight hundred and sixty three, and of the Independence of the United States of America the eighty-seventh.

By the President: ABRAHAM LINCOLN

WILLIAM H. SEWARD, Secretary of State.

4. Fourteenth Amendment (June 1866)

The Thirteenth Amendment, passed by Congress in December 1865, liberated all black slaves. But southern states began to pass black codes to control ex-slaves. The Fourteenth Amendment was passed by Congress in June 1866 to ensure that all blacks, including ex-slaves, were granted U.S. citizenship and that they would have all the rights and privileges any other citizen had.

14TH. AMENDMENT TO THE U.S. CONSTITUTION

Section 1. All persons born or naturalized in the United States, and subject to the jurisdiction thereof, are citizens of the United States and of the State wherein they reside. No State shall make or enforce any law which shall abridge the privileges or immunities of citizens of the United States; nor shall any State deprive any person of life, liberty, or property, without due process of law; nor deny to any person within its jurisdiction the equal protection of the laws.

Section 2. Representatives shall be apportioned among the several States according to their respective numbers, counting the whole number of persons in each State, excluding Indians not taxed. But when the right to vote at any election for the choice of electors for President and Vice President of the United States, Representatives in Congress, the Executive and Judicial officers of a State, or the members of the Legislature thereof, is denied to any of the male inhabitants of such State, being twenty-one years of age, (*See Note 15*) and citizens of the United States, or in any way abridged, except for participation in rebellion, or other crime, the basis of representation therein shall be reduced in the proportion which the number of such male citizens shall bear to the whole number of male citizens twenty-one years of age in such State.

Section 3. No person shall be a Senator or Representative in Congress, or elector of President and Vice President, or hold any office, civil or military, under the United States, or under any State, who, having previously taken an oath, as a member of Congress, or as an officer of the United States, or as a member of any State legislature, or as an executive or judicial officer of any

State, to support the Constitution of the United States, shall have engaged in insurrection or rebellion against the same, or given aid or comfort to the enemies thereof. But Congress may by a vote of two-thirds of each House, remove such disability.

Section 4. The validity of the public debt of the United States, authorized by law, including debts incurred for payment of pensions and bounties for services in suppressing insurrection or rebellion, shall not be questioned. But neither the United States nor any State shall assume or pay any debt or obligation incurred in aid of insurrection or rebellion against the United States, or any claim for the loss or emancipation of any slave; but all such debts, obligations and claims shall be held illegal and void.

Section 5. The Congress shall have power to enforce, by appropriate legislation, the provisions of this article.

5. The Chinese Exclusion Act of 1882

After the California Gold Rush in 1848, a large number of Chinese workers came to California to be used as cheap labor for mining and railroad construction. However, anti-Chinese sentiment was gradually building in California in parallel to the increase in the number of Chinese workers. The increase in anti-Chinese sentiment in California found a receptive audience among Washington politicians and culminated in the passage of the Chinese Exclusion Act in 1882. The original act was to bar Chinese labor immigration for ten years, but Congress extended the ten-year banning of Chinese immigration twice, in 1892 and 1902, and then indefinitely in 1912. It was repealed in 1943, when China was helping the United States in the fight against Japan.

Forty-Seventh Congress. Session I. 1882

Chapter 126.-An act to execute certain treaty stipulations relating to Chinese.

Preamble. Whereas, in the opinion of the Government of the United States the coming of Chinese laborers to this country endangers the good order of certain localities within the territory thereof:

Therefore,

Be it enacted by the Senate and House of Representatives of the United States of America in Congress assembled, That from and after the expiration of ninety days next after the passage of this act, and until the expiration of ten years next after the passage of this act, the coming of Chinese laborers to the United States be, and the same is hereby, suspended; and during such suspension it shall not be lawful for any Chinese laborer to come, or, having so come after the expiration of said ninety days, to remain within the United States.

SEC. 2. That the master of any vessel who shall knowingly bring within the United States on such vessel, and land or permit to be landed, and Chinese laborer, from any foreign port of place, shall be deemed guilty of a misdemeanor, and on conviction thereof shall be punished by a fine of not more than five hundred dollars for each and every such Chinese laborer so brought, and may be also imprisoned for a term not exceeding one year.

SEC. 3. That the two foregoing sections shall not apply to Chinese laborers who were in the United States on the seventeenth day of November, eighteen hundred and eighty, or who shall have come into the same before the expiration of ninety days next after the passage of this act, and who shall produce to such master before going on board such vessel, and shall produce to the collector of the port in the United States at which such vessel shall arrive, the evidence hereinafter in this act required of his being one of the laborers in this section mentioned; nor shall the two foregoing sections apply to the case of any master whose vessel, being bound to a port not within the United States by reason of being in distress or in stress of weather, or touching at any port of the United States on its voyage to any foreign port of place: Provided, That all Chinese laborers brought on such vessel shall depart with the vessel on leaving port.

SEC. 4. That for the purpose of properly identifying Chinese laborers who were in the United States on the seventeenth day of November, eighteen hundred and eighty, or who shall have come into the same before the expiration of ninety days next after the passage of this act, and in order to furnish them with the proper evidence of their right to go from and come to the United States of their free will and accord, as provided by the treaty between the United States and China dated November seventeenth, eighteen hundred and eighty, the collector of customs of the district from which any such Chinese laborer shall depart from the United States shall, in person or by deputy, go on board each vessel having on board any such Chinese laborer and cleared or about to sail from his district for a foreign port, and on such vessel make a list of all such Chinese laborers, which shall be entered in registry-books to be kept for that purpose, in which shall be stated the name, age, occupation, last place of residence, physical marks or peculiarities, and all facts necessary for the identification of each of such Chinese laborers, which books shall be safely kept in the custom-house; and every such Chinese laborer so departing from the United States shall be entitled to, and shall receive, free of any charge or cost upon application therefore, from the collector or his deputy, at the time such list is taken, a certificate, signed by the collector or his deputy and attested by his seal of office, in such form as the Secretary of the Treasury shall prescribe, which certificate shall contain a statement of the name, age, occupation, last place of residence, personal description, and fact of identification of the Chinese laborer to whom the certificate is issued, corresponding with the said list and registry in all particulars. In case any Chinese laborer after having received such certificate shall leave such vessel before her departure he shall deliver his certificate to the master of the vessel, and if such Chinese laborer shall fail to return to such vessel before her departure from port the certificate shall be delivered by the master to the collector of customs for cancellation. The certificate herein provided for shall entitle the Chinese laborer to whom the same is issued to return to and re-enter the United States upon producing and delivering the same to the collector of customs of the district at which such Chinese laborer shall seek to re-enter; and upon delivery of such certificate by such Chinese laborer to the collector of customs at the time of re-entry in the United States, said collector shall cause the same to be filed in the custom house and duly canceled.

SEC. 5. That any Chinese laborer mentioned in section four of this act being in the United States, and desiring to depart from the United States by land, shall have the right to demand and receive, free of charge or cost, a certificate of identification similar to that provided for in section four of this act to be issued to such Chinese laborers as may desire to leave the United States by water; and it is hereby made the duty of the collector of customs of the district next adjoining the foreign country to which said Chinese laborer desires to go to issue such certificate, free of charge or cost, upon application by such Chinese laborer, and to enter the same upon registry-books to be kept by him for the purpose, as provided for in section four of this act.

SEC. 6. That in order to the faithful execution of articles one and two of the treaty in this act before mentioned, every Chinese person other than a laborer who may be entitled by said treaty and this act to come within the United States, and who shall be about to come to the United States, shall be identified as so entitled by the Chinese Government in each case, such identity to be evidenced by a certificate issued under the authority of said government, which certificate shall be in the English language or (if not in the English language) accompanied by a translation into English, stating such right to come, and which certificate shall state the name, title, or official rank, if any, the age, height, and all physical peculiarities, former and present occupation or profession, and place of residence in China of the person to whom the certificate is issued and that such person is entitled conformably to the treaty in this act mentioned to come within the United States. Such certificate shall be prima-facie evidence of the fact set forth therein, and shall be produced to the collector of customs, or his deputy, of the port in the district in the United States at which the person named therein shall arrive.

SEC. 7. That any person who shall knowingly and falsely alter or substitute any name for the name written in such certificate or forge any such certificate, or knowingly utter any forged or fraudulent certificate, or falsely personate any person named in any such certificate, shall be deemed guilty of a misdemeanor; and upon conviction thereof shall be fined in a sum not exceeding one thousand dollars, an imprisoned in a penitentiary for a term of not more than five years.

SEC. 8. That the master of any vessel arriving in the United States from any foreign port or place shall, at the same time he delivers a manifest of the cargo, and if there be no cargo, then at the time of making a report of the entry of vessel pursuant to the law, in addition to the other matter required to be reported, and before landing, or permitting to land, any Chinese passengers, deliver and report to the collector of customs of the district in which such vessels shall have arrived a separate list of all Chinese passengers taken on board his vessel at any foreign port or place, and all such passengers on board the vessel at that time. Such list shall show the names of such passengers (and if accredited officers of the Chinese Government traveling on the business of that government, or their servants, with a note of such facts), and the name and other particulars, as shown by their respective certificates; and such list shall be sworn to by the master in the manner required by law in relation to the manifest of the cargo. Any willful refusal or neglect of any such master to comply with the provisions of this section shall incur the same penalties and forfeiture as are provided for a refusal or neglect to report and deliver a manifest of cargo.

SEC. 9. That before any Chinese passengers are landed from any such vessel, the collector, or his deputy, shall proceed to examine such passengers, comparing the certificates with the list and with the passengers; and no passenger shall be allowed to land in the United States from such vessel in violation of law.

SEC. 10. That every vessel whose master shall knowingly violate any of the provisions of this act shall be deemed forfeited to the United States, and shall be liable to seizure and condemnation on any district of the United States into which such vessel may enter or in which she may be found.

SEC. 11. That any person who shall knowingly bring into or cause to be brought into the United States by land, or who shall knowingly aid or abet the same, or aid or abet the landing in the United States from any vessel of any Chinese person not lawfully entitled to enter the United States, shall be deemed guilty of a misdemeanor, and shall, on conviction thereof, be fined in a sum not exceeding one thousand dollars, and imprisoned for a term not exceeding one year.

SEC. 12. That no Chinese person shall be permitted to enter the United States by land without producing to the proper officer of customs the certificate in this act required of Chinese persons seeking to land from a vessel. And any Chinese person found unlawfully within the United States shall be caused to be removed therefrom to the country from whence he came, by direction of the United States, after being brought before some justice, judge, or commissioner of a court of the United States and found to be one not lawfully entitled to be or remain in the United States.

SEC. 13. That this act shall not apply to diplomatic and other officers of the Chinese Government traveling upon the business of that government, whose credentials shall be taken as equivalent to the certificate in this act mentioned, and shall exempt them and their body and household servants from the provisions of this act as to other Chinese persons.

SEC. 14. That hereafter no State court or court of the United States shall admit Chinese to citizenship; and all laws in conflict with this act are hereby repealed.

SEC. 15. That the words "Chinese laborers", whenever used in this act, shall be construed to mean both skilled and unskilled laborers and Chinese employed in mining.

Approved, May 6, 1882.

6. Excerpt from the Indian Allotment Act (1887)

Congress passed the Indian Allotment Act (Indian Appropriation Act) in 1887. The passage of the Act indicates a major change in the U.S. government's policy toward Native Americans from segregation and separation to assimilation. The Act stipulated that each Indian family be given seventy acres of land. Native Americans considered their land belonging to their tribe, as they had no sense of private property. One main goal of allotting certain acres of land to each Indian family was to teach them the capitalist value of private ownership. But a more important, practical goal of the allotment was to take away land from Indian tribes. The federal government took the remaining tribal lands after allotments to Indian families. Moreover, many Indian families lost their allotted land due to their ignorance of complicated paperwork associated with property ownership.

. . .

Chapter 119—An act to provide for the allotment of lands in severalty to Indians on the various reservations, and to extend the protection of the laws of the United States and Territories over the Indians, and for other purposes. Be it enacted, &c., [For substitute for section 1, see 1891, February 28, c. 383, s. 1, post,].

SEC. 2. That all allotments set apart under the provisions of this act shall be selected by the Indians, heads of families selecting for their minor children, and the agents shall select for each orphan child, and in such manner as to embrace the improvements of the Indians making the selection.

Where the improvements of two or more Indians have been made on the same legal subdivision of land, unless they shall otherwise agree, a provisional line may be run dividing said lands between them, and the amount to which each is entitled shall be equalized in the assignment of the remainder of the land to which they are entitled under this act:

Provided, That if any one entitled to an allotment shall fail to make a selection within four years after the President shall direct that allotments may be made on a particular reservation, the Secretary of the Interior may direct the agent of such tribe or band, if such there be, and if there be no agent, then a special agent appointed for that purpose, to make a selection for such Indian, which selection shall be allotted as in cases where selections are made by the Indians, and patents shall issue in like manner.

SEC. 3. That the allotments provided for in this act shall be made by special agents appointed by the President for such purpose, and the agents in charge of the respective reservations on which the allotments are directed to be made, under such rules and regulations as the Secretary of the Interior may from time to time prescribe, and shall be certified by such agents to the Commissioner of Indian Affairs, in duplicate, one copy to be retained in the Indian Office and the other to be transmitted to the Secretary of the Interior for his action, and to be deposited in the General Land Office.

SEC. 4. That where any Indian not residing upon a reservation, or for whose tribe no reservation has been provided by treaty, act of Congress, or executive order, shall make settlement upon any surveyed or un-surveyed lands of the United States not otherwise appropriated, he or she shall be entitled, upon application to the local land office for the district in which the lands are located, to have the same allotted to him or her, and to his or her children, in quantities and manner as provided in this act for Indians residing upon reservations; and when such settlement is made upon unsurveyed lands, the grant to such Indians shall be adjusted upon the survey of the lands so as to conform thereto; and patents shall be issued to them for such lands in the manner and with the restrictions as herein provided.

And the fees to which the officers of such local land-office would have been entitled has such lands been entered under the general laws for the disposition of the public lands shall be paid to them, from any moneys in the Treasury of the United States not otherwise appropriated, upon a statement of an account in their behalf for such fees by the Commissioner of the General Land Office and certification of such account to the Secretary of the Treasury by the Secretary of the Interior.

SEC. 5. That upon the approval of the allotments provided for in this act by the Secretary of the Interior, he shall cause patents to issue therefore in the name of the allottees, which patents shall be of the legal effect, and declare that the United States does and will hold the land thus allotted for the period of twenty-five years, in trust for the sole use and benefit of the Indian to whom such allotment shall have been made, or, in case of his decease, of his heirs according to the laws of the State or Territory where such land is located, and that at the expiration of said period the Untied States will convey the same by patent to said Indian, or his heirs as aforesaid, in fee, discharged of said trust and free of all charge or incumbrance whatsoever: *Provided*, That the President of the United States may in any case in his discretion extend the period.

And if any conveyance shall be made of the lands set apart and allotted as herein provided, or any contract made touching the same, before the expiration of the time above mentioned, such conveyance or contract shall be absolutely null and void:

Provided, That the law of descent and partition in force in the State or Territory where such lands are situate shall apply thereto after patents therefore have been executed and delivered, except as herein otherwise provided; and the laws of the State of Kansas regulating the descent and partition of real estate shall, so far as practicable, apply to all lands in the Indian Territory which may be allotted in severalty under the provisions of this act:

And provided further, that at any time after lands have been allotted to all the Indians of any tribe as herein provided, or sooner if in the opinion of the President it shall be for the best interests of said tribe, it shall be lawful for the Secretary of the Interior to negotiate with such Indian tribe for the purchase and release by said tribe, in conformity with the treaty or statute under which such reservation is held, of such portions of its reservation not allotted as such tribe shall, from time to time, consent to sell, on such terms and conditions as shall be considered just and equitable between the United States and said tribe of Indians, which purchase shall not be complete until ratified by Congress, and the form and manner of executing such release shall also be prescribed by Congress:

Provided however, That all lands adapted to agriculture, with or without irrigation so sold or released to the United States by any Indian tribe shall be held by the United States for the sole purpose of securing homes to actual settlers and shall be disposed of by the United States to actual and bona fide settlers only in tracts not exceeding one hundred and sixty acres to any one person, on such terms as Congress shall prescribe, subject to grants which Congress may make in aid of education:

And provided further, That no patents shall issue therefore except to the person so taking the same as and for a homestead, or his heirs, and after the expiration of five years occupancy thereof as such homestead; and any conveyance of said lands so taken as a homestead, or any contract touching the same, or lien thereon, created prior to the date of such patent, shall be null and void.

Fees of land officers to be paid from Treasury.

Patent to issue, holding lands in trust; conveyance after twenty-five years.

Contracts, conveyances, etc., before end of twenty-five years void.

Laws of descent and partition.

Negotiations by Secretary of Interior for purchase of lands not allotted.

Agricultural lands so purchased to be held for actual settlers, if arable.

Patent to issue only to persons taking for homestead.

And the sums agreed to be paid by the United States as purchase money for any portion of any such reservation shall be held in the Treasury of the United States for the sole use of the tribe or tribes of Indians to whom such reservations belonged; and the same, with interest thereon at three per cent per annum, shall be at all times subject to appropriation by Congress for the education and civilization of such tribe or tribes of Indian or the members thereof.

The patents aforesaid shall be recorded in the General Land Office, and afterward delivered, free of charge, to the allottee entitled thereto.

And if any religious society or other organization is now occupying any of the public lands to which this act is applicable, for religious or educational work among the Indians, the Secretary of the Interior is hereby authorized to confirm such occupation to such society or organization, in quantity not exceeding one hundred and sixty acres in any one tract, so long as the same shall be so occupied, on such terms as he shall deem just; but nothing herein contained shall change or alter any claim of such society for religious or educational purposes theretofore granted by law.

And hereafter in the employment of Indian police, or any other employees in the public service among any of the Indian tribes or bands affected by this act, and where Indians can perform the duties required, those Indians who have availed themselves of the provisions of this act and become citizens of the United States shall be preferred.

SEC. 6. That upon the completion of said allotments and the patenting of the lands to said allottees, each and every member of the respective bands or tribes of Indians to whom allotments have been made shall have the benefit of and be subject to the laws, both civil and criminal, of the State or Territory in which they may reside; and no Territory shall pass or enforce any law denying any such Indian within its jurisdiction the equal protection of the law.

And every Indian born within the territorial limits of the United States to whom allotments shall have been made under the provisions of this act, or under any law or treaty, and every Indian born within the territorial limits of the Untied States who has voluntarily taken up, within said limits, his residence separate and apart from any tribe of Indians therein, and has adopted the habits of civilized life, [and every Indian in Indian Territory,] is hereby declared to be a citizen of the United States, and is entitled to all the rights, privileges, and immunities of such citizens, whether said Indian has been or not, by birth or otherwise, a member of any tribe of Indians within the territorial limits of the United States without in any manner impairing or otherwise affecting the right of any such Indian to tribal or other property.

SEC. 7. That in cases where the use of water for irrigation is necessary to render the lands within any Indian reservation available for agricultural purposes, the Secretary of the Interior be, and he is hereby, authorized to prescribe such rules and regulations as he may deem necessary to secure a just and equal distribution thereof among the Indians residing upon any such reservations; and no other appropriation or grant of water by any riparian proprietor shall be authorized or permitted to the damage of any other riparian proprietor.

SEC. 8. That the provision of this act shall not extend to the territory occupied by the Cherokees, Creeks, Choctaws, Chickasaws, Seminoles, and Osage, Miamies and Peorias, and Sacs and Foxes, in the Indian Territory, nor to any of the reservations of the Seneca Nation of New York Indians in the State of New York; nor to that strip of territory in the State of Nebraska adjoining the Sioux Nation on the south added by executive order.

SEC. 9. That for the purpose of making the surveys and resurveys mentioned in section two of this act, there be, and hereby is, appropriated, of any monies in the Treasury not otherwise appropriated, the sum of one hundred thousand dollars, to be repaid proportionately out of the proceeds of the sales of such land as may be acquired from the Indians under the provisions of this act.

SEC. 10. That nothing in this act contained shall be so construed as to affect the right and power of Congress to grant the right of way through any lands granted to an Indian, or a tribe of Indians, for railroads or other highways, or telegraph lines, for the public use, or to condemn such lands to public uses, upon making just compensation.

SEC. 11. That nothing in this act shall be so construed as to prevent the removal of the Southern Ute Indians from their present reservation in Southwestern Colorado to a new reservation by and with the consent of a majority of the adult male members of said tribe.

Approved, Feb. 8, 1887
24 Stat., 388

7. *Plessy v. Ferguson* (1896)

After the federal troops withdrew from the South after the Tilden-Hay Compromise of 1878, Southern states began to develop segregation laws to keep whites and blacks separate. By the 1890s, all Southern states had established various segregation laws that required whites and blacks to use separate facilities in public accommodations, such as trains, buses, motels, parks, and schools. *Plessy v. Ferguson* (1896) is the most notorious case in which the U.S Supreme Court ruled "equal but separate" facilities (passenger trains) between whites and black was not a violation of the U.S. Constitution (the equal protection of all citizens guaranteed by the Fourteenth Amendment). The Supreme Court decision reflected the segregationist ideology of the time. It was the *Brown v. Board of Education* case in 1954 that overturned the 1896 decision.

Transcription of the Judgement of the Supreme Court of the United States in *Plessy v. Ferguson*

Supreme Court of the United States,
No. 210, October Term, 1895.
Homer Adolph Plessy,
Plaintiff in Error,
vs.
J. H. Ferguson, Judge of Section "A"
Criminal District Court for the Parish of Orleans
In Error to the Supreme Court of the State of Louisiana

This cause came on to be heard on the transcript of the record from the Supreme Court of the State of Louisiana, and was argued by counsel.

On consideration whereof, It is now here ordered and adjudged by this Court that the judgement of the said Supreme Court, in this cause, be and the same is hereby, affirmed with costs.

per Mr. Justice Brown,
May 18, 1896.
Dissenting:
Mr. Justice Harlan

Transcription of Opinion of the Supreme Court of the United States in *Plessy v. Ferguson*

U.S. Supreme Court
PLESSY v. FERGUSON, 163 U.S. 537 (1896)
163 U.S. 537
PLESSY
v.
FERGUSON.
No. 210.
May 18, 1896.

This was a petition for writs of prohibition and *certiorari* originally filed in the supreme court of the state by Plessy, the plaintiff in error, against the Hon. John H. Ferguson, judge of the criminal district court for the parish of Orleans, and setting forth, in substance, the following facts:

That petitioner was a citizen of the United States and a resident of the state of Louisiana, of mixed descent, in the proportion of seven-eighths Caucasian and one-eighth African blood; that the mixture of colored blood was not discernible in him, and that he was entitled to every recognition, right, privilege, and immunity secured to the citizens of the United States of the white race by its constitution and laws; that on June 7, 1892, he engaged and paid for a first-class passage on the East Louisiana Railway, from New Orleans to Covington, in the same state, and thereupon entered a passenger train, and took possession of a vacant seat in a coach where passengers of the white race were accommodated; that such railroad company was incorporated by the laws of Louisiana as a common carrier, and was not authorized to distinguish between citizens according to their race, but, notwithstanding this, petitioner was required by the conductor, under penalty of ejection from said train and imprisonment, to vacate said coach, and occupy another seat, in a coach assigned by said company for persons not of the white race, and for no other reason than that petitioner was of the colored race; that, upon petitioner's refusal to comply with such order, he was, with the aid of a police officer, forcibly ejected from said coach, and hurried off to, and imprisoned in, the parish jail of New Orleans, and there held to answer a charge made by such officer to the effect that he was guilty of having criminally violated an act of the general assembly of the state, approved July 10, 1890, in such case made and provided.

The petitioner was subsequently brought before the recorder of the city for preliminary examination, and committed for trial to the criminal district court for the parish of Orleans, where an information was filed against him in the matter above set forth, for a violation of the above act, which act the petitioner affirmed to be null and void, because in conflict with the constitution of the United States; that petitioner interposed a plea to such information, based upon the unconstitutionality of the act of the general assembly, to which the district attorney, on behalf of the state, filed a demurrer; that, upon issue being joined upon such demurrer and plea, the court sustained the demurrer, overruled the plea, and ordered petitioner to plead over to the facts set forth in the information, and that, unless the judge of the said court be enjoined by a writ of prohibition from further proceeding in such case, the court will proceed to fine and sentence petitioner to imprisonment, and thus deprive him of his constitutional rights set forth in his said plea, notwithstanding the unconstitutionality of the act under which he was being prosecuted; that no appeal lay from such sentence, and petitioner was without relief or remedy except by writs of prohibition and certiorari. Copies of the information and other proceedings in the criminal district court were annexed to the petition as an exhibit.

Upon the filing of this petition, an order was issued upon the respondent to show cause why a writ of prohibition should not issue, and be made perpetual, and a further order that the record of the proceedings had in the criminal cause be certified and transmitted to the supreme court.

To this order the respondent made answer, transmitting a certified copy of the proceedings, asserting the constitutionality of the law, and averring that, instead of pleading or admitting that he belonged to the colored race, the said Plessy declined and refused, either by pleading or otherwise, to admit that he was in any sense or in any proportion a colored man.

The case coming on for hearing before the supreme court, that court was of opinion that the law under which the prosecution was had was constitutional and denied the relief prayed for by the petitioner (Ex parte Plessy, 45

La. Ann. 80, 11 South. 948); whereupon petitioner prayed for a writ of error from this court, which was allowed by the chief justice of the supreme court of Louisiana.

Mr. Justice Harlan dissenting.

A. W. Tourgee and S. F. Phillips, for plaintiff in error.

Alex. Porter Morse, for defendant in error.

Mr. Justice BROWN, after stating the facts in the foregoing language, delivered the opinion of the court.

This case turns upon the constitutionality of an act of the general assembly of the state of Louisiana, passed in 1890, providing for separate railway carriages for the white and colored races. Acts 1890, No. 111, p. 152.

The first section of the statute enacts "that all railway companies carrying passengers in their coaches in this state, shall provide equal but separate accommodations for the white, and colored races, by providing two or more passenger coaches for each passenger train, or by dividing the passenger coaches by a partition so as to secure separate accommodations: provided, that this section shall not be construed to apply to street railroads. No person or persons shall be permitted to occupy seats in coaches, other than the ones assigned to them, on account of the race they belong to."

By the second section it was enacted "that the officers of such passenger trains shall have power and are hereby required to assign each passenger to the coach or compartment used for the race to which such passenger belongs; any passenger insisting on going into a coach or compartment to which by race he does not belong, shall be liable to a fine of twenty-five dollars, or in lieu thereof to imprisonment for a period of not more than twenty days in the parish prison, and any officer of any railroad insisting on assigning a passenger to a coach or compartment other than the one set aside for the race to which said passenger belongs, shall be liable to a fine of twenty-five dollars, or in lieu thereof to imprisonment for a period of not more than twenty days in the parish prison; and should any passenger refuse to occupy the coach or compartment to which he or she is assigned by the officer of such railway, said officer shall have power to refuse to carry such passenger on his train, and for such refusal neither he nor the railway company which he represents shall be liable for damages in any of the courts of this state."

The third section provides penalties for the refusal or neglect of the officers, directors, conductors, and employees of railway companies to comply with the act, with a proviso that "nothing in this act shall be construed as applying to nurses attending children of the other race." The fourth section is immaterial.

The information filed in the criminal district court charged, in substance, that Plessy, being a passenger between two stations within the state of Louisiana, was assigned by officers of the company to the coach used for the race to which he belonged, but he insisted upon going into a coach used by the race to which he did not belong. Neither in the information nor plea was his particular race or color averred.

The petition for the writ of prohibition averred that petitioner was seven-eighths Caucasian and one-eighth African blood; that the mixture of colored blood was not discernible in him; and that he was entitled to every right, privilege, and immunity secured to citizens of the United States of the white race; and that, upon such theory, he took possession of a vacant seat in a coach where passengers of the white race were accommodated, and was ordered by the conductor to vacate said coach, and take a seat in another, assigned to persons of the colored race, and, having refused to comply with such demand, he was forcibly ejected, with the aid of a police officer, and imprisoned in the parish jail to answer a charge of having violated the above act.

The constitutionality of this act is attacked upon the ground that it conflicts both with the thirteenth amendment of the constitution, abolishing slavery, and the fourteenth amendment, which prohibits certain restrictive legislation on the part of the states.

1. That it does not conflict with the thirteenth amendment, which abolished slavery and involuntary servitude, except a punishment for crime, is too clear for argument. Slavery implies involuntary servitude,-a state of bondage; the ownership of mankind as a chattel, or, at least, the control of the labor and services of one man for the benefit of another, and the absence of a legal right to the disposal of his own person, property, and services. This amendment was said in the Slaughter-House Cases, 16 Wall. 36, to have been intended primarily to abolish slavery, as it had been previously known in this country, and that it equally forbade Mexican peonage or the Chinese coolie trade, when they amounted to slavery or involuntary servitude, and that the use of the word "servitude" was intended to prohibit the use of all forms of involuntary slavery, of whatever class or name. It was intimated, however, in that case, that this amendment was regarded by the statesmen of that day as insufficient to protect the colored race from certain laws which had been enacted in the Southern states, imposing upon the colored race onerous disabilities and burdens, and curtailing their rights in the pursuit of life, liberty, and property to such an extent that their freedom was of little value; and that the fourteenth amendment was devised to meet this exigency.

So, too, in the Civil Rights Cases, 109 U.S. 3, 3 Sup. Ct. 18, it was said that the act of a mere individual, the owner of an inn, a public conveyance or place of amusement, refusing accommodations to colored people, cannot be justly regarded as imposing any badge of slavery or servitude upon the applicant, but only as involving an ordinary civil injury, properly cognizable by the laws of the state, and presumably subject to redress by those laws until the contrary appears. "It would be running the slavery question into the ground," said Mr. Justice Bradley, "to make it apply to every act of discrimination which a person may see fit to make as to the guests he will entertain, or as to the people he will take into his coach or cab or car, or admit to his concert or theater, or deal with in other matters of intercourse or business."

A statute which implies merely a legal distinction between the white and colored races—a distinction which is founded in the color of the two races, and which must always exist so long as white men are distinguished from the other race by color—has no tendency to destroy the legal equality of the two races, or re-establish a state of involuntary servitude. Indeed, we do not understand that the thirteenth amendment is strenuously relied upon by the plaintiff in error in this connection.

2. By the fourteenth amendment, all persons born or naturalized in the

United States, and subject to the jurisdiction thereof, are made citizens of the United States and of the state wherein they reside; and the states are forbidden from making or enforcing any law which shall abridge the privileges or immunities of citizens of the United States, or shall deprive any person of life, liberty, or property without due process of law, or deny to any person within their jurisdiction the equal protection of the laws.

The proper construction of this amendment was first called to the attention of this court in the Slaughter-House Cases, 16 Wall. 36, which involved, however, not a question of race, but one of exclusive privileges. The case did not call for any expression of opinion as to the exact rights it was intended to secure to the colored race, but it was said generally that its main purpose was to establish the citizenship of the negro, to give definitions of citizenship of the United States and of the states, and to protect from the hostile legislation of the states the privileges and immunities of citizens of the United States, as distinguished from those of citizens of the states. The object of the amendment was undoubtedly to enforce the absolute equality of the two races before the law, but, in the nature of things, it could not have been intended to abolish distinctions based upon color, or to enforce social, as distinguished from political, equality, or a commingling of the two races upon terms unsatisfactory to either. Laws permitting, and even requiring, their separation, in places where they are liable to be brought into contact, do not necessarily imply the inferiority of either race to the other, and have been generally, if not universally, recognized as within the competency of the state legislatures in the exercise of their police power. The most common instance of this is connected with the establishment of separate schools for white and colored children, which have been held to be a valid exercise of the legislative power even by courts of states where the political rights of the colored race have been longest and most earnestly enforced.

One of the earliest of these cases is that of Roberts v. City of Boston, 5 Cush. 198, in which the supreme judicial court of Massachusetts held that the general school committee of Boston had power to make provision for the instruction of colored children in separate schools established exclusively for them, and to prohibit their attendance upon the other schools. "The great principle," said Chief Justice Shaw, "advanced by the learned and eloquent advocate for the plaintiff [Mr. Charles Sumner], is that, by the constitution and laws of Massachusetts, all persons, without distinction of age or sex, birth or color, origin or condition, are equal before the law. . . . But, when this great principle comes to be applied to the actual and various conditions of persons in society, it will not warrant the assertion that men and women are legally clothed with the same civil and political powers, and that children and adults are legally to have the same functions and be subject to the same treatment; but only that the rights of all, as they are settled and regulated by law, are equally entitled to the paternal consideration and protection of the law for their maintenance and security." It was held that the powers of the committee extended to the establishment of separate schools for children of different ages, sexes and colors, and that they might also establish special schools for poor and neglected children, who have become too old to attend the primary school, and yet have not acquired the rudiments of learning, to enable them to enter the ordinary schools. Similar laws have been enacted by congress under its general power of legislation over the District of Columbia (sections 281–283, 310, 319, Rev. St. D. C.), as well as by the legislatures of many of the states, and have been generally, if not uniformly, sustained by the courts. State v. McCann, 21 Ohio St. 210; Lehew v. Brummell (Mo. Sup.) 15 S. W. 765; Ward v. Flood, 48 Cal. 36; Bertonneau v. Directors of City Schools, 3 Woods, 177, Fed. Cas. No. 1,361; People v. Gallagher, 93 N. Y. 438; Cory v. Carter, 48 Ind. 337; Dawson v. Lee, 83 Ky. 49.

Laws forbidding the intermarriage of the two races may be said in a technical sense to interfere with the freedom of contract, and yet have been universally recognized as within the police power of the state. State v. Gibson, 36 Ind. 389.

The distinction between laws interfering with the political equality of the negro and those requiring the separation of the two races in schools, theaters, and railway carriages has been frequently drawn by this court. Thus, in Strauder v. West Virginia, 100 U.S. 303, it was held that a law of West Virginia limiting to white male persons 21 years of age, and citizens of the state, the right to sit upon juries, was a discrimination which implied a legal inferiority in civil society, which lessened the security of the right of the colored race, and was a step towards reducing them to a condition of servility. Indeed, the right of a colored man that, in the selection of jurors to pass upon his life, liberty, and property, there shall be no exclusion of his race, and no discrimination against them because of color, has been asserted in a number of cases. Virginia v. Rivers, 100 U.S. 313; Neal v. Delaware, 103 U.S. 370; ush v. Com., 107 U.S. 110, 1 Sup. Ct. 625; Gibson v. Mississippi, 162 U.S. 565, 16 Sup. Ct. 904. So, where the laws of a particular locality or the charter of a particular railway corporation has provided that no person shall be excluded from the cars on account of color, we have held that this meant that persons of color should travel in the same car as white ones, and that the enactment was not satisfied by the company providing cars assigned exclusively to people of color, though they were as good as those which they assigned exclusively to white persons. Railroad Co. v. Brown, 17 Wall. 445.

Upon the other hand, where a statute of Louisiana required those engaged in the transportation of passengers among the states to give to all persons traveling within that state, upon vessels employed in that business, equal rights and privileges in all parts of the vessel, without distinction on account of race or color, and subjected to an action for damages the owner of such a vessel who excluded colored passengers on account of their color from the cabin set aside by him for the use of whites, it was held to be, so far as it applied to interstate commerce, unconstitutional and void. Hall v. De Cuir, 95 U.S. 485. The court in this case, however, expressly disclaimed that it had anything whatever to do with the statute as a regulation of internal commerce, or affecting anything else than commerce among the states.

In the Civil Rights Cases, 109 U.S. 3, 3 Sup. Ct. 18, it was held that an act of congress entitling all persons within the jurisdiction of the United States to the full and equal enjoyment of the accommodations, advantages, facilities, and privileges of inns, public conveyances, on land or water, theaters, and other places of public amusement, and made applicable to citizens of every race and color, regardless of any previous condition of servitude, was unconstitutional and void, upon the ground that the fourteenth amendment was prohibitory upon the states only, and the legislation authorized to be adopted by congress for enforcing it was not direct legislation on matters respecting which the states were prohibited from making or enforcing certain laws, or doing certain acts, but was corrective legislation, such as might be necessary or proper for counter-acting and redressing the effect of such laws or acts. In delivering the opinion of the court, Mr. Justice Bradley observed that the fourteenth amendment "does not invest congress with power to legislate upon subjects that are within the domain of state legislation, but to provide modes of relief against state legislation or state action of the kind referred to. It does not authorize congress to create a code of municipal law for the regulation of private rights, but to provide modes of redress against the operation of state laws, and the action of state officers, executive or judicial, when these are subversive of the fundamental rights specified in the amendment. Positive rights and privileges are undoubtedly secured by the fourteenth amendment; but they are secured by way of prohibition against state laws and state proceedings affecting those rights and privileges, and by power given to congress to legislate for the purpose of carrying such prohibition into effect; and such legislation must necessarily be predicated upon such supposed state laws or state proceedings, and be directed to the correction of their operation and effect."

Much nearer, and, indeed, almost directly in point, is the case of the Louisville, N. O. & T. Ry. Co. v. State, 133 U.S. 587, 10 Sup. Ct. 348, wherein the railway company was indicted for a violation of a statute of Mississippi, enacting that all railroads carrying passengers should provide equal, but separate, accommodations for the white and colored races, by providing two or more passenger cars for each passenger train, or by dividing the passenger cars by a partition, so as to secure separate accommodations. The case was presented in a different aspect from the one under consideration, inasmuch as it was an indictment against the railway company for failing to provide the separate accommodations, but the question considered was the constitutionality of the law. In that case, the supreme court of Mississippi (66 Miss. 662, 6 South. 203) had held that the statute applied solely to commerce within the state, and, that being the construction of the state statute by its highest court, was accepted as conclusive. "If it be a matter," said the court (page 591, 133 U.S., and page 348, 10 Sup. Ct.), "respecting commerce wholly within a state, and not interfering with commerce between the states, then, obviously, there is no violation of the commerce clause of the federal constitution. . . . No question arises under this section as to the power of the state to separate in different compartments interstate passengers, or affect, in any manner, the privileges and rights of such passengers. All that we can consider is whether the state has the power to require that railroad trains within her limits shall have separate accommodations for the two races. That affecting only commerce within the state is no invasion of the power given to congress by the commerce clause."

A like course of reasoning applies to the case under consideration, since the supreme court of Louisiana, in the case of State v. Judge, 44 La. Ann. 770, 11 South. 74, held that the statute in question did not apply to interstate passengers, but was confined in its application to passengers traveling exclusively within the borders of the state. The case was decided largely upon the authority of Louisville, N. O. & T. Ry. Co. v. State, 66 Miss. 662, 6 South, 203, and affirmed by this court in 133 U.S. 587, 10 Sup. Ct. 348. In the present case no question of interference with interstate commerce can possibly arise, since the East Louisiana Railway appears to have been purely a local line, with both its termini within the state of Louisiana. Similar statutes for the separation of the two races upon public conveyances were held to be constitutional in Railroad v. Miles, 55 Pa. St. 209; Day v. Owen 5 Mich. 520; Railway Co. v. Williams, 55 Ill. 185; Railroad Co. v. Wells, 85 Tenn. 613; 4 S. W. 5; Railroad Co. v. Benson, 85 Tenn. 627, 4 S. W. 5;The Sue, 22 Fed. 843; Logwood v. Railroad Co., 23 Fed. 318; McGuinn v. Forbes, 37 Fed. 639; People v. King (N. Y. App.) 18 N. E. 245; Houck v. Railway Co., 38 Fed. 226; Heard v. Railroad Co., 3 Inter St. Commerce Com. R. 111, 1 Inter St. Commerce Com. R. 428.

While we think the enforced separation of the races, as applied to the internal commerce of the state, neither abridges the privileges or immunities of the colored man, deprives him of his property without due process of law, nor denies him the equal protection of the laws, within the meaning of the fourteenth amendment, we are not prepared to say that the conductor, in assigning passengers to the coaches according to their race, does not act at his peril, or that the provision of the second section of the act that denies to the passenger compensation in damages for a refusal to receive him into the coach in which he properly belongs is a valid exercise of the legislative power. Indeed, we understand it to be conceded by the state's attorney that such part of the act as exempts from liability the railway company and its officers is unconstitutional. The power to assign to a particular coach obviously implies the power to determine to which race the passenger belongs, as well as the power to determine who, under the laws of the particular state, is to be deemed a white, and who a colored, person. This question, though indicated in the brief of the plaintiff in error, does not properly arise upon the record in this case, since the only issue made is as to the unconstitutionality of the act, so far as it requires the railway to provide separate accommodations, and the conductor to assign passengers according to their race.

It is claimed by the plaintiff in error that, in an mixed community, the reputation of belonging to the dominant race, in this instance the white race, is "property," in the same sense that a right of action or of inheritance is property. Conceding this to be so, for the purposes of this case, we are unable to see how this statute deprives him of, or in any way affects his right to, such property. If he be a white man, and assigned to a colored coach, he may have his action for damages against the company for being deprived of his so-called "property." Upon the other hand, if he be a colored man, and be so assigned, he has been deprived of no property, since he is not lawfully entitled to the reputation of being a white man.

In this connection, it is also suggested by the learned counsel for the plaintiff in error that the same argument that will justify the state legislature in requiring railways to provide separate accommodations for the two races will also authorize them to require separate cars to be provided for people whose hair is of a certain color, or who are aliens, or who belong to certain nationalities, or to enact laws requiring colored people to walk upon one side of the street, and white people upon the other, or requiring white men's houses to be painted white, and colored men's black, or their vehicles or business signs to be of different colors, upon the theory that one side of the street is as good as the other, or that a house or vehicle of one color is as good as one of another color. The reply to all this is that every exercise of the police power must be reasonable, and extend only to such laws as are enacted in good faith for the promotion of the public good, and not for the annoyance or oppression of a particular class. Thus, in Yick Wo v. Hopkins, 118 U.S. 356, 6 Sup. Ct. 1064, it was held by this court that a municipal ordinance of the city of San Francisco, to regulate the carrying on of public laundries within the limits of the municipality, violated the provisions of the constitution of the United States, if it conferred upon the municipal authorities arbitrary power, at their own will, and without regard to discretion, in the legal sense of the term, to give or withhold consent as to persons or places, without regard to the competency of the persons applying or the propriety of the places selected for the carrying on of the business. It was held to be a covert attempt on the part of the municipality to make an arbitrary and unjust discrimination against the Chinese race. While this was the case of a municipal ordinance, a like principle has been held to apply to acts of a state legislature passed in the exercise of the police power. Railroad Co. v. Husen, 95 U.S. 465; Louisville & N. R. Co. v. Kentucky, 161 U.S. 677, 16 Sup. Ct. 714, and cases cited on page 700, 161 U.S., and page 714, 16 Sup. Ct.; Daggett v. Hudson, 43 Ohio St. 548, 3 N. E. 538; Capen v. Foster, 12 Pick. 485; State v. Baker, 38 Wis. 71; Monroe v. Collins, 17 Ohio St. 665; Hulseman v. Rems, 41 Pa. St. 396; Osman v. Riley, 15 Cal. 48.

So far, then, as a conflict with the fourteenth amendment is concerned, the case reduces itself to the question whether the statute of Louisiana is a reasonable regulation, and with respect to this there must necessarily be a large discretion on the part of the legislature. In determining the question of reasonableness, it is at liberty to act with reference to the established usages, customs, and traditions of the people, and with a view to the promotion of their comfort, and the preservation of the public peace and good order. Gauged by this standard, we cannot say that a law which authorizes or even requires the separation of the two races in public conveyances is unreasonable, or more obnoxious to the fourteenth amendment than the acts of congress requiring separate schools for colored children in the District of Columbia, the constitutionality of which does not seem to have been questioned, or the corresponding acts of state legislatures.

We consider the underlying fallacy of the plaintiff's argument to consist in the assumption that the enforced separation of the two races stamps the colored race with a badge of inferiority. If this be so, it is not by reason of anything found in the act, but solely because the colored race chooses to put that construction upon it. The argument necessarily assumes that if, as has been more than once the case, and is not unlikely to be so again, the colored race should become the dominant power in the state legislature, and should enact a law in precisely similar terms, it would thereby relegate the white race to an inferior position. We imagine that the white race, at least, would not acquiesce in this assumption. The argument also assumes that social prejudices may be overcome by legislation, and that equal rights cannot be secured to the negro except by an enforced commingling of the two races. We cannot accept this proposition. If the two races are to meet upon terms of social equality, it must be the result of natural affinities, a mutual appreciation of each other's merits, and a voluntary consent of individuals. As was said by the court of appeals of New York in People v. Gallagher, 93 N. Y. 438, 448: "This end can neither be accomplished nor promoted by laws which conflict with the general sentiment of the community upon whom they are designed to operate. When the government, therefore, has secured to each of its citizens equal rights before the law, and equal opportunities for improvement and progress, it has accomplished the end for which it was organized, and performed all of the functions respecting social advantages with which it is endowed." Legislation is powerless to eradicate racial instincts, or to abolish distinctions based upon physical differences, and the attempt to do so can only result in accentuating the difficulties of the present situation. If the civil and political rights of both races be equal, one cannot be inferior to the other civilly or politically. If one race be inferior to the other socially, the constitution of the United States cannot put them upon the same plane.

It is true that the question of the proportion of colored blood necessary to constitute a colored person, as distinguished from a white person, is one upon which there is a difference of opinion in the different states; some holding that any visible admixture of black blood stamps the person as belonging to the colored race (State v. Chavers, 5 Jones [N. C.] 1); others, that it depends upon the preponderance of blood (Gray v. State, 4 Ohio, 354; Monroe v. Collins, 17 Ohio St. 665); and still others, that the predominance of white blood must only be in the proportion of three-fourths (People v. Dean, 14 Mich. 406; Jones v. Com., 80 Va. 544). But these are questions to be determined under the laws of each state, and are not properly put in issue in this case. Under the allegations of his petition, it may undoubtedly become a question of importance whether, under the laws of Louisiana, the petitioner belongs to the white or colored race.

The judgment of the court below is therefore affirmed.

Mr. Justice BREWER did not hear the argument or participate in the decision of this case.

Mr. Justice HARLAN dissenting.

By the Louisiana statute the validity of which is here involved, all railway companies (other than street-railroad companies) carry passengers in that state are required to have separate but equal accommodations for white and colored persons, "by providing two or more passenger coaches for each passenger train, or by dividing the passenger coaches by a partition so as to secure separate accommodations." Under this statute, no colored person is permitted to occupy a seat in a coach assigned to white persons; nor any white person to occupy a seat in a coach assigned to colored persons. The managers of the railroad are not allowed to exercise any discretion in the premises, but are required to assign each passenger to some coach or compartment set apart for the exclusive use of is race. If a passenger insists upon going into a coach or compartment not set apart for persons of his race, he is subject to be fined, or to be imprisoned in the parish jail. Penalties are prescribed for the refusal or neglect of the officers, directors, conductors, and employees of railroad companies to comply with the provisions of the act.

Only "nurses attending children of the other race" are excepted from the operation of the statute. No exception is made of colored attendants travel-ing with adults. A white man is not permitted to have his colored servant with him in the same coach, even if his condition of health requires the constant personal assistance of such servant. If a colored maid insists upon riding in the same coach with a white woman whom she has been employed to serve, and who may need her personal attention while traveling, she is subject to be fined or imprisoned for such an exhibition of zeal in the discharge of duty.

While there may be in Louisiana persons of different races who are not cit-izens of the United States, the words in the act "white and colored races" nec-essarily include all citizens of the United States of both races residing in that state. So that we have before us a state enactment that compels, under penal-ties, the separation of the two races in railroad passenger coaches, and makes it a crime for a citizen of either race to enter a coach that has been assigned to citizens of the other race.

Thus, the state regulates the use of a public highway by citizens of the United States solely upon the basis of race.

However apparent the injustice of such legislation may be, we have only to consider whether it is consistent with the constitution of the United States.

That a railroad is a public highway, and that the corporation which owns or operates it is in the exercise of public functions, is not, at this day, to be disputed. Mr. Justice Nelson, speaking for this court in New Jersey Steam Nav. Co. v. Merchants' Bank, 6 How. 344, 382, said that a common carrier was in the exercise "of a sort of public office, and has public duties to perform, from which he should not be permitted to exonerate himself without the assent of the parties concerned." Mr. Justice Strong, delivering the judgment of this court in Olcott v. Supervisors, 16 Wall. 678, 694, said: "That railroads, though con-structed by private corporations, and owned by them, are public highways, has been the doctrine of nearly all the courts ever since such conveniences for passage and transportation have had any existence. Very early the question arose whether a state's right of eminent domain could be exercised by a pri-vate corporation created for the purpose of constructing a railroad. Clearly, it could not, unless taking land for such a purpose by such an agency is taking land for public use. The right of eminent domain nowhere justifies taking prop-erty for a private use. Yet it is a doctrine universally accepted that a state leg-islature may authorize a private corporation to take land for the construction of such a road, making compensation to the owner. What else does this doc-trine mean if not that building a railroad, though it be built by a private cor-poration, is an act done for a public use?" So, in Township of Pine Grove v. Talcott, 19 Wall. 666, 676: "Though the corporation [a railroad company] was private, its work was public, as much so as if it were to be constructed by the state." So, in Inhabitants of Worcester v. Western R. Corp., 4 Metc. (Mass.) 564: "The establishment of that great thoroughfare is regarded as a public work, established by public authority, intended for the public use and benefit, the use of which is secured to the whole community, and constitutes, therefore, like a canal, turnpike, or highway, a public easement." "It is true that the real and personal property, necessary to the establishment and management of the railroad, is vested in the corporation; but it is in trust for the public."

In respect of civil rights, common to all citizens, the constitution of the United States does not, I think, permit any public authority to know the race of those entitled to be protected in the enjoyment of such rights. Every true man has pride of race, and under appropriate circumstances, when the rights of others, his equals before the law, are not to be affected, it is his privilege to express such pride and to take such action based upon it as to him seems proper. But I deny that any legislative body or judicial tribunal may have regard to the race of citizens when the civil rights of those citizens are involved. Indeed, such legislation as that here in question is inconsistent not only with that equality of rights which pertains to citizenship, national and state, but with the personal liberty enjoyed by every one within the United States.

The thirteenth amendment does not permit the withholding or the deprivation of any right necessarily inhering in freedom. It not only struck down the institution of slavery as previously existing in the United States, but it prevents the imposition of any burdens or disabilities that constitute badges of slavery or servitude. It decreed universal civil freedom in this country. This court has so adjudged. But, that amendment having been found inadequate to the protection of the rights of those who had been in slavery, it was followed by the fourteenth amendment, which added greatly to the dignity and glory of American citizenship, and to the security of personal liberty, by declaring that "all persons born or naturalized in the United States, and subject to the jurisdiction thereof, are citizens of the United States and of the state wherein they reside," and that "no state shall make or enforce any law which shall abridge the privileges or immunities of citizens of the United States; nor shall any state deprive any person of life, liberty or property without due process of law, nor deny to any person within its jurisdiction the equal protection of the laws." These two amendments, if enforced according to their true intent and meaning, will protect all the civil rights that pertain to freedom and citizenship. Finally, and to the end that no citizen should be denied, on account of his race, the privilege of participating in the political control of his country, it was declared by the fifteenth amendment that "the right of citizens of the United States to vote shall not be denied or abridged by the United States or by any state on account of race, color or previous condition of servitude."

These notable additions to the fundamental law were welcomed by the friends of liberty throughout the world. They removed the race line from our governmental systems. They had, as this court has said, a common purpose, namely, to secure "to a race recently emancipated, a race that through many generations have been held in slavery, all the civil rights that the superior race enjoy." They declared, in legal effect, this court has further said, "that the law in the states shall be the same for the black as for the white; that all persons, whether colored or white, shall stand equal before the laws of the states; and in regard to the colored race, for whose protection the amendment was primarily designed, that no discrimination shall be made against them by law because of their color." We also said: "The words of the amendment, it is true, are prohibitory, but they contain a necessary implication of a positive immunity or right, most valuable to the colored race,-the right to exemption from unfriendly legislation against them distinctively as colored; exemption from legal discriminations, implying inferiority in civil society, lessening the security of their enjoyment of the rights which others enjoy; and discriminations which are steps towards reducing them to the condition of a subject race." It was, consequently, adjudged that a state law that excluded citizens of the colored race from juries, because of their race, however well qualified in other respects to discharge the duties of jurymen, was repugnant to the fourteenth amendment. Strauder v. West Virginia, 100 U.S. 303, 306, 307 S.; Virginia v. Rives, Id. 313; Ex parte Virginia, Id. 339; Neal v. Delaware, 103 U.S. 370, 386; Bush v. Com., 107 U.S. 110, 116, 1 S. Sup. Ct. 625. At the present term, referring to the previous adjudications, this court declared that "underlying all of those decisions is the principle that the constitution of the United States, in its present form, forbids, so far as civil and political rights are concerned, discrimination by the general government or the states against any citizen because of his race. All citizens are equal before the law." Gibson v. State, 162 U.S. 565, 16 Sup. Ct. 904.

The decisions referred to show the scope of the recent amendments of the constitution. They also show that it is not within the power of a state to prohibit colored citizens, because of their race, from participating as jurors in the administration of justice.

It was said in argument that the statute of Louisiana does not discriminate against either race, but prescribes a rule applicable alike to white and colored citizens. But this argument does not meet the difficulty. Every one knows that the statute in question had its origin in the purpose, not so much to exclude white persons from railroad cars occupied by blacks, as to exclude colored people from coaches occupied by or assigned to white persons. Railroad corporations of Louisiana did not make discrimination among whites in the matter of commodation for travelers. The thing to accomplish was, under the guise of giving equal accommodation for whites and blacks, to compel the latter to keep to themselves while traveling in railroad passenger coaches. No one would be so wanting in candor as to assert the contrary. The fundamental objection, therefore, to the statute, is that it interferes with the personal freedom of citizens. "Personal liberty," it has been well said, "consists in the power of locomotion, of changing situation, or removing one's person to whatsoever places one's own inclination may direct, without imprisonment or restraint, unless by due course of law." 1 Bl. Comm. *134. If a white man and a black man choose to occupy the same public conveyance on a public highway, it is their right to do so; and no government, proceeding alone on grounds of race, can prevent it without infringing the personal liberty of each.

It is one thing for railroad carriers to furnish, or to be required by law to furnish, equal accommodations for all whom they are under a legal duty to carry. It is quite another thing for government to forbid citizens of the white and black races from traveling in the same public conveyance, and to punish officers of railroad companies for permitting persons of the two races to occupy the same passenger coach. If a state can prescribe, as a rule of civil conduct, that whites and blacks shall not travel as passengers in the same railroad coach, why may it not so regulate the use of the streets of its cities and towns as to compel white citizens to keep on one side of a street, and black citizens to keep on the other? Why may it not, upon like grounds, punish whites and blacks who ride together in street cars or in open vehicles on a public road or street? Why may it not require sheriffs to assign whites to one side of a court room, and blacks to the other? And why may it not also prohibit the commingling of the two races in the galleries of legislative halls or in public assemblages convened for the consideration of the political questions of the day? Further, if this statute of Louisiana is consistent with the personal liberty of citizens, why may not the state require the separation in railroad coaches of native and naturalized citizens of the United States, or of Protestants and Roman Catholics?

The answer given at the argument to these questions was that regulations of the kind they suggest would be unreasonable, and could not, therefore, stand before the law. Is it meant that the determination of questions of legislative power depends upon the inquiry whether the statute whose validity is questioned is, in the judgment of the courts, a reasonable one, taking all the circumstances into consideration? A statute may be unreasonable merely because a sound public policy forbade its enactment. But I do not understand that the courts have anything to do with the policy or expediency of legislation. A statute may be valid, and yet, upon grounds of public policy, may well be characterized as unreasonable. Mr. Sedgwick correctly states the rule when he says that, the legislative intention being clearly ascertained, "the courts have no other duty to perform than to execute the legislative will, without any regard to their views as to the wisdom or justice of the particular enactment." Sedg. St. & Const. Law, 324. There is a dangerous tendency in these latter days to enlarge the functions of the courts, by means of judicial interference with the will of the people as expressed by the legislature. Our institutions have the distinguishing characteristic that the three departments of government are co-ordinate and separate. Each much keep within the limits defined by the constitution. And the courts best discharge their duty by executing the will of the law-making power, constitutionally expressed, leaving the results of legislation to be dealt with by the people through their representatives. Statutes must always have a reasonable construction. Sometimes they are to be construed strictly, sometimes literally, in order to carry out the legislative will. But, however construed, the intent of the legislature is to be respected if the particular statute in question is valid, although the courts, looking at the public interests, may conceive the statute to be both unreasonable and impolitic. If the power exists to enact a statute, that ends the matter so far as the courts are concerned. The adjudged cases in which statutes have been held to be void, because unreasonable, are those in which the means employed by the legislature were not at all germane to the end to which the legislature was competent.

The white race deems itself to be the dominant race in this country. And so it is, in prestige, in achievements, in education, in wealth, and in power. So, I doubt not, it will continue to be for all time, if it remains true to its great heritage, and holds fast to the principles of constitutional liberty. But in view of the constitution, in the eye of the law, there is in this country no superior, dominant, ruling class of citizens. There is no caste here. Our constitution is color-blind, and neither knows nor tolerates classes among citizens. In respect of civil rights, all citizens are equal before the law. The humblest is the peer of the most powerful. The law regards man as man, and takes no account of his surroundings or of his color when his civil rights as guarantied by the supreme law of the land are involved. It is therefore to be regretted that this high tribunal, the final expositor of the fundamental law of the land, has reached the conclusion that it is competent for a state to regulate the enjoyment by citizens of their civil rights solely upon the basis of race.

In my opinion, the judgment this day rendered will, in time, prove to be quite as pernicious as the decision made by this tribunal in the Dred Scott Case.

It was adjudged in that case that the descendants of Africans who were imported into this country, and sold as slaves, were not included nor intended to be included under the word "citizens" in the constitution, and could not claim any of the rights and privileges which that instrument provided for and secured to citizens of the United States; that, at time of the adoption of the constitution, they were "considered as a subordinate and inferior class of beings, who had been subjugated by the dominant race, and, whether emancipated or not, yet remained subject to their authority, and had no rights or privileges but such as those who held the power and the government might choose to grant them." 17 How. 393, 404. The recent amendments of the constitution, it was supposed, had eradicated these principles from our institutions. But it seems that we have yet, in some of the states, a dominant race,-a superior class of citizens,-which assumes to regulate the enjoyment of civil rights, common to all citizens, upon the basis of race. The present decision, it may well be apprehended, will not only stimulate aggressions, more or less brutal and irritating, upon the admitted rights of colored citizens, but will encourage the belief that it is possible, by means of state enactments, to defeat the beneficent purposes which the people of the United States had in view when they adopted the recent amendments of the constitution, by one of which the blacks of this country were made citizens of the United States and of the states in which they respectively reside, and whose privileges and immunities, as citizens, the states are forbidden to abridge. Sixty millions of whites are in no danger from the presence here of eight millions of blacks. The destinies of the two races, in this country, are indissolubly linked together, and the interests of both require that the common government of all shall not permit the seeds of race hate to be planted under the sanction of law. What can more certainly arouse race hate, what more certainly create and perpetuate a feeling of distrust between these races, than state enactments which, in fact, proceed on the ground that colored citizens are so inferior and degraded that they cannot be allowed to sit in public coaches occupied by white citizens? That, as all will admit, is the real meaning of such legislation as was enacted in Louisiana.

The sure guaranty of the peace and security of each race is the clear, distinct, unconditional recognition by our governments, national and state, of every right that inheres in civil freedom, and of the equality before the law of all citizens of the United States, without regard to race. State enactments regulating the enjoyment of civil rights upon the basis of race, and cunningly devised to defeat legitimate results of the war, under the pretense of recognizing equality of rights, can have no other result than to render permanent peace impossible, and to keep alive a conflict of races, the continuance of which must do harm to all concerned. This question is not met by the suggestion that social equality cannot exist between the white and black races in this country. That argument, if it can be properly regarded as one, is scarcely worthy of consideration; for social equality no more exists between two races when traveling in a passenger coach or a public highway than when members of the same races sit by each other in a street car or in the jury box, or stand or sit with each other in a political assembly, or when they use in common the streets of a city or town, or when they are in the same room for the purpose of having their names placed on the registry of voters, or when they approach the ballot box in order to exercise the high privilege of voting.

There is a race so different from our own that we do not permit those belonging to it to become citizens of the United States. Persons belonging to it are, with few exceptions, absolutely excluded from our country. I allude to the Chinese race. But, by the statute in question, a Chinaman can ride in the same passenger coach with white citizens of the United States, while citizens of the black race in Louisiana, many of whom, perhaps, risked their lives for the preservation of the Union, who are entitled, by law, to participate in the political control of the state and nation, who are not excluded, by law or by reason of their race, from public stations of any kind, and who have all the legal rights that belong to white citizens, are yet declared to be criminals, liable to imprisonment, if they ride in a public coach occupied by citizens of the white race. It is scarcely just to say that a colored citizen should not object to occupying a public coach assigned to his own race. He does not object, nor, perhaps, would he object to separate coaches for his race if his rights under the law were recognized. But he does object, and he ought never to cease objecting, that citizens of the white and black races can be adjudged criminals because they sit, or claim the right to sit, in the same public coach on a public highway. The arbitrary separation of citizens, on the basis of race, while they are on a public highway, is a badge of servitude wholly inconsistent with the civil freedom and the equality before the law established by the constitution. It cannot be justified upon any legal grounds.

If evils will result from the commingling of the two races upon public highways established for the benefit of all, they will be infinitely less than those that will surely come from state legislation regulating the enjoyment of civil rights upon the basis of race. We boast of the freedom enjoyed by our people above all other peoples. But it is difficult to reconcile that boast with a state of the law which, practically, puts the brand of servitude and degradation upon a large class of our fellow citizens,-our equals before the law. The thin disguise of "equal" accommodations for passengers in railroad coaches will not mislead any one, nor atone for the wrong this day done.

The result of the whole matter is that while this court has frequently adjudged, and at the present term has recognized the doctrine, that a state cannot, consistently with the constitution of the United States, prevent white and black citizens, having the required qualifications for jury service, from sitting in the same jury box, it is now solemnly held that a state may prohibit white and black citizens from sitting in the same passenger coach on a public highway, or may require that they be separated by a "partition" when in the same passenger coach. May it not now be reasonably expected that astute men of the dominant race, who affect to be disturbed at the possibility that the integrity of the white race may be corrupted, or that its supremacy will be imperiled, by contact on public highways with black people, will endeavor to procure statutes requiring white and black jurors to be separated in the jury box by a "partition," and that, upon retiring from the court room to consult as to their verdict, such partition, if it be a movable one, shall be taken to their consultation room, and set up in such way as to prevent black jurors from coming too close to their brother jurors of the white race. If the "partition" used in the court room happens to be stationary, provision could be made for screens with openings through which jurors of the two races could confer as to their verdict without coming into personal contact with each other. I cannot see but that, according to the principles this day announced, such state legislation, although conceived in hostility to, and enacted for the purpose of humiliating, citizens of the United States of a particular race, would be held to be consistent with the constitution.

I do not deem it necessary to review the decisions of state courts to which reference was made in argument. Some, and the most important, of them, are wholly inapplicable, because rendered prior to the adoption of the last amendments of the constitution, when colored people had very few rights which the dominant race felt obliged to respect. Others were made at a time when public opinion, in many localities, was dominated by the institution of slavery; when it would not have been safe to do justice to the black man; and when, so far as the rights of blacks were concerned, race prejudice was, practically, the supreme law of the land. Those decisions cannot be guides in the era introduced by the recent amendments of the supreme law, which established universal civil freedom, gave citizenship to all born or naturalized in the United States, and residing ere, obliterated the race line from our systems of governments, national and state, and placed our free institutions upon the broad and sure foundation of the equality of all men before the law.

I am of opinion that the state of Louisiana is inconsistent with the personal liberty of citizens, white and black, in that state, and hostile to both the spirit and letter of the constitution of the United States. If laws of like character should be enacted in the several states of the Union, the effect would be in the highest degree mischievous. Slavery, as an institution tolerated by law, would, it is true, have disappeared from our country; but there would remain a power in the states, by sinister legislation, to interfere with the full enjoyment of the blessings of freedom, to regulate civil rights, common to all citizens, upon the basis of race, and to place in a condition of legal inferiority a large body of American citizens, now constituting a part of the political community, called the "People of the United States," for whom, and by whom through representatives, our government is administered. Such a system is inconsistent with the guaranty given by the constitution to each state of a republican form of government, and may be stricken down by congressional action, or by the courts in the discharge of their solemn duty to maintain the supreme law of the land, anything in the constitution or laws of any state to the contrary notwithstanding.

For the reason stated, I am constrained to withhold my assent from the opinion and judgment of the majority.

Transcription of the Opinion of the Supreme Court of the United States in Plessy v. Ferguson *courtesy of FindLaw.*
Citation: *Plessy v. Ferguson*, Judgement, Decided May 18, 1886; Records of the Supreme Court of the United States; Record Group 267; *Plessy v. Ferguson*, 163, #15248, National Archives.

8. The National Origins Act of 1924 (Johnson-Reed Act)

This is the most racist U.S. immigration law. It intended to favor northern and western European countries in immigrant visas and to restrict the number of immigrants from southern and eastern European countries. It also completely banned the immigration of non-Europeans who were not eligible for citizenship. As a result, the number of immigrants from southern and eastern European, predominantly non-Protestant, countries, was drastically reduced, and Asian immigration almost came to an end.

The Statutes at Large of the United States of America, from December, 1923 to March, 1925. Vol. XLII, part 1, pp. 153–169. Washington, DC: Government Printing Office, 1925.

SIXTY EIGHTH CONGRESS. SESS.I. CH. 185, 190. 1924.

Be it enacted by the Senate and House of Representatives of the United States of America in Congress assembled, That this Act may be cited as the "Immigration Act of 1924."

SEC. 2. (a) A consular officer upon the application of any immigrant (as defined in section 3) may (under the conditions hereinafter prescribed and subject to the limitations prescribed in this Act or regulations made thereunder as to the number of immigration visas which may be issued by such officer) issue to such immigrant an immigration visa which shall consist of one copy of the application provided for in section 7, visaed by such consular officer. Such visa shall specify (1) the nationality of the immigrant; (2) whether he is a quota immigrant (as defined in section 5) or a non-quota immigrant (as defined in section 4); (3) the date on which the validity of the immigration visa shall expire; and such additional information necessary to the proper enforcement of the immigration laws and the naturalization laws as may be by regulations prescribed.

(b) The immigrant shall furnish two copies of his photograph to the consular officer. One copy shall be permanently attached by the consular officer to the immigration visa and the other copy shall be disposed of as may be by regulations prescribed.

(c) The validity of an immigration visa shall expire at the end of such period, specified in the immigration visa, not exceeding four months, as shall be by regulations prescribed. In the case of a immigrant arriving in the United States by water, or arriving by water in foreign contiguous territory on a continuous voyage to the United States, if the vessel, before the expiration of the validity of his immigration visa, departed from the last port outside the United States and outside foreign contiguous territory at which the immigrant embarked, and if the immigrant proceeds on a continuous voyage to the United States, then, regardless of the time of his arrival in the United States, the validity of his immigration visa shall not be considered to have expired.

(d) If an immigrant is required by any law, or regulations or orders made pursuant to law, to secure the visa of his passport by a consular officer before being permitted to enter the United States, such immigrant shall not be required to secure any other visa of his passport than the immigration visa issued under this Act, but a record of the number and date of his immigration visa shall be noted on his passport without charge therefor. This subdivision shall not apply to an immigrant who is relieved, under subdivision (b) of section 13, from obtaining an immigration visa.

(e) The manifest or list of passengers required by the immigration laws shall contain a place for entering thereon the date, place of issuance, and number of the immigration visa of each immigrant. The immigrant shall surrender his immigration visa to the immigration officer at the port of inspection, who shall at the time of inspection indorse on the immigration visa the date, the port of entry, and the name of the vessel, if any, on which the immigrant arrived. The immigration visa shall be transmitted forthwith by the immigration officer in charge at the port of inspection to the Department of Labor under regulations prescribed by the Secretary of Labor.

(f) No immigration visa shall be issued to an immigrant if it appears to the consular officer, from statements in the application, or in the papers submitted therewith, that the immigrant is inadmissible to the United States under the immigration laws, nor shall such immigration visa be issued if the application fails to comply with the provisions of this Act, nor shall such immigration visa be issued if the consular officer knows or has reason to believe that the immigrant is inadmissible to the United States under the immigration laws.

(g) Nothing in this Act shall be construed to entitle an immigrant, to whom an immigration visa has been issued, to enter the United States, if, upon arrival in the United States, he is found to be inadmissible to the United States under the immigration laws. The substance of this subdivision shall be printed conspicuously upon every immigration visa.

(h) A fee of $9 shall be charged for the issuance of each immigration visa, which shall be covered into the Treasury as miscellaneous receipts.

DEFINITION OF IMMIGRANT.

SEC. 3. When used in this Act the term "immigrant" means an alien departing from any place outside the United States destined for the United States, except (1) a government official, his family, attendants, servants, and employees, (2) an alien visiting the United States temporarily as a tourist or temporarily for business or pleasure, (3) an alien in continuous transit through the United States, (4) an alien lawfully admitted to the United States who later goes in transit from one part of the United States to another through foreign contiguous territory, (5) a bona fide alien seaman serving as such on a vessel arriving at a port of the United States and seeking to enter temporarily the United States solely in the pursuit of his calling as a seaman, and (6) an alien entitled to enter the United States solely to carry on trade under and in pursuance of the provisions of a present existing treaty of commerce and navigation.

NON-QUOTA IMMIGRANTS.

SEC. 4. When used in this Act the term "non-quota immigrant" means-

(a) An immigrant who is the unmarried child under 18 years of age, or the wife, of a citizen of the United States who resides therein at the time of the filing of a petition under section 9;

(b) An immigrant previously lawfully admitted to the United States, who is returning from a temporary visit abroad;

(c) An immigrant who was born in the Dominion of Canada, Newfoundland, the Republic of Mexico, the Republic of Cuba, the Republic of Haiti, the Dominican Republic, the Canal Zone, or an independent country of Central or South America, and his wife, and his unmarried children under 18 years of age, if accompanying or following to join him;

(d) An immigrant who continuously for at least two years immediately preceding the time of his application for admission to the United States has been, and who seeks to enter the United States solely for the purpose of, carrying on the vocation of minister of any religious denomination, or professor of a college, academy, seminary, or university; and his wife, and his unmarried children under 18 years of age, if accompanying or following to join him; or

(e) An immigrant who is a bona fide student at least 15 years of age and who seeks to enter the United States solely for the purpose of study at an accredited school, college, academy, seminary, or university, particularly designated by him and approved by, the Secretary of Labor, which shall have agreed to report to the Secretary of Labor the termination of attendance of each immigrant student, and if any such institution of learning fails to make such reports promptly the approval shall be withdrawn.

EXCLUSION FROM UNITED STATES.

SEC. 13. (a) No immigrant shall be admitted to the United States unless he (1) has an unexpired immigration visa or was born subsequent to the issuance of the immigration visa of the accompanying parent, (2) is of the nationality specified in the visa in the immigration visa, (3) is a non-quota immigrant if specified in the visa in the immigration visa as such, and (4) is otherwise admissible under the immigration laws.

(b) In such classes of cases and under such conditions as may be by regulations prescribed immigrants who have been legally admitted to the United States and who depart therefrom temporarily may be admitted to the United States without being required to obtain an immigration visa.

(c) No alien ineligible to citizenship shall be admitted to the United States unless such alien (1) is admissible as a non-quota immigrant under the provisions of subdivision (b), (d), or (e) of section 4, or (2) is the wife, or the unmarried child under 18 years of age, of an immigrant admissible under such subdivision (d), and is accompanying or following to join him, or (3) is not an immigrant as defined in section 3.

(d) The Secretary of Labor may admit to the United States any otherwise admissible immigrant not admissible under clause (2) or (3) of subdivision (a) of this section, if satisfied that such inadmissibility was not known to, and could not have been ascertained by the exercise of reasonable diligence by, such immigrant prior to the departure of the vessel from the last port outside the United States and outside foreign contiguous territory or, in the case of an immigrant coming from foreign contiguous territory, prior to the application of the immigrant for admission.

(e) No quota immigrant shall be admitted under subdivision (d) if the entire number of immigration visas which may be issued to quota immigrants of the same nationality for the fiscal year already been issued. If such entire number of immigration visas has not been issued, then the Secretary of State, upon the admission of a quota immigrant under subdivision (d), shall reduce by one the number of immigration visas which may be issued to quota immigrants of the same nationality during the fiscal year in which such immigrant is admitted; but if the Secretary of State finds that it will not be practicable to make such reduction before the end of such fiscal year, then such immigrant shall not be admitted.

(f) Nothing in this section shall authorize the remission or refunding of a fine, liability to which has accrued under section 16.

DEPORTATION

SEC. 14. Any alien who at any time after entering the United States is found to have been at the time of entry not entitled under this Act to enter the United States, or to have remained therein for a longer time than permitted under this Act or regulations made thereunder, shall be taken into custody and deported in the same manner as provided for in sections 19 and 20 of the Immigration Act of 1917: Provided, That the Secretary of Labor may, under such conditions and restrictions as to support and care as he may deem necessary, permit permanently to remain in the United States, any alien child who, when under sixteen years of age was heretofore temporarily admitted to the United States and who is now within the United States and either of whose parents is a citizen of the United States.

MAINTENANCE OF EXEMPT STATUS.

SEC. 15. The admission to the United States of an alien excepted from the class of immigrants by clause (2), (3), (4), (5), or (6) of section 3, or declared to be a non-quota immigrant by subdivision (e) of section 4, shall be for such time as may be by regulations prescribed, and under such conditions as may be by regulations prescribed (including, when deemed necessary for the classes mentioned in clauses (2), (3), (4), or (6) of section 3, the giving of bond with sufficient surety, in such sum and containing such conditions as may be by regulations prescribed) to insure that, at the expiration of such time or upon failure to maintain the status under which he was admitted, he will depart from the United States.

SEC 28. As used in this Act-

(a) The term "United States," when used in a geographical sense, means the States, the Territories of Alaska and Hawaii, the District of Columbia, Porto Rico, and the Virgin Islands; and the term "continental United States" means the States and the District of Columbia;

(b) The term "alien" includes any individual not a native-born or naturalized citizen of the United States, but this definition shall not be held to include Indians of the United States not taxed, nor citizens of the islands under the jurisdiction of the United States; (c) The term "ineligible to citizenship," when used in reference to any individual, includes an individual who is debarred from becoming a citizen of the United States under section 2169 of the Revised Statutes, or under section 14 of the Act entitled "An Act to execute certain treaty stipulations relating to Chinese," approved May 6, 1882, or under section 1996, 1997, or 1998 of the Revised Statutes, as amended, or under section 2 of the Act entitled "An Act to authorize the President to increase temporarily the Military Establishment of the United States," approved May 18, 1917, as amended, or under law amendatory of, supplementary to, or in substitution for, any of such sections;

(d) The term "immigration visa" means an immigration visa issued by a consular officer under the provisions of this Act;

(e) The term "consular officer" means any consular or diplomatic officer of the United States designated, under regulations prescribed under this Act, for the purpose of issuing immigration visas under this Act. In case of the Canal Zone and the insular possessions of the United States the term "consular officer" (except as used in section 24) means an officer designated by the President, or by his authority, for the purpose of issuing immigration visas under this Act; (f) The term "Immigration Act of 1917" means the Act of February 5, 1917, entitled "An Act to regulate the immigration of aliens to, and the residence of aliens in, the United States";

(g) The term "immigration laws" includes such Act, this Act, and all laws, conventions, and treaties of the United States relating to the immigration, exclusion, or expulsion of aliens;

(h) The term "person" includes individuals, partnerships, corporations, and associations;

(i) The term "Commissioner General" means the Commissioner General of Immigration;

(j)The term "application for admission" has reference to the application for admission to the United States and not to the application for the issuance of the immigration visa;

(k) The term "permit" means a permit issued under section 10;

(l) The term "unmarried," when used in reference to any as of any time, means an individual who at such time is not married, whether or not previously married;

(m) The terms "child," "father," and "mother," do not include child or parent by adoption unless the adoption took place before January 1, 1924;

(n) The terms "wife" and "husband" do not include a wife husband by reason of a proxy or picture marriage.

9. Executive Order 9066 (February 1942)

In February 1942, President Franklin D. Roosevelt ordered the establishment of internment camps, and the forced evacuation of people of Japanese ancestry settled in the West Coast, with the exception of Hawaii. By this order, more than 100,000 Japanese Americans, including many U.S.-born citizens of Japanese ancestry, were interned in ten camps established in the West. Although the U.S. government's ostensible reason for their internment was the possibility of Japanese Americans engaging in espionage activities to help Japan in the Pacific War, there was no evidence that Japanese Americans were involved in such espionage activities. Many scholars have indicated that racial prejudice against Japanese Americans and white farmers' jealousy of Japanese Americans' success in farming in California led to political lobbies that contributed to the decision to intern Japanese Americans during the war in the Pacific.

AUTHORIZING THE SECRETARY OF WAR TO PRESCRIBE MILITARY AREAS.

Whereas, The successful prosecution of the war requires every possible protection against espionage and against sabotage to national defense material, national defense premises, and national defense utilities as defined in Section 4, Act of April 20, 1918, 40 Stat. 533, as amended by the Act of November 30, 1940, 54 Stat. 1220, and the Act of August 21, 1941, 55 Stat.

655 (U.S.C., Title 50, Sec 104):

Now, therefore, by virtue of the authority vested in me as President of the United States, and Commander in Chief of the Army and Navy, I hereby authorize and direct the Secretary of War, and the Military Commanders whom he may from time to time designate, whenever he or any designated Commander deems such action necessary or desirable, to prescribe military areas in such places and of such extent as he or the appropriate Military Commander may determine, from which any or all persons may be excluded, and with respect to which, the right of any person to enter, remain in, or leave shall be subject to whatever restrictions the Secretary of War or the appropriate Military Commander may determine, from which any or all persons may be excluded, and with respect to which, the right of any person to enter, remain in, or leave shall be subject to whatever restrictions the Secretary of War or the appropriate Military Commander may impose in his discretion. The Secretary of War is hereby authorized to provide for residents of any such area who are excluded therefrom, such transportation, food, shelter, and other accommodations as may be necessary, in the judgment of the Secretary of War or the said Military Commander, and until other arrangements are made, to accomplish the purpose of this order. The designation of military areas in any region or locality shall supersede designations of prohibited and restricted areas by the Attorney General under the Proclamation of December 7 and 8,

1941, and shall supersede the responsibility and authority of the Attorney General under the said Proclamations in respect of such prohibited and restricted areas.

I hereby further authorize and direct the Secretary of War and said Military Commanders to take such other steps as he or the appropriate Military Commander may deem advisable to enforce compliance with the restrictions applicable to each Military area hereinabove authorized to be designated, including the use of Federal troops and other Federal Agencies, with authority to accept assistance of state and local agencies.

I hereby further authorize and direct all Executive Departments, independent establishments and other Federal Agencies, to assist the Secretary of War or the said Military Commanders in carrying out this Executive Order, including the furnishing of medical aid, hospitalization, food, clothing, transportation, use of land, shelter, and other supplies, equipment, utilities, facilities, and services.

This order shall not be construed as modifying or limiting in any way the authority heretofore granted under Executive Order 8972. dated December 12, 1941, nor shall it be construed as limiting or modifying the duty and responsibility of the Federal Bureau of Investigation, with respect to the investigation of alleged acts of sabotage or the duty and responsibility of the Attorney General and the Department of Justice under the Proclamation of December 7 and 8, 1941, prescribing regulations for the conduct and control of alien enemies, except as such duty and responsibility is superseded by the designation of military areas hereunder.

Franklin D. Roosevelt
The White House, February 19, 1942.

10. *Brown v. Board of Education* (May 1954)

In May 1954, the U.S. Supreme Court concluded in the case of *Brown v. the Board of Education* that "in the field of public education, the doctrine of 'separate but equal' has no place" and that "separate facilities are inherently unequal." Thus, the 1954 Supreme Court ruling destroyed the doctrine of separate but unequal facilities supported by the Supreme Court in the 1896 *Plessy v. Ferguson* case. The decision came to have the revolutionary impact of dismantling institutionalized segregation practices not only in education, but in other areas such as public transportation.

Supreme Court of the United States
Brown v. Board of Education, 347 U.S. 483 (1954) (USSC+)
347 U.S. 483
Argued December 9, 1952
Reargued December 8, 1953
Decided May 17, 1954
APPEAL FROM THE UNITED STATES DISTRICT COURT FOR THE
DISTRICT OF KANSAS*
Syllabus

Segregation of white and Negro children in the public schools of a State solely on the basis of race, pursuant to state laws permitting or requiring such segregation, denies to Negro children the equal protection of the laws guaranteed by the Fourteenth Amendment—even though the physical facilities and other "tangible" factors of white and Negro schools may be equal.

(a) The history of the Fourteenth Amendment is inconclusive as to its intended effect on public education.

(b) The question presented in these cases must be determined not on the basis of conditions existing when the Fourteenth Amendment was adopted, but in the light of the full development of public education and its present place in American life throughout the Nation.

(c) Where a State has undertaken to provide an opportunity for an education in its public schools, such an opportunity is a right which must be made available to all on equal terms.

(d) Segregation of children in public schools solely on the basis of race deprives children of the minority group of equal educational opportunities, even though the physical facilities and other "tangible" factors may be equal.

(e) The "separate but equal" doctrine adopted in Plessy v. Ferguson, 163 U.S. 537, has no place in the field of public education.

(f) The cases are restored to the docket for further argument on specified questions relating to the forms of the decrees.

Opinion

MR. CHIEF JUSTICE WARREN delivered the opinion of the Court.

These cases come to us from the States of Kansas, South Carolina, Virginia, and Delaware. They are premised on different facts and different local conditions, but a common legal question justifies their consideration together in this consolidated opinion.

In each of the cases, minors of the Negro race, through their legal representatives, seek the aid of the courts in obtaining admission to the public schools of their community on a nonsegregated basis. In each instance, they had been denied admission to schools attended by white children under laws requiring or permitting segregation according to race. This segregation was alleged to deprive the plaintiffs of the equal protection of the laws under the Fourteenth Amendment. In each of the cases other than the Delaware case, a three-judge federal district court denied relief to the plaintiffs on the so-called "separate but equal" doctrine announced by this Court in Plessy v. Fergson, 163 U.S. 537. Under that doctrine, equality of treatment is accorded when the races are provided substantially equal facilities, even though these facilities be separate. In the Delaware case, the Supreme Court of Delaware adhered to that doctrine, but ordered that the plaintiffs be admitted to the white schools because of their superiority to the Negro schools.

The plaintiffs contend that segregated public schools are not "equal" and cannot be made "equal," and that hence they are deprived of the equal protection of the laws. Because of the obvious importance of the question presented, the Court took jurisdiction. Argument was heard in the 1952 Term, and reargument was heard this Term on certain questions propounded by the Court.

Reargument was largely devoted to the circumstances surrounding the adoption of the Fourteenth Amendment in 1868. It covered exhaustively consideration of the Amendment in Congress, ratification by the states, then-existing practices in racial segregation, and the views of proponents and opponents of the Amendment. This discussion and our own investigation convince us that, although these sources cast some light, it is not enough to resolve the problem with which we are faced. At best, they are inconclusive. The most avid proponents of the post–War Amendments undoubtedly intended them to remove all legal distinctions among "all persons born or naturalized in the United States." Their opponents, just as certainly, were antagonistic to both the letter and the spirit of the Amendments and wished them to have the most limited effect. What others in Congress and the state legislatures had in mind cannot be determined with any degree of certainty.

An additional reason for the inconclusive nature of the Amendment's history with respect to segregated schools is the status of public education at that time. In the South, the movement toward free common schools, supported by general taxation, had not yet taken hold. Education of white children was largely in the hands of private groups. Education of Negroes was almost nonexistent, and practically all of the race were illiterate. In fact, any education of Negroes was forbidden by law in some states. Today, in contrast, many Negroes have achieved outstanding success in the arts and sciences, as well as in the business and professional world. It is true that public school education at the time of the Amendment had advanced further in the North, but the effect of the Amendment on Northern States was generally ignored in the congressional debates. Even in the North, the conditions of public education did not approximate those existing today. The curriculum was usually rudimentary; ungraded schools were common in rural areas; the school term was but three months a year in many states, and compulsory school attendance was virtually unknown. As a consequence, it is not surprising that there should be so little in the history of the Fourteenth Amendment relating to its intended effect on public education.

In the first cases in this Court construing the Fourteenth Amendment, decided shortly after its adoption, the Court interpreted it as proscribing all state-imposed discriminations against the Negro race. The doctrine of "separate but equal" did not make its appearance in this Court until 1896 in the case of Plessy v. Ferguson, supra, involving not education but transportation. American courts have since labored with the doctrine for over half a century. In this Court, there have been six cases involving the "separate but equal" doctrine in the field of public education. In Cumming v. County Board of Education, 175 U.S. 528, and Gong Lum v. Rice, 275 U.S. 78, the validity of the doctrine itself was not challenged. In more recent cases, all on the graduate school level, inequality was found in that specific benefits enjoyed by white students were denied to Negro students of the same educational qualifications. Missouri ex rel. Gaines v. Canada, 305 U.S. 337; Sipuel v. Oklahoma, 332 U.S. 631; Sweatt v. Painter, 339 U.S. 629; McLaurin v. Oklahoma State Regents, 339 U.S. 637. In none of these cases was it necessary to reexamine the doctrine to grant relief to the Negro plaintiff. And in Sweatt v. Painter, supra, the Court expressly reserved decision on the question whether Plessy v. Ferguson should be held inapplicable to public education.

In the instant cases, that question is directly presented. Here, unlike Sweatt v. Painter, there are findings below that the Negro and white schools involved have been equalized, or are being equalized, with respect to buildings, curricula, qualifications and salaries of teachers, and other "tangible" factors. Our decision, therefore, cannot turn on merely a comparison of these tangible factors in the Negro and white schools involved in each of the cases. We must look instead to the effect of segregation itself on public education.

In approaching this problem, we cannot turn the clock back to 1868, when the Amendment was adopted, or even to 1896, when Plessy v. Ferguson was written. We must consider public education in the light of its full development and its present place in American life throughout the Nation. Only in this way can it be determined if segregation in public schools deprives these plaintiffs of the equal protection of the laws.

Today, education is perhaps the most important function of state and local governments. Compulsory school attendance laws and the great expenditures for education both demonstrate our recognition of the importance of education to our democratic society. It is required in the performance of our most basic public responsibilities, even service in the armed forces. It is the very foundation of good citizenship. Today it is a principal instrument in awakening the child to cultural values, in preparing him for later professional training, and in helping him to adjust normally to his environment. In these days, it is doubtful that any child may reasonably be expected to succeed in life if he is denied the opportunity of an education. Such an opportunity, where the state has undertaken to provide it, is a right which must be made available to all on equal terms.

We come then to the question presented: Does segregation of children in public schools solely on the basis of race, even though the physical facilities and other "tangible" factors may be equal, deprive the children of the minority group of equal educational opportunities? We believe that it does.

In Sweatt v. Painter, supra, in finding that a segregated law school for Negroes could not provide them equal educational opportunities, this Court relied in large part on "those qualities which are incapable of objective measurement but which make for greatness in a law school." In McLaurin v. Oklahoma State Regents, supra, the Court, in requiring that a Negro admitted to a white graduate school be treated like all other students, again resorted to intangible considerations: "his ability to study, to engage in discussions and exchange views with other students, and, in general, to learn his profession." Such considerations apply with added force to children in grade and high schools. To separate them from others of similar age and qualifications solely because of their race generates a feeling of inferiority as to their status in the community that may affect their hearts and minds in a way unlikely ever to be undone. The effect of this separation on their educational opportunities was well stated by a finding in the Kansas case by a court which nevertheless felt compelled to rule against the Negro plaintiffs:

> Segregation of white and colored children in public schools has a detrimental effect upon the colored children. The impact is greater when it has the sanction of the law, for the policy of separating the races is usually interpreted as de-

noting the inferiority of the negro group. A sense of inferiority affects the motivation of a child to learn. Segregation with the sanction of law, therefore, has
a tendency to [retard] the educational and mental development of negro children and to deprive them of some of the benefits they would receive in a
racial[ly] integrated school system.

Whatever may have been the extent of psychological knowledge at the time
of Plessy v. Ferguson, this finding is amply supported by modern authority.
Any language in Plessy v. Ferguson contrary to this finding is rejected.

We conclude that, in the field of public education, the doctrine of "separate
but equal" has no place. Separate educational facilities are inherently unequal.
Therefore, we hold that the plaintiffs and others similarly situated for whom
the actions have been brought are, by reason of the segregation complained
of, deprived of the equal protection of the laws guaranteed by the Fourteenth
Amendment. This disposition makes unnecessary any discussion whether such
segregation also violates the Due Process Clause of the Fourteenth Amendment.

Because these are class actions, because of the wide applicability of this decision, and because of the great variety of local conditions, the formulation of
decrees in these cases presents problems of considerable complexity. On reargument, the consideration of appropriate relief was necessarily subordinated
to the primary question—the constitutionality of segregation in public education. We have now announced that such segregation is a denial of the equal
protection of the laws. In order that we may have the full assistance of the
parties in formulating decrees, the cases will be restored to the docket, and
the parties are requested to present further argument on Questions 4 and 5
previously propounded by the Court for the reargument this term. The Attorney General of the United States is again invited to participate. The Attorneys
General of the states requiring or permitting segregation in public education
will also be permitted to appear as amici curiae upon request to do so by September 15, 1954, and submission of briefs by October 1, 1954.

It is so ordered.

*Together with No. 2, Briggs et al. v. Elliott et al., on appeal from the United
States District Court for the Eastern District of South Carolina, argued December 9–10, 1952, reargued December 7–8, 1953; No. 4, Davis et al. v. County
School Board of Prince Edward County, Virginia, et al., on appeal from the
United States District Court for the Eastern District of Virginia, argued December 10, 1952, reargued December 7–8, 1953, and No. 10, Gebhart et al.
v. Belton et al., on certiorari to the Supreme Court of Delaware, argued December 11, 1952, reargued December 9, 1953.

11. The Civil Rights Act of 1964

As a result of the civil rights movement in the latter half of the 1950s
and early 1960s, Congress passed the Civil Rights Act of 1964 to end
practices of racial segregation and other forms of racial discrimination.

It was the most comprehensive legislation in American history that sought to end racial discrimination in the public arena. Its main objective was to end formal discrimination based on race, color, and/or national origin in various areas, such as voting, public accommodation, education, and employment.

An Act

To enforce the constitutional right to vote, to confer jurisdiction upon the district courts of the United States to provide injunctive relief against discrimination in public accommodations, to authorize the Attorney General to institute suits to protect constitutional rights in public facilities and public education, to extend the Commission on Civil Rights, to prevent discrimination in federally assisted programs, to establish a Commission on Equal Employment Opportunity, and for other purposes.

Be it enacted by the Senate and House of Representatives of the United States of America in Congress assembled, That this Act may be cited as the "Civil Rights Act of 1964".

TITLE I—VOTING RIGHTS

TITLE II—INJUNCTIVE RELIEF AGAINST DISCRIMINATION IN PLACES OF PUBLIC ACCOMMODATION

SEC. 201. (a) All persons shall be entitled to the full and equal enjoyment of the goods, services, facilities, and privileges, advantages, and accommodations of any place of public accommodation, as defined in this section, without discrimination or segregation on the ground of race, color, religion, or national origin.

(b) Each of the following establishments which serves the public is a place of public accommodation within the meaning of this title if its operations affect commerce, or if discrimination or segregation by it is supported by State action:

(1) any inn, hotel, motel, or other establishment which provides lodging to transient guests, other than an establishment located within a building which contains not more than five rooms for rent or hire and which is actually occupied by the proprietor of such establishment as his residence;

(2) any restaurant, cafeteria, lunchroom, lunch counter, soda fountain, or other facility principally engaged in selling food for consumption on the premises, including, but not limited to, any such facility located on the premises of any retail establishment; or any gasoline station;

(3) any motion picture house, theater, concert hall, sports arena, stadium or other place of exhibition or entertainment; and

(4) any establishment (A) (i) which is physically located within the premises of any establishment otherwise covered by this subsection, or (ii) within the premises of which is physically located any such covered establishment, and (B) which holds itself out as serving patrons of such covered establishment.

(c) The operations of an establishment affect commerce within the meaning of this title if (1) it is one of the establishments described in paragraph (1) of subsection (b); (2) in the case of an establishment described in paragraph (2) of subsection (b), it serves or offers to serve interstate travelers or a substantial portion of the food which it serves, or gasoline or other products which it sells, has moved in commerce; (3) in the case of an establishment described in paragraph (3) of subsection (b), it customarily presents films, performances, athletic teams, exhibitions, or other sources of entertainment which move in commerce; and (4) in the case of an establishment described in paragraph (4) of subsection (b), it is physically located within the premises of, or there is physically located within its premises, an establishment the operations of which affect commerce within the meaning of this subsection. For purposes of this section, "commerce" means travel, trade, traffic, commerce, transportation, or communication among the several States, or between the District of Columbia and any State, or between any foreign country or any territory or possession and any State or the District of Columbia, or between points in the same State but through any other State or the District of Columbia or a foreign country.

(d) Discrimination or segregation by an establishment is supported by State action within the meaning of this title if such discrimination or segregation (1) is carried on under color of any law, statute, ordinance, or regulation; or (2) is carried on under color of any custom or usage required or enforced by officials of the State or political subdivision thereof; or (3) is required by action of the State or political subdivision thereof.

(e) The provisions of this title shall not apply to a private club or other establishment not in fact open to the public, except to the extent that the facilities of such establishment are made available to the customers or patrons of an establishment within the scope of subsection (b).

SEC. 202. All persons shall be entitled to be free, at any establishment or place, from discrimination or segregation of any kind on the ground of race, color, religion, or national origin, if such discrimination or segregation is or purports to be required by any law, statute, ordinance, regulation, rule, or order of a State or any agency or political subdivision thereof.

SEC. 203. No person shall (a) withhold, deny, or attempt to withhold or deny, or deprive or attempt to deprive, any person of any right or privilege secured by section 201 or 202, or (b) intimidate, threaten, or coerce, or attempt to intimidate, threaten, or coerce any person with the purpose of interfering with any right or privilege secured by section 201 or 202, or (c) punish or attempt to punish any person for exercising or attempting to exercise any right or privilege secured by section 201 or 202.

SEC. 204. (a) Whenever any person has engaged or there are reasonable grounds to believe that any person is about to engage in any act or practice prohibited by section 203, a civil action for preventive relief, including an application for a permanent or temporary injunction, restraining order, or other order, may be instituted by the person aggrieved and, upon timely application, the court may, in its discretion, permit the Attorney General to intervene in such civil action if he certifies that the case is of general public importance. Upon application by the complainant and in such circumstances as the court may deem just, the court may appoint an attorney for such complainant and may authorize the commencement of the civil action without the payment of fees, costs, or security.

(b) In any action commenced pursuant to this title, the court, in its discretion, may allow the prevailing party, other than the United States, a reasonable attorney's fee as part of the costs, and the United States shall be liable for costs the same as a private person.

(c) In the case of an alleged act or practice prohibited by this title which occurs in a State, or political subdivision of a State, which has a State or local law prohibiting such act or practice and establishing or authorizing a State or local authority to grant or seek relief from such practice or to institute criminal proceedings with respect thereto upon receiving notice thereof, no civil action may be brought under subsection (a) before the expiration of thirty days after written notice of such alleged act or practice has been given to the appropriate State or local authority by registered mail or in person, provided that the court may stay proceedings in such civil action pending the termination of State or local enforcement proceedings.

(d) In the case of an alleged act or practice prohibited by this title which occurs in a State, or political subdivision of a State, which has no State or local law prohibiting such act or practice, a civil action may be brought under subsection (a): Provided, That the court may refer the matter to the Community Relations Service established by title X of this Act for as long as the court believes there is a reasonable possibility of obtaining voluntary compliance, but for not more than sixty days: Provided further, That upon expiration of such sixty-day period, the court may extend such period for an additional period, not to exceed a cumulative total of one hundred and twenty days, if it believes there then exists a reasonable possibility of securing voluntary compliance.

SEC. 205. The Service is authorized to make a full investigation of any complaint referred to it by the court under section 204(d) and may hold such hearings with respect thereto as may be necessary. The Service shall conduct any hearings with respect to any such complaint in executive session, and shall not release any testimony given therein except by agreement of all parties involved in the complaint with the permission of the court, and the Service shall endeavor to bring about a voluntary settlement between the parties.

SEC. 206. (a) Whenever the Attorney General has reasonable cause to believe that any person or group of persons is engaged in a pattern or practice of resistance to the full enjoyment of any of the rights secured by this title, and that the pattern or practice is of such a nature and is intended to deny the full exercise of the rights herein described, the Attorney General may bring a civil action in the appropriate district court of the United States by filing with it a complaint (1) signed by him (or in his absence the Acting Attorney General), (2) setting forth facts pertaining to such pattern or practice, and (3) requesting such preventive relief, including an application for a permanent or temporary injunction, restraining order or other order against the person or persons responsible for such pattern or practice, as he deems necessary to insure the full enjoyment of the rights herein described.

(b) In any such proceeding the Attorney General may file with the clerk of such court a request that a court of three judges be convened to hear and determine the case. Such request by the Attorney General shall be accompanied by a certificate that, in his opinion, the case is of general public importance.

A copy of the certificate and request for a three-judge court shall be immediately furnished by such clerk to the chief judge of the circuit (or in his absence, the presiding circuit judge of the circuit) in which the case is pending. Upon receipt of the copy of such request it shall be the duty of the chief judge of the circuit or the presiding circuit judge, as the case may be, to designate immediately three judges in such circuit, of whom at least one shall be a circuit judge and another of whom shall be a district judge of the court in which the proceeding was instituted, to hear and determine such case, and it shall be the duty of the judges so designated to assign the case for hearing at the earliest practicable date, to participate in the hearing and determination thereof, and to cause the case to be in every way expedited. An appeal from the final judgment of such court will lie to the Supreme Court.

In the event the Attorney General fails to file such a request in any such proceeding, it shall be the duty of the chief judge of the district (or in his absence, the acting chief judge) in which the case is pending immediately to designate a judge in such district to hear and determine the case. In the event that no judge in the district is available to hear and determine the case, the chief judge of the district, or the acting chief judge, as the case may be, shall certify this fact to the chief judge of the circuit (or in his absence, the acting chief judge) who shall then designate a district or circuit judge of the circuit to hear and determine the case.

It shall be the duty of the judge designated pursuant to this section to assign the case for hearing at the earliest practicable date and to cause the case to be in every way expedited.

SEC. 207. (a) The district courts of the United States shall have jurisdiction of proceedings instituted pursuant to this title and shall exercise the same without regard to whether the aggrieved party shall have exhausted any administrative or other remedies that may be provided by law.

(b) The remedies provided in this title shall be the exclusive means of enforcing the rights based on this title, but nothing in this title shall preclude any individual or any State or local agency from asserting any right based on any other Federal or State law not inconsistent with this title, including any statute or ordinance requiring nondiscrimination in public establishments or accommodations, or from pursuing any remedy, civil or criminal, which may be available for the vindication or enforcement of such right.

Discrimination because of Race, Color, Religion, Sex, or National Origin

SEC. 703. (a) It shall be an unlawful employment practice for an employer—

(1) to fail or refuse to hire or to discharge any individual, or otherwise to discriminate against any individual with respect to his compensation, terms, conditions, or privileges of employment, because of such individual's race, color, religion, sex, or national origin; or

(2) to limit, segregate, or classify his employees in any way which would deprive or tend to deprive any individual of employment opportunities or otherwise adversely affect his status as an employee, because of such individual's race, color, religion, sex, or national origin.

(b) It shall be an unlawful employment practice for an employment agency to fail or refuse to refer for employment, or otherwise to discriminate against, any individual because of his race, color, religion, sex, or national origin, or to classify or refer for employment any individual on the basis of his race, color, religion, sex, or national origin.

(c) It shall be an unlawful employment practice for a labor organization—

(1) to exclude or to expel from its membership, or otherwise to discriminate against, any individual because of his race, color, religion, sex, or national origin;

(2) to limit, segregate, or classify its membership, or to classify or fail or refuse to refer for employment any individual, in any way which would deprive or tend to deprive any individual of employment opportunities, or would limit such employment opportunities or otherwise adversely affect his status as an employee or as an applicant for employment, because of such individual's race, color, religion, sex, or national origin; or

(3) to cause or attempt to cause an employer to discriminate against an individual in violation of this section.

(d) It shall be an unlawful employment practice for any employer, labor organization, or joint labor-management committee controlling apprenticeship or other training or retraining, including on-the-job training programs to discriminate against any individual because of his race, color, religion, sex, or national origin in admission to, or employment in, any program established to provide apprenticeship or other training.

(e) Notwithstanding any other provision of this title, (1) it shall not be an unlawful employment practice for an employer to hire and employ employees, for an employment agency to classify, or refer for employment any individual, for a labor organization to classify its membership or to classify or refer for employment any individual, or for an employer, labor organization, or joint labor-management committee controlling apprenticeship or other training or retraining programs to admit or employ any individual in any such program, on the basis of his religion, sex, or national origin in those certain instances where religion, sex, or national origin is a bona fide occupational qualification reasonably necessary to the normal operation of that particular business or enterprise, and (2) it shall not be an unlawful employment practice for a school, college, university, or other educational institution or institution of learning to hire and employ employees of a particular religion if such school, college, university, or other educational institution or institution of learning is, in whole or in substantial part, owned, supported, controlled, or managed by a particular religion or by a particular religious corporation, association, or society, or if the curriculum of such school, college, university, or other educational institution or institution of learning is directed toward the propagation of a particular religion.

(f) As used in this title, the phrase "unlawful employment practice" shall not be deemed to include any action or measure taken by an employer, labor organization, joint labor-management committee, or employment agency with respect to an individual who is a member of the Communist Party of the United States or of any other organization required to register as a Communist-action or Communist-front organization by final order of the Subversive Activities Control Board pursuant to the Subversive Activities Control Act of 1950.

(g) Notwithstanding any other provision of this title, it shall not be an unlawful employment practice for an employer to fail or refuse to hire and employ any individual for any position, for an employer to discharge any individual from any position, or for an employment agency to fail or refuse to refer any individual for employment in any position, or for a labor organization to fail or refuse to refer any individual for employment in any position, if—

(1) the occupancy of such position, or access to the premises in or upon which any part of the duties of such position is performed or is to be performed, is subject to any requirement imposed in the interest of the national security of the United States under any security program in effect pursuant to or administered under any statute of the United States or any Executive order of the President; and

(2) such individual has not fulfilled or has ceased to fulfill that requirement.

(h) Notwithstanding any other provision of this title, it shall not be an unlawful employment practice for an employer to apply different standards of compensation, or different terms, conditions, or privileges of employment pursuant to a bona fide seniority or merit system, or a system which measures earnings by quantity or quality of production or to employees who work in different locations, provided that such differences are not the result of an intention to discriminate because of race, color, religion, sex, or national origin, nor shall it be an unlawful employment practice for an employer to give and to act upon the results of any professionally developed ability test provided that such test, its administration or action upon the results is not designed, intended or used to discriminate because of race, color, religion, sex or national origin. It shall not be an unlawful employment practice under this title for any employer to differentiate upon the basis of sex in determining the amount of the wages or compensation paid or to be paid to employees of such employer if such differentiation is authorized by the provisions of section 6(d) of the Fair Labor Standards Act of 1938, as amended (29 U.S.C. 206(d)).

(i) Nothing contained in this title shall apply to any business or enterprise on or near an Indian reservation with respect to any publicly announced employment practice of such business or enterprise under which a preferential treatment is given to any individual because he is an Indian living on or near a reservation.

(j) Nothing contained in this title shall be interpreted to require any employer, employment agency, labor organization, or joint labor-management committee subject to this title to grant preferential treatment to any individual or to any group because of the race, color, religion, sex, or national origin of such individual or group on account of an imbalance which may exist with respect to the total number or percentage of persons of any race, color, religion, sex, or national origin employed by any employer, referred or classified for employment by any employment agency or labor organization, admitted to membership or classified by any labor organization, or admitted to, or employed in, any apprenticeship or other training program, in comparison with the total number or percentage of persons of such race, color, religion, sex, or national origin in any community, State, section, or other area, or in the available work force in any community, State, section, or other area.

Approved July 2, 1964.

LEGISLATIVE HISTORY

HOUSE REPORTS: Nos. 914, 914 pt. 2 (Comm. on the Judiciary).

CONGRESSIONAL RECORD, Vol. 110 (1964):

Jan. 31; Feb. 1, 3–8: Considered in House.

Feb. 10: Considered and passed House.

Feb. 26: Senate placed bill on calendar.

Mar. 9–14, 16–21, 23–25: Senate debated motion to consider bill.

Mar. 26: Senate agreed to motion to consider bill.

Mar. 30, 31; Apr. 1–3, 6–11, 13–18, 20–25, 27–30; May 1,
2, 4–8, 11–16, 18–22, 25–28; June 1–6: Considered in Senate.

June 8: Motion for cloture filed in Senate.

June 9: Considered in Senate.

June 10: Senate adopted motion for cloture.

June 11–13, 15–18: Considered in Senate.

June 19: Considered and passed Senate, amended.

July 2: House concurred in Senate amendments.

Document courtesy of RBP Associates, Inc.
http://rbp.eeomas.com/
Page revised August 13, 1996

12. Excerpt from the Immigration and Naturalization Act of 1965

The Immigration and Naturalization Act of 1965 is the most liberal immigration act. It abolished discrimination in immigration based on race, national origin, and religion; allowed every country to send quota immigrants up to 20,000 per year and additional non-quota immigrants for unmarried children, spouses, and parents of U.S. citizens; and set three main criteria for immigration to the United States: family connections to those already in the United States, possession of occupational skills needed in the U.S. labor market, and vulnerability to persecution in the home country due to their religious or political ideology. Fully enforced in 1968, it has altered U.S. immigration patterns drastically. More than 85 percent of immigrants since 1968 have originated from non-European countries, mostly from Latin American and Asian countries.

U.S. Statutes at Large, Public Law, 89-236, p. 911–922

An Act

To amend the Immigration and Naturalization Act, and for other purposes.

Be it enacted by the Senate and House of Representatives of the United States of America in Congress assembled, That section 201 of the Immigration and Naturalization Act (66 Stat. 175; 8 U.S.C. 1151) be amended to read as follows:

SEC. 201. (a) Exclusive of special immigrants defined in section 101(a)(27), and of the immediate relatives of United States citizens specified in subsection (b) of this section, the number of aliens who may be issued immigrant visas or who may otherwise acquire the status of an alien lawfully admitted to the United States for permanent residence, or who may, pursuant to section 203(a)(7) enter conditionally, (i) shall not in any of the first three quarters of any fiscal year exceed a total of 45,000 and (ii) shall not in any fiscal year exceed a total of 170,000.

(b) The "immediate relatives" referred to in subsection (a) of this section shall mean the children, spouses, and parents of a citizen of the United States: Provided, That in the case of parents, such citizen must be at least twenty-one years of age. The immediate relatives specified in this subsection who are otherwise qualified for admission as immigrants shall be admitted as such, without regard to the numerical limitations in this Act.

(c) During the period from July 1, 1965, through June 30, 1968, the annual quota of any quota area shall be the same as that which existed for that area on June 30, 1965. The Secretary of State shall, not later than on the sixtieth day immediately following the date of enactment of this subsection and again on or before September 1, 1966, and September 1, 1967, determine and proclaim the amount of quota numbers which remain unused at the end of the fiscal year ending on June 30, 1965, June 30, 1966, and June 30, 1967, respectively, and are available for distribution pursuant to subsection (d) of this section.

(d) Quota numbers not issued or otherwise used during the previous fiscal year, as determined in accordance with subsection (c) hereof, shall be transferred to an immigration pool. Allocation of numbers from the pool and from national quotas shall not together exceed in any fiscal year the numerical limitations in subsection (a) of this section. The immigration pool shall be made available to immigrants otherwise admissible under the provisions of this Act who are unable to obtain prompt issuance of a preference visa due to oversubscription of their quotas, or subquotas as determined by the Secretary of State. Visas and conditional entries shall be allocated from the immigration pool within the percentage limitations and in the order of priority specified in section 203 without regard to the quota to which the alien is chargeable.

(e) The immigration pool and the quotas of quota areas shall terminate June 30, 1968. Thereafter immigrants admissible under the provisions of this Act who are subject to the numerical limitations of subsection (a) of this section shall be admitted in accordance with the percentage limitations and in the order of priority specified in section 203.

SEC. 2. Section 202 of the Immigration and Naturalization Act (66 Stat. 175; 8 U.S.C. 1152) is amended to read as follows:

(a) No person shall receive any preference or priority or be discriminated against in the issuance of an immigrant visa because of his race, sex, nationality, place of birth, or place of residence, except as specifically provided in section 101(a)(27), section 201(b), and section 203: Provided, That the total number of immigrant visas and the number of conditional entries made available to natives of any single foreign state under paragraphs (1) through (8) of section 203(a) shall not exceed 20,000 in any fiscal year: Provided further, That the foregoing proviso shall not operate to reduce the number of immigrants who may be admitted under the quota of any quota area before June 30, 1968.

(b) Each independent country, self-governing dominion, mandated territory, and territory under the international trusteeship system of the United Nations, other than the United States and its outlying possessions shall be treated as a separate foreign state for the purposes of the numerical limitation set forth in the proviso to subsection (a) of this section when approved by the Secretary of State. All other inhabited lands shall be attributed to a foreign state specified by the Secretary of State. For the purposes of this Act the foreign state to which an immigrant is chargeable shall be determined by birth within such foreign state except that (1) an alien child, when accompanied by his alien parent or parents, may be charged to the same foreign state as the accompanying parent or of either accompanying parent if such parent has received or would be qualified for an immigrant visa, if necessary to prevent the separation of the child from the accompanying parent or parents, and if the foreign state to which such parent has been or would be chargeable has not exceeded the numerical limitation set forth in the proviso to subsection (a) of this section for that fiscal year; (2) if an alien is chargeable to a different foreign state from that of his accompanying spouse, the foreign state to which such alien is chargeable may, if necessary to prevent the separation of husband and wife, be determined by the foreign state of the accompanying spouse, if such spouse has received or would be qualified for an immigrant visa and if the foreign state to which such spouse has been or would be chargeable has not exceeded the numerical limitation set forth in the proviso to subsection (a) of this section for that fiscal year; (3) an alien born in the United States shall be considered as having been born in the country of which he is a citizen or subject, or if he is not a citizen or subject of any country then in the last foreign country in which he had his residence as determined by the consular officer; (4) an alien born within any foreign state in which neither of his parents was born and in which neither of his parents had a residence at the time of such alien's birth may be charged to the foreign state of either parent.

(c) Any immigrant born in a colony or other component or dependent area of a foreign state unless a special immigrant as provided in section 101(a)(27) or an immediate relative of a United States citizen as specified in section 201(b), shall be chargeable, for the purpose of limitation set forth in section 202(a), to the foreign state, except that the number of persons born in any such colony or other component or dependent area overseas from the foreign state chargeable to the foreign state in any one fiscal year shall not exceed 1 per centum of the maximum number of immigrant visas available to such foreign state.

(d) In the case of any change in the territorial limits of foreign states, the Secretary of State shall, upon recognition of such change, issue appropriate instructions to all diplomatic and consular offices.

U.S. Statutes at Large, Public Law, 89-236, p. 911-922

13. Voting Rights Act of 1965

In the Jim Crow era, Southern states deprived African Americans of voting rights by imposing a few qualifications for voting, such as a literacy test, poll tax, and grandfather clause. Congress passed the Voting Rights Act in 1965 to eliminate all qualifications or prerequisites for voting imposed by states.

Public Law 89–110
Voting Rights Act of 1965
Eighty-ninth Congress of the United States of America
at the First Session
Begun and held at the City of Washington on Monday, the fourth day of
January, One thousand nine hundred and sixty-five
An Act to enforce the fifteenth amendment to the Constitution of the
United States, and for other purposes.
Be it enacted by the Senate and House of Representatives of the
United States of America in Congress assembled, That this Act shall be
known as the "Voting Rights Act of 1965."

SEC. 2. No voting qualifications or prerequisite to voting, or standard, practice, or procedure shall be imposed or applied by any State or political subdivision to deny or abridge the right of any citizen of the United States to vote on account of race or color.

SEC. 3. (a) Whenever the Attorney General institutes a proceeding under any statute to enforce the guarantees of the fifteenth amendment in any State or political subdivision the court shall authorize the appointment of Federal examiners by the United States Civil Service Commission in accordance with section 6 to serve for such period of time and for such political subdivisions as the court shall determine is appropriate to enforce the guarantees of the fifteenth amendment (1) as part of any interlocutory order if the court determines that the appointment of such examiners is necessary to enforce such guarantees or (2) as part of any final judgment if the court finds that violations of the fifteenth amendment justifying equitable relief have occurred in such State or subdivision: Provided, That the court need not authorize the appointment of examiners if any incidents of denial or abridgement of the right to vote on account of race or color (1) have been few in number and have been promptly and effectively corrected by State or local action, (2) the continuing effect of such incidents has been eliminated, and (3) there is no reasonable probability of their recurrence in the future.

(b) If in a proceeding instituted by the Attorney General under any statute to enforce the guarantees of the fifteenth amendment in any State or political subdivision the court finds that a test or device has been used for the purpose or with the effect of denying or abridging the right of any citizen of the United States to vote on account of race or color, it shall suspend the use of tests and devices in such State or political subdivisions as the court shall determine is appropriate and for such period as it deems necessary.

(c) If in any proceeding instituted by the Attorney General under any statute to enforce the guarantees of the fifteenth amendment in any State or political subdivision the court finds that violations of the fifteenth amendment justifying equitable relief have occurred within the territory of such State or political subdivisions, the court in addition to such relief as it may grant, shall retain jurisdiction for such period as it may deem appropriate and during such period no voting qualification or prerequisite to voting, or standard, practice, or procedure with respect to voting different from that in force or effect at the time the proceeding was commenced shall be enforced unless and until the court finds that such qualifications, prerequisite, standard, practice, or procedure does not have the purpose and will not have the effect of denying or abridging the right to vote on account of race or color: Provided, That such qualification, prerequisite, standard, practice, or procedure has been submitted by the chief legal officer or other appropriate official of such State or subdivision to the Attorney General and the Attorney General has not interposed an objection within sixty days after such submission, except that neither the court's findings not the Attorney General's failure to object shall bar a subsequent action to enjoin enforcement of such qualifications, prerequisite, standard, practice, or procedure.

SEC. 4. (a) To assure that the right of citizens of the United States to vote is not denied or abridged on account of race or color, no citizen shall be denied the right to vote in any Federal, State, or local election because of his failure to comply with any test or device in any State with respect to which the determinations have been made under subsection (b) or in any political subdivision with respect to which such determinations have been made as a separate unit, unless the United States District Court for the District of Columbia in an action for a declaratory judgment brought by such State or subdivision against the United States has determined that no such test or device has been used during the five years preceding the filing of the action for the purpose or with the effect of denying or abridging the right to vote on account of race or color: Provided, That no such declaratory judgment shall issue with respect to any plaintiff for a period of five years after the entry of a final judgment of any court of the United States, other than the denial of a declaratory judgment under this section, whether entered prior to or after the enactment of this Act, determining that denials or abridgments of the right to vote on account of race or color through the use of such tests or devices have occurred anywhere in the territory of such plaintiff. An action pursuant to this subsection shall be heard and determined by a court of three judges in accordance with the provisions of section 2284 of title 28 of the United States Code and any appeal shall lie to the Supreme Court. The court shall retain jurisdiction of any action pursuant to this subsection for five years after judgment and shall reopen the action upon motion of the Attorney General alleging that a test or device has been used for the purpose or with the effect of denying or abridging the right to vote on account of race or color. If the Attorney General determines that he has no reason to believe that any such test or device has been used during the five years preceding the filing of the action for the purpose or with the effect of denying or abridging the right to vote on account of race or color, he shall consent to the entry of such judgment.

(b) The provisions of subsection (a) shall apply in any State or in any political subdivision of a state which (1) the Attorney General determines maintained on November 1, 1964, any test or device, and with respect to when (2) the Director of the Census determines that less than 50 per centum of the persons of voting age residing therein were registered on November 1, 1964, or that less than 50 per centum of such persons voted in the presidential election of November 1964. A determination or certification of the Attorney General or of the Director of the Census under this section or under section 6 or section 13 shall not be reviewable in any court and shall be effective upon publication in the Federal Register.

(c) The phrase "test or device" shall mean any requirement that a person as a prerequisite for voting or registration for voting (1) demonstrates the ability to read, write, understand, or interpret any matter, (2) demonstrates any educational achievement of his knowledge of any particular subject, (3) possess good moral character, or (4) prove his qualification by the voucher of registered voters or members of any other class.

(d) For purposes of this section no State or political subdivision shall be determined to have engaged in the use of tests or devices for the purpose or with the effect of denying or abridging the right to vote on account of race or color if (1) incidents of such use have been few in number and have been promptly and effectively corrected by State or local action, (2) the continuing effect of such incidents has been eliminated, and (3) there is no reasonable probability of their recurrence in the future.

(e) (1) Congress hereby declares that to secure the rights under the fourteenth amendment of persons educated in American-flag schools in which the predominant classroom language was other than English, it is necessary to prohibit the States from conditioning the right to vote of such persons on ability to read, write, understand, or interpret any matter in the English language.

(2) No person who demonstrates that he has successfully completed the sixth primary grade in a public school in, or a private school accredited by, any State or territory, the District of Columbia, or the Commonwealth of Puerto Rico in which the predominant classroom language was other than English, shall be denied the right to vote in any Federal, State, or local election because of his inability to read, write, understand, or interpret any matter in the English language, except that in States in which State law provides that a different level of education is presumptive of literacy, he shall demonstrate that he has successfully completed an equivalent level of education in a public school in, or a private school accredited by, any State or territory, the District of Columbia, or the Commonwealth of Puerto Rico in which the predominant classroom language was other than English.

. . .

14. Executive Order 11246 (1965), as Amended

Executive Order 11246, issued by President Lyndon B. Johnson in September 1965, laid the groundwork for affirmative-action policy. It mandated contracts with the government to include a nondiscrimination clause and federal contractors with 100 or more employees to take "affirmative action" to achieve the goal of nondiscrimination in employment, promotion, recruitment, and related areas. It required contractors and their subcontractors to submit compliance reports with information on the practices, policies, programs, and racial composition of their work force.

EXECUTIVE ORDER 11246—EQUAL EMPLOYMENT OPPORTUNITY

Source: The provisions of Executive Order 11246 of September 24, 1965, appear at 30 FR 12319, 12935, 3 CFR, 1964–1965 Comp., p. 339, unless otherwise noted.

Under and by virtue of the authority vested in me as President of the United States by the Constitution and statutes of the United States, it is ordered as follows:

Part I—Nondiscrimination in Government Employment

[Part I superseded by EO 11478 of Aug. 8, 1969, 34 FR 12985, 3 CFR, 1966–1970 Comp., p. 803]

Part II—Nondiscrimination in Employment by Government Contractors and Subcontractors

Subpart A—Duties of the Secretary of Labor

SEC. 201. The Secretary of Labor shall be responsible for the administration and enforcement of Parts II and III of this Order. The Secretary shall adopt such rules and regulations and issue such orders as are deemed necessary and appropriate to achieve the purposes of Parts II and III of this Order.

[Sec. 201 amended by EO 12086 of Oct. 5, 1978, 43 FR 46501, 3 CFR, 1978 Comp., p. 230]

Subpart B—Contractors' Agreements

SEC. 202. Except in contracts exempted in accordance with Section 204 of this Order, all Government contracting agencies shall include in every Government contract hereafter entered into the following provisions:

During the performance of this contract, the contractor agrees as follows:

(1) The contractor will not discriminate against any employee or applicant for employment because of race, color, religion, sex, or national origin. The contractor will take affirmative action to ensure that applicants are employed, and that employees are treated during employment, without regard to their race, color, religion, sex or national origin. Such action shall include, but not be limited to the following: employment, upgrading, demotion, or transfer; recruitment or recruitment advertising; layoff or termination; rates of pay or other forms of compensation; and selection for training, including apprenticeship. The contractor agrees to post in conspicuous places, available to employees and applicants for employment, notices to be provided by the contracting officer setting forth the provisions of this nondiscrimination clause.

(2) The contractor will, in all solicitations or advancements for employees placed by or on behalf of the contractor, state that all qualified applicants will receive consideration for employment without regard to race, color, religion, sex or national origin.

(3) The contractor will send to each labor union or representative of workers with which he has a collective bargaining agreement or other contract or

understanding, a notice, to be provided by the agency contracting officer, advising the labor union or workers' representative of the contractor's commitments under Section 202 of Executive Order No. 11246 of September 24, 1965, and shall post copies of the notice in conspicuous places available to employees and applicants for employment.

(4) The contractor will comply with all provisions of Executive Order No. 11246 of Sept. 24, 1965, and of the rules, regulations, and relevant orders of the Secretary of Labor.

(5) The contractor will furnish all information and reports required by Executive Order No. 11246 of September 24, 1965, and by the rules, regulations, and orders of the Secretary of Labor, or pursuant thereto, and will permit access to his books, records, and accounts by the contracting agency and the Secretary of Labor for purposes of investigation to ascertain compliance with such rules, regulations, and orders.

(6) In the event of the contractor's noncompliance with the nondiscrimination clauses of this contract or with any of such rules, regulations, or orders, this contract may be cancelled, terminated, or suspended in whole or in part and the contractor may be declared ineligible for further Government contracts in accordance with procedures authorized in Executive Order No. 11246 of Sept. 24, 1965, and such other sanctions may be imposed and remedies invoked as provided in Executive Order No. 11246 of September 24, 1965, or by rule, regulation, or order of the Secretary of Labor, or as otherwise provided by law.

(7) The contractor will include the provisions of paragraphs (1) through (7) in every subcontract or purchase order unless exempted by rules, regulations, or orders of the Secretary of Labor issued pursuant to Section 204 of Executive Order No. 11246 of September 24, 1965, so that such provisions will be binding upon each subcontractor or vendor. The contractor win take such action with respect to any subcontract or purchase order as may be directed by the Secretary of Labor as a means of enforcing such provisions including sanctions for noncompliance: Provided, however, that in the event the contractor becomes involved in, or is threatened with, litigation with a subcontractor or vendor as a result of such direction, the contractor may request the United States to enter into such litigation to protect the interests of the United States. [Sec. 202 amended by EO 11375 of Oct. 13, 1967, 32 FR 14303, 3 CFR, 1966–1970 Comp., p. 684, EO 12086 of Oct. 5, 1978, 43 FR 46501, 3 CFR, 1978 Comp., p. 230]

SEC. 203. Each contractor having a contract containing the provisions prescribed in Section 202 shall file, and shall cause each of his subcontractors to file, Compliance Reports with the contracting agency or the Secretary of Labor as may be directed. Compliance Reports shall be filed within such times and shall contain such information as to the practices, policies, programs, and employment policies, programs, and employment statistics of the contractor and each subcontractor, and shall be in such form, as the Secretary of Labor may prescribe.

(b) Bidders or prospective contractors or subcontractors may be required to state whether they have participated in any previous contract subject to the provisions of this Order, or any preceding similar Executive order, and in that event to submit, on behalf of themselves and their proposed subcontractors, Compliance Reports prior to or as an initial part of their bid or negotiation of a contract.

(c) Whenever the contractor or subcontractor has a collective bargaining agreement or other contract or understanding with a labor union or an agency referring workers or providing or supervising apprenticeship or training for such workers, the Compliance Report shall include such information as to such labor union's or agency's practices and policies affecting compliance as the Secretary of Labor may prescribe: Provided, That to the extent such information is within the exclusive possession of a labor union or an agency referring workers or providing or supervising apprenticeship or training and such labor union or agency shall refuse to furnish such information to the contractor, the contractor shall so certify to the Secretary of Labor as part of its Compliance Report and shall set forth what efforts he has made to obtain such information.

(d) The Secretary of Labor may direct that any bidder or prospective contractor or subcontractor shall submit, as part of his Compliance Report, a statement in writing, signed by an authorized officer or agent on behalf of any labor union or any agency referring workers or providing or supervising apprenticeship or other training, with which the bidder or prospective contractor deals, with supporting information, to the effect that the signer's practices and policies do not discriminate on the grounds of race, color, religion, sex or national origin, and that the signer either will affirmatively cooperate in the implementation of the policy and provisions of this Order or that it consents and agrees that recruitment, employment, and the terms and conditions of employment under the proposed contract shall be in accordance with the purposes and provisions of the order. In the event that the union, or the agency shall refuse to execute such a statement, the Compliance Report shall so certify and set forth what efforts have been made to secure such a statement and such additional factual material as the Secretary of Labor may require.

[Sec. 203 amended by EO 11375 of Oct. 13, 1967, 32 FR 14303, 3 CFR, 1966–1970 Comp., p. 684; EO 12086 of Oct. 5, 1978, 43 FR 46501, 3 CFR, 1978 Comp., p. 230]

SEC. 204 (a) The Secretary of Labor may, when the Secretary deems that special circumstances in the national interest so require, exempt a contracting agency from the requirement of including any or all of the provisions of Section 202 of this Order in any specific contract, subcontract, or purchase order.

(b) The Secretary of Labor may, by rule or regulation, exempt certain classes of contracts, subcontracts, or purchase orders (1) whenever work is to be or has been performed outside the United States and no recruitment of workers within the limits of the United States is involved; (2) for standard commercial supplies or raw materials; (3) involving less than specified amounts of money or specified numbers of workers; or (4) to the extent that they involve subcontracts below a specified tier.

(c) Section 202 of this Order shall not apply to a Government contractor or subcontractor that is a religious corporation, association, educational institution, or society, with respect to the employment of individuals of a particular religion to perform work connected with the carrying on by such corporation, association, educational institution, or society of its activities. Such contractors and subcontractors are not exempted or excused from complying with the other requirements contained in this Order.

(d) The Secretary of Labor may also provide, by rule, regulation, or order, for the exemption of facilities of a contractor that are in all respects separate and distinct from activities of the contractor related to the performance of the contract: provided, that such an exemption will not interfere with or impede the effectuation of the purposes of this Order: and provided further, that in the absence of such an exemption all facilities shall be covered by the provisions of this Order.

[Sec. 204 amended by EO 13279 of Dec. 16, 2002, 67 FR 77141, 3 CFR, 2002 Comp., pp. 77141–77144]

Subpart C—Powers and Duties of the Secretary of Labor and the Contracting Agencies

SEC. 205. The Secretary of Labor shall be responsible for securing compliance by all Government contractors and subcontractors with this Order and any implementing rules or regulations. All contracting agencies shall comply with the terms of this Order and any implementing rules, regulations, or orders of the Secretary of Labor. Contracting agencies shall cooperate with the Secretary of Labor and shall furnish such information and assistance as the Secretary may require.

[Sec. 205 amended by EO 12086 of Oct. 5, 1978, 43 FR 46501, 3 CFR, 1978 Comp., p. 230]

SEC. 206. The Secretary of Labor may investigate the employment practices of any Government contractor or subcontractor to determine whether or not the contractual provisions specified in Section 202 of this Order have been violated. Such investigation shall be conducted in accordance with the procedures established by the Secretary of Labor.

(b) The Secretary of Labor may receive and investigate complaints by employees or prospective employees of a Government contractor or subcontractor which allege discrimination contrary to the contractual provisions specified in Section 202 of this Order.

[Sec. 206 amended by EO 12086 of Oct. 5, 1978, 43 FR 46501, 3 CFR, 1978 Comp., p. 230]

SEC. 207. The Secretary of Labor shall use his/her best efforts, directly and through interested Federal, State, and local agencies, contractors, and all other available instrumentalities to cause any labor union engaged in work under Government contracts or any agency referring workers or providing or supervising apprenticeship or training for or in the course of such work to cooperate in the implementation of the purposes of this Order. The Secretary of Labor shall, in appropriate cases, notify the Equal Employment Opportunity Commission, the Department of Justice, or other appropriate Federal agencies whenever it has reason to believe that the practices of any such labor organization or agency violate Title VI or Title VII of the Civil Rights Act of 1964 or other provision of Federal law.

[Sec. 207 amended by EO 12086 of Oct. 5, 1978, 43 FR 46501, 3 CFR, 1978 Comp., p. 230]

SEC. 208. The Secretary of Labor, or any agency, officer, or employee in the executive branch of the Government designated by rule, regulation, or order of the Secretary, may hold such hearings, public or private, as the Secretary may deem advisable for compliance, enforcement, or educational purposes.

(b) The Secretary of Labor may hold, or cause to be held, hearings in accordance with Subsection of this Section prior to imposing, ordering, or recommending the imposition of penalties and sanctions under this Order. No order for debarment of any contractor from further Government contracts under Section 209(6) shall be made without affording the contractor an opportunity for a hearing.

Subpart D—Sanctions and Penalties

SEC. 209. In accordance with such rules, regulations, or orders as the Secretary of Labor may issue or adopt, the Secretary may:

(1) Publish, or cause to be published, the names of contractors or unions which it has concluded have complied or have failed to comply with the provisions of this Order or of the rules, regulations, and orders of the Secretary of Labor.

(2) Recommend to the Department of Justice that, in cases in which there is substantial or material violation or the threat of substantial or material violation of the contractual provisions set forth in Section 202 of this Order, appropriate proceedings be brought to enforce those provisions, including the enjoining, within the limitations of applicable law, of organizations, individuals, or groups who prevent directly or indirectly, or seek to prevent directly or indirectly, compliance with the provisions of this Order.

(3) Recommend to the Equal Employment Opportunity Commission or the Department of Justice that appropriate proceedings be instituted under Title VII of the Civil Rights Act of 1964.

(4) Recommend to the Department of Justice that criminal proceedings be brought for the furnishing of false information to any contracting agency or to the Secretary of Labor as the case may be.

(5) After consulting with the contracting agency, direct the contracting agency to cancel, terminate, suspend, or cause to be cancelled, terminated, or suspended, any contract, or any portion or portions thereof, for failure of the contractor or subcontractor to comply with equal employment opportunity provisions of the contract. Contracts may be cancelled, terminated, or suspended absolutely or continuance of contracts may be conditioned upon a program for future compliance approved by the Secretary of Labor.

(6) Provide that any contracting agency shall refrain from entering into further contracts, or extensions or other modifications of existing contracts, with any noncomplying contractor, until such contractor has satisfied the Secretary of Labor that such contractor has established and will carry out personnel and employment policies in compliance with the provisions of this Order.

(b) Pursuant to rules and regulations prescribed by the Secretary of Labor, the Secretary shall make reasonable efforts, within a reasonable time limitation, to secure compliance with the contract provisions of this Order by methods of conference, conciliation, mediation, and persuasion before proceedings shall be instituted under subsection (a)(2) of this Section, or before a contract shall be cancelled or terminated in whole or in part under subsection (a)(5) of this Section.

[Sec. 209 amended by EO 12086 of Oct. 5, 1978, 43 FR 46501, 3 CFR, 1978 Comp., p. 230]

SEC. 210. Whenever the Secretary of Labor makes a determination under Section 209, the Secretary shall promptly notify the appropriate agency. The agency shall take the action directed by the Secretary and shall report the results of the action it has taken to the Secretary of Labor within such time as the Secretary shall specify. If the contracting agency fails to take the action directed within thirty days, the Secretary may take the action directly.

[Sec. 210 amended by EO 12086 of Oct. 5, 1978, 43 FR 46501, 3 CFR, 1978 Comp., p. 230]

SEC. 211. If the Secretary shall so direct, contracting agencies shall not enter into contracts with any bidder or prospective contractor unless the bidder or prospective contractor has satisfactorily complied with the provisions of this Order or submits a program for compliance acceptable to the Secretary of Labor.

[Sec. 211 amended by EO 12086 of Oct. 5, 1978, 43 FR 46501, 3 CFR, 1978 Comp., p. 230]

SEC. 212. When a contract has been cancelled or terminated under Section 209(a)(5) or a contractor has been debarred from further Government contracts under Section 209(a)(6) of this Order, because of noncompliance with the contract provisions specified in Section 202 of this Order, the Secretary of Labor shall promptly notify the Comptroller General of the United States.

[Sec. 212 amended by EO 12086 of Oct. 5, 1978, 43 FR 46501, 3 CFR, 1978 Comp., p. 230]

Subpart E—Certificates of Merit

SEC. 213. The Secretary of Labor may provide for issuance of a United States Government Certificate of Merit to employers or labor unions, or other agencies which are or may hereafter be engaged in work under Government contracts, if the Secretary is satisfied that the personnel and employment practices of the employer, or that the personnel, training, apprenticeship, membership, grievance and representation, upgrading, and other practices and policies of the labor union or other agency conform to the purposes and provisions of this Order.

SEC. 214. Any Certificate of Merit may at any time be suspended or revoked by the Secretary of Labor if the holder thereof, in the judgment of the Secretary, has failed to comply with the provisions of this Order.

SEC. 215. The Secretary of Labor may provide for the exemption of any employer, labor union, or other agency from any reporting requirements imposed under or pursuant to this Order if such employer, labor union, or other agency has been awarded a Certificate of Merit which has not been suspended or revoked.

Part III—Nondiscrimination Provisions in Federally Assisted Construction Contracts

SEC. 301. Each executive department and agency, which administers a program involving Federal financial assistance shall require as a condition for the approval of any grant, contract, loan, insurance, or guarantee thereunder, which may involve a construction contract, that the applicant for Federal assistance undertake and agree to incorporate, or cause to be incorporated, into all construction contracts paid for in whole or in part with funds obtained from the Federal Government or borrowed on the credit of the Federal Government pursuant to such grant, contract, loan, insurance, or guarantee, or undertaken pursuant to any Federal program involving such grant, contract, loan, insurance, or guarantee, the provisions prescribed for Government contracts by Section 202 of this Order or such modification thereof, preserving in substance the contractor's obligations thereunder, as may be approved by the Secretary of Labor, together with such additional provisions as the Secretary deems appropriate to establish and protect the interest of the United States in the enforcement of those obligations. Each such applicant shall also undertake and agree (1) to assist and cooperate actively with the Secretary of Labor in obtaining the compliance of contractors and subcontractors with those contract provisions and with the rules, regulations and relevant orders of the Secretary, (2) to obtain and to furnish to the Secretary of Labor such information as the Secretary may require for the supervision of such compliance, (3) to carry out sanctions and penalties for violation of such obligations imposed upon contractors and subcontractors by the Secretary of Labor pursuant to Part II, Subpart D, of this Order, and (4) to refrain from entering into any contract subject to this Order, or extension or other modification of such a contract with a contractor debarred from Government contracts under Part II, Subpart D, of this Order.

[Sec. 301 amended by EO 12086 of Oct. 5, 1978, 43 FR 46501, 3 CFR, 1978 Comp., p. 230]

SEC. 302. "Construction contract" as used in this Order means any contract for the construction, rehabilitation, alteration, conversion, extension, or repair of buildings, highways, or other improvements to real property.

(b) The provisions of Part II of this Order shall apply to such construction contracts, and for purposes of such application the administering department or agency shall be considered the contracting agency referred to therein.

(c) The term "applicant" as used in this Order means an applicant for Federal assistance or, as determined by agency regulation, other program participant, with respect to whom an application for any grant, contract, loan, insurance, or guarantee is not finally acted upon prior to the effective date of this Part, and it includes such an applicant after he/she becomes a recipient of such Federal assistance.

SEC. 303. The Secretary of Labor shall be responsible for obtaining the compliance of such applicants with their undertakings under this Order. Each administering department and agency is directed to cooperate with the Secretary of Labor and to furnish the Secretary such information and assistance as the Secretary may require in the performance of the Secretary's functions under this Order.

(b) In the event an applicant fails and refuses to comply with the applicant's undertakings pursuant to this Order, the Secretary of Labor may, after consulting with the administering department or agency, take any or all of the following actions: (1) direct any administering department or agency to cancel, terminate, or suspend in whole or in part the agreement, contract or other arrangement with such applicant with respect to which the failure or refusal occurred; (2) direct any administering department or agency to refrain from extending any further assistance to the applicant under the program with respect to which the failure or refusal occurred until satisfactory assurance of future compliance has been received by the Secretary of Labor from such applicant; and (3) refer the case to the Department of Justice or the Equal Employment Opportunity Commission for appropriate law enforcement or other proceedings.

(c) In no case shall action be taken with respect to an applicant pursuant to clause (1) or (2) of subsection (b) without notice and opportunity for hearing.

[Sec. 303 amended by EO 12086 of Oct. 5, 1978, 43 FR 46501, 3 CFR, 1978 Comp., p. 230]

SEC. 304. Any executive department or agency which imposes by rule, regulation, or order requirements of nondiscrimination in employment, other than requirements imposed pursuant to this Order, may delegate to the Secretary of Labor by agreement such responsibilities with respect to compliance standards, reports, and procedures as would tend to bring the administration of such requirements into conformity with the administration of requirements imposed under this Order: Provided, That actions to effect compliance by recipients of Federal financial assistance with requirements imposed pursuant to Title VI of the Civil Rights Act of 1964 shall be taken in conformity with the procedures and limitations prescribed in Section 602 thereof and the regulations of the administering department or agency issued thereunder.

Part IV—Miscellaneous

SEC. 401. The Secretary of Labor may delegate to any officer, agency, or employee in the Executive branch of the Government, any function or duty of the Secretary under Parts II and III of this Order.

[Sec. 401 amended by EO 12086 of Oct. 5, 1978, 43 FR 46501, 3 CFR, 1978 Comp., p. 230]

SEC. 402. The Secretary of Labor shall provide administrative support for the execution of the program known as the "Plans for Progress."

SEC. 403. Executive Orders Nos. 10590 (January 19, 1955), 10722 (August 5, 1957), 10925 (March 6, 1961), 11114 (June 22, 1963), and 11162 (July 28, 1964), are hereby superseded and the President's Committee on Equal Employment Opportunity established by Executive Order No. 10925 is hereby abolished. All records and property in the custody of the Committee shall be transferred to the Office of Personnel Management and the Secretary of Labor, as appropriate.

(b) Nothing in this Order shall be deemed to relieve any person of any obligation assumed or imposed under or pursuant to any Executive Order superseded by this Order. All rules, regulations, orders, instructions, designations, and other directives issued by the President's Committee on Equal Employment Opportunity and those issued by the heads of various departments or agencies under or pursuant to any of the Executive orders superseded by this Order, shall, to the extent that they are not inconsistent with this Order, remain in full force and effect unless and until revoked or superseded by appropriate authority. References in such directives to provisions of the superseded orders shall be deemed to be references to the comparable provisions of this Order.

[Sec. 403 amended by EO 12107 of Dec. 28, 1978, 44 FR 1055, 3 CFR, 1978 Comp., p, 264]

SEC. 404. The General Services Administration shall take appropriate action to revise the standard Government contract forms to accord with the provisions of this Order and of the rules and regulations of the Secretary of Labor.

SEC. 405. This Order shall become effective thirty days after the date of this Order.

www.dol.gov/esa
U.S. Department of Labor
Frances Perkins Building
200 Constitution Avenue, NW
Washington, DC 20210

15. Excerpt from the Kerner Commission Report (1968)

The Kerner Commission was formed by President Lyndon B. Johnson in July 1967 to investigate the causes and implications of full-scale urban riots in black sections of major American cities in 1967. The report, issued in 1968, stated that pervasive racial discrimination and segregation in employment, education, and housing had excluded African Americans from the benefits of economic progress. It concluded that racial segregation and racial inequality were the major causes of race riots. It recommended sweeping changes to moderate racial inequality so that further race riots could be prevented.

Washington, DC: United States Government Publication Office, 1968. 73–77.

THE RESERVOIR OF GRIEVANCES IN THE NEGRO COMMUNITY

Our examination of the background of the surveyed disorders revealed a typical pattern of deeply held grievances which were widely shared by many members of the Negro community. The specific content of the expressed grievances varied somewhat from city to city. But in general, grievances among Negroes in all the cities related to prejudice, discrimination, severely disadvantaged living condition, and a general sense of frustration about their inability to change those conditions. Specific events or incidents exemplified and reinforced the shared sense of grievance. News of such incidents spread quickly throughout the community and added to the reservoir. Grievances about police practices, unemployment and underemployment, housing, and other objective conditions in the ghetto were aggravated in the minds of many Negroes by the inaction of municipal authorities.

Out of this reservoir of grievance and frustration, the riot process began in the cities which we surveyed.

PRECIPITATING INCIDENTS

In virtually every case a single triggering or precipitating incident can be identified as having immediately preceded within a few hours and in generally the same location—the outbreak of disorder. But this incident was usually a relatively minor, even trivial one, by itself substantially disproportionate to the scale of violence that followed. Often it was an incident of a type which had occurred frequently in the same community in the past without provoking violence.

We found that violence was generated by an increasingly disturbed social atmosphere, in which typically not one, but a series of incidents occurred over a period of weeks or months prior to the outbreak of disorder. Most cities had three or more such incidents. Houston had 10 over a 5-month period. These earlier or prior were linked in the minds of many Negroes to the pre-existing reservoir of underlying grievances. With each such incident, frustration and tension grew until at some point a final incident, often similar to the incidents preceding it, occurred and was followed almost immediately by violence.

As we see it, the prior incidents and the reservoir of underlying grievances contributed to a cumulative process of mounting tension that spilled over into violence when the final incident occurred.

This chain describes the central trend in the disorders we surveyed and not necessarily all aspects of the riots or of all rioters. For example, incidents have not always increased tension; and tension has not always resulted in violence. We conclude only that the processes did occur in the disorders we examined.

Similarly, we do not suggest that all rioters shared the conditions or grievances of their Negro neighbors: some may deliberately have exploited the chaos created out of the frustration of others; some may have been drawn into the melee merely because they identified with, or wished to emulate, others. Some who shared the adverse conditions and grievances did not riot.

We found that the majority of the rioters did share the adverse conditions and grievances, although they did not necessarily articulate in their own minds the connection between that background and their actions.

THE PROFILE OF A RIOTER

The typical rioter in the summer of 1967 was a Negro, unmarried male between the ages of 15 and 24. He was in many ways very different from the stereotype. He was not a migrant. He was born in the state and was a lifelong resident of the city in which the riot took place. Economically his position was about the same as his Negro neighbors who did not actively participate in the riot. Although he had not, usually, graduated from high school, he was somewhat better educated than the average inner-city Negro, having at least attended high school for a time.

Nevertheless he was more likely to be working in a menial or low status job as an unskilled laborer. If he was employed, he was not working full time and his employment was frequently interrupted by periods of unemployment.

He feels strongly that he deserves a better job and that he is barred from achieving it, not because of lack of training, ability, or ambition, but because of discrimination by employers.

He rejects the white bigot stereotype of the Negro as ignorant and shiftless. He takes great pride in his race and believes that in some respects Negroes are superior to whites. He is extremely hostile to whites, but his hostility is more apt to be a product of social and economic class than of race; he is almost equally hostile toward middle class Negroes.

He is substantially better informed about politics than Negroes who were not involved in the riots. He is more likely to be actively engaged in civil rights efforts, but is extremely distrustful of the political system and of political leaders.

THE PROFILE OF THE COUNTERRIOTER

The typical counterrioter, who risked injury and arrest to walk the streets urging rioters to cool it, was an active supporter of existing social institutions. He was, for example, far more likely than either the rioter or the noninvolved to feel that his country is worth defending in a major war. His actions and his attitudes reflected his substantially greater stake in the social system; he was considerably better educated and more affluent than either the rioter or the noninvolved. He was somewhat more likely than the rioter, but less likely than the noninvolved, to have been a migrant. In all other respects he was identical to the noninvolved.

THE PATTERN OF DISADVANTAGE

Social and economic conditions in the riot cities constituted a clear pattern of severe disadvantage for Negroes as compared with whites, whether the Negroes lived in the disturbance area or outside of it. When ghetto conditions are compared with those for whites in the suburbs, the relative disadvantage for Negroes is even greater.

In all the cities surveyed, the Negro population increased between 1950 and 1960 at a median rate of 75 percent.

Meanwhile the white population decreased in more than half the cities including six which experienced the most severe disturbances in 1967. The increase in nonwhite population in four of these cities was so great that their total population increased despite the decrease in white population. These changes were attributable in large part to heavy in-migration of Negroes from rural poverty areas and movement of whites from the central cities to the suburbs.

ORIGINAL WRITINGS

16. Excerpts from President Abraham Lincoln's "Letter to James C. Conkling" (August 26, 1863)

Source: Roy P. Basler, ed., *Abraham Lincoln: His Speeches and Writings* (New York: Da Capo Press, 1990, 721–723).

Many people erroneously believe that President Abraham Lincoln issued the Emancipation Proclamation mainly for the sake of black slaves because he personally considered it important to abolish slavery. But his views about slavery were complicated; although he opposed it, he did not believe it could be abolished without compensating the owners for the loss of their properties. A man, James C. Conkling, sent President Lincoln a letter complaining about the Emancipation Proclamation. The following excerpt from Lincoln's response to Conkling shows that he made the Emancipation Proclamation mainly to give black slaves the motivation to fight for the Union Army instead of helping the enemy.

You dislike the emancipation proclamation; and, perhaps, would have it retracted. You say it is unconstitutional—I think differently. I think the constitution invests its Commander-in-chief, with the law of war, in time of war. The most that can be said, if so much, is, that slaves are property. Is there—has there ever been—any question that by the law of war, property, both of enemies and friends, may be taken when needed? And is it not needed whenever taking it, helps us, or hurts the enemy? Armies, the world over, destroy enemie's property when they can not use it; and even destroy their own to keep it from the enemy. Civilized belligerents do all in their power to help themselves, or hurt the enemy, except a few things regarded as barbarous or cruel. Among the exceptions are the massacre of vanquished foes, and noncombatants, male and female. . . .

You say you will not fight to free negroes. Some of them seem willing to fight for you; but, no matter. Fight you, then exclusively to save the Union. I issued the proclamation on purpose to aid you in saving the Union. Whenever you shall have conquered all resistance to the Union, if I shall urge you to continue fighting, it will be an apt time, then, for you to declare you will not fight to free negroes.

I thought that in your struggle for the Union, to whatever extent the negroes should cease helping the enemy, to that extent it weakened the enemy in his resistance to you. Do you think differently? I thought that whatever negroes can be got to do as soldiers, leaves just so much less for white soldiers to do, in saving the Union. Does it appear otherwise to you? But negroes, like other people, act upon motives. Why should they do any thing for us, if we will do nothing for them? If they stake their lives for us, they must be prompted by the strongest motive—even the promise of freedom. And the promise being made, must be kept.

17. Excerpt from W.E.B. Du Bois's *The Souls of Black Folk* (1903)

Source: See W.E.B. Du Bois, *The Souls of Black Folk* (New York: Vintage Books, 1986, 16).

In his classic 1903 book, *The Souls of Black Folk,* W.E.B. Du Bois used the metaphor of the "color line" to indicate racial segregation and racial inequality in the United States in the early twentieth century. When he was writing the book, all Southern states maintained a rigid form of racial segregation enforced by Jim Crow laws and practices. Du Bois was the most prominent black intellectual in the late nineteenth and early twentieth centuries to demand radical social changes for racial equality.

The problem of the twentieth century is the problem of the color-line,— the relation of the darker to the lighter races of men in Asia and Africa, in America and the islands of the sea. It was a phase of this problem that caused the Civil War; and however much they who marched South and North in 1861 may have fixed on the technical points of union and local autonomy as a shibboleth, all nevertheless knew, as we know, that the question of Negro slavery was the real cause of the conflict. Curious it was, too, how this deeper question ever forced itself to the surface despite effort and disclaimer. No sooner had Northern armies touched Southern soil than this old question, newly guised, sprang from the earth—What shall be done with Negroes? Peremptory military commands, this way and that, could not answer the query; the Emancipation Proclamation seemed but to broaden and intensify the difficulties; and the War Amendments made the Negro problems of today.

18. Excerpts from Madison Grant's *The Passing of the Great Race* (1916)

Source: Madison Grant, *The Passing of the Great Race* (New York: Ayer Publishing, 1916, 228).

The first decade of the twentieth century was the decade of biological racism, the racist ideology that the people of "Nordic" or northern and western European ancestry are intellectually superior to other racial groups. Madison Grant was the champion of biological racism at that time. His book, *The Passing of the Great Race*, published in 1916, popularized the racist ideology. The excerpt from the conclusion of the book most succinctly reflects his campaign for the restriction of immigration from southern and eastern European countries, as well as his argument for Nordic superiority.

In concluding this revision of the racial foundations upon which the history of Europe has been based, it is scarcely necessary to point out that the actual results of the spectacular conquests and invasions of history have been far less permanent than those of the more insidious victories arising from the crossing of two diverse races, and that in such mixtures the relative prepotency of the various human subspecies in Europe appears to be in inverse ratio to their social value.

The continuity of physical traits and the limitation of the effects of environment to the individual only are now so thoroughly recognized by scientists that it is at most a question of time when the social consequences which result from such crossings will be generally understood by the public at large. As soon as the true bearing and import of the facts are appreciated by lawmakers, a complete change in our political structure will inevitably occur, and our present reliance on the influences of education will be superseded by a readjustment based on racial values. . . .

We Americans must realize that the altruistic ideals which have controlled our social development during the past century, and the maudlin sentimentalism that has made America "an asylum for the oppressed," are sweeping the nation toward a racial abyss. If the "Melting Pot" is allowed to boil without control, and we continue to follow our national motto and deliberately blind ourselves to all "distinctions of race, creed, or color," the type of native American of colonial descent will become as extinct as the Athenian of the age of Pericles, and the Viking of the days of Rollo.

19. Excerpt from Gunnar Myrdal's *An American Dilemma: The Negro Problem and Modern Democracy* (1944)

Source: Gunnar Myrdal, *An American Dilemma: The Negro Problem and Modern Democracy* (New York: Harper and Row, 1962, lxxi).

Gunnar Myrdal was a Swedish social critic who wrote one of the most-often-quoted books on race relations in the United States. In this classic 1944 book, Myrdal considered the conflict between the American creed, which emphasized freedom and equality, and the black-white racial tension and inequality to be the American moral dilemma, the fundamental problem of American society. The excerpt from the introduction reflects the central thesis of his book.

The American Negro problem is a problem in the heart of the American. It is there that the interracial tension has its focus. It is there that the decisive struggle goes on. This is the central viewpoint of this treatise. Though our study includes economic, social, and political race relations, at bottom our problem is the moral dilemma of the American—the conflict between his moral valuations on various levels of consciousness and generality. The "American Dilemma," referred to in the title of this book, is the ever-raging conflict between, on the one hand, the valuations preserved on the general plane which we shall call the "American Creed," where the American thinks, talks, and acts under the influence of high national and Christian precepts, and, on the other hand, the valuations on specific planes of individual and group living, where personal and local interests; economic, social, and sexual jealousies; considerations of community prestige and conformity; group prejudice against particular persons or types of people; and all sorts of miscellaneous wants, impulses, and habits dominate his outlook.

20. Excerpt from Martin Luther King Jr.'s "Letter from a Birmingham Jail" (1963)

Source: See Martin Luther King Jr., *I Have a Dream: Writings and Speeches That Changed the World,* James Melvin Washington, ed. (San Francisco: HarperSanFrancisco, 1992, 89).

King wrote this essay as an open letter on April 16, 1963 while serving a sentence for participating in civil rights demonstrations in Birmingham, Alabama. Earlier, in January 1963, eight prominent white Alabama clergymen had published an open letter that asked King to engage in the integration movement without breaking laws. In this essay, he tried to defend his position to use rule-breaking by making a distinction between "just and unjust" laws. He wrote that since segregation ordinances were morally wrong, unjust laws, he could urge people to disobey segregation ordinances.

You express a great deal of anxiety over our willingness to break laws. This is certainly a legitimate concern. Since we so diligently urge people to obey the Supreme Court's decision of 1954 outlawing segregation in the public schools, it is rather strange and paradoxical to find us consciously breaking laws. One may well ask, "How can you advocate breaking some laws and obeying others?" The answer is found in the fact that there are two types of laws: *just* and *unjust* laws. I would agree with Saint Augustine that "an unjust law is no law at all."

Now what is the difference between the two? How does one determine when a law is just or unjust? A just law is a man-made code that squares with the moral law or the law of God. An unjust law is a code that is out of harmony with the moral law. To put it in the terms of Saint Thomas Aquinas, an unjust law is a human law that is not rooted in eternal and natural law. Any law that uplifts human personality is just. Any law that degrades human personality is unjust. All segregation statutes are unjust because segregation distorts the soul and damages the personality. It gives the segregator a false sense of superiority, and the segregated a false sense of inferiority. To use the words of Martin Buber, the great Jewish philosopher, segregation substitutes an "I-it" relationship for the "I-thou" relationship, and ends up relegating persons to the status of things. Hence segregation is not only politically, economically and sociologically unsound, but it is morally wrong and awful. Paul Tillich said that sin is separation. Isn't segregation an existential expression of man's tragic separation, an expression of his awful estrangement, his terrible sinfulness? Thus it is that I can urge men to disobey segregation ordinances, for they are morally wrong.

21. Excerpt from Martin Luther King Jr.'s "I Have a Dream" Speech (1963)

Source: See Martin Luther King Jr., *I Have a Dream: Writings and Speeches That Changed the World*, James Melvin Washington ed. (San Francisco: HarperSanFrancisco, 1992, 104–105).

The "I Have a Dream" speech is King's most widely cited speech. He delivered the speech before the Lincoln Memorial on August 28, 1963, at the March on Washington.

I say to you, my friends, that even though we face the difficulties of today and tomorrow, I still have a dream. It is a dream deeply rooted in the American dream that one day this nation will rise up and live out the true meaning of its creed—we hold these truths to be self-evident, that all men are created equal.

I have a dream that one day on the red hills of Georgia, sons of former slaves and sons of former slave-owners will be able to sit down together at the table of brotherhood.

I have a dream that one day even the state of Mississippi, a state sweltering with the heat of injustice, sweltering with the heat of oppression, will be transformed into an oasis of freedom and justice.

I have a dream my four little children will one day live in a nation where they will not be judged by the color of their skin but by the content of their character. I have a dream today!

I have a dream that one day down in Alabama, with its vicious racists, with its governor having his lips dripping with the words of interposition and nullification; that one day right there in Alabama, little black boys and black girls will be able to join hands with little white boys and white girls as sisters and brothers. I have a dream today!

I have a dream that one day every valley shall be exalted, every hill and mountain shall be made low, the rough places shall be made plain, and the crooked places shall be made straight and the glory of the Lord will be revealed and all flesh shall see it together.

22. Excerpt from Malcolm X's *The Autobiography of Malcolm X* (1965)

Source: See Malcolm X, *The Autobiography of Malcolm X* (New York: Ballantine Books, 1992, 411–412).

Malcolm X was the most prominent figure in the Black Nationalist Movement. Black Nationalists did not allow white people to join their organizations, while black Civil Rights leaders worked closely with white liberals. In the following paragraph, Malcolm X tells why white people cannot help to fight white racism.

When I say that here now, it makes me think about that little co-ed I told you about, the one who flew from her New England college down to New York and came up to me in the Nation of Islam's restaurant in Harlem, and I told her that there was "nothing" she could do. I regret that I told her that. I wish that now I knew her name, or where I could telephone her, or write to her, and tell her what I tell white people now when they present themselves as being sincere, and ask me, one way or another, the same thing that she asked.

The first thing I tell them is that at least where my own particular Black Nationalist organization, the Organization of Afro-American Unity, is concerned, they can't *join* us. I have these very deep feelings that white people who want to join black organizations are really just taking the escapist way to salve their consciences. By visibly hovering near us, they are "proving" that they are "with us." But the hard truth is this *isn't* helping to solve America's racist problem. The Negroes aren't the racists. Where the really sincere white people have got to do their "proving" of themselves is not among the black *victims*, but out on the battle lines of where America's racism really *is*—and that's in their own home communities; America's racism is among their own fellow whites. That's where the sincere whites who really mean to accomplish something have got to work.

23. Excerpt from James Mooney's *The Ghost-Dance Religion and the Sioux Outbreak of 1890*

Source: See James Mooney, *The Ghost-Dance Religion and the Sioux Outbreak of 1890* (Chicago and London: The University of Chicago Press, 1965, 41).

In the story of ghost dancing, the Ogalala heard that the Son of God was truly on earth in the west from their country. This was in the year 1889. The first people knew about the messiah to be on earth were the Shoshoni and Arapaho. So in 1889 Good Thunder with four or five others visited the place where Son of God said to be. These people went there without permission. They said the messiah was there at the place, but he was there to help the

Indians and not the whites; so this made the Indians happy to find this out. Good Thunder, Cloud Horse, Yellow Knife, and Short Bull visited the place again in 1890 and saw the messiah. Their story of their visit to the messiah is as follows:

"From the country where the Arapaho and Shoshoni we start in the direction of northwest in train for five nights and arrived at the foot of the Rocky mountains. Here we saw him and also several tribes of Indians. The people said that the messiah will come at a place in the woods where the place was prepare for him. When we went to the place a smoke descended from heaven to the place where he was to come. When the smoke disappeared, there was a man of about forty, which was the Son of God. The man said:

" 'My grandchildren! I am glad you have come far away to see your relatives. This are your people who have come back from your country.' When he said he want us to go with him, we looked and we saw a land created across the ocean on which all the nations of Indians were coming home, but, as the messiah looked at the land which was created and reached across the ocean, again disappeared, saying that it was not time for that to take place. The messiah then gave to Good Thunder some paints—Indian paint and a white paint—a green grass [sagebrush twigs?]; and said, 'My grandchildren, when you get home, go to farming and send all your children to school. And on way home if you kill any buffalo cut the head, the tail, and the four feet and leave them, and that buffalo will come to live again. When the soldiers of the white people chief want to arrest me, I shall stretch out my arms, which will knock them to nothingness, or, if not that, the earth will open and swallow them in. My father commanded me to visit the Indians on a purpose. I have came to the white people first, but they not good. They killed me, and you can see the marks of my wounds on my feet, my hands, and on my back. My father has given you life—your old life—and you have come to see your friends, but you will not take me home with you at this time. I want you to tell when you get home your people to follow my examples. Any one Indian does not obey me and tries to be on white's side will be covered over by a new land that is to come over this old one. You will, all the people, use the paints and grass I give you. In the spring when the green grass comes, your people who have gone before you will come back, and you shall see your friends then, for you have come to my call.' "

The people from every tipi send for us to visit them. They are people who died many years ago. Chasing Hawk, who died not long ago, was there, and we went to his tipi. He was living with his wife, who was killed in war long ago. They live in a buffalo skin tipi—a very large one—and he wanted all his friends to go there to live. A son of Good Thunder who died in war long ago was one who also took us to his tipi so his father saw him. When coming we come to a herd of buffaloes. We killed one and took everything except the four feet, head, and tail, and when we came a little ways from it there was the buffaloes come to life again and went off. This was one of the messiah's word came to truth. The messiah said, "I will short your journey when you feel tired of the long ways, if you call upon me." This we did when we were tired. The night came upon us, we stopped at a place, and we called upon the messiah to help us, because we were tired of long journey. We went to sleep and in the morning we found ourselves at a great distance from where we stopped.

24. Excerpt from the Aryan Nations Platform

Source: http://www.aryannations.org/an/index.html.
Aryan Nations World Headquarters

> Aryan Nations is the most representative group of the Christian Identity Church Movement, a white-supremacist movement. Aryan Nations is a para-military organization with a few hundred members. Its compound is in Hayden Lake, Idaho. It is exceedingly anti-Semitic, as its platform indicates.

Aryan Nations is the on-going work of Jesus The Christ re-gathering His people, calling His people to a state for their nation to bring in His Kingdom! We hail His Victory!

WE BELIEVE in the preservation of our Race, individually and collectively, as a people as demanded and directed by Yahweh. We believe our Racial Nation has a right and is under obligation to preserve itself and its members.

WE BELIEVE that Adam, man of Genesis, is the placing of the White Race upon this earth. Not all races descend from Adam. Adam is the father of the White Race only. (Adam in the original Hebrew is translated: "to show blood in the face; turn rosy.") Genesis 5:1

. . .

WE BELIEVE that there are literal children of Satan in the world today. These children are the descendants of Cain, who was a result of Eve's original sin, her physical seduction by Satan. We know that because of this sin there is a battle and a natural enmity between the children of Satan and the children of The Most High God (Yahweh). Genesis 3:15; 1 John 3:12

WE BELIEVE that the Cananite Jew is the natural enemy of our Aryan (White) Race. This is attested by scripture and all secular history. The Jew is like a destroying virus that attacks our racial body to destroy our Aryan culture and the purity of our Race. Those of our Race who resist these attacks are called "chosen and faithful." John 8:44; 1 Thessalonians 2:15; Revelations 17:14

25. Excerpt from the American Sociological Association's "The Importance of Collecting Data and Doing Social Scientific Research on Race" (2003)

Source: Washington, DC: American Sociological Association, 2003. Reprinted with permission of the American Sociological Association.

The question of whether to collect statistics that allow the comparison of differences among racial and ethnic groups in the census, public surveys, and administrative databases is not an abstract one. Some scholarly and civic leaders believe that measuring these differences promotes social divisions and fuels a mistaken perception that race is a biological concept. California voters are likely to face a referendum in 2004 to prohibit the collection of racial data by most state government agencies. As the leading voice for 13,000 academic and practicing sociologists, the ASA takes the position that calls to end the collection of data using racial categories are ill advised, although racial categories do not necessarily reflect biological or genetic categories. The failure to gather data on this socially significant category would preserve the status quo and hamper progress toward understanding and addressing inequalities in primary social institutions. The ASA statement highlights significant research findings on the role and consequences of race relations in social institutions such as schools, labor markets, neighborhoods, and health care scholarship that would not have been possible without data on racial categories. The longstanding debate over racial classification in the United States is certain to generate greater public interest as our population becomes more diverse. The ASA hopes to continue to play a meaningful role in that important dialogue.

Executive Summary

Race is a complex, sensitive, and controversial topic in scientific discourse and in public policy. Views on race and the racial classification system used to measure it have become polarized. At the heart of the debate in the United States are several fundamental questions: What are the causes and consequences of racial inequality? Should we continue to use racial classification to assess the role and consequences of race? And, perhaps most significantly, under what conditions does the classification of people by race promote racial division, and when does it aid the pursuit of justice and equality? The answers to these questions are important to scientific inquiry, but they are not merely academic. Some scholarly and civic leaders have proposed that the government stop collecting data on race altogether. Respected voices from the fields of human molecular biology and physical anthropology (supported by research from the Human Genome Project) assert that the concept of race has no validity in their respective fields. Growing numbers of humanist scholars, social anthropologists, and political commentators have joined the chorus in urging the nation to rid itself of the concept of race.

However, a large body of social science research documents the role and consequences of race in primary social institutions and environments, including the criminal justice, education and health systems, job markets, and where people live. These studies illustrate how racial hierarchies are embedded in daily life, from racial profiling in law enforcement, to 'red-lining' communities of color in mortgage lending, to sharp disparities in the health of members of different population groups. Policymakers, in fact, have recognized the importance of research into the causes of racial disparities. For example, the 2000 Minority Health and Health Disparities Research and Education Act directed the National Institutes of Health to support continued research on health gaps between racial groups, with the ultimate goal of eliminating such disparities. Moreover, growth among some racial and ethnic groups (notably, Asians and Hispanics), and the diversification of the nation's racial and ethnic composition underscore the need for expanded research on the health and socio-economic status of these groups.

Sociologists have long examined how race, a social concept that changes over time, has been used to place people in categories. Some scientists and policymakers now contend that research using the concept of race perpetuates the negative consequences of thinking in racial terms. Others argue that measuring differential experiences, treatment, and outcomes across racial categories is necessary to track disparities and to inform policymaking in order to achieve greater social justice.

The American Sociological Association (ASA), an association of some 13,000 U.S. and international sociologists, finds greater merit in the latter point of view. Sociological scholarship on "race" provides scientific evidence in the current scientific and civic debate over the social consequences of the existing categorizations and perceptions of race; allows scholars to document how race shapes social ranking, access to resources, and life experiences; and advances understanding of this important dimension of social life, which in turn advances social justice. Refusing to acknowledge the fact of racial classification, feelings, and actions, and refusing to measure their consequences will not eliminate racial inequalities. At best, it will preserve the status quo.

When a concept is central to societal organization, examining how, when, and why people in that society use the concept is vital to understanding the organization and consequences of social relationships. The following statement sets forth the basis for ASA's position and illustrates the importance of data on race to further scientific investigation and informed public discourse. ASA fully recognizes the global nature of the debate over race, racial classification, and the role of race in societies; this statement focuses attention on the treatment of race in the United States and the scholarly and public interest in continuing to measure it.

Racial Classifications as the Basis For Scientific Inquiry

Race is a complex, sensitive, and controversial topic in scientific discourse and in public policy. Views on race and the racial classification system used to measure it, have become polarized. In popular discourse, racial groups are viewed as physically distinguishable populations that share a common geographically based ancestry. "Race" shapes the way that some people relate to each other, based on their belief that it reflects physical, intellectual, moral, or spiritual superiority or inferiority. However, biological research now suggests that the substantial overlap among any and all biological categories of race undermines the utility of the concept for scientific work in this field.

How then, can it be the subject of valid scientific investigation at the social level? The answer is that social and economic life is organized, in part, around race as a social construct. When a concept is central to societal organization, examining how, when, and why people in that society use the concept is vital to understanding the organization and consequences of social relationships.

Sociological analysis of the family provides an analogue. We know that families take many forms; for example, they can be nuclear or extended, patrilineal or matrilineal. Some family categories correspond to biological categories; others do not. Moreover, boundaries of family membership vary, depending on a range of individual and institutional factors. Yet regardless of whether families correspond to biological definitions, social scientists study families and use membership in family categories in their study of other phenomena, such as well-being. Similarly, racial statuses, although not representing biological differences, are of sociological interest in their form, their changes, and their consequences.

1. The federal government defines race categories for statistical policy purposes, program administrative reporting, and civil rights compliance, and sets forth minimum categories for the collection and reporting of data on race. The current standards, adopted in October 1997, include five race categories: American Indian or Alaska Native; Asian; Black or African American; Native Hawaiian or Other Pacific Islander; and White. Respondents to federal data collection activities must be offered the option of selecting one or more racial designations. Hispanics or Latinos, whom current standards define as an ethnic group, can be of any race. However, before the government promulgated standard race categories in 1977, some U.S. censuses designated Hispanic groups as race categories (e.g., the 1930 census listed Mexicans as a separate race).

The Social Concept of Race

Individuals and social institutions evaluate, rank, and ascribe behaviors to individuals on the basis of their presumed race. The concept of race in the United States, and the inevitable corresponding taxonomic system to categorize people by race has changed, as economic, political, and historical contexts have changed (19). Sociologists are interested in explaining how and why social definitions of race persist and change. They also seek to explain the nature of power relationships between and among racial groups, and to understand more fully the nature of belief systems about race, the dimensions of how people use the concept and apply it in different circumstances.

Social Reality and Racial Classification

The way we define racial groups that comprise "the American mosaic" has also changed, most recently as immigrants from Asia, Latin America, and the Caribbean have entered the country in large numbers. One response to these demographic shifts has been the effort (sometimes contentious) to modify or add categories to the government's official statistical policy on race and ethnicity, which governs data collection in the census, other federal surveys, and administrative functions. Historically, changes in racial categories used for administrative purposes and self-identification have occurred within the context of a polarized biracialism of Black and White; other immigrants to the United States, including those from Asia, Latin America, and the Caribbean, have been "racialized" or ranked in between these two categories (26).

Although racial categories are legitimate subjects of empirical sociological investigation, it is important to recognize the danger of contributing to the popular conception of race as biological. Yet refusing to employ racial categories for administrative purposes and for social research does not eliminate their use in daily life, both by individuals and within social and economic institutions. In France, information on race is seldom collected officially, but evidence of systematic racial discrimination remains (31, 10). The 1988 Eurobarometer revealed that, of the 12 European countries included in the study, France was second (after Belgium) in both anti-immigrant prejudice and racial prejudice (29). Brazil's experience also is illustrative: The nation's then-ruling military junta barred the collection of racial data in the 1970 census, asserting that race was not a meaningful concept for social measurement. The resulting information void, coupled with government censorship, diminished public discussion of racial issues, but it did not substantially reduce racial inequalities. When racial data was collected again in the 1980 census, they revealed lower socioeconomic status for those with darker skin (38).

The Consequences of Race and Race Relations in Social Institutions

Although race is a social construct (in other words, a social invention that changes as political, economic, and historical contexts change), it has real consequences across a wide range of social and economic institutions. Those who favor ignoring race as an explicit administrative matter in the hope that it will cease to exist as a social concept, ignore the weight of a vast body of sociological research that shows that racial hierarchies are embedded in the routine practices of social groups and institutions.

Primary areas of sociological investigation include the consequences of racial classification as:

- A sorting mechanism for mating, marriage and adoption.
- A stratifying practice for providing or denying access to resources.
- An organizing device for mobilization to maintain or challenge systems of racial stratification.
- A basis for scientifically investigating proximate causes.

Race as a Sorting Mechanism for Mating, Marriage, and Adoption

Historically, race has been a primary sorting mechanism for marriage (as well as friendship and dating). Until anti-miscegenation laws were outlawed in the United States in 1967, many states prohibited interracial marriage. Since then, intermarriage rates have more than doubled to 2.2 percent of all marriages, according to the latest census information (14, 28). When Whites (the largest racial group in the United States) intermarry, they are most likely to marry Native Americans/American Indians and least likely to marry African Americans. Projections to the year 2010 suggest that intermarriage and, consequently, the universe of people identifying with two or more races is likely to increase, although most marriages still occur within socially designated racial groupings (7).

Race as a Stratifying Practice

Race serves as a basis for the distribution of social privileges and resources. Among the many arenas in which this occurs is education. On the one hand, education can be a mechanism for reducing differences across members of racial categories. On the other hand, through "tracking" and segregation, the primary and secondary educational system has played a major role in reproducing race and class inequalities. Tracking socializes and prepares students for different education and career paths. School districts continue to stratify by race and class through two-track systems (general and college prep/advanced) or systems in which all students take the same courses, but at different levels of ability. African Americans, Hispanics, American Indians, and students from low socioeconomic backgrounds, regardless of ability levels, are over-represented in lower-level classes and in schools with fewer Advanced Placement classes, materials, and instructional resources (11, 13, 20, 23).

Race as an Organizing Device for Mobilization to Maintain or Challenge Systems of Racial Stratification

Understanding how social movements develop in racially stratified societies requires scholarship on the use of race in strategies of mobilization. Racial stratification has clear beneficiaries and clear victims, and both have organized on racial terms to challenge or preserve systems of racial stratification. For example, the apartheid regime in South Africa used race to maintain supremacy and privilege for whites in nearly all aspects of economic and political life for much of the twentieth century. Blacks and others seeking to overthrow the system, often were able to mobilize opposition by appealing to its victims, the black population. The American civil rights movement was similarly successful in mobilizing resistance to segregation, but it also provoked some white citizens into organizing their own power base (for example, by forming White Citizens' Councils) to maintain power and privilege (2, 24).

Race and Ethnicity as a Basis for the Scientific Investigation of Proximate Causes and Critical Interactions

Data on race often serve as an investigative key to discovering the fundamental causes of racially different outcomes and the "vicious cycle" of factors affecting these outcomes. Moreover, because race routinely interacts with other primary categories of social life, such as gender and social class, continued examination of these bases of fundamental social interaction and social cleavage is required. In the health arena, hypertension levels are much higher for African Americans than other groups. Sociological investigations suggests that discrimination and unequal allocation of society's resources might expose members of this racial group to higher levels of stress, a proximate cause of hypertension (40).

Similarly, rates of prostate cancer are much higher for some groups of men than others. Likewise, breast cancer is higher for some groups of women than others. While the proximate causes may appear to be biological, research shows that environmental and socio-economic factors disproportionately place at greater risk members of socially subordinated racial and ethnic groups. For example, African Americans' and Hispanics' concentration in polluted and dangerous neighborhoods result in feelings of depression and powerlessness that, in turn, diminish the ability to improve these neighborhoods (35, 40, 41). Systematic investigation is necessary to uncover and distinguish what social forces, including race, contribute to disparate outcomes.

Whites and African Americans tend to live in substantially homogenous communities, as do many Asians and Hispanics.

Research Highlights: Race and Ethnicity as Factors in Social Institutions

The following examples highlight significant research findings that illustrate the persistent role of race in primary social institutions in the United States, including the job market, neighborhoods, and the health care system. This scientific investigation would not have been possible without data on race.

Job Market

Sociological research shows that race is substantially related to workplace recruitment, hiring, firing, and promotions. Ostensibly neutral practices can advantage some racial groups and adversely affect others. For example, the majority of workers obtain their jobs through informal networks rather than through open recruitment and hiring practices. Business-as-usual recruitment and hiring practices include recruiting at predominantly white schools, advertising only in suburban newspapers, and employing relatives and friends of current workers.

Young, white job seekers benefit from family connections, studies show. In contrast, a recent study revealed that word-of-mouth recruitment through family and friendship networks limited job opportunities for African Americans in the construction trades. Government downsizing provides another example of a "race neutral" practice with racially disparate consequences: Research shows that because African Americans have successfully established employment niches in the civil service, government workforce reductions displace disproportionate numbers of African American, and increasingly, Hispanic-employees. These and other social processes, such as conscious and unconscious prejudices of those with power in the workplace, affecting the labor market largely explain the persistent two-to-one ratio of black to white unemployment (4, 5, 9, 15, 32, 39, 42, 43).

Neighborhood Segregation

For all of its racial diversity, the highly segregated residential racial composition is a defining characteristic of American cities and suburbs. Whites and African Americans tend to live in substantially homogenous communities, as do many Asians and Hispanics. The segregation rates of blacks have declined slightly, while the rates of Asians and Hispanics have increased. Sociological research shows that the "hyper-segregation" between blacks and whites, for example, is a consequence of both public and private policies, as well as individual attitudes and group practices. Sociological research has been key in understanding the interaction between these policies, attitudes, and practices. For example, according to attitude surveys, by the 1990s, a majority of whites were willing to live next door to African Americans, but their comfort level fell as the proportion of African Americans in the neighborhood increased. Real estate and mortgage-industry practices also contribute to neighborhood segregation, as well as racially disparate homeownership rates (which, in turn, contribute to the enormous wealth gap between racial groups). Despite fair housing laws, audit studies show, industry practices continue to steer African American homebuyers away from white neighborhoods, deny African Americans information about available loans, and offer inferior property insurance. Segregation profoundly affects quality of life. African American neighborhoods (even relatively affluent ones) are less likely than white neighborhoods to have high quality services, schools, transportation, medical care, a mix of retail establishments, and other amenities. Low capital investment, relative lack of political influence, and limited social networks contribute to these disparities (1, 6, 8, 9, 17, 21, 22, 25, 30, 35, 36, 37, 42, 44).

Health

Research clearly documents significant, persistent differences in life expectancy, mortality, incidence of disease, and causes of death between racial groups. For example, African Americans have higher death rates than whites for eight of the ten leading causes of death. While Asian-Pacific Islander babies have the lowest mortality rates of all broad racial categories, infant mortality for Native Hawaiians is nearly three times higher than for Japanese Americans. Genetics accounts for some health differences, but social and economic factors, uneven treatment, public health policy, and health and coping behaviors play a large role in these unequal health outcomes.

Socio-economic circumstances are the strongest predictors of both life span and freedom from disease and disability. Unequal life expectancy and mortality reflect racial disparities in income and incidence of poverty, education, and to some degree, marital status.

Many studies have found that these characteristics and related environmental factors such as overcrowded housing, inaccessibility of medical care, poor sanitation, and pollution adversely impact life expectancy and both overall and cause-specific mortality for groups that have disproportionately high death rates.

Race differences in health insurance coverage largely reflect differences in key socio-economic characteristics. Hispanics are least likely to be employed in jobs that provide health insurance and relatively fewer Asian Americans are insured because they are more likely to be in small low-profit businesses that make it hard to pay for health insurance. Access to affordable medical care also affects health outcomes. Sociological research shows that highly segregated African American neighborhoods are less likely to have health care facilities such as hospitals and clinics, and have the highest ratio of patients to physicians. In addition, public policies such as privatization of medicine and lower Medicaid and Medicare funding have had unintended racial consequences; studies show a further reduction of medical services in African American neighborhoods as a result of these actions.

Even when health care services are available, members of different racial groups often do not receive comparable treatment. For example, African Americans are less likely to receive the most commonly performed diagnostic procedures, such as cardiovascular and orthopedic procedures. Institutional discrimination, including racial stereotyping by medical professionals, and systemic barriers, such as language difficulties for newer immigrants (the majority of whom are from Asia and Latin America), partly explain differential treatment patterns, stalling health improvements for some racial groups.

All of these factors interact to produce poorer health outcomes, indicating that racial stratification remains an important explanation for health disparities (3, 12, 16, 18, 21, 27, 33, 34, 40, 41).

Summary: The Importance of Sociological Research On Race

A central focus of sociological research is systematic attention to the causes and consequences of social inequalities. As long as Americans routinely sort each other into racial categories and act on the basis of those attributions, re-search on the role of race and race relations in the United States falls squarely within this scientific agenda. Racial profiling in law enforcement activities, "redlining" of predominantly minority neighborhoods in the mortgage and in-surance industries, differential medical treatment, and tracking in schools, ex-emplify social practices that should be studied. Studying race as a social phenomenon makes for better science and more informed policy debate. As the United States becomes more diverse, the need for public agencies to con-tinue to collect data on racial categories will become even more important. Sociologists are well qualified to study the impact of "race"—and all the ram-ifications of racial categorization—on people's lives and social institutions. The continuation of the collection and scholarly analysis of data serves both sci-ence and the public interest. For all of these reasons, the American Sociolog-ical Association supports collecting data and doing research on race.

References

1. Alba, Richard D., John R. Logan, and Brian J. Stults. 2000. "The Changing Neighborhood Contexts of the Immigrant Metropolis." *Social Forces* 79:587–621.

2. Bloom, Jack M. 1987. *Class, Race and the Civil Rights Movement*. Bloom-ington: Indiana University Press.

3. Bobo, Lawrence D. 2001. "Racial Attitudes and Relations at the Close of the Twentieth Century." Pp. 264–201, In *America Becoming: Racial Trends and Their Consequences*, vol. 2, edited by Neil J. Smelser, William J. Wilson, and Faith Mitchell. Washington, DC: National Research Council.

4. Bobo, Lawrence D., Devon Johnson, and Susan Suh. 2002. "Racial Atti-tudes and Power in the Workplace: Do the Haves Differ from the Have-Nots?" Pp. 491–522, In *Prismatic Metropolis: Inequality in Los Angeles*, edited by Lawrence D. Bobo, Melvin J. Oliver, James H. Johnson, Jr., and Abel Valenzuela Jr. New York, NY: Russell Sage Foundation.

5. DiTomaso, Nancy. 2000. "Why Anti-Discrimination Policies Are Not Enough: The Legacies and Consequences of Affirmative Inclusion—For Whites." Presented at the 95th annual meeting of the American Sociological Association, August 16, Anaheim, CA.

6. Drier, Peter, John Mollenkopf, and Todd Swanstrom. 2001. *Place Matters: Metropolitics in the 21st Century*. Lawrence: University of Kansas Press.

7. Edmonston, Barry, Sharon M. Lee, and Jeffrey Passel. (in press). "Recent Trends in Intermarriage and Immigration, and Their Effects on the Future Racial Composition of the U.S. Population." In *The New Race Question*, edited by Joel Perlmann and Mary C. Waters. New York, NY: Russell Sage Foundation.

8. Farley, Reynolds. 1996. *The New American Reality: Who We Are, How We Got Here, Where We Are Going?* New York, NY: Russell Sage Foundation.

9. Farley, Reynolds, Sheldon Danzinger, and Harry Holzer. 2001. *Detroit Di-vided*. New York, NY: Russell Sage Foundation.

10. Galap, Jean. 1991. "Phenotypes et Discrimination des Noirs en France: Question de Methode." *Intercultures* 14 (Juillet): 21–35.

11. Hallinan, Maureen T. 2001. "Sociological Perspectives on Black-White In-equalities in American Schooling." *Sociology of Education* (Extra Issue 2001): 50–70.

12. Hayward, Mark D., Eileen M. Crimmins, Toni P. Miles, and Yu Yang. 2000. "Socioeconomic Status and the Racial Gap in Chronic Health Conditions." *American Sociological Review* 65:910–930.

13. Heubert, Jay P., and Robert M. Hauser, eds. 1999. *High Stakes: Testing for Tracking, Promotion, and Graduation*. Washington, DC: National Research Council.

14. Jones, Nicholas A., and Amy Symens Smith. 2001. The Two or More Races Population 2000: Census 2000 Brief. U.S. Bureau of the Census (November). Retrieved June 19, 2002. (http:www.census.gov/population/www/cen2000/briefs.html.)

15. Kirshenman, Joleen, and Kathryn M. Neckerman. 1992. "We'd Love to Hire Them, But . . . : The Meaning of Race for Employers." Pp. 203–234, In *The Urban Underclass*, edited by C. Jencks and P. Peterson. Washington, DC: The Brookings Institution.

16. Klinenberg, Eric. 2002. *Heat Wave: A Social Autopsy of Disaster in Chicago*. Chicago, IL: University of Chicago Press.

17. LaVeist, Thomas. 1992. "The Political Empowerment and Health Status of African Americans: Mapping a New Territory." *American Journal of Sociology* 97:1080–1095.

18. LaViest, Thomas A., C. Diala, and N.C. Jarrett. 2000. "Social Status and Perceived Discrimination: Who Experiences Discrimination in the Health Care System and Why?" Pp. 194–208, In *Minority Health in America*, edited by Carol J.R. Hogue, Martha A. Hargraves, and Karen Scott-Collins. Baltimore, MD: Johns Hopkins University Press.

19. Lee, Sharon M. 1993. "Racial Classifications in the U.S. Census: 1890–1990." *Ethnic and Racial Studies* 16:75–94.

20. Lucas, Samuel Roundfield. 1999. *Tracking Inequality: Stratification and Mobility in American High Schools*. New York, NY: Teachers College Press.

21. Massey, Douglas S. 2001. "Residential Segregation and Neighborhood Conditions in U.S. Metropolitan Areas." Pp. 391–434, In *America Becoming: Racial Trends and Their Consequences*, vol. 1, edited by Neil J. Smelser, William J. Wilson, and Faith Mitchell. Washington, DC: National Research Council.

22. Massey, Douglas S., and Nancy Denton. 1993. *American Apartheid: Segregation and the Making of the Underclass*. Cambridge, MA: Harvard University Press.

23. Mikelson, Roslyn A. 2002. "What Constitutes Racial Discrimination in Education? A Social Science Perspective." Prepared for workshop on Measuring Racial Disparities and Discrimination in Elementary and Secondary Education, National Research Council Committee on the National Statistics Center for Education, July 2002. For a grant from the Ford Foundation and National Science Foundation.

24. Morris, Aldon D. 1986. *The Origins of the Civil Rights Movement: Black Communities Organizing for Change*. New York, NY: The Free Press.

25. Oliver, Melvin L., and Thomas J. Shapiro. 1995. *Black Wealth? White Wealth?: A New Perspective on Racial Inequality*. New York, NY: Routledge.

26. Omi, Michael. 2001. "The Changing Meaning of Race." Pp. 243–263, In *America Becoming: Racial Trends and Their Consequences*, edited by Neil J.

Smelser, William J. Wilson, and Faith Mitchell. Washington, DC: National Academy Press.

27. Quadagno, Jill. 2000. "Promoting Civil Rights through the Welfare State: How Medicare Integrated Southern Hospitals." *Social Problems* 47:68–89.

28. Qian, Zhenchao. 1997. "Breaking the Racial Barriers: Variations in Interracial Marriage Between 1980 and 1990." *Demography* 34:263–276.

29. Quillian, Lincoln. 1995. "Prejudice as a Response to Perceived Group Threat: Population Composition and Anti-Immigrant and Racial Prejudice in Europe." *American Sociological Review* 60:586–611.

30. Rankin, Bruce H., and James M. Quane. 2000. "Neighborhood Poverty and Social Isolation of Inner-City African American Families." *Social Forces* 79: 139–164.

31. Raveau, F., B. Kilborne, L. Frere, J. M. Lorin, and G. Trempe. 1976. "Perception Sociale de la Couleur et Discrimination." *Cahiers d'Anthropologie* 4: 23–42.

32. Reskin, Barbara F. 1998. The Realities of Affirmative Action in Employment. Washington, DC: The American Sociological Association.

33. Rogers, Richard, Robert Hummer, Charles B. Nam, Kimberly Peters. 1996. "Demographic, Socioeconomic, and Behavioral Factors Affecting Ethnic Mortality by Cause." *Social Forces* 74:1419–1438.

34. Ross, Catherine E., and John Mirowsky. 2001. "Neighborhood Disadvantage, Disorder, and Health." *Journal of Health and Social Behavior* 42: 258–276.

35. Sampson, Robert J., Gregory D. Squires, and Min Zhou. 2001. How Neighborhoods Matter: The Value of Investing at the Local Level. Washington, DC: The American Sociological Association.

36. Schuman, Howard, Charlotte Steeh, Lawrence Bobo, and Maria Kryson. 1997. *Racial Attitudes in America*. 2nd ed. Cambridge, MA: Harvard University Press.

37. Squires, Gregory D., and Sally O'Connor. 2001. *Color and Money: Politics and Prospects for Community Reinvestment in Urban America*. Albany, NY: SUNY Press.

38. Telles, Edward. 2002. "Racial Ambiguity among the Brazilian Population." *Ethnic and Racial Studies* 25:415–441.

39. Waldinger, Roger. 1996. *Still the Promised City? African-Americans and New Immigrants in Postindustrial New York*. Cambridge, MA: Harvard University Press.

40. Williams, David R. 2001. "Racial Variations in Adult Health Status: Patterns, Paradoxes, and Prospects," Pp. 371–410, In *America Becoming: Racial Trends and Their Consequences*, vol. 2, edited by Neil J. Smelser, William J. Wilson, and Faith Mitchell. Washington, DC: National Research Council.

41. Williams, David R., and Chiquita Collins. (in press). "Racial Residential Segregation: A Fundamental Cause of Racial Disparities in Health." Public Health Reports.

42. Wilson, William J. 1996. *When Work Disappears: The World of the New Urban Poor*. New York, NY: Alfred A. Knopf, Inc.

43. Woo, Deborah. 2000. *Glass Ceilings and Asian Americans: The New Face of Workplace Barriers*. Walnut Creek, CA: AltaMira Press.

44. Yinger, John. 1995. *Closed Doors, Opportunities Lost*. New York, NY: Russell Sage Foundation.

26. Poem by Haunani-Kay Trask, "Settlers, Not Immigrants" (2000)

Source: *Amerasia Journal* vol. 26, no. 2 (2000).

Settlers, not immigrants,
    from America, from Asia.
        Come to settle, to take.
            To take from the Native
                that which is Native:
                    Land, water, women,
                        sovereignty.

Settlers, not immigrants,
    bringing syphilis and leprosy,
        Jehovah and democracy,
            Settlers, settling,
                our Native Hawai'i,
                    inscribing their
                        lies of discovery,
                            of penury, of victory.

Settlers, not immigrants
    Killing us off,
        disease by disease, lie by lie,
        one by one.

SELECTED BIBLIOGRAPHY

GENERAL

Allport, Gordon W. *The Nature of Prejudice*. Reading, MA: Addison-Wesley, 1954.

American Sociological Association. "The ASA Statement on the Importance of Collecting Data and Doing Social Science Research on Race." American Sociological Association, 2003.

Anders, Stephen. *Manifest Destiny: American Expansionism and the Empire of Right*. New York: Hill and Wang, 1996.

Anderson, Elijah, and Douglas S. Massey, eds. *Problem of the Century*. New York: Russell Sage Foundation, 2004.

Anderson, Margaret L., and Patricia Hill Collins, eds. *Race, Class, and Gender*. 2nd ed. New York: Wadsworth, 1995.

Baca, Zinn M., and B. T. Dill, eds. *Women of Color in the United States*. Philadelphia: Temple University Press, 1993.

Banks, James A. *Multicultural Education, Transformative Knowledge, and Action: Historical and Contemporary Perspectives*. New York: Teachers College Press, 1996.

Banks, James A., and Cherry A. Banks, eds. *Handbook of Research on Multicultural Education*. 2nd ed. San Francisco: Jossey-Bass, 2004.

Bernardi, Daniel, ed. *Classic Hollywood, Classic Whiteness*. Minneapolis: University of Minnesota Press, 2001.

Blauner, Robert. *Racial Oppression in America*. New York: Harper & Row, 1972.

Bogardus, Emory S. *Social Distance*. Los Angeles: Antioch Press, 1959.

Bonilla-Silva, Eduardo. *Racism without Racists: Color-Blind Racism and the Persistence of Racial Inequality in the United States*. Lanham, MD: Rowman & Littlefield, 2003.

———. *White Supremacy and Racism in the Post Civil Rights Era*. Boulder, CO: L. Rienner, 2003.

Bowser, Benjamin P., and Raymond G. Hunt. *Impacts of Racism on White Americans*. 2nd ed. Thousand Oaks, CA: Sage Publications, 1996.

Bureau of National Affairs. *The Civil Rights Act of 1964*. Washington, DC: Bureau of National Affairs, 1964.

Burris, Val, Emery Smith, and Ann Strahm. "White Supremacist Networks on the Internet." *Sociological Focus* 33 (2000): 215-235.

Chesler, M. A. "Contemporary Sociological Theories of Racism." In *Towards the Elimination of Racism*, edited by P. A. Katz, 21-71. New York: Pergamon, 1976.

Cole, David. *No Equal Justice: Race and Class in the American Criminal Justice System*. New York: The New Press, 1999.

Correspondents of the New York Times. *How Race Is Lived in America: Pulling Together, Pulling Apart*. New York: Henry Holt, 2001.

Crawford, James. *Hold Your Tongue: Bilingualism and the Politics of "English Only."* Boston: Addison-Wesley, 1992.

Crenshaw, Kimberlé, et al., eds. *Critical Race Theory: The Key Writings That Formed the Movement*. New York: New Press, 1995.

Delgado, Richard. "Words That Wound: A Tort Action for Racial Insults, Epithets, and Name-Calling." *Harvard Civil Rights-Civil Liberties Law Review* 17 (1982).

Delgado, Richard, and Jean Stefancic. *Critical Race Theory*. New York: New York University Press, 2001.

Doob, Christopher Bates. *Racism: An American Cauldron*. 3rd ed. New York: Longman, 1999.

Elias, Robert. *Baseball and the American Dream: Race, Class, Gender and the American Pastime*. Armonk, NY: M. E. Sharpe, 2001.

Farely, R., and W. R. Allen. *The Color Line and the Quality of Life in America*. New York: Oxford University Press, 1989.

Ferber, Amy. *White Man Falling: Race, Gender, and White Supremacy*. New York: Rowman & Littlefield, 1998.

Foner, Nancy. *New Immigrant in New Work*. New York: Columbia University Press, 2001.

Frankenberg, Erika, Chungmei Lee, and Gary Orfield. *"A Multiracial Society with Segregated Schools: Are We Losing the Dream?"* The Civil Rights Project. Cambridge, MA: Harvard University, 2003.

Gallagher, Charles A. *Rethinking the Color Line*. California: Mayfield, 1999.

Gans, Herbert J. "Second Generation Decline: Scenarios for the Economic and Ethnic Futures of the Post-1965 American Immigrants." *Ethnic and Racial Studies* 15, no. 2 (April 1992): 173-192.

Geschwender, James A. *Racial Stratification in America*. Dubuque, IA: W. C. Brown Co., 1978.

Gibson, James L. *Overcoming Apartheid*. New York: Russell Sage Foundation, 2004.

Glazer, Nathan. *Affirmative Discrimination: Ethnic Inequality and Public Policy*. New York: Basic Books, 1974.

Grant, Madison. *The Passing of the Great Race*. New York: Charles Scribner's Sons, 1916.

Green, Jonathan. *Words Apart: The Language of Prejudice*. London: Kyle Cathie Publishing, 1996.

Harris, A. "Whiteness as Property." *Harvard Law Review* 106 (1993): 1707-1791.

Hate Crimes Today: An Age-Old Foe in Modern Dress. http://www.apa.org/pubinfo/hate/.

Healey, Joseph F. *Race, Ethnicity, Gender, and Class*. Thousand Oaks, CA: Pine Forge Press, 1998.

Herrnstein, Richard J., and Charles Murray. *The Bell Curve: Intelligence and Class Structure in American Life*. New York: Free Press, 1994.

Higham, John. *Strangers in the Land*. New York: Atheneum, 1955.

Hogue, Carol J. R., Martha A. Hargraves, and Karen Scott-Collins. *Minority Health in America*. Baltimore, MD: Johns Hopkins University Press, 2000.

Jaret, Charles. *Contemporary Ethnic and Race Relations*. New York: HarperCollins, 1995.

———. "Troubled by Newcomers: Anti-Immigrant Attitudes and Action During Two Eras of Mass Immigration to the United States." *Journal of American Ethnic History* 18 (1999): 9–39.

Jenness, Valerie, and Ryken Grattet. *Making Hate a Crime*. New York: Russell Sage Foundation, 2004.

Jordan, W. D. *The White Man's Burden: Historical Origins of Racism in the United States*. New York: Oxford University Press, 1974.

Knowles, Louis L., and Kenneth Prewitt, eds. *Institutional Racism in America*. Englewood Cliffs, NJ: Prentice Hall, 1969.

Kovel, Joel. *White Racism: A Psychohistory*. New York: Pantheon, 1970.

Lamm, Richard D., and Gary Imhoff. *The Immigration Time Bomb: The Fragmenting of America*. New York: Truman Talley and Dutton, 1985.

Lamont, Michele. *The Cultural Territories of Race: Black and White Boundaries*. Chicago: The University of Chicago and the Russell Sage Foundation, 1999.

Lapchick, Richard E. *Broken Promises: Racism in American Sports*. New York: St. Martin's Press, 1984.

Lehmann, Nicholas. *The Big Test: The Secret History of the American Meritocracy*. New York: Farrar, Straus and Giroux, 1999.

Lewis, Oscar. "The Culture of Poverty." *Scientific American* 115 (1966): 19–25.

Liberson, Stanley. "A Societal Theory of Race and Ethnic Relations." *American Sociological Review* 26 (1961): 902–910.

———. *A Piece of the Pie: Blacks and White Immigrants since 1880*. Berkeley: University of California Press, 1980.

Liebow, Elliot. *Tally's Corner*. Lanham, MD: Rowman & Littlefield, 2003.

Lincoln, C. Eric. *Race, Religion, and the Continuing American Dilemma*. New York: Hill and Wang, 1999.

Loevy, Robert, ed. *The Civil Rights Act of 1964: The Passage of the Law That Ended Racial Segregation*. Albany: State University of New York Press, 1997.

Lucas, Samuel Roundfield. *Tracking Inequality: Stratification and Mobility in American High Schools*. New York: Teachers College Press, 1999.

Marger, Martin. *Race and Ethnic Relations: American and Global Perspectives*. 5th ed. Belmont, CA: Wadsworth, 2000.

Merton, Robert. "Discrimination and the American Creed." In *Discrimination and National Welfare*, edited by R. M. McIver, 99–126. New York: Institute for Religious and Social Studies, 1949.

Miller, Randall, ed. *Ethnic Images in American Film and Television*. Philadelphia: The Balch Institute, 1978.

Montagy, Ashiley. *Man's Most Dangerous Myth*. Walnut Creek, CA: AltaMira Press, 1998.

Moore, Robert B. *Racism in the English Language*. New York: Council on Interracial Books for Children, 1976.

Murray, Charles. *Losing Ground: American Social Policy, 1950–1980*. New York: Basic Books, 1984.

Omi, Michael, and Howard Winant. *Racial Formation in the United States, from the 1960s to the 1990s*. 2nd ed. New York: Routledge, 1994.

Perea, Juan F., ed. *Immigrants Out: The New Nativism and the Anti-Immigrant Impulse in the United States*. New York: New York University Press, 1997.

Perlmann, Joel, and Mary C. Waters, eds. *The New Race Question: How the Census Counts Multiracial Individuals*. New York: Russell Sage Foundation, 2000.

Portes, Alejandro, and Min Zhou. "The New Second Generation: Segmented Assimilation and Its Variants." *Annals of the American Academy of Political and Social Sciences* 530 (1993): 74–96.

Portes, Alejandro, and Rubén G. Rumbaut. *Immigrant America: A Portrait.* 2nd ed. Berkeley: University of California Press, 1996.

———. *Legacies: The Story of the Immigrant Second Generation.* New York: Russell Sage Foundation, 2001.

Raffel, Jeffrey. *Historical Dictionary of School Segregation and Desegregation: The American Experience.* Westport, CT: Greenwood Press, 1998.

Roediger, David. *The Wages of Whiteness: Race and the Making of the American Working Class.* New York: Verso, 1996.

Roosens, E. E. *Creating Ethnicity: The Process of Ethnogensis.* Newbury Park, CA: Sage, 1989.

Rosenthal, E. "Acculturation without Assimilation." *American Journal of Sociology* 66 (1960): 275–288.

Ross, Stephen, and John Yinger. *The Color of Credit: Mortgage Discrimination, Research Methodology, and Fair-Lending Enforcement.* Cambridge, MA: MIT Press, 2002.

Rotenberg, Paula S. *White Privilege: Essential Readings on the Other Side of Racism.* New York: Worth Publishers, 2002.

Ryan, William. *Blaming the Victim.* New York: Vintage Books, 1976.

Schuman, Howard, Charlotte Steeh, Lawrence Bobo, and Maria Krysan. *Racial Attitudes in America: Trends and Interpretations.* Rev. ed. Cambridge, MA: Harvard University Press, 1997.

Shlay, Anne B. "Social Science Research and Contemporary Studies of Homelessness." *Annual Review of Sociology* 18 (1989): 129–160.

Smelser, Neil J., William J. Wilson, and Faith Mitchell, eds. *America Becoming: Racial Trends and Their Consequences.* Vol. 2. Washington, DC: National Research Council, 2001.

Spring, Joel. *Deculturalization and the Struggle for Equality: A Brief History of the Education of Dominated Cultures in the United States.* 4th ed. Boston: McGraw-Hill, 2003.

Squires, Gregory D., and Sally O'Connor. *Color and Money.* Albany: State University of New York Press, 2001.

Steinberg, Stephen. *The Ethnic Myth: Race, Ethnicity, and Class in America.* 2nd ed. Boston: Beacon Press, 1988.

———. *Turning Back: The Retreat from Racial Justice in American Thought and Policy.* Boston: Beacon Press, 1995.

Szymanski, Al. "Racial Discrimination and White Gains." *American Sociological Review* 41 (June 1976): 403–414.

Takaki, Ronald. *Iron Cages: Race and Culture in 19th Century America.* New York: Knopf, 1979.

Thernstrom, Stephan, ed. *Harvard Encyclopedia of American Ethnic Groups.* Cambridge, MA: Harvard University Press, 1980.

Tonry, Michael. *Malign Neglect: Race, Crime, and Punishment in America.* New York: Oxford University Press, 1995.

Toplin, Robert B., ed. *Hollywood as a Mirror: Changing Views of "Outsiders" and "Enemies" in American Movies.* Westport, CT: Greenwood Press, 1993.

Vidmar, Neil, and Milton Rokeach. "Archie Bunker's Bigotry." *Journal of Communication* 24 (1974): 36–47.

Waters, Mary. *Ethnic Options: Choosing Identities in America.* Berkeley: University of California Press, 1990.

Williams, David R. "The Health of Men: Structured Inequalities and Opportunities." *American Journal of Public Health* 93 (2003): 720–727.

Wilson, John K. *The Myth of Political Correctness: The Conservative Attack on Higher Education*. Durham, NC: Duke University Press, 1995.

AFRICAN AMERICANS

Anderson, Wayne. *Plessy v. Ferguson: Legalizing Segregation*. New York: Rosen Publishing Group, 2003.

Baldwin, James. *Black Anti-Semitism and Jewish Racism*. New York: R. W. Baron, 1969.

Barrera, Mario. *Race and Class in the Southwest: A Theory of Racial Inequality*. Notre Dame, IN: University of Notre Dame Press, 1979.

Blauner, Robert. *Black Lives, White Lives*. Berkeley: University of California Press, 1989.

————. "Some Self-Critical Reflections on Colonized and Immigrant Minorities." In *Still the Big News: Racial Oppression in America*, edited by Robert Blauner, 189–192. Philadelphia: Temple University Press, 2001.

Blockson, Charles L. *The Underground Railroad*. New York: Prentice Hall, 1987.

Bobo, Lawrence, James R. Kluegel, and Ryan A. Smith. "Laissez-Faire Racism: The Crystallization of a 'Kinder, Gentler' Anti-Black Ideology." In *Racial Attitudes in the 1990s: Continuity and Change*, edited by Steven Tuch and Jack Martin. Westport, CT: Praeger, 1997.

Carmichael, Stokely, and Charles V. Hamilton. *Black Power*. New York: Vintage Books, 1967.

Cole, J. B. "Culture: Negro, Black, and Nigger." *Black Scholar* 1 (June 1970): 40–44.

Collins, Patricia H. *Black Feminist Thought*. New York: Routledge and Chapman and Hall, 1990.

Cox, Oliver C. *Caste, Class, and Race*. Garden City, NY: Doubleday, 1948.

Davis, Angela. "Rape, Racism, and the Myth of the Black Rapist." In *Feminism and 'Race,'* edited by Kum-Kum Bhavnani, 50–64. Oxford: Oxford University Press, 2001.

Davis, David Brion. *The Problem of Slavery in Western Culture*. Ithaca, NY: Cornell University Press, 1966.

Drake, S. C., and H. R. Cayton. *Black Metropolis*. Rev. ed. New York: Harper Torchbooks, 1962.

Du Bois, W.E.B. *The Souls of the Black Folks*. New York: Fawcett, 1903.

————. *Black Reconstruction in the United States: 1860–1880*. New York: Atheneum, 1907.

————. "The Negro Race in the United States of America." In *W.E.B. Du Bois: On Sociology and the Black Community*, edited by D. S. Green and E. D. Driver, 85–111. Chicago: University of Chicago Press, 1911.

Entman, Robert M., and Andrew Rojecki. *The Black Image in the White Mind: Media and Race in America*. Chicago: The University of Chicago Press, 2001.

Farley, Reynolds, Sheldon Danziger, and Harry Holzer. *Detroit Divided*. New York: Russell Sage Foundation, 2001.

Farley, Reynolds, Charlotte Steeh, Maria Krysan, Tara Jackson, and Keith Reeves. "Stereotypes and Segregation: Neighborhoods in the Detroit Area." *American Journal of Sociology* 100 (1994): 750–780.

Feagin, Joe. *Discrimination, American Style*. Englewood, NJ: Prentice Hall, 1978.

————. *Discrimination American Style: Institutional Racism and Sexism*. Malabar, FL: Robert E. Krieger, 1986.

————. "The Continuing Significance of Race: Anti-Black Discrimination in Public Places." *American Sociological Review* 56 (1991): 101–116.

Feagin, Joe R., and Karyn D. McKinney. *The Many Costs of Racism*. Lanham: Rowman & Littlefield, 2002.

Feagin, Joe, and Melvin P. Sikes. *Living with Racism: The Black Middle-Class Experience*. Boston: Beacon Press, 1994.

Fischer, Claude S., et al. *Inequality by Design: Cracking the Bell Curve Myth*. Princeton, NJ: Princeton University Press, 1996.

Folgelson, R. *Violence as a Protest: A Study of Riots and Ghettos*. New York: Doubleday, 1971.

Foner, Nancy, and George M. Fredrickson, eds. *Not Just Black and White*. New York: Russell Sage Foundation, 2004.

Fordham, Signithia, and John U. Ogbu. "Black Students' School Success: Coping with the Burden of 'Acting White.'" *The Urban Review* 18, no. 3 (1996): 176–206.

Franklin, John Hope. *From Slavery to Freedom*. 3rd ed. New York: Knopf, 1967.

Franklin, John Hope, and Alfred A. Moss Jr. *From Slavery to Freedom: A History of Negro Americans*. New York: McGraw-Hill, 1988.

Frederickson, George. *White Supremacy: A Comparative Study of American and South African History*. New York: Oxford University Press, 1981.

————. *The Arrogance of Race: Historical Perspectives on Slavery, Racism, and Social Inequality*. Middletown, CT: Wesleyan University Press, 1998.

Fremon, K. David. *The Jim Crow Laws and Racism*. New York: Enslow Publishers, 2000.

Friedman, R. "Institutional Racism: How to Discriminate Without Really Trying." In *Racial Discrimination in the United States*, edited by T. F. Pettigrew, 384–407. New York: Harper & Row, 1975.

Garrod, Andrew, Janie Ward, Tracy Robinson, and Robert Kilkenny, eds. *Souls Looking Back: Life Stories about Growing Up Black*. New York: Routledge, 1999.

Genovese, Eugene. *Roll, Jordan, Roll: The World the Slaves Made*. New York: Vintage Books, 1972.

Gibson, Margaret A., and John U. Ogbu. *Minority Status and Schooling: A Comparative Study of Immigrant and Involuntary Minorities*. New York: Garland, 1991.

Hacker, Andrew. *Two Nations: Black and White, Separate, Hostile, Unequal*. 2nd ed. New York: Random House, 1995.

Haley, Alex, and Malcolm X. *The Autobiography of Malcolm X*. New York: Ballantine Books, 1964.

Hallinan, Maureen T. "Sociological Perspectives on Black and White Inequalities in American Schooling." Extra issue, *Sociology of Education* (2001): 50–70.

Heuman, Gad, and James Walvin, eds. *The Slavery Reader*. New York: Routledge, 2003.

Humphrey, H. Hubert, ed. *School Desegregation: Documents and Commentaries*. New York: Thomas Y. Crowell, 1964.

Jencks, Christopher, and Meredith Phillips, eds. *The Black-White Test Score Gap*. Washington, DC: Brookings Institution Press, 1998.

Jensen, Arthur R. "How Can We Boost IQ and Scholastic Achievement?" *Harvard Educational Review* 39 (1969): 1–123.

————. "The Debunking of Scientific Fossils and Straw Persons." *Contemporary Education Review* 1, no. 2 (1982): 121–135.

Kasinitz, Philip. *Caribbean New York: Black Immigrants and the Politics of Race*. Ithaca, NY: Cornell University Press, 1992.

Kennedy, Randall. *Nigger: The Strange Career of a Troublesome Word*. New York: Vintage, 2003.

King, Martin Luther, Jr. *I Have a Dream: Writings and Speeches That Changed the World*. New York: HarperCollins, 1992.

Kirshenman, Joleen, and Kathryn M. Neckerman. "We'd love To Hire Them, But . . .: The Meaning of Race for Employers." In *The Urban Underclass*, edited by C. Jencks and P. Peterson, 203–234. Washington, DC: The Brookings Institution Press, 1992.

Kluger, Richard. *Simple Justice: The History of Brown v. Board of Education and Black America's Struggle for Equality*. New York: Knopf, 1976.

Knopf, Terry Ann. *Rumors, Race, and Riots*. New Brunswick, NJ: Transaction Publications, 1975.

LaVeist, Thomas. "The Political Empowerment and Health Status of African Americans: Mapping a New Territory." *American Journal of Sociology* 97 (1992): 1080–1095.

Leeming, David. *James Baldwin: A Biography*. New York: Henry Holt, 1994.

Lowery, Charles D., and John F. Marszalek, eds. *The Greenwood Encyclopedia of African American Civil Rights: From Emancipation to the Twenty-First Century*. Westport, CT: Greenwood Press, 2003.

Marsh, Charles. *The Last Days: A Son's Story of Sin and Segregation at the Dawn of a New South*. New York: Basic Books, 2002.

Massey, Douglass, and Nancy Denton. *American Apartheid: Segregation and the Making of the Underclass*. Cambridge, MA: Harvard University Press, 1993.

———. *American Apartheid*. Cambridge, MA: Harvard University Press, 1998.

Mathabane, Mark, and Gail Mathabane. *Love in Black and White: The Triumph of Love over Prejudice and Taboo*. New York: HarperCollins, 1992.

McKivigan, John R., ed. *History of the American Abolitionist Movement*. 5 vols. New York: Garland, 1999.

Meyer, Stephen Grant. *As Long as They Don't Move Next Door: Segregation and Racial Conflict in American Neighborhoods*. Lanham, MD: Rowman & Littlefield, 2000.

Mittelberg, David, and Mary Waters. "The Process of Ethnogenesis among Haitian and Israeli Immigrants in the United States." *Ethnic and Racial Studies* 15 (1992): 412–435.

Morris, Aldon D. *The Origins of the Civil Rights Movement: Black Communities Organizing for Change*. New York: The Free Press, 1984.

Morrison, Toni. *Playing in the Dark: Whiteness and the Literary Imagination*. Cambridge, MA: Harvard University Press, 1992.

Moynihan, Daniel. *The Negro Family: The Case for National Action*. Washington, DC: U.S. Department of Labor, 1965.

National Advisory Commission. *Report of the National Advisory Survey*. Chicago: NORC, 1968.

Ogbu, John. "Immigrant and Involuntary Minorities in Comparative Perspective." In *Minority Status and Schooling: A Comparative Study of Immigrant and Involuntary Minorities*, edited by Margaret Gibson and John Ogbu. New York: Garland Publishing, 1991.

Oliver, Melvin L., and Thomas M. Shapiro. *Black Wealth/White Wealth: A New Perspective on Racial Inequality*. New York: Routledge, 1995.

Parks, Rosa. *Rosa Parks: My Story*. New York: Dial Books, 1992.

Perry, Bruce. *Racially Separate or Together?* New York: McGraw-Hill, 1971.

———. *Malcolm: The Life of a Man Who Changed Black America*. Barrytown, NY: Station Hill Press, 1991.

Pettigrew, Thomas, ed. *Racial Discrimination in the United States*. New York: Harper & Row, 1975.

————. "The Changing—Not Declining—Significance of Race." Symposia on *The Declining Significance of Race* in *Contemporary Sociology* 9, no. 1 (1980).

Porter, Kenneth. *Black Seminoles: History of a Freedom-Seeking People*. Gainesville: University of Florida Press, 1996.

Portes, Alejandro, and Alex Stepick. "Unwelcome Immigrants: The Labor Market Experience of 1980 (Mariel) Cuban and Haitian Refuges in South Florida." *American Sociological Review* 50, no. 4 (1985): 493-514.

Poston, D. L., D. Alvarez, and M. Tienda. "Earnings Differences between Anglo and Mexican American Male Workers in 1960 and 1970: Changes in the 'Cost' of Being Mexican American." *Social Science Quarterly* 57 (1976): 618-631.

Rankin, Bruce H., and James M. Quane. "Neighborhood Poverty and Social Isolation of Inner-City African American Families." *Social Forces* 79 (2000): 139-164.

Raper, Arthur. *The Tragedy of Lynching*. Chapel Hill: University of North Carolina Press, 1933.

Robinson, Randall. *The Debt: What America Owes to Blacks*. New York: Penguin Putnam, 2000.

Rudwick, Elliot. *W.E.B. Du Bois: Voice of the Black Protest Movement*. Champaign-Urbana: University of Illinois Press, 1960.

Seigal, Paul. "The Cost of Being a Negro." *Sociological Inquiry* 35 (1965): 1.

Shlay, Anne B. "Not in That Neighborhood: The Effects of Population and Housing on the Distribution of Mortgage Finance within the Chicago SMSA." *Social Science Research* 17 (1988): 152-163.

Stampp, Kenneth. *The Peculiar Institution: Slavery in the Ante-Bellum South*. New York: Vintage Books, 1956.

Steele, Shelby. *A Dream Deferred*. New York: HarperCollins, 1998.

Stepick, Alex. *Pride against Prejudice: Haitians in the United States*. Boston: Allyn & Bacon, 1998.

Stevenson, Brenda. *Life in Black and White: Family and Community in the Slave South*. New York: Oxford University Press, 1996.

Tatum, Beverly D. *"Why Are All the Black Kids Sitting Together in the Cafeteria?" and Other Conversations about Race*. New York: Basic Books, 1997.

Taylor, Ronald L. "Black Ethnicity and the Persistence of Ethnogesis." *American Journal of Sociology* 84 (1979):1401-1423.

Terkel, Studs. *Race: How Blacks and White Think and Feel about American Obsession*. New York: New Press, 1992.

U.S. Immigration Commission. *Brief Statement of the Conclusions and Recommendation of the Immigration Commission with the View of the Minority*. Washington, DC: U.S. Government Printing Office, 1910.

Vickerman, Milton. *Crosscurrents: West Indian Immigrants and Race*. New York: Oxford University Press, 1999.

Waldinger, Roger. *Still the Promised City: African Americans and New Immigrants in Postindustrial New York*. Cambridge, MA: Harvard University Press, 1996.

Waldinger, Roger, and Michael I. Richter. *How the Other Half Works: Immigration and the Social Organization of Race*. Berkeley: University of California Press, 2003.

Waters, Mary. *Black Identities: West Indian Immigrant Dreams and American Realities*. New York: Russell Sage Foundation, 1999.

West, Cornel. *Race Matters*. New York: Vintage Books, 1994.

Williams, David R., and Ruth Williams-Morris. "Racism and Mental Health: The African-American Experience." *Ethnicity and Health* 5, no. 3 (2000): 243-268.

Wilson, William Julius. *The Declining Significance of Race*. Chicago: University of Chicago Press, 1978.

————. *The Truly Disadvantaged: The Inner City, the Underclass, and Public Policy*. Chicago: University of Chicago Press, 1987.

Winbush, Raymond, ed. *Should America Pay? Slavery and the Raging Debate on Reparations*. New York: Amistad, 2003.

Woodward, C. Vann. *The Strange Career of Jim Crow*. 2nd ed. Oxford: Oxford University Press, 1966.

Yinger, John. *Closed Doors, Opportunities Lost: The Continuing Costs of Housing Discrimination*. New York: Russell Sage Foundation, 1995.

NATIVE AMERICANS

Banks, Dennis, and Richard Erdoes. *Ojibwa Warrior: Dennis Banks and the Rise of the American Indian Movement*. Norman: University of Oklahoma Press, 2004.

Berkhoffer, Robert F. Jr. *The White Man's Indian: Images of the American Indian from Columbus to the Present*. New York: Knopf, 1978.

Brown, Dee Alexander. *Bury My Heart at Wounded Knee: An Indian History of the American West*. 30th anniversary ed. New York: Henry Holt, 2001.

Cornell, Stephen. *The Return of the Native: American Indian Political Resurgence*. New York: Oxford University Press, 1988.

Deloria, V. Jr. *Red Earth, White Lies: Native Americans and the Myth of Scientific Fact*. New York: Scribner, 1995.

Deloria, V. Jr., and C. M. Lytle. *American Indians, American Justice*. Austin: University of Texas Press, 1983.

Fixico, D. L. *The Invasion of Indian Country in the Twentieth Century: American Capitalism and Tribal Natural Resources*. Niwot: University Press of Colorado, 1998.

Forman, Grant. *Indian Removal: The Emigration of the Five Civilized Tribes of Indians*. Norman: University of Oklahoma Press, 1953.

Hanson, Jeffery, and Linda Rouse. "Dimensions of Native American Stereotyping." *American Indian Culture and Research Journal* 11 (1987): 33–58.

Hittman, Michael. *Wovoka and the Ghost Dance*. Edited by Don Lynch. Expanded ed. Lincoln: University of Nebraska Press, 1998.

Huhndorf, Shari M. *Going Native: Indians in the American Cultural Imagination*. Ithaca, NY: Cornell University Press, 2002.

Jacobson, C. K. "Internal Colonialism and Native Americans: Indian Labor in the United States from 1871 to World War II." *Social Science Quarterly* 65 (1984): 158–171.

Johansen, Bruce Elliott. *The Encyclopedia of Native American Legal Tradition*. Westport, CT: Greenwood Press, 1998.

Lazarus, Edward. *Black Hills/White Justice: The Sioux Nation versus the United States, 1775 to the Present*. New York: HarperCollins, 1991.

Mooney, James. *The Ghost-Dance Religion and Wounded Knee*. New York: Dover Publications, 1991.

Nagel, J. *American Indian Ethnic Renewal: Red Power and the Resurgence of Identity and Culture*. New York: Oxford University Press, 1997.

Ostler, Jeffrey. *The Plains Sioux and U.S. Colonialism from Lewis and Clark to Wounded Knee*. New York: Cambridge University Press, 2004.

Porter, Kenneth. *Black Seminoles: History of a Freedom-Seeking People*. Gainesville: University of Florida Press, 1996.

Snipp, C. Matthew. *American Indians: The First of This Land*. New York: Russell Sage Foundation, 1989.

Stannard, D. E. *American Holocaust*. New York: Oxford University Press, 1992.

Thornton, Russell. *American Indian Holocaust Survival: A Population History Since 1492*. Norman: University of Oklahoma Press, 1987.

———. *Studying Native America: Problems and Prospects*. Madison: University of Wisconsin Press, 1998.

Viola, Herman J. *Trail to Wounded Knee: Last Stand of the Plains Indians, 1860–1890*. Washington, DC: National Geographic Society, 2003.

Vogel, Virgil, ed. *This Country Was Ours: A Documentary History of the American Indian*. New York: Harper & Row, 1972.

Wright, Ronald. *Stolen Continents: The Americas Through Indian Eyes Since 1492*. Boston: Houghton Mifflin, 1992.

LATINOS

Acuna, Rodolfo. *Occupied America: The Chicano's Struggle Toward Liberation*. San Francisco: Canfield Press, 1972.

———. *Occupied America: A History of Chicanos*. 4th ed. New York: Longman, 2000.

Bean, Frank, and Marta Tienda. *The Hispanic Population of the United States*. New York: Russell Sage Foundation, 1987.

Cruz, J. *Identity and Power: Puerto Rican Politics and the Challenge of Ethnicity*. Philadelphia: Temple University Press, 1998.

Davidson, Chandler, and Charles M. Gaitz. " 'Are the Poor Different?' A Comparison of Work Behavior and Attitudes among the Urban Poor and Nonpoor." *Social Problems* 22 (1974): 229–245.

Escobar, Edward J. *Race, Police, and the Making of a Political Identity: Mexican Americans and the Los Angeles Police Department 1900–1945*. Berkeley: University of California Press, 1999.

Fitzpatrick, Joseph P. *Puerto Rican Americans: The Meaning of Migration to the Mainland*. 2nd ed. Englewood Cliffs, NJ: Prentice Hall, 1987.

Frazier, Donald S., ed. *The United States and Mexico at War: Nineteenth Century Expansionism and Conflict*. New York: Macmillan Reference USA, 1998.

Garcia, Ignacio. *The Forging of a Militant Ethos among Mexican Americans*. Tucson: University of Arizona Press, 1997.

Grasmuck, Sherri, and Patricia R. Pessar. *Between Two Islands: Dominican International Migration*. Berkeley: University of Chicago Press, 1991.

Grenier, Guillermo J., and Alex Stepick, eds. *Miami Now! Immigration, Ethnicity, and Social Change*. Gainesville: University Press of Florida, 1992.

Gutiérrez, David G. *Mexican Americans, Mexican Immigrants, and the Politics of Ethnicity*. Berkeley: University of California Press, 1995.

Gutiérrez, Ramón. "Ethnic Mexican in Historical and Social Science Scholarship." In *Handbook of Research on Multicultural Education*, edited by James A. Banks and Cherry A. McGee Banks, 261–287. San Francisco: Jossey-Bass, 2004.

Horsman, Reginald. *Race and Manifest Destiny: The Origins of American Racial Anglo-Saxonism*. Cambridge, MA: Harvard University Press, 1981.

Lewis, Oscar. *The Children of Sanchez*. New York: Random House, 1961.

Lopez, Adalberto, and James Petras. *Puerto Rico and Puerto Ricans*. Cambridge, MA: Schenkman Pub. Co., 1974.

Lopez-Strafford, Gloria. *A Place in El Paso: A Mexican-American Childhood*. Albuquerque: University of New Mexico Press, 1996.

Martinez, Corinne, Zeus Leonardo, and Carlos Tejeda, eds. *Charting Terrains of Chicana(o)/Latina(o) Education*. Cresskill, NJ: Hampton Press, 2000.

Massey, Douglas, Rafael Alarcon, Jorge Durand, and Humberto Gonzalez. "Latinos,

Poverty, and the Underclass: A New Agenda for Research." *Hispanic Journal of Behavioral Science* 15 (1993): 449–475.

―――. *Return to Aztlan: The Social Process of International Migration from Western Mexico*. Berkeley: University of California Press, 1987.

McLemore, S. Dale. "The Origins of Mexican American Subordination in Texas." *Social Science Quarterly* 53 (1973): 656–679.

Montejano, David. *Anglos and Mexicans in the Making of Texas, 1836–1986*. Austin: University of Texas Press, 1987.

Moore, Joan W. "Colonialism: The Case of the Mexican American." *Social Problems* 17 (1970): 463–472.

―――. *Mexican Americans*. 2nd ed. Englewood Cliffs, NJ: Prentice Hall, 1976.

Munoz, Carlos. *The Chicano Movement: Youth, Identity, and Power.* New York: Verso Books, 2003.

Navarro, Armando. *La Raza Unida Party: A Chicano Challenge to the U.S. Two-Party Dictatorship*. Philadelphia: Temple University Press, 2000.

Ortiz, Vilma. "Women of Color: A Demographic Overview." In *Women of Color in U.S. Society*, edited by Maxine Baca Zinn and Bonnie Thorton Dill. Philadelphia: Temple University Press, 1994.

Padilla, Felix. *Latino Ethnic Consciousness*. Notre Dame, IN: University of Notre Dame Press, 1985.

―――. *Puerto Rican Chicago*. Notre Dame, IN: University of Notre Dame Press, 1987.

Portes, Alejandro, and Robert L. Bach. *Latin Journey: Cuban and Mexican Immigrants in the United States*. Berkeley: University of California Press, 1985.

Rochin, Refugio I., and Dennis N. Valdes, eds. *Voices of a New Chicana/o History*. East Lansing: Michigan State University Press, 2000.

Rodriguez, C. E. *Puerto Ricans: Born in the U.S.A*. Boston: Unwin and Hymann, 1991.

Rodriguez, C. E., and Korrol V. Sanchez, eds. *Historical Perspectives on Puerto Rican Survival in the United States*. Princeton, NJ: Markus Wiener, 1996.

Torres, A. *Between Melting Pot and Mosaic: African Americans and Puerto Ricans in the New York Political Economy*. Philadelphia: Temple University Press, 1994.

ASIAN AMERICANS

Bonacich, Edna. "A Theory of Middleman Minorities." *American Sociological Review* 38 (1973): 583–594.

Bulosan, Carlos. *America Is in the Heart*. Seattle: University of Washington Press, 1973.

Chan, Sucheng. *Asian Americans*. Boston: Twayne, 1991.

Commission on Wartime Relocation and Internment of Civilians. *Personal Justice Denied: Report of the Commission on Wartime Relocation and Internment of Civilians*. Washington, DC: U.S. Government Printing Office, 1982.

Cooper, M. *Fighting for Honor: Japanese Americans and World War II*. New York: Houghton Mifflin, 2000.

Daniels, R. *Prisoners without Trial: Japanese Americans in World War II*. New York: Hill and Wang, 1993.

Espiritu, Yen Le. *Asian American Panethnicity: Bridging Institutions and Identities*. Philadelphia: Temple University Press, 1992.

―――. *Asian American Women and Men*. Thousand Oaks, CA: Sage, 1997.

Gibson, Margaret. *Accommodation without Assimilation: Sikh Immigrants in an American High School*. Ithaca, NY: Cornell University Press, 1998.

Hall, Patricia Wong, and Victor M. Hwang. *Anti-Asian Violence in North America: Asian American and Asian Canadian Reflections on Hate, Healing and Resistance*. Walnut Creek, CA: AltaMira, 2001.

Hing, Bill Ong. *Making and Remaking of Asian America through Immigration Policy*. Stanford, CA: Stanford University Press, 1993.

Hirschman, Charles, and Morrison Wong. "Trends in Socioeconomic Achievement among Immigrant and Native-Born Asian Americans, 1960–1976." *Sociological Quarterly* 22 (1981): 495–513.

Hurh, Won Moo, and Kwang Chung Kim. "The 'Success' Image of Asian Americans: Its Validity and Its Practical Implications." *Ethnic and Racial Studies* 12 (1989): 512–538.

Inada, L. F. *Only What We Could Carry: The Japanese American Internment Experience*. Oakland: Heyday Books, 2000.

Kailin, Julie. *Antiracist Education*. Lanham, MD: Rowman & Littlefield, 2002.

Lee, Jennifer, and Min Zhou. *Asian American Youth*. New York: Routledge, 2004.

Lee, Robert G. *Orientals: Asian Americans in Popular Culture*. Philadelphia: Temple University Press, 2000.

Lowe, Lisa. *Immigrant Acts*. Durham, NC: Duke University Press, 1996.

McClain, Charles, ed. *Japanese Immigrants and the American Law: The Alien Land Laws and Other Issues*. New York: Garland, 1994.

Min, Pyong Gap. *Caught in the Middle: Korean Communities in New York and Los Angeles*. Berkeley and Los Angeles: University of California Press, 1996.

———. "Social Science Research on Asian Americans." In *Handbook of Research on Multicultural Education*, edited by James A. Banks and Cherry A. McGee Banks, 332–348. San Francisco: Jossey-Bass, 2004.

Min, Pyong Gap, and Rose Kim, eds. *Struggle for Ethnic Identity: Narratives by Asian American Professionals*. Walnut Creek, CA: AltaMira Press, 1999.

Okihiro, Gary Y. *Margins and Mainstreams: Asians in American History and Culture*. Seattle: University of Washington Press, 1994.

Said, Edward. *Orientalism*. New York: Random House, 1979.

Salyer, Lucy E. *Laws Harsh as Tigers: Chinese Immigrants and the Shaping of Modern Immigration Law*. Chapel Hill: University of North Carolina Press, 1995.

Saxton, Alexander. *The Indispensable Enemy: The Labor and the Anti-Chinese Movement in California*. Berkeley, CA: University of California Press, 1971.

Synott, Marcia Graham. *The Half-Opened Door: Discrimination and College Admissions at Harvard, Yale, and Princeton*. Westport, CT: Greenwood Press, 1979.

Takagi, Dana Y. *The Retreat from Race*. New Brunswick, NJ: Rutgers University Press, 1992.

Takaki, Ronald. *Strangers from a Different Shore: A History of Asian Americans*. Boston: Little, Brown, 1989.

Tuan, Mia. *Forever Foreigners or Honorary Whites? The Asian Ethnic Experience Today*. New Brunswick, NJ: Rutgers University Press, 1999.

U.S. Commission on Civil Rights. *Civil Rights Issues Facing Asian Americans in the 1990s*. Washington, DC: U.S. Government Printing Office, 1992.

Wei, William. *The Asian American Movement*. Philadelphia: Temple University Press, 1993.

Woo, Deborah. *Glass Ceilings and Asian Americans: The New Face of Workplace Barriers*. Walnut Creek, CA: AltaMira Press, 2000.

Wu, Frank H. *Yellow: Race in America Beyond Black and White*. New York: Basic Books, 2002.

Yu, Henry. *Thinking Orientals: Migration, Contact, and Exoticism in Modern America*. Oxford: Oxford University Press, 2002.

Zhou, Min, and Y. Kamo. "An Analysis of Earnings Patterns for Chinese, Japanese, and Non-Hispanic White Males in the United States." *Sociological Quarterly* 35 (1994): 581–602.

MIDDLE EASTERN REFERENCES

Afridi, Sam. *Muslims in America: Identity, Diversity, and the Challenge of Under-standing*. New York: Carnegie Corporation of New York, 2001.

Cole, David. *Enemy Aliens: Double Standards and Constitutional Freedoms in the War on Terrorism*. New York: The New Press, 2003.

Ghayur, M. A. "Muslims in the United States." *Annals of the American Academy of Political and Social Science* 454 (March 1981): 150–163.

Haddad, Yevonne Yazbeck, ed. *The Muslims of America*. New York: Oxford University Press, 1991.

———. *Muslim Minorities in the West*. Walnut Creek, CA: AltaMira Press, 2002.

Haddad, Yevonne Yazbeck, and Jane I. Smith, eds. *Muslim Communities in North America*. Albany: State University of New York Press, 1994.

Haddad, Yevonne Yazbeck, and John L. Espositio, eds. *Muslims on the Americanization Path?* New York: Oxford University Press, 2000.

Leonard, Karen Isaksen. *Muslims in the United States*. New York: Russell Sage Foundation, 2003.

Said, Edward. *Orientalism*. New York: Random House, 1979.

Shaheen, Jack G. *Reel Bad Arabs: How Hollywood Vilifies a People*. New York: Olive Branch Press, 2001.

Smith, Jane I. *Islam in America*. New York: Columbia University Press, 1999.

Tarbush, Susannah. "The Arab Image in the West." A Report based on the 1998 Conference held at Oxford. Jordan: Royal Institute of Inter-Faith Studies, 1998.

Younis, Adele, and Philip M. Kayal. *The Coming of the Arabic-Speaking People to the United States*. Staten Island: Center for Migration Studies, 1995.

WHITE ETHNIC GROUPS

Baldwin, James. *Black Anti-Semitism and Jewish Racism*. New York: R. W. Baron, 1969.

Brodkin, Karen. *How Jews Became White Folks and What That Says About Race in America*. New Brunswick, NJ: Rutgers University Press, 1999.

Carr, Steven Alan. *Hollywood and Anti-Semitism: A Cultural History Up to World War II*. Cambridge: Cambridge University Press, 2001.

Foner, Nancy. *From Ellis Island to J.F.K. Airport: Immigrants to New York City*. New Haven, CT: Yale University Press, 2001.

Gambino, Richard. *Blood of My Blood: The Dilemma of the Italian-Americans*. Garden City, NY: Doubleday, 1974.

———. *Vendetta: The True Story of the Worst Lynching in America, the Mass Murder of Italian-Americans in New Orleans in 1891, the Vicious Motivations Behind It, and the Tragic Repercussions that Linger to this Day*. Garden City, NY: Doubleday, 1977.

Gerson, W. "Jews at Christmas Time: Role-Strain and Strain Reducing Mechanisms." In *Social Problems in a Changing World*, edited by W. Gerson, 65–76. New York: Thomas Y. Crowell, 1969.

Greeley, Andrew M. *That Most Distressful Nation: The Taming of the American Irish*. Chicago: Quadrangle Books, 1972.

Ignatiev, Noel. *How the Irish Became White*. New York: Routledge, 1995.

Jaher, Frederic Cople. *A Scapegoat in the New Wilderness: The Origins and Rise of Anti-Semitism in America*. Cambridge, MA: Harvard University Press, 1994.

Laxton, Edward. *The Famine Ships: The Irish Exodus to America 1846–51*. New York: Henry Holt, 1996.

Mayo, Louise A. *The Ambivalent Image: Nineteenth-Century America's Perception of the Jew*. Rutherford, NJ: Fairleigh Dickenson University Press, 1988.

Slavin, Stephen L., and Mary A. Pratt. *The Einstein Syndrome: Corporate Anti-Semitism in America Today*. New York: World Publishers, 1982.

Sleznick, Gertrude Jaeger, and Stephan Steinberg. *The Tenacity of Prejudice: Anti-Semitism in Contemporary America*. New York: Harper & Row, 1969.

INDEX

Page numbers in bold type refer to main entries in the encyclopedia.

AAFE. *See* Asian Americans for Equality
AAI. *See* Arab American Institute
AALDEF. *See* Asian American Legal Defense and Education Fund (AALDEF)
Abernathy, Ralph, 316, 407, 475, 594
Abolitionist movement, **1–2**, 136, 186–87, 583, 585, 621–22
Abolition of slavery, **135–37**
Abourezk, James, 19
Abrams, Charles, 554
Absconder initiative, 245, 562
Academic racism, **3–4**
Academy Awards, 266
ACCESS. *See* Arab Community Center for Economic and Social Services (ACCESS)
Accommodation, policy of, 192, 239, 641, 642
ACLU. *See* American Civil Liberties Union (ACLU)
"Acting white," **5–6**; ethnic retention and, 212; internalized racism and, 307–8; "passing," 477–78; social identity and, 144, 145, 463
Active bigots. *See* Bigots, types of
Actors, minority, **266–68**
Adaptive discrimination, **6–7**
ADC. *See* American-Arab Anti-Discrimination Committee (ADC)
ADL. *See* Anti-Defamation League of B'nai Brith (ADL)

Adventures of Huckleberry Finn (Twain), xxxv, 25–26, 177–78
AEL. *See* Asiatic Exclusion League (AEL)
Affirmative action, **7–13**; arguments against, xxi, xli, 14, 193, 194, 359, 361; arguments for, 10, 359, 541–43; black middle class and, 169; court cases, xlii, xliii, xlv, 13, 127–28, 523–25, 538–39; in education, 139; Executive Orders regarding, xxxix, 9, 727–36; reverse discrimination and, 537–38. *See also* California Ballot Proposition, 209
Affirmative Discrimination: Ethnic Inequality and Public Policy (Glazer), xli, **14**
Afghanistan, 17–18, 19
African American Methodist Episcopal (AME) church, 526
African Americans, xiii–xiv; anti-Semitism and, 38, 67–69, 329–30, 457; Asian Americans and, 52, 74–75, 368; Caribbean immigrants and, 107–8, 489–90; Cuban Americans and, 265; Irish immigrants and, 310; Latino immigrants and, 368
African Heritage Association, 328
Afrocentrism, **14–15**, 192
AGIF. *See* American GI Forum (AGIF)
Agricultural workers, 88, 112–13, 201–2, 390, 564–65, 611. *See also* Plantation system; United Farm Workers (UFW)
Agricultural Workers Organizing Committee, xli

Agriculture, U.S. Department of, 230
Aguinaldo, Emilio, 481–82
Aid to Families with Dependent Children (AFDC). *See* Welfare
AIM. *See* American Indian Movement (AIM)
Ain't No Makin' It (McLeod), 162
Al-Arian, Sami Amin, 311
Alaska Native Claims Settlement Act of 1971, xli, **15–16**
Alcatraz Island, xli, 23, **292**, 293, 523
Alcohol, Tobacco, and Firearms, Bureau of, 337
Alianza Federal de Pueblos Libres (Federal Alliance of Land Grant), xxxix, 617
Alien and Sedition Acts of 1798, 446
Alien Land Laws, xv–xvi, xxxvi, xxxviii, **16**, 49, 318
All-African People's Revolutionary Party, 112
All-black resorts, **17**
All in the Family (TV show), xli, 45–46
Allport, Gordon, xxxviii, 448
All-weather bigots. *See* Bigots, types of
All-weather liberals. *See* Bigots, types of; Fair-weather liberals
Al Qaeda, xliii, xlv, **17–19**, 245, 332
American Anti-Slavery Society (AASS), xxxiii, 1
American Apartheid (Massey and Denton), 336
American-Arab Anti-Discrimination Committee (ADC), xlii, **19–20**, 423, 559
American Arab Chamber of Commerce, 44
American Citizens for Justice, 473
American Civil Liberties Union (ACLU), xxxvi, **20–21**
American Dilemma: The Negro Problem and Modern Democracy, An (Myrdal), 72, **739**
American Dream ideology, **21–22**
American Federation of Labor (AFL), 351
American Federation of Musicians, 416, 417
American Friends Service Committee, 130
American GI Forum (AGIF), xxxviii, **22–23**
American Honda Finance Company, 229
American Indian Movement (AIM), xl, xli, **23–24**, 522–23, 599
American Indians. *See* Native Americans
Americanization Movement, **29–31**. *See also* Nativism and anti-immigrant movements
American Jewish Committee, 40
American literature and racism, xxxv, **24–27**, 36, 177–78, 409–10
American Muslim Law Enforcement Officers Association, 43–44
American Nazi Party, xxxviii, **27–28**. *See also* White-supremacist groups

American "Obsession with Race," **28–29**, 509
American Revolution, 582–83, 637
American Sociological Association, 745–56
Amnesty International, 105
Amsterdam, Anthony, 237
Angelou, Maya, 400
Anglo conformity, **31–32**, 495. *See also* Nativism and anti-immigrant movements
ANP. *See* American Nazi Party
Anthony, Susan B., 621
Anti-Catholicism, xvi, xix, **32–34**, 310, 442, 445, 446, 525
Anti-Chinese sentiments. *See* Chinese immigrants
Anti-Defamation League of B'nai Brith (ADL), xxxvi, **34**, 40, 233, 347, 571–72
Anti-Immigration movements. *See* Nativism and anti-immigrant movements
Anti-Iranian stereotypes. *See* Iran hostage crisis and anti-Iranian stereotypes
Anti-Semitism, xvi, 34, **35–41**, 525, 646, 648, 651; black, 38, 67–69, 327, 328, 329–30, 457; Henry Ford and, 230–31; John Birch Society, 336–37; Leo Frank and, 232–33. *See also* White-supremacist groups
Anti-Zionism, 39–40
Apartheid system, xiv, xvii
Apprentice laws, 332
Arab American Bar Association, 43
Arab American Institute, xlii, **41–42**
Arab Americans, xli, xlii; American-Arab Anti-Discrimination Committee, 19–20; American Civil Liberties Union (ACLU) and, 21; Arab/Muslim advocacy organizations, 41–42, 42–43, 43–45; hate crimes against, 559–61; Japanese American Citizens League (JACL) and, 318; media and, 228, 338; racial profiling, 28, 157; terrorism and, 245–48, 557, 561–64. *See also* Middle Easterners; Muslims
Arab Community Center for Economic and Social Services (ACCESS), xli, **42–43**
Arab-Israeli War (1967), 394
Arab/Muslim advocacy organizations, **43–45**
Archie Bunker bigotry, **45–46**
Aristide, Bertrand, 253
Ariyoshi, George, 326
Armenians, 397
Arnout, Enaam, 419
Arrest statistics, 154–55
Arthur, Chester Alan, 118
Aryan National Alliance, 48
Aryan Nations, xlii, **46–48**, 451, 648, **743**
Aryan Youth Movement, 572

Ashcroft, John, 245

Asian American Legal Defense and Education Fund (AALDEF), xlii, **48**

Asian Americans, xix, xxxv, xxxvi, **50–53**, discrimination against, 48–50, 231; education and, xli, 139, 211, 212, 356, 546–47; ethnicity and, 184, 210–11; in films, 227–28; housing and, 531; intelligence of, 4, 328; intermarriage and, 305; land ownership, xv–xvi, xxxvi, xxxviii, 16, 49, 318; model-minority thesis, 160, 162, 403–5; pan-Asian solidarity, 472–73; perceived as foreigners, **51**, 338; racial earnings gap, 505; racial violence and, 116–17, 185–86; South Asians, ambiguity in racial identity among, 592–94; stereotypes of, 236, 465–66, 653; Wen Ho Lee case and, 358–59. *See also* specific ethnicities

Asian Americans for Equality (AAFE), **50–51**

Asian immigrants, xxxvi, 282–83, 285, 286, 319, 377, 442. *See also* Coolie; specific nationalities

Asian Indians. *See* South Asians

Asiatic Barred Zone, **54**, 377, 432

Asiatic Exclusion League (AEL), xxxv, **54–55**

Asociacion Tepeyac de New York, 392

Assimilation: Caribbean immigrants and, 108–9; colonialism and, 306, 510; cultural, 5, 31–32; ethnogenesis and, 215, 216; of immigrants, xix, 29–30, 184, 441, 443, 444–45, 494–96; "second-generation decline," 550–51; segmented-assimilation theory, 551–53. *See also* Black nationalist movements

Assimilation theory, **55–56**

Association for the Study of Classical African Civilizations, 14, 328

Association of Community Organizations for Reform Now (ACORN), 229

Association of Patriotic Arab-Americans in the Military (APAAM), 44

Atkins v. Virginia, 106, 237

Atlanta Braves, 600

Atlanta Compromise, 642

Attucks, Crispus, 582

Austin, Moses, 384

Austin, Stephen, 384, 611

Autobiography of Malcolm X, excerpt from, **741**

Aversive racism. *See* Racism, aversive versus dominative

Aviation and Transportation Security Act of 2001, 245

Avoidance of contact with minorities, 406

Awful Disclosure of the Hotel Dieu Nunnery of Montreal (Monk), 33

Back-to-Africa movement, **57**, 76, 77, 239, 363

Baker, Josephine, 219

Bakke, Allan, 523–24

Bakke decision. *See Regents of the University of California v. Bakke*

Baldwin, James, 25, 26, 219

Baldwin, Roger, 21

Banfield, Edward, 161

Banking. *See* Financial institutions, discrimination and

Banks, Dennis, 522

Barrios, **58**, 386, 387. *See also* Racial ghettos

Barron, Charles, 79

Baton Rouge bus boycott, 130–31, 407

Batts, Valerie, 406

Becker, Gary S., 196

Beecher, Lyman, 33

Being Black, Living in the Red (Conley), 505

Bell Curve: Intelligence and Class Structure in American Life, The (Herrnstein and Murray), xliv, 4, 65

Bellingham riots, xxxv, **58–59**

Benevolence International Foundation (BIF), 418, 419, 563

Bensonhurst incident, xliii, **59–60**

Berbrier, Mitch, 649, 650

Berger, Ronald J., 154

Bernal, Martin, 14

Bernstein, Leonard, 644

Berry, Shawn, 96

Beyond the Melting Pot (Glazer and Moynihan), 378, 643

BIA. *See* Bureau of Indian Affairs (BIA)

Bias crimes. *See* Hate crimes

Big Foot, Chief, 569

Bigots, types of, 6–7, 45–46, **61**, 223–24

Bilingual education, xliv, 31, 32, **61–63**, 199–200; California Ballot Proposition 227, xliv, 62, 100–101; English-only movement and, 204, 205; ethnic retention and school performance, 211, 212; *Lau v. Nichols*, 356; multiculturalism and, 414, 415. *See also* Ebonics

Bilingual Education Act of 1968, xl, 61–62, 414

Bindra, Hansdip Singh, 560

Binet, Alfred, 300, 302

Bin Laden, Osama, xliii, xlv, 17, 332

Biological racism, xvi–xvii, xx, xxi, **63–67**; genotype versus phenotype, 240; hereditarians versus environmentalists, 261–62; one-drop rule

and, 460-61, 511, 646, 654; *The Passing of the Great Race* (Grant), xxxvi, 478-80, 740. *See also* Eugenics movement; Intelligence tests
Birch, John, 336
Birmingham protests, 133
Birth of a Nation (film), xxxvi, 24, 226, 346, 647
Black, Don, 650
Black and Conservative (Schuyler), 69
Black anti-Semitism, 38, **67–69**, 327, 328, 329-30, 457
Black Athena: The Afroasiatic Roots of Classical Civilization (Bernal), 14
Black Codes, 332-33, 519
Black conservatives, **69–71**, 614-15
Black Economic Development Conference, 134
Black English (Ebonics), xlii, **71**. *See also* Bilingual education
Black family instability thesis, **71–73**, 159-60, 280-81, 449
Black Identities: West Indian Immigrant Dreams and American Realities (Waters), xliv, **73**
Black-Jewish conflicts, **329–30**, 457. *See also* Black anti-Semitism
Black-Korean conflicts, **74–75**, 444, 457
Black Like Me (Griffin), xxxix, 150
Blackmun, Harry, 8, 10, 105
Black Muslims. *See* Nation of Islam
Black nationalist movements, 68, **76–80**, 134, 412; back-to-Africa movement, 57, 239-40; Black Panther Party, xl, 78-79, 81, 134; Congress of Racial Equality (CORE), xxxvii, 111, 148-49, 148-49, 234, 372, 375; Olympic Project for Human Rights, 597; Organization of Afro-American Unity (OAAU), 464; Stokely Carmichael and, 111-12; W.E.B. Du Bois and, 193. *See also* Malcolm X; Nation of Islam
Black Panther Party, xl, 78-79, **81**, 134
Black political disenfranchisement, **82**. *See also* Voting rights
Black Power movement. *See* Black nationalist movements
Black Power: The Politics of Liberation in America (Carmichael and Hamilton), xx, xl, 76, 79, **82–83**, 295
Black Star Line, 57, 77
Black Wealth/White Wealth: A New Perspective on Racial Inequality (Oliver and Shapiro), xliv, **83–84**, 505
Black Worker (periodical), 516

Blaming-the-victim argument, 72, **86–87**, 208, 404, 406
Blauner, Robert, xli, 140, 142-43, 306, 510
Block-busting, **87**, 221, 272
Boaz, Franz, 396
Bobo, Lawrence, 353
Bogardus, Emory, 591
Bogardus Social Distance Scale, 591
Bond, Julian, 429
Bonds, Barry, 598
Bond servants. *See* Indentured servants
Boone, Daniel, 434
Boone, Pat, 417
Border Patrol, U.S., **625–26**
Bowler, Jack, 575
Boycotts, 74, 75, **87–88**, 130-31, 407-8
Bracero Program, xxxvii, xxxix, 58, **88–89**, 388, 392, 462
Bremer, Arthur Herman, 636
Brennan, William Jr., 236
Brett, G. S., 300
Brewer, Lawrence Russell, 95, 96
Brooklyn Dodgers, xxxvii, 540, 598
Brotherhood of Sleeping Car Porters, 352, 376, 407, 516
Browder v. Gayle, 131
Brown, Henry Billings, 555-56
Brown, John, xxxiv, 2, 586
Brown, Linda, 335
Brown Berets, 78
Brown University, 138
Brown v. Board of Education of Topeka, xxxviii, **89–91**, 335, 709-13; busing and, 93; de jure and de facto segregation, 173; Fourteenth Amendment and, 232; NAACP and, 428
Bryant, Kobe, 518
Buchanan v. Warley, 272, 335, 536
Buckley, William, Jr., 337
Buck v. Bell, 217
Buffalo Soldiers, **91–92**, 637
Bunche, Ralph, 133
Bunker, Archie (TV character), xli, **45–46**
Bureau of Indian Affairs (BIA), xxxiii, xxxiv, 23, **92–93**, 294-95, 381
Bureau of Refugees, Freedmen and Abandoned Lands. *See* Freedmen's Bureau
Burke Act of 1906, 92
Burlingame-Seward Treaty of 1869, 118
Bush, George H.W., 128, 251, 491
Bush, George W.: African American appointees, 70, 487, 488; government response to terror-

ism and, 190, 245, 309; Mexican immigration and, 392-93

Business ownership, 68, 74-75, 121-22, 229, 397, 444

Busing, **93–95**, 197

Butler, Richard G., xlii, 46, 47, 648

Byrd, James Jr., xliv, **96**

CAIR. *See* Council on American Islamic Relations (CAIR)

California, settlement of, xv, 384

California Ballot Initiative to Ban Racial Data. *See* California Ballot Proposition

California Ballot Proposition 54, xxii, xlv, **97–99**, 146

California Ballot Proposition 187, xix, xliii, **99–100**, 382, 392, 442-43, 444, 623

California Ballot Proposition 209, xliv, 11, 97, **100**

California Ballot Proposition 227, xliv, 62, **100–101**

California Civil Rights Initiative. *See* California Ballot Proposition

Callendar's Minstrels, 402

Caló, **101–2**

Campinis, Al, 598

Campus ethnoviolence, **102–3**

Capitalism, **103–4**, 361, 493

Capital punishment, xli, xlii, **105–7**, 156, 236-37

Caribbean immigrants, xiii, xviii, **108–11**, African Americans and, 107-8, 489-90; racial violence and, 276; social identity of, 463

Car loans, 229

Carlos, Juan, 597

Carmichael, Stokely, **111–12**; black nationalist movements and, 76, 79, 80, 603; *Black Power: The Politics of Liberation in America* (Carmichael and Hamilton), xx, xl, 82, 295

Carson, Kit, 435

Carter, Jimmy, 308, 327

Catholic Church. *See* Anti-Catholicism

Cato, Gavin, 68

Censorship, 25

Census Bureau, U.S., 502

Chamberlain, Houston S., 479

Charities, 418-19, 563

Charles C. Green v. County School Board of New Kent County, 548

Chavez, Cesar, xxxix, **112–13**, 201, 338, 624

Chavis, Benjamin E. Jr., 429

Chenault, Kenneth, 299

Cherokee Indians, 435, 438, 579

Cherokee Nation v. Georgia, xxxiii, **113–14**

Cheyney University, 138

Chicano movement, **114–15**, 252, 306-7, 617; Chicano Youth Liberation Front, 244; La Raza Unida, 354-56; National Chicano Moratorium, xli, 429-30

Children: "acting white" stage of life, 5-6; racial socialization and, 513-14; of slaves, 574-75. *See also* Education

Chin, Lily, 116

Chin, Vincent, xlii, 52, **116–17**, 317, 318, 473

Chinese Americans, xli, 464-65

Chinese Exclusion Act of 1882, xv, xxxv, 49, 54, **117–21**, 431, 678-81

Chinese immigrants, xv, xxxiv, 51, **121–25**, 149-50; bilingual education and, 356; middleman minorities and, 397; prejudice against, 319, 443-44; racial violence and, 366; Wen Ho Lee, 357-59. *See also* Chinese Exclusion Act of 1882

Choy, Christine, 116

Christian Identity Movement, xx, 47, 527, 648-49, 651

Christianity. *See* Religion

Chronology of race and racism, xxxiii–xlv

Churches, black, 130, 257, 526

Church of Jesus Christ of Latter-Day Saints, 526

CIO. *See* Congress of Industrial Organizations (CIO)

Citizens for Justice, 116

Citizenship, xxxvi, 16, 49, 442, 469, 624-25; Americanization and, 29-30, 31; Fourteenth Amendment to the Constitution, 231, 677-78; for Japanese Americans, 318, 320, 323; marriage and, 432; McCarran-Walter Act of 1952 and, xxxviii, 284, 377; for Mexican Americans, 386, 387; for Native Americans, 290, 291; Naturalization Act of 1790, xxxiii, 447-48. *See also* Chinese Exclusion Act of 1882

City of Angels (TV show), 609

City of Richmond v. J.A. Croson Company. See Richmond v. Croson

Civil disobedience, 132-33. *See also* Civil rights movement

"Civil Disobedience" (Thoreau), 386

Civil Liberties Act of 1988, xliii, 318, 326, 345

Civil Rights, U.S. Commission on. *See* U.S. Commission on Civil Rights (USCCR)

Civil Rights Act of 1870, 231

Civil Rights Act of 1957, xxxviii, 626

Civil Rights Act of 1964, xxxix, 9, **125–27**, 713-20; Asian Americans and, 50; education and,

139, 414; employment and, 84, 178, 207; en-
forcement of, 133; housing and, 628; labor
movement and, 353, 636; voting rights and,
82, 365
Civil Rights Act of 1968, **127**. *See also* Fair
Housing Act of 1968
Civil Rights Act of 1991, xliii, **127–28**
Civil rights movement, **128–35**, 279, 335–36,
500, 603. *See also* King, Martin Luther Jr.
Civil War, **135–37**, 187–88, 362–64, 586, 637. *See
also* Emancipation Proclamation; Reconstruc-
tion era
Clansman, The (Dixon), 24
Clark, Kenneth B., 340
Clark, Mark, 81
Class. *See* Socioeconomic status
Cleaver, Eldridge, 81
Cleveland Indians, 599–600
Clinton, Bill, 12, 316, 618
*Closed Doors, Opportunities Lost: The Continu-
ing Costs of Housing Discrimination*
(Yinger), xliv, **137–38**
Cloward, Richard, 639
Cobell, Elouise, 93
Cobell v. Norton, 92–93
Cold War, 129
Cole, David, 248
Coleman, Bill, 219
College admissions, discrimination in, **138–40**
Collier, John, 293
Colonialism, 129, 140, 140–45, 306–7, 398–99,
510. *See also* Minorities, involuntary; Neocolo-
nialism
Colonialization complex, **140**
Colonized versus immigrant minorities, **140–45**,
462–63, 510
Color-blind racism, xxii–xxii, **146**, 406, 527
Color-blind society, 97, 98, 361
Colored Troops, Bureau of, 637
Color hierarchy, **146**
Color line, **147**
"Color Line, The" (Douglass), 147
Columbus, Christopher, 147, 148, 433
Columbus Day controversy, **147–48**
Combs, Sean, 417
Commission for Racial Justice, 618
Commission for Social Justice/Sons of Italy in
America, 244
Commission on Civil Rights, U.S. *See* U.S. Com-
mission on Civil Rights
Commission on Wartime Relocation and Intern-
ment of Civilians, 318, 324, 327

Common Sense (Paine), 471˙
Communications Act of 1934, 266
Communism, 104, 219, 337
Community colleges, 200–201
Community Reinvestment Act of 1977, 275, 522
Compensation argument for affirmative action,
10
Competitive race relations. *See* Race relations,
paternalistic vs. competitive
Compromise of 1850, xxxiv, 333
Confessions of Nat Turner, The (Styron), 24
Congress of Industrial Organizations (CIO), 351,
352–53
Congress of Racial Equality (CORE), xxxvii, 111,
148–49, 234, 372, 375
Conkling, James C., letter to, 738–39
Conley, Dalton, 505
Connerly, Ward, xxii, 97
Conservatives. *See* Black conservatives; Liberal
and conservative views of racial inequality
Constitution, U.S., 583, 649. *See also* specific
amendments; Supreme Court, U.S.
*Construction Compliance Program Operations
Manual*, 10
Conyers, John, Jr., 258, 476, 528
Coolidge, Calvin, 239, 432
Coolie, **149–50**. *See also* Derogatory terms
CORE. *See* Congress of Racial Equality (CORE)
Cortina Wars, 390
Cosby, Bill, 177
Costilla, Miguel Hidalgo, 384
"Cost of being a Negro," **150–52**. *See also* Racial
earnings gap; Wage discrimination
Cottrell, Leonard, 639
Coughlin, Charles, 37
Council of Conservative Citizens, 445
Council on American Islamic Relations (CAIR),
xliv, 44, **152–53**, 418, 420, 423, 560
Counter-productivity argument, 11
Covert discrimination, **153**
Creation generation, **153–54**
Creativity movement, 526
Creek Indians, 435, 579
Creppy, Michael, 245
Crime and race, **154–56**, 171, 298–99, 430–31,
491, 517–18, 567–68
Criminal justice system. *See* Justice system
Crisis, The (periodical), 192, 428
Crusade for Justice, 114, 244, 355
Cuba, Spanish-American War and, 595
Cuban immigrants, 253–54, 265
Cuffe, Paul, 57

Cultural-ecological theory, 144–45

Cultural explanations for socioeconomic problems, 86, 195–96, 208, 354, 404

Cultural genocide, **158**

Cultural inversion. *See* "Acting white"

Cultural pluralism. *See* Multiculturalism

Culture, oppositional, 198

Culture and ethnicity, 107-8, 108-9

Culture of poverty thesis, **158–63**, 208

Cumming v. Richmond County Board of Education, 335

"Curveball" (Gould), 66

Custer, George, 436, 569

Custred, Glynn, 100

Dana, Richard, 383

Darwin, Charles. *See* Social Darwinism

Data collection, race and, xxii, xlv, 97–98, 146, 502-3, 745-56

Davenport, Charles Benedict. *See* Eugenics movement

Davidson, Chandler, 161

Davis, Benjamin, 400

Davis, Gray, 97

Davis, Miles, 219

Davis, Sammy Jr., 46

Dawes Act of 1887. *See* Indian Allotment Act of 1887

Death penalty. *See* Capital punishment

Decatur Federal Savings and Loan Association, 229

Declaration of Independence, 583

Declining Significance of Race (Wilson), xviii, xlii, 151, **165–70**

De facto segregation. *See* De jure and de facto segregation

Deindustrialization, xviii, **170–72**

De jure and de facto segregation, **172–73**, 548-49, 629

Democracy in America (Tocqueville), xxxiii, **173–74**

Democratic Party, 244, 355

Denny, Reginald, 367

Deportations. *See* Repatriations, Mexican; September 11 attacks; Undocumented immigrants

Derogatory terms, **174–79**

Desegregation. *See* Segregation

De Tocqueville, Alexis, xxxiii, 173

Detroit Race Riot of 1943, xxxvii, **179–80**

Detroit Race Riot of 1967, xl, **180–81**

Dewey, George, 481

Dewey, John, 263

DeWitt, John L., 217, 321

Diallo, Amadou, xliv, **181–82**

Dillingham, William P., xxxv

Dillingham Report, xxxv, **182**, 388, 431

Dinkins, David, 60, 69

Dinnerstein, Leonard, 602

Discrimination: adaptive discrimination, 6-7; against Asian Americans, 48-50, 53; bigots, types of, 45-46, 61, 223-24; against Caribbean immigrants, 110-11; covert vs. overt, 153; economics of, 196-97; in education, 138-40, 197-201; in employment, 151, 152; employment and, 506; financial institutions and, 228-30; in housing, 221-23, 270-75, 533-34; against Irish immigrants, 309-10; against Latino Americans, 264-66; against Muslims and Sikhs, 420-21; against Native Americans, 439-40; in refugee policies, 253-54; reverse discrimination, 537-38. *See also* Affirmative action; Prejudice

Discrimination, American Style (Feagin), xlii, **183–84**

Dissimilarity, index of, **289–90**, 530-31. *See also* Social distance

Diversity, ethnic and racial, 10, 12, 13, 30, 32, **184–85**, 445

Dixon, Thomas, 24

Doi, Carole, 322

Dominative racism, xxi. *See* Racism, aversive versus dominative

Dot buster attacks, **185–86**

Do the Right Thing (film), 60

Douglass, Frederick, xxxiii, 2, 147, **186–87**, 621, 638

Dow, George, 396

Dow v. United States, 396

Draft, military, 323

Draft riot of 1863, xxxiv, **187–88**

Dred Scott Decision, xxxiv, 136, **188**, 586

"Driving while black," 28, 157, **189–90**

Drug laws, 156-57, 298-99, 625

D score. *See* Dissimilarity, index of

Dual housing markets, **190–91**

Du Bois, W.E.B., **191–93**; black family instability thesis and, 72; Booker T. Washington and, 239, 642; color line and, xiv, 147; on derogatory terms, 178-79; labor movement and, 352; NAACP and, 428; Niagara Movement, 452; *The Souls of Black Folk*, xxxv, 739-40

Dukakis, Michael, 491, 545

Duke, David, **193–94**, 347, 445, 647, 649, 651

Dyer, Leonidas, 428
Dyer, Richard, 588
Dysfunctional rescuing, 406

Earnings gap, racial, xviii, xxxix, 84–86, 151, 152, 196, 505–7
Easley v. Cromartie, 565
Eastern Orthodox immigrants, xvi
Ebens, Ronald, 116, 117
Ebonics. *See* Black English (Ebonics)
Economic conditions, xiv, xxxix; black conservatives and, 70; black-Korean conflicts and, 74–75; black nationalism and, 79; economic responsibility, 315; employment of immigrants and, 281, 443–44; middleman minorities and, 396–97; racial violence and, 51–52; wealth, 83–84. *See also* Socioeconomic status
Economic Opportunity Act of 1964, 639
Economics and Politics of Race, The (Sowell), xlii, **195–96**
Economics of discrimination, **196–97**
Economics of Discrimination, The (Becker), 196
Economic systems: capitalism, 103–4, 361, 493; communism, 104, 219, 337; deindustrialization, xviii, 170–72; industrialization, 166–67; plantation system, 483–85, 577, 578, 583–84; race relations and, 493; slave economy, 135–36, 166, 483–84
Education: academic racism and, 3–4; affirmative action and, 12, 13, 541–42; Afrocentrism and, 13–14; Asian Americans and, xli, 50, 356, 546–47; barriers to, 144, 477–78; black English (Ebonics), xlii, 71; busing and, 93–95; Catholic school system, 310, 312; collection of data on race and, 98; community colleges, 200–201; discrimination in, 37–38, 126, 138–40, 197–201; ethnic retention and school performance, 211–13; ethnic studies, 199, 213–15, 277–78, 413–14, 466, 613; Head Start program, xxi, xl, 3–4, 65, 357; hidden curriculum and, 262–64; Higher Education and Reauthorization Act of 1998, 258; institutional racism in, xx, 297; multiculturalism in, 31–32, 199, 212, 413–14; Native Americans and, 295; segregation in, xxxv, xxxviii, 173, 365–66, 548–50; sports mascots and, 600; standardized testing, 139, 198, 199, 200, 300–302, 303, 619; tracking, 619; wages and, 84, 505–6. *See also* Bilingual education; *Brown v. Board of Education of Topeka*
Education, U.S. Department of, xlii

Education Amendments of 1972, 414
Education of All Handicapped Children Act of 1975, 414
Edwards, Harry, 597
Effective argument for affirmative action, 11
Eisenhower, Dwight D., xxxviii, 337, 365
Elections, presidential, xxxiv–xxxv, 260–61, 315, 636
El-Shabazz, El-Hajj Malik. *See* Malcolm X
El Teatro Campensino, xxxix, **201–2**
Emancipation Proclamation, xxxiv, **202**, 362–64, 363–64, 586, **675–77**, 736–37
Emergency Labor Program. *See* Bracero Program
Emerson, John, 188
Emerson, Ralph Waldo, 378
Emmons, D. C., 320
Employment: affirmative action in, 9; anti-Semitism and, 38; Asian Americans and, 48, 50, 53; assimilation and, 31; automobile industry, 230–31; Black Codes and, 333; Bracero Program, xxxvii, xxxix, 58, 88–89, 388, 392, 462; Chinese immigrants and, 117, 118, 119, 121–23, 124; Civil Rights Act of 1991, 127–28; deindustrialization and, 170–72; discrimination in, 421, 560–61; earnings gap and, xviii, 84–86, 151, 152, 505–7; economics of discrimination, 196–97, 601–2; Equal Employment Opportunity Act of 1972, 207–8; government jobs, 168; immigrants and, 281, 310, 443–44; institutional racism and, 299; Mexican Americans and, 388, 390; mismatch hypothesis, 402–3; race relations and, 492–93; racial violence and, xlii, 58–59, 116, 500, 501; training, 23; undocumented immigrants and, 392, 622–23. *See also* Labor movement; Socioeconomic status
Encyclopedia Africana, The, 193
English Language Education for Children in Public Schools Initiative (Proposition 227). *See* California Ballot Proposition 227
English Language Empowerment Act of 1996, 204
English-only movement, **203–5**, 445. *See also* California Ballot Proposition 227
English-Plus, 205
English Unity Act of 2003, 204
Enhanced Border Security and Visa Entry Reform Act of 2002, 246
Entertainment industry: films, 226–28, 243–44, 266–68, 453, 644–45; minstrelsy, 401–2; music industry, 416–18; sports, 597–99, 599–601;

stereotypes in, 466; television shows, 46–47, 607-8, 608–10
Entrepreneurship. *See* Business ownership
Environmentalists, 446. *See also* Hereditarians versus environmentalists
Environmental Protection Agency, 618
Environmental racism, **206–7**, 618
Equal Credit Opportunity Act of 1974, 275
Equal Employment Opportunity Act of 1972, xli, **207–8**
Equal Employment Opportunity Commission (EEOC), 9, 207, 421, 560, 614
Equal Pay Act of 1963, 414
Ertegun, Ahmet, 416
ER (TV show), 609–10
Ethnicity: Caribbean immigrants and, 107–8; marriage and, 303, 304, 305; melting pot metaphor and, 378; Mestizo, 381; origin of ethnic stratification theory, 467–68; pan-ethnic movements, 473–75; South Asians, ambiguity in racial identity among, 592-94; whiteness and, 588–89
Ethnicity in the United States: A Preliminary Reconnaissance (Greeley), 215–16
Ethnic Myth: Race, Ethnicity and Class in America (Steinberg), xliii, **208–9**
Ethnic options, **209–11**
Ethnic Options: Choosing Identities in America (Waters), 209
Ethnic retention and school performance, **211–13**
Ethnic studies, 199, **213–15**, 277-78, 413-14, 466, 613
Ethnocentrism, **215**, 467. *See also* Afrocentrism
Ethnogenesis, **215–16**
Ethnoviolence. *See* Campus ethnoviolence
Eugenics movement, xvii, 3, 4, 64, **216–17**, 302, 458, 597. *See also* Biological racism
Eurocentrism, 13
European-American Unity and Rights Organization, 194
Evers, Medger, 133
Executive Order 1962, 628
Executive Order 8802, 516
Executive Order 9066, xxxvii, **217–18**, 318, 321, 345, 708-9
Executive Order 9980, 218
Executive Order 9981, xxxvii, **218**, 516, 637
Executive Order 10925, xxxix, 8-9
Executive Order 11063, 273
Executive Order 11246, 9, 725-34
Executive Order 11375, 9

Executive Order 12898, 618
Expansionism, U.S., 373-75, 383-84, 385
Expatriation, **218–19**
Exposure index, **219–20**. *See also* Dissimilarity, index of

Fair Employment Board, 218
Fair Employment Practices Committee, 8
Fair Housing Act of 1968, xl, 127, **221–22**, 274, 533-34, 628, 645
Fair Housing Amendments Act of 1988, xliii, **222**
Fair-housing audits, **223**, 271, 274
Fair-weather liberals, 7, **223–24**
Families: black family instability thesis, 71-73, 159-60, 449; illegitimacy and, 280-81; John Birch Society and, 337; poverty and, 504; slave families, 574-75, 584; socioeconomic status of, 86; welfare and, 643-44
Fard, Wallace D. *See* Muhammad, Wali Farad
Farley, Reynolds, 513
Farm ownership, 230. *See also* Agricultural workers
Farmworkers Theater. *See* El Teatro Campensino
Farrakhan, Louis, **224–25**; anti-Semitism and, 69, 328, 329, 457; Million Man March, xliv, 400–401, 427
Faubus, Orval, 90
Faulkner, William, 26
FBI, 79, 81, 154
Feagin, Joe, xvii, xlii, 168, 183-84, 256, 295, 298
Federal Contract Compliance Programs, Office of (OFCCP), 9-10
Federal Housing Administration (FHA), xxxvii, **225–26**, 533, 628. *See also* U.S. Department of Housing and Urban Development (HUD)
Federal Office of Thrift and Supervision, 298
Federation for American Immigration Reform (FAIR), 204, 442
Feigham, Edward, 284
Fellowship of Reconciliation, 130
Ferber, Amy, 649
Ferguson, John Howard, 334
FHA. *See* Federal Housing Administration (FHA)
Fifteenth Amendment to the Constitution, 333, 364, 519, 631-32
Films, stereotypes and, **226–28**, 243-44, 422-23, 644-45
Final Call, The, 225
Financial institutions, discrimination and, **228–30**; Chinese immigrants and, 121-22; fair housing and, 191, 221, 271, 272, 274-75, 534;

mortgage lending, 221, 226; redlining, 272, 298, 521-22, 521-22, 629

Finney, Charles G., 2

First Confiscation Act, 362

Fix, Michael, 444

Forced relocation. *See* Native Americans

Ford, Gerald, 9

Ford, Henry, xvi, 29, 37, **230–31**

Ford, Wallace, 371

Ford Foundation, 382

Foreign Conspiracy against the Liberties of the United States (Morse), 33

Foreigners, Asian Americans perceived as, 50-51

Foreign Miners License Tax of 1852, xxxiv, 117-18, 123, **231**

Foreign Terrorist Tracking Task Force, 245

Forrest, Nathan Bedford, 346

Forsyth, James, 569

Foster, Mike, 194

Fourteenth Amendment to the Constitution, xxxiv, xliii, **231–32**, 333, 346, 519, 677-78

Frank, Leo, xxxvi, 34, **232–33**

Fraser, Nancy, 644

Frazier, E. Franklin, 72

Free blacks, xiii, **235**, 582-83. *See also* Slavery

Freedmen's Bureau, xxxiv, **233–34**

Freedom Riders, xxxix, 132, **234**, 647

Free speech, right of, 103, 486

Frémont, John, 362

French and Indian War, 434

Fugitive Slave Act of 1850, xxxiv, 622

Fu Manchu (character), **236**, 653

Furman v. Georgia, xli, 105-6, **236–37**

Gadsden Purchase of 1854, 375

Gaitz, Charles M., 161

Galton, Francis, 64, 216

Gandhi, Mahatma, 342

Gangs, xliii, 101, 313

Gans, Herbert, 210, 550, 552

Garcia, Hector P., xxxviii, 22

Garrison, William Lloyd, 1, 2

Garvey, Marcus, xxxvi, 57, 76-77, **239–40**, 371, 426

Gay rights, 415

Geary Act of 1892, 119

Gender, earnings gap and, 85, 506

Gender roles: Chinese immigrants and, 121-22; Million Man March and, 400; Orientalism and, 466; religious right and, 528

General Motors, 229

Genotype versus phenotype, **240**

Gentlemen's Agreement of 1908, xxxv, 49, **240–41**, 547. *See also* Chinese Exclusion Act of 1882; National Origins Act of 1924

Georgia Minstrels, 402

Gerrymandering, racial, **241**. *See also* Redistricting

Ghettos, racial, 508. *See also* Barrios; Housing

Ghost Dance religion, **242–43**, 436, 569, 741-43

Ghost-Dance Religion and the Sioux Outbreak of 1890, The (Mooney), excerpt from, **741–43**

GI Bill of Rights, 22, 138

Giddings, Joshua, 386

Gideon v. Wainwright, 156

Glazer, Nathan, xli, 14, 378, 643

Global Relief Foundation (GRF), 418, 419, 563

Gobineau, Arthur de, 458, 479

Goddard, Henry H., 3, 66, **243**, 442

Godfather, The (film), **243–44**

Goffman, Erving, 514

Goldman, Ron, xliv, 567

Gone with the Wind (film), 226

Gonzales, Rodolfo "Corky", 114, **244**, 355

"Gook," use of, 175

Gordon, Linda, 644

Gordon, Milton, 55-56

Gould, C.W., xvii-xvii

Gould, Stephen Jay, 65-66, 262, 328, 329

Government, federal: affirmative action in, 8-10; Civil Rights Act of 1964, 126; employment and, 168; multiculturalism and, 414-15; response to September 11 attacks, 245-48, 557-59, 561-64; Wen Ho Lee and, 357-59

Graham, Franklin, 526, 559

Grant, Madison, xxxvi, 63-64, 217, 442, 477-78, 738

Grant, Ulysses S., 250, 260

Gratz v. Bollinger, xlv, 13

Gray Panthers, 78

Great Migration, 129, 166-67, 231, 501

Great Society. *See* War on Poverty and the Great Society

Greeley, Andrew, 215-16

Greeley, Horace, 250

"Green Menace," **249**

Greenstone, David, 215

Gregg v. Georgia, xlii, 106

Gregorio T. v. Wilson, 382

Grierson, Benjamin, 91

Griffin, John Howard, xxxix, 150

Griffith, D.W., xxxvi, 24

Griffith, Michael, xliii, 276

Grimes, Timothy, 276
Grutter, Barbara, 13
Grutter v. Bollinger, xlv, 13
Guadalupe Hidalgo, Treaty of, xv, xxxiv, 153, **250–51**, 611, 672-75. *See also* Mexican-American War
Guinn v. United States, 335, 428
Gulf War, **251**
Gutierrez, Jose Angel, **252**, 355

Hacker, Andrew, xvii, xviii, 360, 361
Haitian refugees, **253–54**
Haley, Alex, xlii, 28, 77, 543-44
Hall, Prescott Farnsworth, 288
Hamas, 311, 419
Hamilton, Charles, xx, xl, 76, 80, 82, 295
Hammerskin Nation, 648
Hampton, Fred, 81
Hardy, Ken, 178
Harlan, John M., 556
Harlem Renaissance, **254–55**
Harlem Riot of 1964, xxxix, **255–56**
Harper's Ferry, Virginia, xxxiv, 586
Harrington, Michael, 639, 640
Harrison, Benjamin, 568
Harrison, William Henry, 434-35
Hart-Cellar Immigration Act. *See* Immigration and Nationality Act of 1965
Hate crimes, **256–58**; after September 11 attacks, xx, 19, 557-58, 559-61; anti-Semitism, 38; against Arab Americans, 20, 152; campus ethnoviolence and, 102; National Crime Victimization Survey, 431. *See also* White supremacist groups
Hate Crimes Statistics Act of 1990, xliii, **258**
Hate Crimes Statistics Improvement Act of 2003, 258
Hate speech. *See* Derogatory terms
Hawaii, annexation of, xxxv, **258–60**
Hawkins, Yusef, xliii, 59
Hayakawa, S. I., 203-4
Hayes, Rutherford B., xxxiv–xxxv, 118, 260, 333
Hayes-Tilden Compromise of 1877, **260–61**, 519
HCSA. *See* Hate Crimes Statistics Act of 1990
Head Start program, xxi, xl, 3-4, 65, 357
Health, 206, 296-97, 380, 619-20
Heart of Atlanta Motel v. United States, 126
Hebrew Immigrant Aid Society, 36
Hereditarians versus environmentalists, 64, **261–62**
Hernandez v. The State of Texas, 23, 357
Herrera, Jóse Joaquin de, 385

Herrnstein, Richard, xxi, xliv, 4, 65-66
Hidden curriculum, **262–64**
Higham, John, xxxviii, 602
Higher Education and Reauthorization Act of 1998, 258
Highlander Folk School, 130
High yellows. *See* Yellows
Hijab, 560
Hill, Anita, 614-15
Hilliard, David, 78
Himes, Chester, 219
Hindu immigrants, xix-xx, xxxv, 624-25
Hinduism, 526-27, 527-28
Hispanic Americans. *See* Latino Americans
Hitler, Adolph, 27
Hollywood and minority actors, **266–68**. *See also* Entertainment industry
Holocaust revisionists, 38, 648, 650
Holy Land Foundation for Relief and Development (HLF), 418-19, 563
Homeland Security, Department of, 247, 563-64, 625
Homeland Security Council, 245
Homelessness, **268–70**
Home Mortgage Disclosure Act of 1975, 275, 521-22
Hoover, Herbert, 482
Hoover, J. Edgar, 77, 79
Horton, Willie, 491
Housing, **270–75**; aversive racism and, xxi; block-busting, 87, 221, 272; *Closed Doors, Opportunities Lost: The Continuing Costs of Housing Discrimination* (Yinger), xliv, 137-38; dual housing markets, 190-91; fair-housing audits, 223, 271, 274; Federal Housing Administration (FHA), xxxvii, 225-26, 533, 628; homelessness, 268-70; low-income, 48; racial ghettos and, 58, 386, 387, 508; restrictive covenants, xxxviii, 273, 536-37, 566; segregation in, xvii–xviii, 28, 297-98, 336, 530-36, 530-36; U.S. Department of Housing and Urban Development (HUD), xxxix, xliii, 222, 271, 533, 628-29; white flight, 553, 645. *See also* Fair Housing Act of 1968; Financial institutions, discrimination and
Housing and Community Development Act of 1974, 628
Housing and Urban Development, Department of (HUD). *See* U.S. Department of Housing and Urban Development (HUD)
Houston, Sam, 612
Howard, Oliver O., 234

Howard Beach incident, xliii, 59, **276**

"How Can We Boost IQ and Scholastic Achievement?" (Jensen), 65

Huerta, Dolores, xxxix, 112, 624

Hughes, Langston, 219

Hughes, Sarah, 50–51

Human trafficking. *See* Indentured servants; Slave trade

Hunter, David, 362

Hurston, Zora Neale, 69

Hussein, Saddam, 251

ICC. *See* Indian Claims Commission (ICC)

Identity politics, **277–79**. *See also* Pan-ethnic movements

"I Have a Dream" speech, xxxix, 133, **279–80**, 342, 375, 742–43

Illegal aliens. *See* Undocumented immigrants

Illegal Immigration Reform and Immigrant Responsibility Act of 1996, 623

Illegitimacy and race, **280–81**

Immigrant minorities. *See* Colonized versus immigrant minorities

Immigrant preference in employment, **281**

Immigrant Reform and Control Act of 1986 (IRCA), 622–23

Immigrants, illegal. *See* Undocumented immigrants

Immigrants and immigration: anti-Catholicism and, 32–34; assimilation of, 5, 29–30, 31–32, 494–96; biological racism and, 63, 65, 217, 479; Bracero Program, xxxvii, xxxix, 58, 88–89, 388, 392, 462; citizenship and, xv–xvi; colonialism and, 140–45, 450; Dillingham Report, xxxv, 182, 388, 431; employment and, 48, 281, 506-7; English-only movement and, 203–5, 445; ethnicity, 184, 209-11, 211–13, 215, 216; Federation for American Immigration Reform (FAIR), 442; intelligence tests and, 3, 66, 243, 302; Know-Nothing Party and, xxxiv, 33–34, 344–45; McCarran-Walter Act of 1952, xxxviii, 49, 284, 377; melting pot metaphor and, 377–79, 412; Naturalization Act of 1790, xxxiii, 49, 446, 447–48; proximal host and, 489–90; response to September 11 attacks and, 19, 245-48, 561-64; "second-generation decline," 550–51; segmented-assimilation theory, 551–53. *See also* Chinese Exclusion Act of 1882; National Origins Act of 1924; Nativism and anti-immigrant movements; specific nationalities and ethnic groups; Undocumented immigrants

Immigration Act of 1917, 49, 54, 432

Immigration Act of 1924. *See* National Origins Act of 1924

Immigration Act of 1990, 286, 442

Immigration and Naturalization Act of 1965, xl, 120, 184, **282–88**, 378-79, 720-22

Immigration and Naturalization Service, xxxviii, 245, 246, 253, 309, 388

Immigration Reform and Control Act of 1986, 286

Immigration Restriction League, xxxv, 34, **288**, 442

"Importance of Collecting Data and Doing Social Scientific Research on Race, The" (American Sociological Association), 743-54

In Black and White: Race and Sports in America (Shropshire), 598

Indentured servants, **288–89**, 581. *See also* Coolie

Indian Allotment Act of 1887, xxxv, 92, **290–91**, 294, 380, 681–85

Indian Appropriation Act of 1871, 435

Indian Citizenship Act of 1924, xxxvi, **291**

Indian Claims Commission (ICC), xxxvii, **291–92**

Indian Education Act of 1972, 414

Indian Removal Act of 1830, 435, 437–38

Indian Reorganization Act of 1934 (IRA), xxxvii, 92, 291, **293**, 294, 381, 430

Indian reservations, **293**, 380-81, 435, 436, 438

Indians. *See* Native Americans; South Asians

Indian Self-Determination and Education Assistance Act of 1976 (ISDEAA), xlii, **294–95**

Indians of All Tribes, 522, 523

Indian Territory, 435, 437, 438

Indigenous subordination. *See* Migrant superordination and indigenous subordination

Indigenous superordination, 141–42

Individualism, 21

Individual racism, xx

Industrialization, 166–67

Ineffectiveness argument, 11

Inoue, Daniel, 326

Insidious Dr. Fu Manchu, The (Rohmer), 236

Institutional racism, xx, 6, **295–300**

Integration. *See* Assimilation; Segregation

Intelligence, xl, xliv, 3–4, 328–29

Intelligence tests, **300–303**, biological racism and, xvi–xvii, xxi, 63, 610; cultural biases in, 65–66, 199, 263; eugenics movement and, 64–65; immigrants and, 243. *See also* Standardized testing

Intermarriage, 28, **303–6**; Asian Americans, xix; biological racism and, xvii, 479, 511; ethnicity and, 209, 210-11; Jim Crow laws, 332; one-drop rule, 460, 461; racial classification and, 98

Internal colonialism, **306–7**, 510

Internalized racism, **307–8**. *See also* "Acting white"

International Association of Firefighters v. City of Cleveland, 8

International Jew, The (Ford), 230

International slave trade. *See* Slave trade

Internet, white-supremacist groups and, 650

Internment camps. *See* Japanese American internment

Involuntary minorities. *See* Colonized versus immigrant minorities

Involuntary segregation. *See* Segregation

IQ tests. *See* Intelligence tests

IRA. *See* Indian Reorganization Act of 1934 (IRA)

Iran hostage crisis and anti-Iranian stereotypes, **308–9**, 394

Iranian immigrants, 562-63

Iraq, 251

Irish Americans, 379-80

Irish immigrants, xxxiv, 32, 33, 187-88, **309–10**, 345

Irish Riot of 1863. *See* Draft riot of 1863

ISDEAA. *See* Indian Self-Determination and Education Assistance Act of 1976 (ISDEAA)

Islam, 78, 331-32, 455, 526. *See also* Arab Americans; Muslims; Nation of Islam

Islamic Committee for Palestine, 311

Islamic fundamentalism, 249, 311

Islamic Jihad, **311**

Israel, 39-40, 68, 330

Israeli immigrants, 490

Italian American Heritage Foundation, 244

Italian Americans, 147, 243-44, **311–14**, 545-46

Italian immigrants, xvi

Ito, Midori, 322

"I've Been to the Mountaintop" speech, 342

Jackson, Andrew, 435, 437

Jackson, Jesse, xlii, 59-60, **315–17**, 515, 594

JACL. *See* Japanese American Citizens League (JACL)

James Byrd Foundation for Racial Healing, 96

Janitors for Justice (JFJ), 353

Japan bashing, **317**

Japanese American Citizens League (JACL), xxxvi, **317–18**, 324, 326

Japanese American internment, xvi, xxxvii, 49, 317, **318–26**, 345, 640-41. *See also* Executive Order 9066

Japanese Americans, xxxvi, xliii, 217-18, 469, 546-47

Japanese Americans, redress movement for, **326–27**, 641

Japanese and Korean Exclusion League. *See* Asiatic Exclusion League

Japanese immigrants, xv–xvi, xxxv, xxxvi, 51, 52, **240–41**

Jaret, Charles, 443

JDL. *See* Jewish Defense League (JDL)

Jefferson, Thomas, 583

Jeffries, Leonard, 66, **327–28**, 457

Jemison, T. J., 130, 407

Jensen, Arthur, xxi, xl, 3-4, 65, 262, **328–29**

Jewish Americans, xxxvi; Anti-Defamation League of B'nai Brith, xxxvi, 34, 40, 233, 347, 571-72; college admissions and, 138; Israeli immigrants and, 490; media bias and, 338; middleman minorities and, 397; racism of, 330. *See also* Anti-Semitism

Jewish-Black conflicts, **329–30**, 457

Jewish Defense League (JDL), 40, **330–31**

Jewish immigrants, xvi, xix, 285-86, 490

Jewish Supremacism (Duke), 194

Jihad, **331–32**

Jim Crow, origin of term, 402

Jim Crow laws, xxxv, **332–36**; Civil Rights Act of 1964, 125, 126; Ku Klux Klan (KKK) and, 647; laissez-faire racism and, 354; marriage and, 304-5; segregation and, xiv, 172, 554; voting rights and, 82

John Birch Society, xxxviii, **336–37**

Johnson, Andrew, 234, 528

Johnson, James Weldon, 192

Johnson, Lyndon B.: affirmative action, 8, 9; Civil Rights Act of 1964, 125; immigration and, 284; National Advisory Commission on Civil Disorders, xl, 339, 427; Vietnam War an, 638; War on Poverty and the Great Society, 244, 369, 639-40

Johnson-Reed Act. *See* National Origins Act of 1924

Johnson v. Transportation Agency, Santa Clara County, 8

Jones Act of 1916, 482

Journalism, stereotypes and, **337–38**

Justice system, 28, 105-7, 116, 154-56, **156–58**, 171

Kahlil Gibran: Spirit of Humanity Awards, 41

Kain, John, 402

Kallen, Horace, 412

Kansas-Nebraska Act of 1854, xxxiv, 188, 585

Karenga, Maulana, xl, 349

Kasarda, John, 402–3

Kasinitz, Philip, 107–8

Kaufman, Charles, 116, 473

Kearney, Denis, 443

Kearney, Stephen Watts, 386

Kellor, Frances A., 29–30

Kemetic Institute of Chicago, 14

Kennedy, John F.: affirmative action, xxxix, 8; civil rights movement and, 125, 639; Freedom Riders, 234; housing and, 628; immigration and, 284; Irish Americans and, 310

Kent, Jacob, 596

Kerner, Otto, 339, 427

Kerner Commission. *See* National Advisory Commission on Civil Disorders

Kerner Commission Report, **339–41**, 736–38

Khomeini, Ayatollah, 308

Khoury, George, 42

King, Alberta Williams, 342

King, Bernice, 342

King, Coretta Scott, 316, 342

King, Dexter, 342

King, John William, *95*, *96*

King, Martin Luther III, 342, 594

King, Martin Luther Jr., 131, 133, **341–44**; death of, 134, 221, 427; "I Have a Dream" speech, xxxix, 279–80, 742–43; Jesse Jackson and, 315, 316; "Letter from a Birmingham Jail," 359–60, 739–40; Malcolm X and, 371, 372; Montgomery Bus Boycott, 88, 335, 407, 408, 475; Southern Christian Leadership Conference (SCLC), 594; voting rights and, 631

King, Martin Luther Sr., 342

King, Rodney. *See* Rodney King beating

King, Steve, 204

King, Yolanda, 342

King Philip's War, 434

Kingston, Alex, 610

KKK. *See* Ku Klux Klan (KKK)

Knights of Labor, 352

Knights of Mary Phagan, 233

Know-Nothing Party, xxxiv, 33–34, **344–45**

Knox, Frank, 320

Koch, Ed, 60

Koehl, Matthias, 451, 647

Koppel, Ted, 598

Korean Americans: black-Korean conflicts, 52, 74–75, 367, 444; boycotts and, 88; middleman minorities and, 456, 457; segregation and, 546–47

Korean immigrants, 368

Korean War, 638

Korematsu v. United States, xxxvii, 324, **345**

Kovel, Joel, xxi

Ku Klux Klan (KKK), **345–48**, 647; anti-Semitism and, xvi, xx, 37, 233; George Wallace and, 636; lynching and, 370; Malcolm X and, 77, 371; membership of, 183, 257; origins of, xiii–xiv, xxxiv, xxxvi, 24, 519. *See also* White supremacist groups

Kwan, Michelle, 50

Kwanzaa, xl, **348–49**

Labor movement, **351–53**; affirmative action and, 8; American Federation of Musicians, 416, 417; Brotherhood of Sleeping Car Porters, 352, 376, 407, 516; deindustrialization and, 170; Japanese American internment and, 321; racial violence and, 59, 601; strikebreakers, 59, 118, 124; undocumented immigrants, 392; United Auto Workers, 351; United Farm Workers (UFW), xxxix, xli, 112–13, 114, 201, 202, 338, 624; Wagner Act of 1935, xxxvii, 635–36

Labor rights, 48

Ladone, Jason, 276

Laissez-faire racism, **353–54**

Lamarck, Jean-Baptiste, 64, 596–97

Lampman, Robert, 639

Land ownership, xv–xvi; Alien Land Laws, xv–xvi, xxxvi, xxxviii, 16, 49, 318; Mexican Americans and, xxxix, 250–51, 386–87, 387–88, 389–90, 617; Native Americans and, xxxv, 15–16, 92–93, 290–91, 293–94

Language: black English (Ebonics), xlii, 71; Caló, 101–2; derogatory terms and, 174–79; English-only movement, xix, 100–101, 203–5, 445; immigrants and, 29–30, 31–32; political correctness and, 486; Spanish, xv, 265; voting rights and, xlii, 633. *See also* Bilingual education

La Raza Unida, 115, 244, 252, **354–56**

LaSalle, Eriq, 609, 610

Latino Americans: American GI Forum, xxxviii, 22–23; barrios and, 58, 386, 387; Caló and, 101–2; culture of poverty thesis and, 159; discrimination against, 264–66; El Teatro Campensino, xxxix, 201–2; ethnicity and, 184, 211, 378, 379; in films, 227; housing and, 269, 530–31; League of United Latin American Citizens (LULAC), xxxvi, 356–57; mestizo, 381; Mexican American Legal Defense and Education

Fund (MALDEF), xl, 382; racial earnings gap, 505, 506. *See also* Bilingual education; Chicano movement; specific nationalities

Latino immigrants, xviii–xix, 285, 287, 368

Laundry businesses, 121, 122

Lau v. Nichols, xli, **356**, 415

Law enforcement: Birmingham protests and, 133; crime and race, 154–56, 171, 298–99, 430–31, 491, 517–18, 567–68; "driving while black," 28, 157, 189–90; FBI, 79, 81, 154; immigration and, 246, 625–26; institutional racism and, 298–99; *Miranda* rights, xl; police brutality, xliii, xliv, 181, 366–67, 451, 500, 501, 522–23, 540–41; response to September 11 attacks, 558; Texas Rangers, 611–12. *See also* Race riots; Violence, racial

League of United Latin American Citizens (LULAC), xxxvi, **356–57**

Lear, Norman, xli, 45, 46

Lee, Heon, 74

Lee, Jennifer, 74

Lee, Robert E., 346

Lee, Spike, 60, 77

Lee, Wen Ho, xliv, **357–59**

Legacy of past discrimination argument, **359**

Lester, Jon, 276

"Letter from a Birmingham Jail" (King), xxxix, 342, **359–60**, 741–42

"Letter to James C. Conkling" (Lincoln), 736–37

Lewis, Al, 17

Lewis, John, 79

Lewis, Oscar, 159, 161

Liberal and conservative views of racial inequality, 69–71, **360–62**, 527–28, 614–15

Liberator, The (periodical), 2

Lieberson, Stanley, 141–42, 398, 399

Lieu, Ted, 51

Light in August (Faulkner), 26

Liliuokalani, Queen, 259

Limited-English-proficiency. *See* Bilingual education

Lincoln, Abraham, xxxiv, 25, 136–37, **362–64**; draft riot of 1863, 187, 188; election of, 586; Emancipation Proclamation, 202, 675–77, 736–37

Lincoln County Wars, 390

Lipinski, Tara, 50

Literacy tests, **364–65**, 631

Literature. *See* American literature and racism

Little, Earl, 77, 371

Little, Louise, 77, 371

Little, Malcolm. *See* Malcolm X

Little, Reginald, 77

Little Richard, 417

Little Rock Central High School, integration of, xxxviii, **365–66**

Liu, Jon, 473

Livingston, Sigmund, 34

Lóme, Enrique Dupuy de, 595

Longoria, Felix, 23

Loo, Jim, 52

Los Alamos Research Laboratory, xliv, 357

Los Angeles Riot of 1871, **366**

Los Angeles Riot of 1992, **366–69**, 540

Losing Ground: American Social Policy, 1950–1980 (Murray), xlii, **369**

Lott, Trent, 616

Loury, Glenn C., 70

Luce-Celler Act of 1946, 49

LULAC. *See* League of United Latin American Citizens (LULAC)

Lynching, xiv, 333–34, **369–70**, 428; of Italian immigrants, xvi, 313–14; of Jewish Americans, xxxvi, 34, 232–33; of Mexican Americans, xv; race riots and, 497

Mafia, stereotypes and, 312

Magnet schools, 200

Malcolm X, 77–78, **371–73**; Elijah Muhammad and, 410–11; excerpt from *The Autobiography of Malcolm X,* 743; Louis Farrakhan and, 224; Organization of Afro-American Unity (OAAU), xxxix, 464

MALDEF. *See* Mexican American Legal Defense and Education Fund (MALDEF)

Maloney, Carolyn, 258

Mandatory sentencing, 156–57

Manifest destiny, xxxiv, **373–75**, 595–96. *See also* Mexican-American War; Philippine-American War

March on Washington movement, **376–77**, 516

March on Washington (1963), xxxix, 133, 279, 342, **375–76**, 376–77, 516

Marriage, 280, 573, 574. *See also* Intermarriage

Marshall, Thurgood, 236, 428, 539

Martí, Jose, 595–96

Martin, Tony, 457

Marx, Karl, 103–4

Massasoit, 434

"Matter of Whiteness, The" (Dyer), 588

McCarran-Walter Act of 1952, xxxviii, 49, 284, **377**

McCarthy, Joseph, 219

McCleskey v. Kemp, 105

McDaniel, Hattie, *267*

McKinley, William, 481, 595, 596

McLeod, Jay, 162

McVeigh, Timothy, 459, 647–48

Mead, Lawrence, 161

Measure of Man, The (King), 342

MEChA (Chicano Student Movement of Aztlán), xli, 115

Media: bias in, 50–51, 152, 249, 388, 396, 440; immigrants and, 185; Japanese American internment and, 320; journalism, 337–38; National Coalition for Sports and Racism in the Media (SCRSM), 599; white-supremacist groups and, 649–50. *See also* Entertainment industry

Medical research, 619–20

Mein Kampf (Hitler), 27

Melting pot, **377–79**, 412

Melting Pot, The (Zangwill), 378

Memphis race riot of 1866, **379–80**

Mental health, 297

Meriam, Lewis M., 380

Meriam Report, xxxvi, 293, **380–81**

Merton, Robert K., 61, 223–24

Messenger, The (periodical), 516

Mestizo, **381**

Metacomet, 434

Metro Broadcasting v. FCC, 8

Metzger, Tom, 572

Mexican American Legal Defense and Education Fund (MALDEF), xl, **382**, 633

Mexican Americans, xv, 264–65, 282, **387–91**; Alianza Federal de Pueblos Libres (Federal Alliance of Land Grant), xxxix, 617; colonialism and, 306–7; creation generation, 153–54; La Raza Unida, 115, 224, 252, 354–56; media bias and, 337–38; wage discrimination and, 151; Zoot Suit Riots, xxxvii, 388, 390, 656–57. *See also* Chicano movement; Guadalupe Hidalgo, Treaty of; Mexican-American War

Mexican-American War, 373, 375, **382–87**, 611, 637. *See also* Guadalupe Hidalgo, Treaty of

Mexican immigrants, xviii–xix, xxxviii, 58, 252, **391–93**. *See also* Bracero Program

Mexican repatriations, **393**, 442, 461–62

Mexico, U.S. relations with, 383–84, 384–85, 612

Mfume, Kweisi, 429

MidAmerica Bank, 229

Middlebury Female Seminary, 138

Middle class, 83, 167, 168

Middle Easterners, **394–96**. *See also* Arab Americans; Muslims

Middleman minorities, 75, **396–98**, 456

Migrant farm workers. *See* Agricultural workers

Migrant superordination and indigenous subordination, 141, 142, **398–99**

Military: American Revolution and, 582–83; Buffalo Soldiers, 91–92; Civil War, 202, 364, 586; integration of, xxxvii, 8, 218, 516, 637–38; Japanese American internment and, 323; Latino Americans and, 114–15. *See also* Veterans; War and racial inequality

Militia movement. *See* White-supremacist groups

Miller, Kelly, 192

Milliken v. Bradley, 549

Million Man March, xliv, 69, 225, **400–401**, 427

Min, Pyong Gap, 74

Mineta, Norman, 326

Minorities: actors, 266–68; assimilation of, 495; capitalism and, 103–4; ethnic studies and, 213–14; group names, 414; involuntary, 140–45, 154, 398–99, 462–63; model-minority thesis, 160, 162, 227, 317, 403–5; negative self-image, 449

Minstrelsy, **401–2**, 416

Miranda v. Arizona, xl, 156

Mismatch hypothesis, **402–3**

Mismeasure of Man, The (Gould), 66

Mississippi Freedom Democratic Party, 603

Missouri Compromise, xxxiii, xxxiv, 135, 188, **403**, 585

Missouri ex rel. Gaines v. Canada, 548

Mitchell, George, 41, 522

Mittleberg, David, 489

Model-minority thesis, 160, 162, 227, 317, **403–5**

Modern racism, **405–7**

Mody, Navroze, 185

Monk, Maria, 33

Montana Freemen, 649

Montgomery Bus Boycott, xxxviii, 88, 130–31, 335, 342, **407–8**, 475–76. *See also* Civil rights movement

Montgomery Improvement Association, 408

Mooney, James, 741–43

Moorish Science Temple. *See* Nation of Islam

Mormons. *See* Church of Jesus Christ of Latter-Day Saints

Morrison, Toni, 25, **409–10**

Morse, Samuel F. B., 33

Mortgage disinvestment. *See* Redlining

Mortgage lending. *See* Financial institutions, discrimination and

Movies. *See* Films, stereotypes and

Moynihan, Daniel Patrick, xl, 71–72, 86, 159–60, 280, 378, 449, 643

Moynihan Report. *See Negro Family in America: The Case for National Action, The* (Moynihan)

Muhammad, Elijah, 77, 78, 224, 371, **410–11**, 425

Muhammad, Wali Farad, xxxvi, 69, 410, 425

Muhammad, Wallace, 224

Mulatto, **411**, 654

Multiculturalism, 184–85, **411–16**, 443; assimilation and, 495; collection of data on race and, 98; in education, 31–32, 199, 413–14; ethnic studies, 213–15, 277–78, 413–14, 466, 613; ethnogenesis and, 216; identity politics and, 277–78; melting pot metaphor and, 377–79, 412; Third World Movement, 613–14

Murphy, Frank, 345

Murray, Charles: *The Bell Curve: Intelligence and Class Structure in American Life* (Herrnstein and Murray), xliv, 4; biological racism and, xxi, 65–66; cultural explanations for socioeconomic problems, 86, 280, 643–44; *Losing Ground: American Social Policy, 1950–1980* (Murray), xlii, 369

Music industry, racism in, **416–18**

Muslim philanthropic organizations, **418–19**, 563

Muslim Public Affairs Council, 423

Muslims, **420–23**; anti-Iranian stereotypes, 308–9; Council on American Islamic Relations (CAIR), xliv, 44, 152–53, 418, 420, 423, 560; hate crimes against, 559–61; immigrants, xix–xx; media bias and, 338; religious right and, 527–28; terrorism and, 245–48, 557, 561–64. *See also* Arab Americans; Islam; Middle Easterners

Muzzey, David Saville, 250

My Country versus Me (Lee), 358

Myrdal, Gunnar, 72, 739

9/11. *See* September 11 attacks

NAACP. *See* National Association for the Advancement of Colored People (NAACP)

Nader, Ralph, 41

Narrative of the Life of Frederick Douglass (Douglass), xxxiii

National Advisory Commission on Civil Disorders, xl, 299, 339–41, **427**

National Alliance, 451, 647–48

National Association for the Advancement of Colored People (NAACP), **428–29**; civil rights

movement, 129, 130, 234, 375; David Duke and, 649; founding of, xxxv, 192; media and, 266; Montgomery Bus Boycott and, 407, 475; Stokely Carmichael and, 111–12; television and, 609. *See also Brown v. Board of Education of Topeka*

National Association for the Advancement of White People (NAAWP), 649

National Baptist Convention, 526

National Chicano Moratorium, xli, 114–15, **429–30**

National Coalition for Redress Reparations (NCRR), 327

National Coalition for Sports and Racism in the Media (SCRSM), 599

National Collegiate Athletic Association (NCAA), 303

National Committee Against Discrimination in Housing, 273

National Community Reinvestment Coalitions, 229

National Congress of American Indians (NCAI), xxxvii, **430**, 522

National Council for Japanese American Redress (NCJAR), 326–27

National Crime Victimization Survey, 154, **430–31**

National Farm Workers Association (NFWA). *See* United Farm Workers (UFW)

National Indian Youth Council (NIYC), 522

National Italian American Foundation, 243

National Labor Relations Act of 1935. *See* Wagner Act of 1935

National Negro Labor Council, 353

National Organization for European American Rights (NOFEAR), 445

National Origins Act of 1924, xxxvi, 283, **431–33**, 703–8; Asian immigrants, xv, 49, 54, 120; biological racism and, 3, 4, 63, 65; Dillingham Report and, 182; McCarran-Walter Act, 377; nativism and anti-immigrant movements, 34, 36, 442

National Population Council, Mexican, 391

National Security Entry-Exit Registration System (NSEERS), 246, 247, 562

National Socialist White People's Party. *See* New Order, the

Nation of Islam, xxxvi, **425–27**; anti-Semitism of, 38, 69, 328, 457; Louis Farrakhan and, 224–25; Malcolm X and, 77–78, 371; Million Man March, xliv, 400–401; Muhammad, Elijah and, 410–11. *See also* Islam

Native Americans, xiv, xxxv, xxxvii, **433–40**; Alaska Native Claims Settlement Act of 1971, xli, 15–16; American Indian Movement (AIM), xl, xli, 23–24, 522–23, 599; Buffalo Soldiers and, 91–92; Bureau of Indian Affairs (BIA), xxxiii, xxxiv, 23, 92–93, 294–95, 381; Cherokee Indians, 113–14, 435, 438, 579; Civil Rights Act of 1968, 127; colonialism and, 307; Columbus Day controversy, 147–48; cultural genocide, 158; ethnocentrism and, 215; Ghost Dance religion, 242–43, 436, 569, 741–43, 743–45; housing and, 531–32; Indian Allotment Act of 1887, xxxv, 92, 290–91, 294, 380, 681–85; Indian Appropriation Act of 1871, 435; Indian Citizenship Act of 1924, xxxvi, 291; Indian Claims Commission (ICC), xxxvii, 291–92, 291–92; Indian Education Act of 1972, 414; Indian Removal Act of 1830, 435, 437–38; Indian Reorganization Act of 1934 (IRA), xxxvii, 92, 291, 292–93, 294, 381, 430; Indian reservations, 293–94, 380–81, 435, 436, 438; Indian Self-Determination and Education Assistance Act of 1976 (ISDEAA), xlii, 294–95, 294–95; Indians of All Tribes, 522, 523; intermarriage and, 305; Irish immigrants and, 309–10; manifest destiny and, 374; Meriam Report, xxxvi, 293, 380–81; National Congress of American Indians (NCAI), xxxvii, 430, 522; National Indian Youth Council (NIYC), 522; Navajo Indians, 294, 435; occupation of Alcatraz, xli, 292, 293; psychosocial passing and, 477–78; racism of, 456; Red Power movement, 522–23; self-governance of, xxxvii; Seminole Indians, 438, 579; Sioux Indians, xxxv, 436, 568–70, 743–45; slavery and, 578–79; sports mascots and, 599–601; stereotypes of, 454; Trail of Broken Treaties, 23; Trail of Tears, xxxiii, 438. *See also* Minorities, involuntary
Nativism and anti-immigrant movements, xvi, xix, xxxviii, **440–47**, 602–3; Americanization Movement, 29–31; Anglo conformity, 31–32, 495; anti-Catholicism and, 33–34; Asiatic Exclusion League, xxxv, 54–55; ethnocentrism and, 215; Know-Nothing Party, xxxiv, 344–45
Naturalization. *See* Citizenship
Naturalization, Bureau of, 31. *See also* Immigration and Naturalization Service
Naturalization Act of 1790, xxxiii, 49, 446, **447–48**
Nature of Prejudice, The (Allport), xxxviii, **448**
Navajo Indians, 294, 435

Nazi Party, American, xxxviii, 27–28, 451
Nazi Party, German, 65, 458
Nazism, 217, 230, 302, 450–51
NCAI. *See* National Congress of American Indians (NCAI)
NCVS. *See* National Crime Victimization Survey
Negative eugenics. *See* Eugenics movement
Negative self-image, **449**
Negro Family in America: The Case for National Action, The (Moynihan), xl, 71–72, 86, 159–60, **449–50**
Negro in the United States, The (Frazier), 72
Nelson, Lemrick, 68
Neocolonialism, **450**
Neo-Nazism, **450–51**, 647–48
Network of Arab-American Professionals, 44
Newark riots of 1967, xl, **451–52**, 501–2
Newman, Katherine, 162
New Order, the, 28, 451, 647
New Philadelphia, Illinois, xxxiii, 17
New Politics of Poverty, The (Mead), 161
Newton, Huey, xl, 78, 81
Niagara Movement, xxxv, 192, **452–53**
Nichols, Terry, 459
Nietzsche, Friedrich, 458
Nigger, use of, 25, 175–77, **453**
Nitz, Michael, 116
Nixon, E. D., 131, 407
Nixon, Richard, 9, 16, 523
Nkrumah, Kwame, 193
Nobel Peace Prize, 342
Noble savage, **454**
Noel, Donald, 467, 468
Non-Judeo-Christian immigrant groups, violence against, **454–56**
Nonmeritocracy argument, 11
Nonviolence, 131–32
Nonwhite racism, 425, **456–58**. *See also* Black anti-Semitism
Nordic superiority, **458**, 479
North Star (periodical), 2
Norton, Gale, 93
No Shame in My Game: The Working Poor in the Inner City (Newman), 162
Notes of a Native Son (Baldwin), 25

OAAU. *See* Organization of Afro-American Unity (OAAU)
Oakes, Richard, 292
Oberlin College, 138
Obsession with race. *See* American "Obsession with Race"

OCA. *See* Organization of Chinese Americans (OCA)

O'Connor, "Bull," 133

O'Connor, Carroll, 45, 46

O'Connor, Sandra Day, 10, 13

Ogbu, John, 144–45, 198, 462, 477

Ohlin, Lloyd, 639

Oil embargo, 394

Oklahoma City bombing, xliv, 394, 420, **459–60**, 647-48

Oliver, Melvin L., xliv, 83, 505

Olympic Games, 50–51, 597

Olympic Project for Human Rights, 597

Omi, Michael, xliii, 507

One-drop rule, **460–61**, 511, 646, 654

"On the Cost of Being Negro" (Siegel), xxxix, 151

Operation Desert Storm. *See* Gulf War

Operation TIPS, 247, 563–64

Operation Wetback, xxxviii, **461–62**

Oppositional identity, 198, **462–64**

Oregon Boarder Treaty of 1846, 375

Organization of Afro-American Unity (OAAU), xxxix, 77, 78, **464**

Organization of Chinese Americans (OCA), xli, **464–65**

Oriental Exclusion Act of 1924. *See* National Origins Act of 1924

Orientalism, **465–67**

Orientalism (Said), 395, 465

Origin of ethnic stratification theory, **467–68**

O'Sullivan, John L., xxxiv, 373, 383–84

Other America, The (Harrington), 639

"Our Sacred Mission" (Jeffries), 66

Overt discrimination, **153**

Owen, Chandler, 516

Oyama v. California, xxxviii, 16

Ozawa v. United States, xxxvi, 49, **469**, 625

Pacific Islanders. *See* Pan-Asian solidarity

Page Law of 1875, 118

Pahlavi, Reza Shah, 308

Paine, Thomas, **471–72**

Palestinian Islamic Jihad. *See* Islamic Jihad

Palestinians, 311

Paley, William, 46

Pan-African Conferences (Paris), 192

Pan-Asian solidarity, **472–73**, 593–94

Pan-ethnic movements, **473–75**, 613–14

Panic-peddling. *See* Block-busting

Pan-Indian movements. *See* Red Power movement

"Paper-son" strategy, 120

Paredes, Mariano, 385

Park, Robert, 55, 494–96, 591, 592

Parker, Charlie, 219

Parker, I. A., 70

Parker, James A., 358

Parks, Rosa, xxxviii, 131, 335, 400, 407, **475–77**

Parris, Fred, 416

Parsons, Richard, 299

Passel, Jeffrey, 444

Passing, psychosocial, **479–80**

Passing of the Great Race, The (Grant), xxxvi, 63–64, 217, **477–78**, 740

Paternalistic race relations. *See* Race relations, paternalistic vs. competitive

Patriot Act of 2001, xlv, 19, 21, 245, 420, 446, 561

Patterson, John, 636

P.C. *See* Political correctness

Peculiar Institution: Slavery in the Ante-Bellum South, The (Stampp), xxxviii, **480–81**

Peltier, Leonard, 24

People v. Hall, 118, 124

Perkins, Joseph, 70

Perry, Rick, 96

Personal Responsibility and Work Opportunity Reconciliation Act. *See* Welfare Reform Law of 1996

Pfaelzer, Mariana, 100

Phagan, Mary, 232

Phenotype. *See* Genotype versus phenotype

Philadelphia Negro, The (Du Bois), 72, 191

Philippine-American War, **481–83**, 596

Philippine Organic Act of 1902, 482

Pierce, William, 451, 459, 460, 647, 648, 651

Pierre-Louis, Francois, xx

PIJ. *See* Islamic Jihad

Plantation system, **483–85**, 577, 578, 583–84

Platt Amendment, 596

Playing in the Dark: Whiteness and the Literary Imagination (Morrison), 25

Plea for the West, The (Beecher), 33

Plessy, Homer, 334, 555

Plessy v. Fergusson, xxxv, 334–35, 548, 555–57, 685–703; color line and, 147; Fourteenth Amendment to the Constitution and, 232; segregation and, 89, 125, 172–73. *See also* *Brown v. Board of Education of Topeka*

Police. *See* Law enforcement

Police brutality: Amadou Diallo shooting, xliv; justice system and, 155; Native Americans and, 522–23; riots and, 451, 500, 501; Rodney

King beating, xliii, 366–67, 540–41; Texas
    Rangers and, 611
Political correctness, **485–87**, 617–18
Political parties: Democratic Party, 244, 355;
    Know-Nothing Party, 344–45; La Raza Unida,
    115, 244, 252, 354–56; Mississippi Freedom
    Democratic Party, 603; Republican Party, 12,
    69, 70; U.S. Commission on Civil Rights
    (USCCR), 627; Workingmen's Party of Califor-
    nia (WPC), 122, 351, 443
Politics: anti-Semitism and, 38–39; Arab American
    Institute and, 41; identity politics, 277–78; im-
    migrants and, 445–46; liberal and conserva-
    tive views of racial inequality, 69–71, 360–62,
    527–28, 614–15; Mexican Americans and, 244;
    pan-ethnic movements, 473, 474; race card in
    political campaigns, 491–92; white supremac-
    ists and, 193–94. *See also* Elections, presi-
    dential; Voting rights
Polk, James K., 385, 386
Poll taxes, **487**, 631
Poole, Elijah. *See* Muhammad, Elijah
Poor People's March of 1968, 244
Populist Observer, The (periodical), 650
Portes, Alejandro, 551
Posse Comitatus, 649
Posser, Gabriel, 575, 576
Poussaint, Alvin, 46
Poverty: culture of poverty thesis, 158–63,
    208; racial differences in rate of, 503–4;
    War on Poverty and the Great Society, 244,
    369, 639–40; welfare, 72, 280–81, 349, 444,
    623, 640, 643–44. *See also* Socioeconomic
    status
Powell, Colin, 70, 251, 289, 299, **487–88**
Powell, Laurence, 366
Powell, Lewis F. Jr., 542
Powhatan Indians, 434
Preferential treatment. *See* Affirmative action
Prejudice, 6–7, 45–46, 61, 223–24, 448, **488–89**,
    547–48. *See also* Discrimination
Prejudice Institute, 102
Prison population, xx
Problem of Indian Administration, The. See
    Meriam Report
Property holding. *See* Racial differences in prop-
    erty holding
Property holding, racial differences in, 504–5
Proposition 54. *See* California Ballot Proposition
    54
Proposition 187. *See* California Ballot Proposi-
    tion 187

Proposition 203 (Arizona), 62
Proposition 209. *See* California Ballot Proposi-
    tion 209
Proposition 227. *See* California Ballot Proposi-
    tion 227
Prosser, Gabriel, xxxiii
Prostitutes, 118, 124
Protestant Ethic and the Spirit of Capitalism
    (Weber), 21
Protocols of the Elders of Zion, The, 36, 69, 655
Proximal host, **489–90**
Public Health Service, U.S., xxxvii, 619
Public housing projects, 273
Public policy, 3–4, 14, 168–69
Puerto Rican immigrants, xix, 265, 644–45
PUSH (People United to Save Humanity), 315,
    516

Quakers, 1, 583
Quota Act of 1924. *See* National Origins Act of
    1924
Quotas, 12, 34, 138, 139, 330. *See also* Affirma-
    tive action
Qutb, Sayyid, 332

Race: American obsession with, 28–29; classifica-
    tion of, 502–3; concept of, 67; marriage and,
    303, 304–5; of Middle Easterners, 395–96;
    South Asians, ambiguity in racial identity
    among, 592–94; white, 587–89
Race and Economics (Sowell), 69–70
Race card in political campaigns, **491–92**
Race Matters (West), xliv, **492**
Race relations, paternalistic vs. competitive,
    492–94
Race-relations cycle, **494–96**
Race riots, xiv, xxxiv, xxxvi, xxxvii, xl, 134,
    496–502; anti-Chinese, xxxiv; Bellingham
    Riots, xxxv; Crown Heights riots, 68–69; De-
    troit race riot of 1943, 179–80; Detroit race
    riot of 1967, 180–81; draft riot of 1863, 187–
    88; Harlem riot of 1964, xxxix, 255–56; in
    Japanese American internment camps, 323;
    Los Angeles riots, xliii, 74, 366, 366–69; Mem-
    phis race riot of 1866, 379–80; National Advi-
    sory Commission on Civil Disorders, xl, 339–
    41, 427, 734–36; Newark riots of 1967, xl,
    451–52; St. Louis riot of 1917, 601; Watts
    riots, xl; Zoot Suit riots, 388, 390, 656–57
Racial classification of population, **502–3**
Racial differences in poverty rate, **503–4**
Racial differences in property holding, **504–5**

Racial earnings gap, **505–7**

Racial epithets. *See* Derogatory terms

Racial Formation in the United States From the 1960s to the 1980s (Omi and Winant), xliii, **507–8**

Racial ghettoes, **508**. *See also* Barrios; Housing

Racialism, 28–29, **509**

Racial Isolation in the Public Schools, 93

Racialization, **509–10**

Racial Oppression in America (Blauner), xli, 306, **510–11**

Racial Privacy Initiative (Proposition 54). *See* California Ballot Proposition 54

Racial profiling: "driving while black," 28, 157, 189–90; institutional racism and, 298; terrorism and, 325, 420, 558–59, 559–60, 563

Racial purity, **511**

Racial segregation, white and black preferences as a cause of. *See* Segregation

Racial socialization, **513–14**

Racial stigmatization, **514–15**

Racism: academic racism, 3–4; definition of, xiii; environmental, 206–7; institutional, 295–300; internalized, 307–8; laissez-faire, 353–54; literature and, 24–27; modern, 405–7; nonwhite, 425, 456–58; persistence of, xvii–xx; rape and, 517–18; symbolic, 604–5; types of, xx–xxii. *See also* Biological racism

Racism, aversive versus dominative, xxi, 406, **515**

Rainbow Coalition, xlii, 315, **515–16**

Rainbow/PUSH Action Network, 315, 516

Randolph, A. Philip, 352, 375, 376, 407, **516**

Rape and racism, **517–18**

Ray, James Earl, 343

Reagan, Ronald, 310

Reconstruction era, xiii–xiv, xxxv, **518–20**; Fourteenth Amendment to the Constitution and, 231; Hayes-Tilden Compromise of 1877, 260–61; Jim Crow laws and, 125, 333; Memphis race riot of 1866, 379–80; reparations and, 528; voting rights and, 82. *See also* Freedmen's Bureau

Red Cloud, Chief, 569

Redfaeirn, Harold Ray, 648

Red Guard, 78

Redistricting, 241, **520–21**, 565–66

Redlining, 228, 229, 272, 298, **521–22**, 629

Red Power movement, **522–23**

Redress movement. *See* Japanese Americans, redress movement for

Refugees, 36–37, 65, 120, 233, 253–54

Regents of the University of California v. Bakke, xlii, 8, **523–25**

Re: Halladjian, 395–96

Rehnquist, William, 13

Reimers, David, 602

Religion, xv, xix–xx, **525–27**; anti-Catholicism, xvi, xix, 32–34, 310, 312, 442, 445, 446, 525; Anti-Defamation league of B'nai Brith, 34; black churches, 130, 257, 526; Ghost Dance religion, 436, 569, 743–45; Hinduism, 526–27, 527–28; immigrants and immigration, xvi, 282, 287, 309; Islam, xliv, 17–18, 43–45, 78, 311, 331–32, 455, 526; Islamic fundamentalism, 249; marriage and, 303–4; Native American, 242–43; reparations for African Americans, 134; violence against non-Judeo-Christian groups, 454–56. *See also* Anti-Semitism

Religious right, **527–28**

Reparations for African Americans, 134, **528–29**. *See also* Japanese Americans, redress movement for

Repatriations, Mexican, **393**

Republican Party, 12, 69, 70

Reservations. *See* Indian reservations

Residential segregation, **530–36**

Resorts, all-black, **17**

Resources, competition for, 467–68

Restrictive covenants, xxxviii, 273, **536–37**, 566

Reverse discrimination, 11, **537–38**

Rice, Condoleezza, 70, 299

Rice, Thomas "Daddy," 332, 402

Rice Funeral Home, 22–23

Richmond v. Croson, xliii, **538–39**

Richter, Michael, xviii

Ridge, Tom, 247

Riff-raff theory, 497, 498

Rights of Men (Paine), 471

Riots. *See* Race riots

Robb, Thomas, 347, 649

Robbins, Jerome, 644

Roberts, Michael, xiv

Robertson, Pat, 559

Robert S. Rankin Civil Rights Library, 627

Robert v. City of Boston, 548

Robinson, Frank, 540

Robinson, Jackie, xxxvii, **539–40**, 598

Robinson, Jo Ann, 131, 407

Rock, Chris, 453

Rockefeller Drug Laws of 1973, xx, 298–99

Rockwell, George Lincoln, xxxviii, 27–28, 451, 647

Rodney King beating, xliii, 366–67, **540–41**

Rohmer, Sax, 236

Role-model argument for affirmative action, **541–43**

Roosevelt, Franklin D.: African American employment and, 8, 376, 516; Columbus Day and, 147; Federal Housing Administration (FHA), 225; Japanese American internment and, xxxvii, 217, 320, 321, 345, 640; Jewish refugees and, 37; military and, 637; Native Americans and, 293

Roosevelt, Theodore, 30, 240, 547, 596, 642

Roots: The Saga of an American Family (Haley), xlii, 28, **543–44**

Rosa and Raymond Parks Institute for Self-Development, 476

Rosenbaum, Yankel, xliii, 68–69

Ross, John, 435

Rossi, Peter, 269

Rule of hypo-descent. *See* One-drop rule

Rushton, J. Phillipe, 4

Rustin, Bayard, 378

Ryan, William, 161–62

Sacco and Vanzetti case, xvi, xxxvi, 313, **545–46**

Said, Edward, 395, 465

Salaries. *See* Wage discrimination

Salazar, Ruben, 115, 430

Sampson, Calvin T., 118, 124

Sandiford, Cedric, 276

San Francisco School Board Crisis of 1906, xxxv, **546–47**

Santa Anna, Antonio López de, 385, 612

Save our State Initiative. *See* California Ballot Proposition 187

Scalia, Antonin, 189–90

Scalping, 439–40

Scapegoat theory of racial prejudice, **547–48**

Schindler's List (film), 231

School choice, 200

School performance. *See* Ethnic retention and school performance

Schools. *See* Education

School segregation, **548–50**

Schur, Edwin, 555

Schuyler, George S., 69

Schwarzenegger, Arnold, 97

Schwarzkopf, Norman, 251

SCLC. *See* Southern Christian Leadership Conference (SCLC)

Scott, Dred, 136

Scott, Winfield, 386, 435

Scott Act of 1888, 119

Scottsboro Boys, 517

Seale, Bobby, xl, 78, 81

Second Confiscation Act, 363

"Second-generation decline," **550–51**

Secret Relationship between Blacks and Jews, The, 69

Segmented-assimilation theory, **551–53**

Segregation, 28–29, **511–13**, 532–33, **553–54**; color line, 147; de jure and de facto, 172–73; in education, xxxv, xxxviii, 93–95, 197, 356, 546–47, 548–50; exposure index, 219–20; George Wallace and, 636; housing and, xvii–xviii, 58, 190–91, 226, 270–75, 297–98; index of dissimilarity, 289–90; integration of Little Rock Central High School, 365–66; in labor movement, 351–53; in military, 218, 637–38; recreation and, 17; W.E.B. Du Bois and, 192–93; William Faulkner on, 26. *See also Brown v. Board of Education of Topeka*; Discrimination; Jim Crow laws

Sei Fujii v. the State of California, 49

Selective Service Act of 1940, 637

Self-fulfilling prophecy, **555**

Self-image, negative, 449

Selma-Montgomery march, 133

Seminole Indians, 438, 579

Separate but equal doctrine, **555–57**. *See also Plessy v. Fergusson*

September 11 attacks, xlv, 245–48, **557–64**; Al Qaeda, 19; Arab Americans and, 20, 41–42, 43–44; government response to, 309, 311, 325, 418–19, 420, 446; Middle Easterners and, 395, 396; Sikh community and, 455–56

SER—Jobs for Progress, 23

Service Employees International Union (SEIU), 353

Sexuality, 122, 461, 465. *See also* Gay rights

Shabazz, Betty, 78, 372

Shakur, Tupac, 177, 453

Shalala, Donna, 41

Shallah, Ramadan, 311

Shannon, Wilson, 385

Shapiro, Thomas M., xliv, 83, 505

Sharecropping, **564–65**

Sharpton, Al, 60

Shawnee Indians, 434–35

Shaw v. Hunt, xliv, **565–66**

Sheatsley, Paul, 256

Sheet Metal Workers v. EEOC, 8

Shelley v. Kraemer, xxxviii, 273, 536–37, **566**
Sheridan, Philip, 91
Shlay, Anne, 269
Shockley, William, 3
Shropshire, Kenneth, 598
Siegel, Paul M., xxxix, 151
Sikes, Melvin, xvii
Sikh community, xix–xx, 455–56, 527–28, 557, 560
Simmel, Georg, 591–92
Simmons, Russell, 417
Simon Wiesenthal Center, 40
Simpson, Nicole Brown, xliv, 567
Simpson, O.J., xliv, 518, **567–68**
Sioux Indians, xxxv, 436
Sioux outbreak of 1890, **568–70**, 741–43
Sit-ins, 132, 336, **570–71**. *See also* Civil rights movement
Sitting Bull, 436, 569
Skinheads, 451, **571–72**, 648. *See also* White-supremacist groups
Slaton, John, 232
Slave auctions, **572–73**
Slave codes, **573**, 582, 584–85, 660–72, 660–72
Slave families, **574–75**
Slave revolts and white attacks on black slaves, xxxiii, **575–76**, 585
Slavery, xiii, xxxiii, xxxiv, xxxviii, **580–87**; abolition of, 1–2, 135–37, 346, 362–63; education and, 197; families and, 574–75; Jewish people and, 68; lingering impact of, 360–61; Missouri Compromise, xxxiii, xxxiv, 135, 188, 403; Native Americans and, xiv, 578–79; *The Peculiar Institution: Slavery in the Ante-bellum South* (Stampp), 480–81; plantation system, 483–85, 577, 578; race relations systems and, 166; religion and, 525; slave auctions, 572–73; slave codes, 573, 582, 584–85, 660–72; slave trade, 577–78, 580–81, 582; Thomas Paine on, 471–72. *See also* Free blacks; Indentured servants
Slavery and American Indians, **578–79**
Slavery reparations. *See* Reparations for African Americans
Slave trade, **577–78**, 580–81, 582
Slidell, John, 385
Small-business loans, 229
Smith, John, 451
Smith, Tommie, 597
SNCC. *See* Student Nonviolent Coordinating Committee (SNCC)
Social construction of whiteness, **587–89**

Social Darwinism, 64, 216, 261, **589–91**, 596. *See also* Biological racism
Social distance, xxi, **591–92**. *See also* Dissimilarity, index of
Social identity, 5–6, 29–30, 79–80, 587–89
Socialization, racial, 513–14, 607
Social Security, 640
"Societal Theory of Race and Ethnic Relations, A" (Lieberson), 398
Socioeconomic status: affirmative action and, 12, 361–62; American Dream ideology and, 21–22; of Asian Americans, xix; biological racism and, 65–66, 479–80, 590; capitalism and, 104; civil rights movement and, 129–30; class conflict, 166; crime and, 156; cultural explanations for, 72, 86–87, 158–63, 402–3; *Declining Significance of Race* (Wilson), 165–70; earnings gap, 150–52; *Economics and Politics of Race, The* (Sowell), 195–96; education and, 95, 198; housing and, xvii–xviii, 532–33; of immigrants, 108–10, 550–51; intelligence tests and, 302; middle class, 83, 167, 168; model-minority thesis, 160, 162, 227, 317, 403–5; of Native Americans, 380–81; racial differences in poverty rate, 503–4; wealth and, 83, 504–5; welfare, 72, 280–81, 349, 623, 640; of white people, 588–89; *White Trash: Race and Class in America* (Wray and Newitz), 589
Sodhi, Balbar Singh, 455–56, 557
Sopranos, The (TV show), 243–44
Souls of Black Folk, The (Du Bois), xxxv, 147, 191, 737–38
South Asians, xliii, 16, 49, 185–86, **592–94**
Southern Baptist Convention, 526–27
Southern Christian Leadership Conference (SCLC), xxxviii, 131–32, 315, 342, 375, **594**, 631
Southern Homestead Act, 528
Southern Poverty Law Center, 451, 646
Soviet Lenin Peace Prize, 193
Sowell, Thomas, xlii, 11, 69–70, 167, 195–96
Spanish-American War, 375, 481, **595–96**, 637
Spencer, Herbert, 64, 589, 590, **596–97**
Spielberg, Steven, 231
Sports and racism, xxxvii, **597–99**. *See also* Robinson, Jackie
Sports mascots, **599–601**
Springarn, Joel, 192
Stampp, Kenneth, xxxviii, 480–81
Standardized testing, 139, 198, 199, 200, 300–302, 619. *See also* Intelligence tests

Standards-based education, 200

Statistical discrimination, 196, **601–2**

Steele, Claude, 198–99

Steele, Shelby, 70

Steele v. Louisville and Nashville Railroad, 635

Steinberg, Stephen, xliii, 168, 208

Stereotypes: affirmative action and, 11; of Asian Americans, 236, 404–5, 653; crime and race, 517–18; education and, 198–99, 263; examples of, xvi, 489; of Italian Americans, 312; journalism and, 337–38; of Mexican Americans, xv, 388, 389; of Middle Easterners, 308–9, 394, 395–96, 557; minstrelsy and, 401–2; of Muslims, 19, 249, 422–23; of Native Americans, 439–40, 454; Orientalism, 465–67; self-fulfilling prophesy, 555; standardized testing and, 301; symbolic racism and, xx–xxi; in TV and film, 226–28, 243–44, 267, 607–8, 609. *See also* Derogatory terms; Racialization

Sterilization, 3, 4, 217

Stevens, Thaddeus, 260

Stigmatization, racial, 514–15

Still the Big News (Blauner), 510

St. Louis Riot of 1917, **601**

Stowe, Harriet Beecher, xxxiv, 2, 24–25

Strangers in the Land (Higham), xxxviii, **602–3**

Strikebreakers, 59, 118, 124

Structure vs. agency discourse, 160–61

Student and Exchange Visitor System (SEVIS), 246, 562

Student Nonviolent Coordinating Committee (SNCC), xxxviii, 132, **603**; Freedom Riders, 234; Malcolm X and, 372; March on Washington (1963), 375; Stokely Carmichael and, 79, 111, 112

Students for a Democratic Society, 132

Styron, William, 24

Suhayda, Rocky, 28

Sumner, Charles, 260

Sumner, William, 597

Supreme Court, U.S., xxxiii, xxxiv, xxxv; capital punishment and, xli, xlii, 105–6, 236–37; citizenship, xxxvi, 49, 469; Clarence Thomas and, 22, 70, 477, 614–15; Dred Scott Decision, 136, 188, 586; education and, 356, 548–49; eugenics movement and, 217; Fourteenth Amendment and, 232; housing and, xxxviii, 272, 273, 335, 536–37, 566; immigration and, 624–25; Japanese American internment and, xxxvii, 324, 345; labor movement and, 635–36; land ownership, xxxviii, 16; law enforcement and, xl, 156, 189–90; Native Americans and, 113–14; voting rights and, xliv, 335, 521, 565–66. *See also* Affirmative action; *Brown v. Board of Education of Topeka*; *Plessy v. Fergusson*

Swift, Wesley, 46–47

Sylvester, Curtis, 276

Symbolic racism, xx–xxi, **604–5**. *See also* Color-blind racism; Covert discrimination

Taft, William Howard, 182, 482, 642

Tajima, Renee, 116

Takao Ozawa v. United States. See Ozawa v. United States

Taliban, the, 19

Tanton, John, 204

Tappan, Lewis, 2

Taxes, 117–18, 123–24, 231, 431, 487, 631

Taylor, Zachary, 385

Tecumseh, 435

Television shows, 46–47, 243, 244, 543–44, **607–10**

Teller Amendment, 596

Temporary Assistance to Needy Families (TANF). *See* Welfare

Ten Years' War, 595

Terman, Lewis, xvii–xvii, 64–65, **610–11**

Terrell, Mary Church, 428

Terrorism: Al Qaeda, xliii, xlv, 17–19, 245, 332; Hamas, 311, 419; Islamic fundamentalism, 311, 331, 332; Jewish Defense League (JDL), 330; Muslims' image and, 422–23; Oklahoma City bombing, 459–60; racial profiling and, 190, 394. *See also* September 11 attacks; White supremacist groups

Terry v. Ohio, 189

Texas, xv, xxxiv, 373, 382, 384–85, **611**, 612

Texas Rangers, **611–12**

Texas Rebellion, The, **612–13**

Theater, 201–2

Thind, Bhagat Singh, 49

Thind v. United States. See United States v. Thind

Third World Movement, **613–14**. *See also* Pan-ethnic movements

Thirteenth Amendment to the Constitution, 346, 364

Thomas, Clarence, 22, 70, 477, **614–15**

Thompson, Robert, 366

Thoreau, Henry David, 2, 250, 386, 621

Thirteenth Amendment to the Constitution, xxxiv

Thurmond, Strom, **615–16**

Tierra Amarrilla Courthouse raid, 617

Tijerina, Reies Lopez, xxxix, **617**
Tilden, Samuel J., 260
Timid bigots. *See* Bigots, types of
Title VII, 84
Tokenism, **617–18**
Toxic neighborhoods, **618**
Toyota Motor Credit Corporation, 229
Tracking, **619**
Trail of Broken Treaties, 23
Trail of Tears, xxxiii, 438
Transcontinental railroad, 123, 124
Transportation Security Administration (TSA), 245
Treaties, Native Americans and, 434–35
Treaty of Guadalupe Hidalgo. *See* Guadalupe Hidalgo, Treaty of
Truman, Harry S., xxxvii, 8, 218, 516, 637, 641
Truong, Hung, 53
Tuan, Mia, 210
Tubman, Harriet, 621
Tuchman, Gloria, 101
Tule Lake Relocation Center, 641
Tulsa race riot of 1921, 498
Ture, Kwame. *See* Carmichael, Stokely
Turner, Nat, xxxiii, 24, 575, 576
Turner Diaries, The (Pierce), 459–60, 647–48
Tuskegee Institute, 641–42
Tuskegee Study of Untreated Syphilis in the Negro Male, xxxvii, **619–20**
TV shows. *See* Television shows
Twain, Mark, xxxv, 25, 178
Twenty-Fourth Amendment to the Constitution, 487
Tydings-McDuffie Act of 1934, 482

UFW. *See* United Farm Workers (UFW)
Uncle Tom's Cabin (Stowe), xxxiv, 24–25
Underground Railroad, 1, 585, **621–22**
Undocumented immigrants, 391–93, **622–24**; amnesty for, 286; California Ballot Proposition 187, xix, xliii, 99–100, 382, 392, 442–43, 444; employment of, 507; Mexican, 390, 462; U.S. Border Patrol, 625–26
Uniform Crime Reports (UCR), 154, 155, 258
Unions. *See* Labor movement
United Auto Workers, 351
United Church of Christ Commission for Racial Justice, 206
United Defense League (UDL), 130
United Farm Workers (UFW), xxxix, xli, 112–13, 114, 201, 202, 338, **624**

United Mine Workers, 351
United States v. Paradise, 8
United States v. Thind, xxxvi, 16, 49, 469, **624–25**
United Steelworkers of American v. Weber, 8
Universal Negro Improvement Association (UNIA), xxxvi, 57, 76–77, 239, 371, 426
Universities, 12, 37–38, 39, 102–3, 138–39, 213, 303. *See also* Community colleges
University of Michigan affirmative action ruling, xlv, 10, 13
Unz, Ron, 62, 101
Up from Slavery (Washington), 641
USCCR. *See* U.S. Commission on Civil Rights (USCCR)
U.S. Commission on Civil Rights (USCCR), xxxviii, 93, 247, **626–28**, 629
U.S. Commission on Immigration. *See* Dillingham Report
U.S. Department of Housing and Urban Development (HUD), xxxix, xliii, 222, 271, 533, **628–29**
U.S. English, 204
USS Maine, 595
USS St. Louis, 37
U.S. Visitor and Immigrant Status Indication Technology (U.S. VISIT), 247

Vagrancy laws, 332
Valdez, Luis, xxxix, 201
Van de Berghe, Pierre, 492, 494
Van den Haag, Ernest, 106
Vanzetti, Bartolomeo. *See* Sacco and Vanzetti case
Vesey, Denmark, xxxiii, 576
Veteran Outreach Program, 23
Veterans, 22–23
Victims of Trafficking and Violence Protection Act of 2000 (TVPA), 289
Vietnamese immigrants, 211
Vietnam War, xli, 114–15, 134, 429, 613, 638, 639–40
Vigilantes, 462
Violence, racial, xliii, xliv; anti-Italian, 313–14; Asian Americans and, xix, xlii, 51–53, 116–17, 123, 473; assassination of Malcolm X, 78; Bensonhurst incident, 59–60; campus ethnoviolence, 102–3; dot buster attacks, 185–86; Howard Beach incident, 276; James Byrd Jr., 96; against Mexican Americans, 389–91; against non-Judeo-Christian groups, xx, 454–56; slave revolts and white attacks on black

slaves, xxxiii, 575–76, 585. *See also* Hate crimes; Lynching; Police brutality; Race riots
Violent Crime Control and Law Enforcement Act of 1994, 258
Voluntary minorities. *See* Segregation
Voluntary segregation. *See* Segregation
Voting rights, xliv, 82, 133, 428, 627; Arab Americans and, 44; Asian Americans and, 48; Civil Rights Act of 1964, 126; Jesse Jackson and, 315; Jim Crow laws and, 333; literacy tests, 364–65; poll taxes, 487, 631; redistricting and, 241, 520–21, 565–66
Voting Rights Act of 1965, xl, xlii, 133, 336, 414, **631–32**, 723–25
Voting Rights Amendments of 1975, **632–33**
Voting Rights Amendments of 1982, 521
Vouchers, school, 200

Wage discrimination, xviii, 84–86, 151, 152, 196
Wagner, Robert, 635
Wagner Act of 1935, xxxvii, **635–36**
Walcott, Louis Eugene. *See* Farrakhan, Louis
Waldinger, Roger, xviii
Walker, David, 575
Wallace, George, 90, **636–37**
Wall Street Project, 315
Wampanoag Indians, 434
War and racial inequality, **637–39**
War Brides Act, 120
Ward, Arthur Henry Sarsfield, 236
Ward, Robert DeCourcy, 288
War of 1812, 637
War on Drugs, 156–57
War on Poverty and the Great Society, 244, 369, **639–40**
War on Terrorism, 18–19. *See also* September 11 attacks
War Relocation Authority (WRA), xxxvii, 321–22, 324, **640–41**
Warren, Charles, 288
Warren, Earl, 89–90, 335
War Resisters League, 130
Washington, Booker T., 76, 192, 239, 453, **641–42**
WASPs, **642–43**
Waters, Mary: *Black Identities: West Indian Immigrant Dreams and American Realities* (Waters), xliv, 73; on Caribbean immigrants, xviii, 107, 109, 111, 463; *Ethnic Options: Choosing Identities in America* (Waters), 209; proximal host and, 489
Watson, Tom, 232

Watts riots, xl
Wealth, 83–84
Weaver, Randy, 648–49
Weber, Max, 21
Welch, Robert, xxxviii, 336
Weld, Theodore, 2
Welfare, 72, 280–81, 369, **643–44**
Welfare Reform Law of 1996, 444, 623, 640
Wells-Barnett, Ida B., 428
West, Cornel, xliv, 492
West Indian immigrants, xlv, 73, 109
West Side Story (film), xxxix, **644–45**
Weyler, Valeriano, 595
Wheeler-Howard Act of 1934. *See* Indian Reorganization Act of 1934
White Aryan Resistance, 572
White flight, 553, **645**
Whiteness, social construction of, 587–89
White people, xvi–xvii, 496, 499–500, 511–13, 642–43
White-supremacist groups, xx, 38, **645–51**; American Nazi Party, 27–28; Aryan Nations, xlii, 46–48, 451, 745; David Duke and, 193–94, 193–94, 347, 445, 647, 649, 651; National Organization for European American Rights (NOFEAR), 445; neo-Nazism, 450–51; The New Order, 28, 451; Oklahoma City bombing, xliv, 394, 420, 459–60, 647–48; religion and, 526, 527; skinheads, 571–72; white-supremacist underground, 651–52; William Pierce, 451, 459, 460, 647, 648, 651; Zionist Occupied Government (ZOG), 655–56
White-supremacist underground, **651–52**
White Trash: Race and Class in America (Wray and Newitz), 589
White Youth Alliance, 193
Who Killed Vincent Chin? (film), 116–17
Whren et al. v. United States, 189–90
Why We Can't Wait (King), 342
Willard, Emma, 138
Williams, Walter E., 70
Willis, Paul, 263
Wilson, Jack. *See* Wovoka
Wilson, Pete, 367
Wilson, William Julius, xviii, xlii, 151, 165–70
Wilson, Woodrow, 54
Winant, Howard, xliii, 507
Winthrop, Robert C., 384
Wofford, Chloe Anthony. *See* Morrison, Toni
Women. *See* Gender roles
Wood, Thomas, 100
Woodson, Robert, 70

Worcester, Samuel, 113
Work, Hubert, 380
Work ethic, 161
Workingmen's Party of California (WPC), 122, 351, 443
World and Islam Studies Enterprise (WISE), 311
World Bank, 614
World Church of the Creator, 526
"World Jewish conspiracy," xvi
World Peace Council, 193
World Trade Organization, 614
World War I, 637
World War II, xvi, 637. *See also* Japanese American internment
Wounded Knee, South Dakota, xxxv, xli, 23, 436, 523, 568, 569
Wovoka, 242, 569
WRA. *See* War Relocation Authority (WRA)
Wright, Richard, 219
Wu, David, 51
Wygant v. Jackson Board of Education, 542

Yamaguchi, Jim, 322
Yamaguchi, Kristi, 322
Yellow Peril, **653**
Yellows, **654**
Yerkes, Robert, 66
Yinger, John, xliv, 137, 270
Yorkin, Bud, 46
"Yo Soy Joaquin" (Gonzales), 244
Young, Lester, 219
Young Lords, 78

Zangwill, Israel, 378
Zhou, Min, 551
Zionist Occupied Government (ZOG), **655–56**
ZOG. *See* Zionist Occupied Government (ZOG)
Zogby, James, 41
Zoning, racial, 272–73, 536, 629
Zoot Suit Riots, xxxvii, 388, 390, **656–57**
Zundel, Ernst, 650

About the Editor

PYONG GAP MIN is Professor of Sociology at Queens College and the Graduate Center of the City University of New York. His research interests are immigration, ethnic identity, ethnic business, religion, and family/gender, with a special focus on Asian Americans. He is the author of three books, including *Caught in the Middle: Korean Communities in New York and Los Angeles* (1996), and the winner of two national book awards. He is the editor or co-editor of five books, including *Struggle for Ethnic Identity: Personal Narratives by Asian American Professionals* (1999) and *Mass Migration to the United States: Classical and Contemporary Periods* (2002).